Palgrave Studies on Children and Development

Series Editors
Michael Bourdillon
University of Zimbabwe
Harare, Zimbabwe

Joy Boyden
Department of International Development
University of Oxford
Oxford, UK

Roy Huijsmans
Institute of Social Studies
Erasmus University Rotterdam
Den Haag, The Netherlands

Nicola Ansell
Social and Political Sciences
Brunel University London
Uxbridge, UK

The series focuses on the interface between childhood studies and international development. Children and young people often feature as targets of development or are mobilized as representing the future in debates on broader development problems such as climate change. Increased attention to children in international development policy and practice is also fuelled by the near universally ratified United Nations Convention on the Rights of the Child and the recently adopted Sustainable Development Goals.

Nonetheless, relatively little has been written on how the experience of childhood and youth is shaped by development as well as how young people as social actors negotiate, appropriate or even resist development discourses and practices. Equally, the increased emphasis in research on children and young people's voices, lived experiences and participation has yet to impact policy and practice in substantial ways.

This series brings together cutting-edge research presented in a variety of forms, including monographs, edited volumes and the Palgrave Pivot format; and so furthers theoretical, conceptual and policy debates situated on the interface of childhood and international development. The series includes a mini-series from Young Lives, a unique 15-year longitudinal study of child childhood poverty in developing countries. A particular strength of the series is its inter-disciplinary approach and its emphasis on bringing together material that links issues from developed and developing countries, as they affect children and young people. The series will present original and valuable new knowledge for an important and growing field of scholarship.

More information about this series at
http://www.springer.com/series/14569

Roy Huijsmans
Editor

Generationing Development

A Relational Approach to Children, Youth and Development

Editor
Roy Huijsmans
International Institute of Social Studies (ISS), Erasmus University
Rotterdam, The Hague, The Netherlands

Palgrave Studies on Children and Development
ISBN 978-1-137-55622-6 (hardcover)   ISBN 978-1-137-55623-3   (eBook)
ISBN 978-1-349-71755-2 (softcover)
DOI 10.1057/978-1-137-55623-3

Library of Congress Control Number: 2016956380

This Palgrave Macmillan imprint is published by Springer Nature
The registered company is Macmillan Publishers Ltd.
The registered company address is: The Campus, 4 Crinan Street, London, N1 9XW, United Kingdom

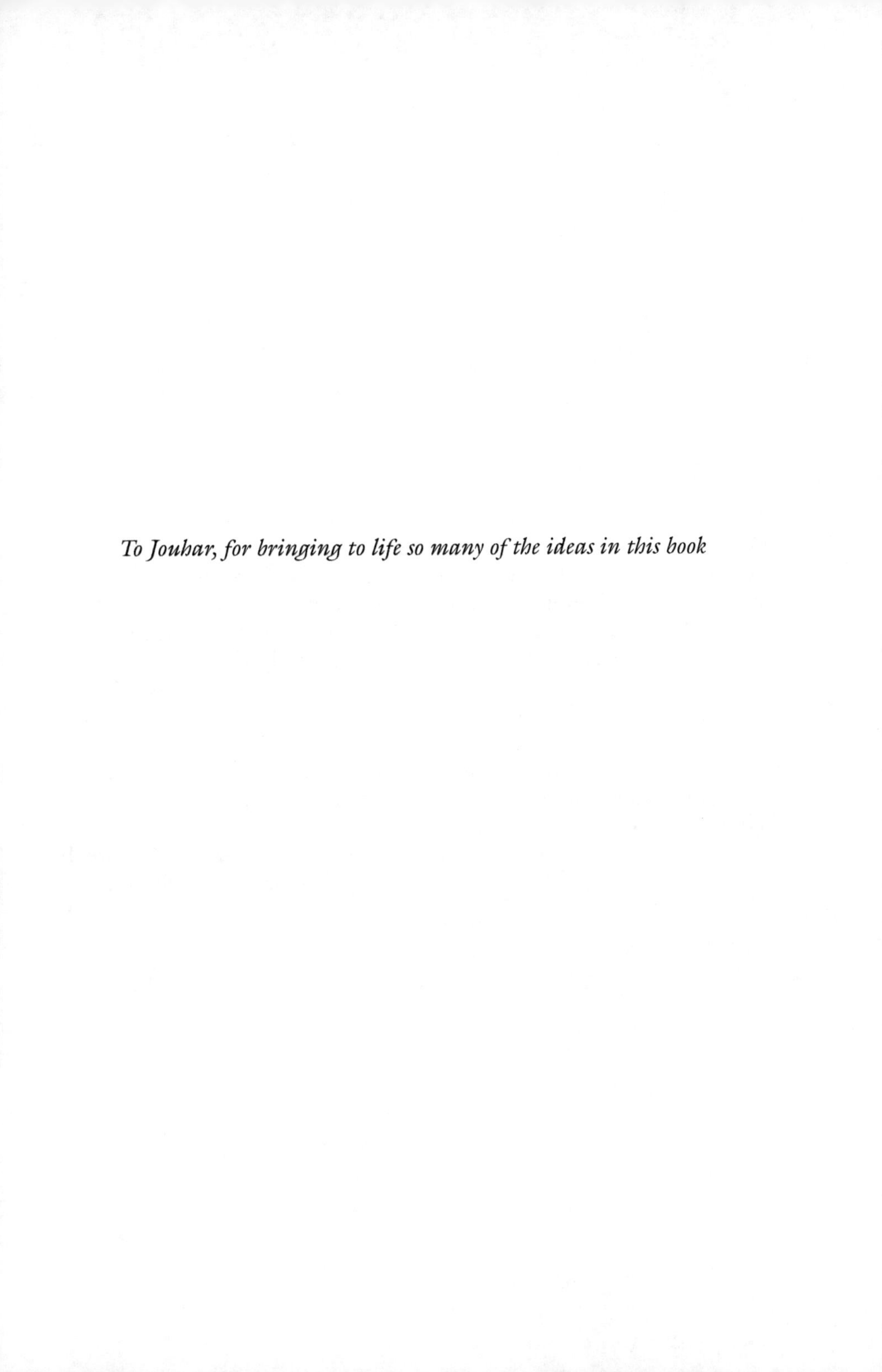

To Jouhar, for bringing to life so many of the ideas in this book

Preface

Unlike many edited volumes, this title has *not* grown out of a conference panel or workshop. The ideas and arguments brought together here have emerged from a range of places and institutions, and matured through various interactions involving plenty of people. A few deserve special mention here. First, the book is in part a product of and reflection on some years of teaching classes and courses on childhood and youth studies as part of degree-level programmes in International Development Studies—first, at the University of Amsterdam, and subsequently at the International Institute of Social Studies (ISS) in the Hague (part of Erasmus University Rotterdam). The ideas presented here have benefited from numerous conversations with both students and colleagues at these two institutes. The chapters by Degwale Gebeyehu Belay, Sara Vida Coumans, Elyse Mills, María Gabriela Palacio, Mahardhika Sjamsoeoed Sadjad, Wedadu Sayibu, and Sharada Srinivasan require special mention. These chapters are all based on research that, in one way or the other, has been shaped by staff and students at, as well as the broader intellectual environment of the ISS. Second, this volume builds on an earlier collaborative publication on 'generationing' development that I guest-edited together with Sandra Evers, Shanti George, and Roy Gigengack for the *European Journal of Development Research* (EJDR 2014, Volume 26, issue 2). The chapters by Lidewyde Berckmoes and Ben White, Jason Hart, Karuna Moraji, and Sharada Srinivasan are modified and updated versions of articles that appeared under the same title in the EJDR Special Issue. In addition, discussions generated by presentations of this early work in a seminar series organized by the VU University (Amsterdam)-based Anthropology of Children and Youth Network have certainly informed this volume. Third, the volume has benefited from the support provided by Palgrave, including the constructive feedback of anonymous reviewers on the initial proposal and final manuscript. A word of thanks also goes out to my fellow series editors, Michael Bourdillon and Jo Boyden, for their constant encouragement and generous feedback (always delivered with amazing speed and sharpness) at various points in the process. Lastly, the chapters could not have been written without the children, young people, and their families who shared so much about their lives.

RH, The Hague, March 2016

Contents

NOTES ON THE CONTRIBUTORS

Nicola Ansell is Reader in Human Geography at Brunel University London. Her research focuses on social and cultural change in the lives of young people, mainly in southern Africa. She is currently exploring the impacts of social cash transfers on generational relations in rural communities in Lesotho and Malawi and will shortly begin a study of the relationships between schooling and aspiration in remote rural communities. The second edition of her book *Children, Youth and Development* is due to be published in 2016. She also runs Brunel's Masters in Children, Youth and International Development.

Degwale G. Belay is Lecturer in the School of Governance and Development Studies, Hawassa University, Ethiopia. He holds an MA degree in 'Regional and Local Development Studies' from Addis Ababa University, Ethiopia. He also has an MA degree in Development Studies (Major in 'Social Policy for Development', specialisation in 'Children and Youth Studies') from the International Institute of Social Studies of Erasmus University Rotterdam, the Netherlands. Degwale's research interest lies with issues of children and young people's work, employment, and migration.

Lidewyde H. Berckmoes holds degrees in anthropology, African studies, and international developments studies. She is affiliated as a postdoc researcher to the Anthropology Department, University of Amsterdam, the Netherlands. In her work, she is interested in the ways people shape their lives in challenging circumstances and the transmission of hardship across generations. She has written on youth, parenting, and violence and peace-building in Burundi.

Christina Clark-Kazak is Associate Professor (International Studies) and Associate Principal (Research and Graduate Studies) at York University's bilingual Glendon College. She serves as Acting Director of York University's Centre for

Refugee Studies and Editor-in-chief of *Refuge: Canada's Journal on Refugees*. Prior to becoming an academic, she worked for eight years as a development practitioner with the Canadian government.

Sara Vida Coumans is a Dutch national born in Nicaragua and spent her childhood in the Philippines. She has been a member of the youth-led organisations CHOICE for youth and sexuality and the Youth Coalition for Sexual and Reproductive Rights. She was involved in advocacy efforts around the ICPD Beyond 2014 review process and co-chaired (with Rishita Nandagiri) the Bali Global Youth Forum in 2012. Sara holds a Master's degree in International Development Studies (major in Social Policy for Development and a specialization in Children and Youth Studies) from the International Institute of Social Studies of Erasmus University Rotterdam. Sara currently works at Amnesty International as International Youth Coordinator. Sara's chapter is written in her personal capacity and it does not necessarily reflect the views of Amnesty International.

Jason Hart is Senior Lecturer at the University of Bath, a research associate at the Refugee Studies Centre, University of Oxford, and a visiting professor at the Norwegian Technical University, Trondheim. His research has explored the experiences of young people in settings of armed conflict and displacement, and the nature of institutional responses to these young people. Hart has worked in South Asia, East Africa, and the Middle East, particularly Israel/occupied Palestinian territories and Jordan. He has been employed as a consultant author, researcher, evaluator, and trainer by various UN and non-governmental organisations, and has served as an advisor to the UN in the formulation of studies, guidelines, and policies.

Paul Horton is a Senior Lecturer in Education at the Department of Behavioural Sciences and Learning at Linköping University, Sweden. His research has focused on school bullying, power relations, and issues of gender and sexuality in the northern Vietnamese contexts of Haiphong and Hanoi. He has also previously written about school bullying in New Zealand and Denmark. His publications include *Bullied into it: Bullying, Power and the Conduct of Conduct*, which is part of the Ethnography and Education book series.

Roy Huijsmans holds degrees in education, development studies, and human geography. He is currently Senior Lecturer in Children and Youth Studies at the International Institute of Social Studies in the Hague, the Netherlands (part of Erasmus University Rotterdam). He has written on childhood, youth, and migration, the generational dynamics of multilocal householding, and on nationalism, youth, and mobile telephony.

Elyse Mills holds an MA in Agrarian and Environmental Studies, with a specialization in Agriculture and Rural Development from the International Institute of

Social Studies in The Hague (part of Erasmus University Rotterdam), Netherlands. She has conducted research on young farmers in Canada, Chinese land investments in Southeast Asia, and the development of the bioeconomy in the European Union (EU). Her research interests include future farming trajectories, access to farmland in the Global North, 'sustainable' agricultural agendas and agrofuels, and small-scale production in fisheries and agriculture. She is currently researching corporate land deals globally, EU fisheries policies, collaborates on research with the Initiatives in Critical Agrarian Studies (ICAS), and works in the ICAS secretariat.

Karuna Morarji is an independent educator affiliated with the Centre for Holistic Learning (http://www.jeevanshala.org/). She lives with her husband and two home-schooled children in a village in South India. Karuna has a long-standing concern with understanding relationships between education and visions of human possibility and development. As an educator, she enjoys sharing an appreciation for critical social theory as a lens to see relationships between things that often appear independent and disconnected. Other current interests include food, film, processual/historical analysis, and collaborative ways of teaching, learning, and living. Karuna was educated in Sweden, India, and the USA.

María Gabriela Palacio is a PhD researcher at the International Institute of Social Studies of the Erasmus University Rotterdam. She holds degrees in economics, social economy, and poverty studies. Her current research explores the gendered aspects of social protection in Ecuador as an ideal case to examine the challenges of providing targeted welfare via cash transfers in a highly segregated context.

Mahardhika Sjamsoeoed Sadjad is an ISS alumna (International Institute of Social Studies of Erasmus University Rotterdam). Her award-winning Research Paper titled 'An Autoethnographic Study on Dutch Society', weaves together narratives of whiteness, neighbourhoods, and the complexity of religious identities through the perspectives of young *allochtoon* Dutch Muslims. After completing her studies at ISS, Mahardhika is interested to continue doing ethnographic research on Muslim identities, transnational movement of people, and narratives of solidarity in Indonesia.

Wedadu Sayibu is a development practitioner currently working as Programme manager with the Regional Advisory Information and Network Systems (RAINS), a local non-governmental organization in Tamale, Ghana. She holds an MA degree in Peace and Development Studies from the University of Cape Coast, Ghana, and an MA degree in Development Studies (major in Human Rights Gender and Conflict Studies: Social Justice Perspectives) from the International Institute of Social Studies of Erasmus University Rotterdam, the Netherlands. Wedadu's research interests lie with children, working children, and children's rights issues.

Sharada Srinivasan is Canada Research Chair in Gender, Justice, and Development and Associate Professor of International Development at the University of Guelph. Her research is located within the broad field of gender and development, focusing on gender-based discrimination and violence. Since receiving her PhD in Development Studies from the International Institute of Social Studies of Erasmus University Rotterdam in the Netherlands, she has undertaken research on various facets and consequences of daughter deficit in India and China. Her current research focuses on the relative contributions of daughters and sons to their parents' well-being, and the trajectories of youth into farming.

Ben White is Emeritus Professor of Rural Sociology at the International Institute of Social Studies, the Hague (part of Erasmus University Rotterdam). His research and teaching has focused mainly on processes of agrarian change and the anthropology and history of childhood and youth, especially in Indonesia. His recent books or edited volumes include *Rights and Wrongs of Children's Work* (2010) and *Growing Up in Indonesia: Experience and Diversity in Youth Transitions* (2012).

List of Figures

LIST OF TABLES

CHAPTER 1

Generationing Development: An Introduction

Roy Huijsmans

PRESENTING THE CASE

A growing body of research on childhood and youth in the context of development has brought lots, yet still too little. The 'new sociology of childhood' that gained shape in the 1990s transformed the field (Tisdall and Punch 2012). Its key premises, appreciating childhood as a social construct and children as social actors, countered the socialisation approaches and development psychology perspectives that long dominated knowledge production about children (Ansell 2009: 190). In this new wave of research, qualitative, participatory, ethnographic, and especially so-called child-centred methods were typically favoured over standardised questionnaires (Christensen and James 2000). This generated a wealth of knowledge about children in their current condition *as children*, privileging their own perspectives and experiences, and challenging any singular understanding of childhood leading some to speak about 'multiple' childhoods (Balagopalan 2014: 11–14).

The story about youth is different.[1] Their agency was never in question, albeit seldom studied in relation to young women, and mostly seen as a problem or a particularity. Unlike childhood studies, qualitative research

R. Huijsmans (✉)
International Institute of Social Studies of Erasmus University Rotterdam, Kortenaerkade 12, 2518 AX The Hague, Netherlands

R. Huijsmans (ed.), *Generationing Development*,
DOI 10.1057/978-1-137-55623-3_1

is a respected tradition within youth studies (Willis 1981; Mead 2001 [1928]). Research conducted in rich countries still dominates the field, with numerous articles and books on the various 'crises' attributed to (male) youth and particular sub-cultural formations. This epistemological frame has also influenced emerging youth research in the Global South (Amit-Talai and Wulff 1995; Honwana and De Boeck 2005). It is only in recent years that youth studies have started paying serious attention to more-or-less ordinary youth and the potential of studying their everyday lives for rethinking development (Jeffrey et al. 2008; Jeffrey 2010; Woronov 2016).

Nonetheless, a key motivation driving this book is that both childhood and youth studies have informed debates in development studies only marginally. Or more precisely, it is particularly these more recent perspectives and approaches in the respective fields that have failed to impact development thinking despite their potential. For it must be recognised that research coming out of economics, medical science, and development psychology, on children especially, has made more than just a dent in development thinking and practice. This is evident from the global uptake of conditional cash transfer programmes (see Palacio this volume) as well as renewed interest in early childhood programmes (Young, 2007). Driven by the interaction between neuroscience, development psychology, and neoclassical economics, such interventions are considered highly efficient approaches to simultaneously alleviating poverty and building human capital for facilitating economic growth. Such child research, thus, speaks directly to dominant global development agendas while also offering the robust 'large-n' causal analyses demanded by inter-governmental donors and national governments alike. However, this research treats childhood as a site of intervention ignoring children's active engagement with and appropriation of programmes, important contextual variations in how interventions play out, the constantly evolving relational and generational fabric within which children and young people live their lives and in which programmes intervene, as well as the temporal dimension that would show that at least some children may 'do well' later in life despite initial hardships and deprivations (Boyden et al. 2015).

At its core, development studies and practice have remained adult-centric. This influences the questions that drive most research about young people within the field. This adult-centrism is seldom, however, sufficiently marked, and it can be easily missed because of the vast volume of (evaluation) research on the incorporation of children into development interventions, frequent rhetorical references to 'young people as the future', and sub-debates on the fringes of the discipline about specific 'child', 'adolescent' or 'youth'-related themes such as 'child poverty', 'adolescent sexuality', and 'youth employment'. Children may thus have 'become prominent "clients" of international development discourse and intervention' (Boyden and Zharkevich forthcoming), and the idea of the 'youth bulge' continues to ignite debates on youth as either a danger or potential for development (e.g. World Bank 2006). Yet, the conceptual and theoretical innovations that have come out of the qualitative research on childhood and youth have hardly impacted the terms of thinking about development.

Perhaps, this state of affairs is partly the prize of success. Much of the qualitative research in childhood and youth studies, including work on young people in the context of development, is published in the specialised childhood and youth studies journals and book series launched in recent decades (Tisdall and Punch 2012: 252). In contrast to the early days (e.g. Goddard and White 1982; Nieuwenhuys 1994), only a fraction of this work appears in, or seems to inform in any substantial way, debates in development studies circles (Huijsmans et al. 2014: fn1). Others have pointed at the failure of much childhood and youth research to employ a political economy perspective (see Mills this volume), and thereby speak more directly to larger global processes (Hart 2008; Côté 2014; Woronov 2016).

This volume is a modest contribution to bridging gaps in order to facilitate conceptual dialogue between these strands of research. That is, between childhood and youth studies, and between those two fields and development studies (other major works include Young Lives; Katz 2004; Ansell 2005; Jeffrey et al. 2008; Wells 2009). To this end, the volume brings together a total of 14 chapters. The three parts of the book, 'theorising age and generation in young lives', 'everyday relationalities: school, work and belonging', and 'negotiating development' consist of four chapters each and are complemented with an introductory chapter setting out the conceptual and theoretical parameters and a commentary by Nicola Ansell that closes the volume.

Analytically, the volume coheres around a relational approach. Relational thinking can take many forms, but in essence it is about tying together different things, actors, dimensions, dynamics, or forces. It emphasises relationships, networks, friction, interaction, negotiation, the everyday and power. At an ontological level, relational thinking, thus, seeks to overcome static agency–structure binaries (Worth 2014). At a minimum, the relational exercise presented in this volume is about bringing into critical conversation some of the conceptual and theoretical contributions of childhood and youth studies with debates and perspectives in development studies. In addition, the chapters in this volume also retain the important relational exercise of investigating the interactions between constructs of childhood and youth and the lived experience of being young (see for example Alma Gottlieb's (2004) work on the interplay between the understanding of the personhood attributed to babies and practices of child rearing). However, the specific contribution of the volume lies in its attempt to capture the twofold dynamic of how development, in its various conceptualisations, restructures generational social landscapes, and also how young people themselves, as constrained agents of development, renegotiate their role and position vis-à-vis others and in particular places and spaces of development.

The next section sets out an analytical frame underpinning the relational approach informing this book. This framework is given specific childhood and youth studies content by mobilising age and generation, in their various interpretations, as key concepts. Next, the general approach to development is sketched followed by an outline of the organisation of the book and a brief introduction to the contributing chapters.

RELATIONAL THINKING

In recent years, there has been somewhat of a revival of relational approaches. This is evident not only in work on 'space' (Jones 2009), 'the state' (Thelen et al. 2014), 'poverty' (Mosse 2010) but also in research with young people (e.g. Punch 2002b; Kraftl 2013; Worth 2014). Thelen et al. (2014: 2) posit that by making relations the entry point of analysis, we gain new insights into how things work. The rationale for foregrounding generational relations is, thus, to gain a deeper understanding of how development, in its diverse conceptualisations, works in a generational manner—and especially, though not exclusively, how this pertains to young people.

Thelen et al.'s (2014) relational anthropology of studying the state is driven by a problematique that maps well onto childhood and youth studies because of its concern with the interplay between 'formations', 'representations', and 'practices'. In the context of childhood and youth studies, formations can be operationalised as 'generational structures', representations can be taken to refer to 'discourses about young people', and practices can direct attention to the 'lived experiences of being young'. Thelen et al. (2014: 2) propose studying these interconnected dimensions with an analytical framework comprising of three axes: 'relational modalities, boundary work, and the embeddedness of actors'.

The idea of modalities captures the different ontologies in which notions of childhood and youth exist and the various understandings of age that come with it. We could, thus, speak of 'generational modalities'. In Sara Vida Coumans' chapter, different modalities are clearly illustrated through policies seeking to regulate sex work. These policies are articulated in terms of chronological age and legitimised on the basis of neuroscience. However, there is also the modality of the embodied dimension of age that shapes sex work as practice. Similarly, in Lidewyde Berckmoes and Ben White's contribution, young people hopefully articulate the rights and obligations associated with kinship descent. According to this generational modality, parents support their children in setting up an adult life. However, under conditions in which such support is lacking young women and young men must mobilise their youthfulness in other ways in order to 'find a life', amongst other things, by resorting to cross-border labour migration, 'illegal marriages', and for some urban youth also by becoming involved in 'political participation', the latter giving rise to discourses about the destructive and disruptive potential of idle male youth (see also Izzi 2013). Berckmoes and White's chapter shows that these different modalities are neither mutually exclusive nor discrete and especially in times of rapid change, crises or transformation people draw on various modalities, at times simultaneously, in their efforts to get by (see also Vigh 2006).

The concept of boundary work draws attention to the fuzzy and fluid boundaries of age-based categories, and the constant work that gives these artificial boundaries the gloss of fixity and puts them beyond question. It is precisely these boundaries that are poorly covered in childhood and youth studies. The work of Sally McNamee and Julie Seymour (2013) suggests that research on age-based categories gravitates to the centre. On the basis of a review of 320 articles published between 1993 and 2010 in three leading childhood journals, they conclude that the scholarly attention is unevenly distributed across the age range the journals claim to cover: the articles most commonly report about 10–12 year olds, there is very little coverage of the 'under 5s' and also relatively little attention to young people aged 17 years and older. If, however, the objective is to understand how age-based categories affect the lived experiences of being young, it is of methodological importance to work across age boundaries. This is of particular importance in relation to phenomena such as migration and sex work that typically straddle (inter)national boundaries between age of minority and majority (O'Connell Davidson 2005; Huijsmans 2015a: 18), and Alma Gottlieb's (2004) ethnography of babies demonstrates it is no less important at the other end of the childhood age-scale.

The relevance of boundary work for understanding how development policies intervening in generational landscapes play out is vividly illustrated by Mariá Gabriela Palacio in her discussion on teenage mothers (Chap. 11 this volume). Attaining motherhood prior to turning 18 frictions with the social logic underpinning the conditional cash transfer scheme. Social workers are aware that these young mothers are often the most needy, yet conservative Catholicism holds them back from bending the boundaries of the programme out of fear of creating a perverse incentive. Similarly, young mothers do boundary work by opting for practicing motherhood in the margins of their lives as a consequence of choosing employment rather than claiming financial support even once they have reached the age at which they have become admissible to the programme. Attention to boundary work is also demonstrated in the chapters by Wedadu Sayibu and Degwale Belay, respectively. Their work does not only investigate why children enter begging arrangements and street-based work, a question that is commonly addressed in childhood studies, but it also unravels why young people cease to be involved in or aim to exit this work some years later.

The third axis of analysis in Thelen et al's scheme (2014) is the embeddedness of actors. As Karuna Morarji's contribution illustrates, even within one locality various actors are situated very differently in webs of social relations. The teachers who work in the remote mountainous areas of Northern India position themselves firmly as agents of the modernising project of mass education. This allows them to mobilise starkly different relational modalities then the rural students and their parents. In addition, through mass schooling and (rural-to-urban) migration, young rural folk become embedded in relational fields other than the place-based community and kinship relations they have been raised into. Young people experience first-hand the conflicts and contradictions between the different ways they are embedded in these respective social fields. They respond to this with a search for 'balance'. The precise shape such balancing takes would depend however on the extent to which they are able to mobilise some of the social relations they are embedded in. Here, Morarji's chapter underscores the importance of viewing the embeddedness of actors not only through a generational lens but also through a gender lens. She shows that modern schooling is perceived to have a very different effect on, and offering possibilities for, young men as opposed to their female peers. Although the importance of the intersection between gender and generation transpires from virtually all contributions, this is perhaps most powerfully illustrated by Sharada Srinivasan on the basis of her research in a southern Indian study context characterised by 'daughter aversion'. She demonstrates that in their 'bargaining with patriarchy' young women have little other option than to mobilise another set of exploitative relations: the capitalist forces underpinning the *sumangali* scheme. Submitting to capital to exploit their youthful, feminine labour power allows them to delay marriage, attain additional schooling, and save for a dowry (compare with Mills 1999; Utrata 2011).

Beyond Categorisation: Age and Generation as Relational Concepts

Relationality in research with children and young people is first and foremost a critique of the categorisation fashion that has come to characterise a good part of both the childhood and youth studies literature. Peter Hopkins and Rachel Pain (2007: 288) even write about a 'politics of fetishizing the social-chronological margins'. With this, they take issue with the isolationist fashion in which research on children and youth and to a lesser extent older people has developed into vibrant sub-fields, while the adult centre has been left unmarked (see also Vanderbeck and Worth 2015: 3).

Responding to Hopkins and Pains' critique comes with methodological implications. Childhood and youth researchers have long argued for child and youth friendly, or -centred methods (Punch 2002a; Alderson and Morrow 2004). The chapters in this volume, however, are rather characterised by research that *decentres* adults. Adults, in their various capacities like teachers, parents, employers, social workers, researchers, are deliberately included in the research, while simultaneously creating the space for children and young people's own experiences and perspectives on matters (see also Hoang and Yeoh 2015; Punch 2016: 188). Where possible, research was conducted in so-called 'natural settings' in order to capture how generational relations work in practice, be it on the streets of Addis Ababa, secondary schools in Northern Vietnam, health clinics in Ecuador, or a Sufi centre in Kall, Germany.

Hopkins and Pain note further that despite much awareness of the constructed nature of categorisations on the basis of age and the variations in which people experience age, 'age has been given a fixity' (ibid 2007: 288). Research that uncritically embraces such age-based categories risks missing sight of how:

> ...identities of children and others are produced *through* interactions with other age/generational groups and are in a constant state of flux. Therefore, children and childhood interact with others in family and community settings and so are *more than* children alone; studying them in context adds new layers to our understanding. (Hopkins and Pain 2007: 289, original emphasis)[2]

Hopkins and Pains' call for 'more relational geographies of age', however, does not fully delineate how notions of generation and age are understood precisely (Hopkins and Pain 2007: 291). In fact, the aforementioned quote leaves unclear whether or the extent to which age and generation are conceptually distinct. Since both terms are widely used in everyday parlance and subject to many interpretations, I present a brief overview.

Understanding Age

Despite the centrality of the idea of age in childhood and youth studies, and in development practice too, it is seldom subject to much conceptual scrutiny (Laz 1998: 85; Thorne 2004: 404). Cheryl Laz (1998: 86) argues that age 'involves much more than the number of years since one's birth' leading her to argue that 'age is not natural or fixed'.

Chronological Age

When the term 'age' is used, this often refers to its chronological conceptualisation; the figure identifying the number of (Gregorian) calendar years that have passed since birth. Taking issue with an understanding of age as 'a chronological fact and as something every individual simply *is*', Laz (1998: 85, original emphasis) calls for a sociology of age:

…in which we theorize and study empirically how age as a concept and institution is created, maintained, challenged, and transformed; how assumptions and beliefs about age in general and about particular age categories inform and are reinforced by social statuses, norms, roles, institutions, and social structures; and how age patterns individual lives and experiences even as individuals accomplish age. (Laz 1998: 90)

Some questions such a framework raises would include: how one particular conceptualisation of age (chronological age) has become hegemonic, what it mutes, and how it matters? The work of Philippe Ariès (1962) and James Scott (1998) shed light on this from a history of childhood and development studies' perspective, respectively (see also Grieg 1994: 32). Their work confirms Laz's assertion (1998: 92, original emphasis) that 'chronological age is *made* important in particular social and historical contexts'.

In Scott's terms, chronological age can be seen as a form of state simplification; characteristic of modernising states' efforts to make legible its population. State simplifications allow for 'discriminating interventions' (Scott 1998: 3) which include (and exclude) segments of the population on the basis of the unidimensional measure of chronological age. Key examples include mass schooling (Horton this volume), mass organisations for the young (Valentin 2007; Semedi 2016), minimum age regulations (Melchiorre 2004; Bourdillon et al. 2009), and the very idea of a separate set of rights specifically for children (Van Bueren 1995; Hanson and Nieuwenhuys 2013; Twum-Danso Imoh and Ansell 2013). In other instances, 'discriminating interventions' employ age in combination with additional characteristics such as sex, in case of boy scouts and girl guides (Proctor 2009) income in the case of conditional cash transfer programmes (Palacio this volume), social class (as proposed by Mills, this volume), or migrant status (Sadjad, this volume Hopkins and Hill 2010). These examples illustrate that age, in its chronological conceptualisation, is evidently *made* important not only by the state but also through work of non-govermental and inter-governmental organisations—amongst other things through development related interventions. However, Scott (1998: 8) cautions that 'global capitalism is perhaps the most powerful force for homogenization'. Indeed, where states and their non-governmental partners have failed or do not fully succeed in making young people identify with their date of birth, it is increasingly the digital capitalism of companies like *Facebook*,[3] and mobile services providers that succeed in doing so (Huijsmans 2015b), while simultaneously providing chronological age with new meanings, possibilities (Boellstorff 2008: 122; Alexander 2014), and risks (Kierkegaard 2008).

Relative Age and Social Age
Although chronological age has by no means displaced alternative conceptualisations of age, creating the conceptual space for understanding age otherwise requires some efforts—especially in environments where chronological age dominates such as in the classroom and policy arenas (see Horton, this volume; Clark-Kazak, this volume). In my teaching with mostly mature MA-level students from diverse professional, geographical and cultural backgrounds I have, to this end, been using a short exercise. In pairs, students ask each other about:

1. their (chronological) age;
2. the day of the week they were born;
3. the time of the day they were born;
4. whether they can identify fellow students that are older/younger than them; and
5. whether they consider themselves youth, adults, etc.

Next, students explain to one another why they were struggling with some answers and had no problems with others (which usually is the case).

Should there be any Korean students or other East Asian students who are aware of traditional age systems, the first question already challenges the singularity of chronological age.[4] The second and third question shed light on what in some places are very important biographical data (e.g. used in name-giving or in astrology to calculate auspicious dates or identify suitable marriage partners) yet virtually unknown by lots of people in other contexts. The fourth question turns the spotlight onto 'relative age' (Huijsmans 2014a). In many parts of the world, it is in everyday interactions often more important to be aware of differences in relative age (i.e. whether one is older or younger) than the precise chronological age. This is evident from the use of different personal pronouns depending on relative positions in relations of seniority between individuals (Enfield 2007; Szymańska-Matusiewicz 2014).[5] The fifth question refers to the concept of 'social age'. Christina Clark-Kazak (2009: 1310) has defined social age as 'the socially constructed meanings applied to physical development and roles attributed to infants, children, young people, adults and elders, as well as their intra- and inter-generational relationships' (for a concrete application see Huijsmans 2010: Chap. 5). Although (inter)national definitions of childhood and youth define these life phases firmly in chronological terms (Herrera 2006), in everyday contexts however social age has a strong performative dimension and is always contextual, embodied, and gendered (Laz 1998; Huijsmans and Baker 2012: 935; Huijsmans 2013).[6]

Interpreting Generation

Unlike the concept of age, generation in its various interpretations *has* received its share of attention in the relevant recent literature (e.g. Koning 1997; Alanen 2001; Edmunds and Turner 2005; Cole and Durham 2007; Herrera and Bayat 2010; Jeffrey 2010; Naafs and White 2012; Punch 2016). Although age and generation are sometimes used interchangeably, they are conceptually distinct even though some interpretations of generation presuppose a concept of age. The preceding discussion has illustrated that age is foremost a principle of social differentiation (La Fontaine 1978). In its various conceptualisations, age is helpful in understanding some of the relations of power shaping everyday interactions between individuals. In addition, at a macro-level age is a key variable employed in policies and social analysis. Generation, on the other hand, is useful for understanding how societies are structured on the basis of age-based groupings and how this may relate to larger processes of change and continuity (Thorne 2004: 404).

Kinship Descent
In the kinship descent interpretation of generation, generation refers mostly to parent–child relations. This interpretation of generation has proven useful for conceptualising the generational dimension of intra-household relations (Xu 2015). For example, it can be recognised in Samantha Punch's work (2002b, 2015) on the idea of 'negotiated and constrained interdependencies'; a critique to conventional youth transition models which view young people as moving in a fairly unconstrained and linear manner from a condition of dependence to one of independence. The idea of generation as kinship descent also transpires through the notion of the 'inter-generational contract' (Hoddinott 1992; Kabeer 2000; Whitehead et al. 2007; Evans 2015).

The idea of interdependence and the inter-generational contract may be understood in relation to the nuclear family residing in the same locality. Yet, it can also be employed in the context of differently composed and dispersed family formations (e.g. Sayibu, this volume; Carsten 2004; Mazzucato and Schans 2011) and possibly to fictive kinship formations entirely outside of any conventional understanding of the household as Sarada Balagopalan's (2014: 142–145) work on street children suggests (see also Belay, this volume; Heinonen 2013). In modalities of kinship descent the generational positions, such as child and parent, are permanent locations regardless of people's chronological age. However, as both children and their parents age their rights and obligations to one another shift within the loose frame of the inter-generational contract (Huijsmans 2010: 129–130). It is at this point that we see how generation in its interpretation of kinship descent overlaps with generation as a life phase situated in a generational order. It is further important to note that the loose set of generational relations comprising the intergenerational contract and negotiated interdependence is always gendered and subject to reinterpretation as circumstances change—something which is especially evident in the context of migration (Mazzucato et al. 2006; Punch 2007; Huijsmans 2013, 2014a; Hoang and Yeoh 2015; Punch 2015).

Life Phase

In contrast to generation as kinship descent, generation as a life phase directs the analytical gaze towards the interplay between institutional dimensions and individual biographies.[7] Närvänen and Näsman (2004: 84) explain that 'age-related life phases, such as childhood, come into being through complex processes and are institutionalized but can also change over time'. Although the phrase institutionalisation often refers to forces of the state Anoop Nayak and Mary Jane Kehily (2013: 12) note that 'contemporary Western childhood cannot be read outside of market forces but is constituted in and through relations of capital'. Poor people in poor countries have long been recognised as an important consumer base and recently been 'rediscovered' in terms of 'the bottom of the pyramid' (Kolk et al. 2013). Nayak and Kehily's claim, thus, is unlikely to be limited to the West (for an early hint into this direction see White 1996: 830). However, the little research that critically investigates the role of consumption and the market in the constitution of young lives tends to be limited to the life phase of youth (e.g. Lukose 2005; Beazley and Chakraborty 2008).

Närvänen and Näsman (2004: 85) stress that life phases are relational because they define each other within 'the framework of their relative positions in the life course as a whole'. Such a life course perspective sits uncomfortably in both childhood and youth studies because it is seen as inviting a reductionist view on children and youth as 'becomings'. Yet, especially in relation to development, a hesitant engagement with the becoming part of being young must be reconsidered. It delimits the analytical scope as it means losing sight of how the temporal dimension of development interacts with the embodied and gendered experience of being young and growing up (Cole and Durham 2008).

The interplay between these different rhythms of continuity and change is not only of analytical interest, but also of political relevance. For the adult population, young people constitute a means to access, and also a site to influence the future (Smith 2013). This is partly because the young are seen as more malleable. Making them a key target for projects seeking to bring about politico-economic and socio-cultural change (Evans 1998: 159; Christie 2015: 260–1). The interplay between brain research and human capital theory has added scientific clout to this long-standing popular idea and, more importantly, given rise to an understanding of childhood as the life phase with the highest returns to investment (Young 2007). Next, the interplay between the temporality of development and human maturation also transpires from interventions and practices seeking to safeguard continuity. It is through young people that one may attempt to secure particular pasts and presents in the future (Lall and Vickers 2009; Huijsmans 2011; Sinha-Kerkhoff 2011).

Attending to futurity neither means viewing children or youth as 'blank slates' onto which any future can be written, even if adults represent children as such (see Moraji, this volume), nor going back to visions about children and young people as incomplete and adults-in-making. Indeed, it is fully compatible with viewing young people as social actors because 'looking forward to what a child "becomes" is arguably an important part of "being" a child' (Uprichard 2008: 306). Several of the chapters included in this volume illustrate this argument (Berckmoes & White; Hart; Morarji; Palacio; Srinivasan). For example, Palacio's chapter shows that the way in which the human capital theory and development psychology underpinning conditional cash transfer programmes is mapped onto the life course renders childhood a site of investment. She, then, proceeds to investigate how this particular understanding of the life phase of childhood affects how children think of themselves in relation to the future. This brings out important gender differences. The idea of succeeding in the labour market gels well with masculine ideas of adulthood while it is perceived as out of sync with the gendered opportunity structures girls growing up in poverty have become aware of.

Generation in its interpretation of life phase is also associated with the idea of transitions (i.e. school-to-work transitions). Transition thinking has been especially influential in questions concerning youth in development (Camfield 2011). This is illustrated by the World Bank's 2007 World Development Report framed around the idea of 'youth transitions' (World Bank 2006) and the International Labour Office's school-to-work transition survey (e.g. Elder 2014). The linearity and directionality of many youth transitions models has been a subject to substantial critique. Scholars like Johanna Wyn and Rob White (1997: 97–8), for example, argue the importance of adding a 'vertical perspective' to the idea of youth transition in order to capture generational continuities in terms of class, ethnicity, religion and gender (see also Mills, this volume). They further note that the metaphor of 'transitions' suggests a landscape of 'pathways' leading to a certain destination (adulthood). Even if these institutional 'pathways' are well trodden by many, they are often invisible or inaccessible to others (ibid 1997: 99; Punch 2015). A more relational and non-teleological understanding of how young people develop their lives is found in the idea of 'vital conjunctures' (Johnson-Hanks 2002), emphasising the importance of understanding key life course events as indeterminant and multi-directional. Similarly, the concept of 'social navigation' (Vigh 2009) sheds light on how in conditions of extreme volatility people make decisions in relation to potential possibilities and risks (instead of established 'pathways'). These conceptual contributions are all critical of the linearity and determinacy of conventional transition models without, however, throwing out the idea of life phases and the life course.

When life phases are attributed particular properties and set within the inflexible frame of chronological age this produces something that we may call 'age-normativity: certain rights, responsibilities, and places, as well as the evaluation of the appropriateness of particular activities carried out by young people, become normatively (dis)associated to life phases demarcated by the universal measure of chronological age' (Huijsmans 2015a: 10). Development policies often breathe age-normativity (i.e. World Bank 2006). This is not necessarily bad news. In fact, it has led to an increase in social services targeted at specific age-based populations (the young, but also the old) such as the *Education for All* campaign (Gerber and Huijsmans 2016) and programmes aimed at protecting the development and survival of the very young (Myers and Bourdillon 2012: 438). At the same time though, age-normativity pathologises young lives that do not conform with such globalised middle-class ideas of age-appropriate behaviour, often with adverse effects as critical research on children's work, young people's migration and teenage motherhood has shown (Liebel 2004; Wilson and Huntington 2006; Howard 2014; Maconachie and Hilson 2016). Importantly, the voices of young people living their lives in contradiction to normative ideas about childhood and youth remain mostly excluded from policy making and programmatic interventions, not in the least because institutional contexts and other dimensions of positionality often have a normalising effect on such voices (Montgomery 2007: 421; Spyrou 2011: 155).

Mannheim

Next to kinship descent and life phase, the term 'generation' has also been used in its meaning of 'cohort'. This simply refers to people born in the same year(s). In demographic approaches to development cohorts are used as 'a tool to observe, to describe, and sometimes to explain social change' (Corsten 1999: 255). However, for childhood and youth studies, the Mannheimian development of the idea of cohorts is of greater relevance. In his essay on *The Problem of Generations*, Karl Mannheim presents a formal sociological analysis of the generation phenomenon with the aim of better understanding some of the dynamics of historical development (Mannheim 1952). According to this schema, not all cohorts develop into a generation (ibid 1952: 310). For this to happen, there must be a 'stratification of experience' (Mannheim, in Corsten 1999: 256). This means that sharing the same historical time at which they were born (in Mannheim terms 'generational location') is a necessary, yet not a sufficient condition for the formation of an actual generation. For people to start identifying as an 'actual generation', they must also belong to a 'cultural and historical region' (Närvänen and Näsman 2004: 78–9). Specifying the generational dimension of belonging further, Corsten (1999: 258) defines 'actual generations' as cohorts 'who do not only have something in common, they have also a (common) sense for (a kind of knowledge about) the fact that they have something in common'. Mannheim further coined the phrase 'generational units'. These are different groups of young people within the same actual generation that have experienced and respond to the same historical events very differently (Mannheim 1952: 304).

Given development studies' concern with social transformation, the Mannheimian interpretation of generation has much immediate intuitive appeal—and indeed, the generationally marked use of social media and digital technologies only adds to this (Barendregt 2008; Shah and Abraham 2009; Mesch and Talmud 2010; Ezbawy 2012; Meek 2012; Buckingham et al. 2014; Huijsmans and Trần Thị Hà Lan 2015).[8] While the Mannheimian interpretation of generation also echoes through the widely used development slogan of 'youth as agents of change', there are also questions and concerns.

First, Mannheim placed the formative period of generational identities in the youth stage of the life course. Leena Alanen (2001: 16) rightly asks whether it is not in childhood that generations are formed. Second, at what point in the life course can we truly speak of an actual generation? 'Reflective participation in intellectual issues and shared experiences' (Närvänen and Näsman 2004: 79) is, in part, also produced by the increased intensity of the institutionalisation of the life phases of childhood and youth, yet does that render cohorts of young people into actual generations or can this only be ascertained if at later points in the life course this is still observable? Third, the Mannheimian interpretation of generation contributes to reinforcing a common feature in the cultural studies of youth, in that a disproportionate share of scholarly attention goes out to so-called 'spectacular youth' such a punkers, skinheads, skaters, and those youth involved in social movements, with relatively little attention paid to ordinary, and especially, rural youth (Robson et al. 2007). Fourth, attention to spectacular youth easily equates the idea of youth with young men. This leads to a gender-blind perspective of youth because it leaves female youth out of sight while the male dimension too often remains unmarked (Sadjad, this volume; Huijsmans 2014b).

The aforementioned discussion has not more than scratched the surface of the multiple ways in which ideas of age and generation have been conceptualised. Even so, I hope to have demonstrated the relevance of these relational concepts for a firmer analytical anchoring of research on childhood and youth in the field of development studies. Table 1.1 pulls together the discussion. It outlines the main concepts of age various interpretations of generation presuppose, the key relations they capture and also how each of these different interpretations of generation comes with its own cluster of connecting concepts.

As all tables, Table 1.1 is not more than a heuristic device. The various interpretations of generation flow into one another (Vanderbeck and Worth 2015: 2) and are here separated for analytical purposes only. For example, the life phase understanding of generation overlaps with the

Table 1.1   Concepts of generation and age in relational approaches to childhood and youth

Interpretation of 'generation'	Pre-supposing concepts of age	Relationality	Clustering 'age' conceptually with	Examples
Kinship descent	Relative age, social age	Relations between household members (possibly spatially dispersed and fictive kin)	Kinship, gender, generational reciprocity, negotiation, socialisation, parenting, childing, the home	Parent-child and sibling relations, intra-household bargaining
Life phase	Chronological age, social age	Relation between social institutions and individual biographies	Social institutions and norms, consumption and market forces, gender, age-based identities, place, life course, transitions, performativity	Youth transitions, schooling, children's work
Mannheimian understanding of generation	Social age, chronological age	Relation between the coming of age of a cohort, and the possible formation of generationally distinct political subjectivities, with events in historical time	Historical events, media and communication technologies, collective generational identities, sub-cultures, movements, resistance	Youth sub-cultures, post-Apartheid generation in South Africa, Đổi Mới generation (economic reform in Vietnam)

idea of social age. What sets the two apart is less empirical than analytical and thus defined by the questions we ask and the conceptual frames we employ.[7] Furthermore, conceptual innovation is often achieved by working across different interpretations. For example, Samantha Punch's (2015) notion of 'negotiated and constrained interdependencies' for understanding youth transitions combines the idea of generation as a life phase and generation in terms of kinship descent.

The conceptual journey through different understandings of age and generation that is presented in this section adds childhood and youth studies specific substance to Thelen et al.'s (2014) relational framework. More specifically, it provides a conceptual basis for different ways of understanding the idea of generational modalities, a starting point for how 'boundary' work might look like in relation to different concepts of age, and together this sheds light on how to understand the embeddedness of actors in generational and age-related terms.

Approaching Development

Development is a highly contested concept and the study of development has branched out into various intellectual directions (Thomas 2000). Within this scholarly landscape, the approach to development informing this book can best be described as people-centred and empirically rooted in the everyday. This means that local lives, structures, and processes are taken as the starting point for explaining why things work the way they do (Rigg 2007: 7–8).

A focus on the everyday is explicitly relation; the messy, fluid, and net-worked characteristics of the everyday amount to unmaking the seemingly fixed and clear-cut categories that inform so much scholarly work on children and youth (Balagopalan 2014: 183) and development too (Mosse 2005). This does not mean that I consider the local scale and the everyday in isolation from larger structures, relations, and histories—quite the contrary. Drawing on the ethnography of development and globalisation, I treat the local and the global as constantly interacting, co-constituting (Appadurai 1996: 32; Katz 2004; Maira and Soep 2005; Mosse 2005), and historically particular (Morrison 2015; Huijsmans 2016; Woronov 2016). In this view the everyday, even in out-of-the-way places is, drawing on Charles Piot (1999), 'remotely global'.

In line with contemporary approaches to development studies (McMichael 2004) and practice (United Nations 2016), this volume adopts a global approach. Next to the more conventional case studies, this volume, thus, includes three chapters based on research conducted in the Global North and a chapter that concentrates on the global development framework of the Sustainable Development Goals. The chapter by Sara Vida Coumans concentrates on the Dutch debate about regulating sex work. Since 'sexual and reproductive health and rights' is one of the four central themes of Dutch development cooperation it is worthwhile unravelling the specific ideas underpinning the Dutch debate as these are likely to have an effect on Dutch development cooperation on this theme.

The chapter by Elyse Mills addresses the challenges faced by Canadians aspiring to become 'young farmers'. The generational problem of farming is receiving much attention in research in the global South (e.g. White 2012). Mills' work shows that the dynamics that exclude many young people from farming futures in the Global South, especially the increase in large-scale, capital intensive agriculture, are not very different in the Canadian context. International migration is one of the factors that have reconfigured the geographies of development. This is vividly illustrated by Mahardhika Sjamsoeoed Sadjad, who, as a young, female, Muslim, Indonesian researcher reflects on her research encounters with young Dutch Muslims from migrant backgrounds as part of her MA in Development Studies. She not only makes a strong case for attending to positionality in the relational exercise of doing research, her work also contributes to redrawing the geographical boundaries of development studies.

Structure of the Book

Next follow 12 full chapters and a commentary by Nicola Ansell. Part I of the book ('theorising age and generation in young lives') starts off with a chapter by Jason Hart that argues the importance of attending to 'age-position' in studying and working with young refugees. He draws on four different interpretations of the notion of generation and develops and illustrates these with reference to his work with young Palestinian refugees in Jordan. Hart argues that attending to age-position is important for appreciating the historicity of young refugee lives as well as to comprehend the forces that shape and reshape the particular needs and aspirations of young male refugees. Sara Vida Coumans' contribution takes us to the Netherlands. Drawing on recent policy debates about the increase of the minimum age of prostitution, she explores two very different dimensions of age that shape sex work and vividly illustrates the idea of 'boundary work' in relation to age (Thelen et al. 2014). Chronological age dominates in policy discussions, yet it is the corporeal dimension of age that matters in sex work as practice. Coumans' chapter also shows that age, in its various, conceptualisations never works in isolation but always intersects with other relations of social differentiation such as gender. Elyse Mills furthers the theme of intersectionality in her chapter on becoming a young farmer in Nova Scotia, Canada, by analysing the interaction between age and social class. This leads her to propose the idea of 'age-class', which shows that Canadian policies meant to support young people in becoming a young farmer are of little use for large groups of (aspiring) young farmers. She also emphasises the importance of the collective agency of young farmers' organisations especially for (aspiring) young farmers from middle-class and lower-class backgrounds both in terms of a support structure as well as a lobbying organisation for rethinking agrarian futures. Part I closes with Christina Clark-Kazak's chapter. She employs the concept of social age and the idea of 'age-mainstreaming' as lenses to critically assess the way age has been incorporated in the Sustainable Development Goals.

Part II of the book coheres around 'everyday relationalities: school, work and belonging'. On the basis of ethnographic research in two secondary schools in the Northern Vietnamese city of Haiphong, Paul Horton unravels the generational dimension of school bullying. Countering perspectives that understand school bullying at the level of individual children, Horton proposes that school bullying is deeply connected to the ways power works in the generational organisation of the school and that some students learn to utilise bullying in such a context as a means to influence the behaviour of others. In both Degwale Belay's and Wedadu Sayibu's contribution, the street is treated as an important everyday space and a key site of children's work. The street is an important meeting place for different 'relational modalities' (Thelen et al. 2014) as various registers of meaning interact (Gigengack 2014). This renders street-based work deeply relational. The two chapters also show that children's street-based work is intricately connected to the wider, gendered and generationally organised street-based urban economy. The chapters refute quick generalisations about children's street-based work. Shoe-shining, lottery vending, and accompanying blind adult beggars constitute very different relational modalities, subject to different moral registers, set within different economic relations and presenting their own set of vulnerabilities and opportunities. Mahardhika Sjamsoeoed Sadjad's chapter closes part II with a discussion of the relationality of the idea of home and belonging drawing on research with Dutch Muslim youth with migrant backgrounds. Her auto-ethnographic contribution brings out in vivid detail the important, yet too little acknowledged, relational dimension of doing research. Sadjad's reflection on her positionality also extends Hart's (this volume) discussion of the idea of 'having been' (in addition 'being' and 'becoming') in research with children and young people.

Part III of the book is themed 'negotiating development'. It shows how development interventions reshape generational landscapes and how young people from their particular position in society negotiate the various contradictions of development and work hard to 'have a life' as one of the young people in Lidewyde Berckmoes and Ben White's chapter put it. Karuna Morarji's chapter is also written in an ethnographic fashion, but unlike Sadjad's Dutch setting Morarji's chapter is set in a remote mountainous area of northern India. She illustrates how young men and women negotiate the contradictions of schooling as a modernising project that is part and parcel of the broader cultural politics of development yet distinctly differentiated by class, gender, and generation. María Gabriela Palacio focuses in her chapter on another widespread development intervention that targets the young: conditional cash transfers (CCTs). Despite the wealth of literature on CCTs and the centrality of children in the theory of change underpinning these schemes, relatively little has been written about how these affect the lived experience of being young and growing up (a notable exception includes: Streuli 2012). Drawing on research in Loja, Ecuador, Palacio's chapter investigates how children's recipient status affects their relational position within the family, between children and vis-à-vis the state. Sharada Srinivasan's chapter explicitly addresses the theme of gender, another long-standing concern in development studies and practice. Srinivasan asks what it means for girls to grow up in contexts characterised by poverty and daughter aversion. This brings to the surface the particular ways in which gender discrimination manifests and is negotiated by these girls over the first two decades of their lives. Part III closes with a contribution from Lidewyde Berckmoes and Ben White based on research in rural eastern Burundi. The chapter illuminates young people's highly gendered and 'fleeting responses' to the challenges of building a livelihood and successful generational transitions in the aftermath of conflict and under conditions of extreme poverty. In contrast to various other studies, Berckmoes and White argue that young people's apparent turnaway from farming has less to do with an aversion to farming futures but is rather attributable to structural limitations over which young people have little influence.

The volume closes with a commentary by Nicola Ansell. She points out that age and generation are produced and deployed in the exercise of power in societies, and thus fundamental concepts for understanding contexts in which development interventions play out.

Children and young people are central to questions of development. This argument is mostly made in reference to demographic data showing that especially in poorer parts of the world typically a large share of the population falls in the childhood and youth category (Ansell 2005: 3; World Bank 2006: 4). The relational perspective running through the chapters of this book demands adjusting this oft-repeated argument. Although sheer numbers matter, generationing development is ultimately an analytical exercise.[9] Research with and on children and youth constitutes a unique window on processes of social change and continuity for the ways in which the temporal dimension of development interacts with the embodied and gendered experience of being young and growing up (Cole and Durham 2008; MacDonald 2011; Woronov 2016). Similarly, processes of development are key for childhood and youth studies precisely because development plays out in generational landscapes. Thereby, development transforms the opportunities structures shaping young lives, reshuffles the parameters within which young people negotiate their generational position and within which they give new meaning to the very idea of childhood and youth. The chapters in this volume thus stimulate further thinking on how ideas of age and generation help coming to grips with development as a generational process—especially, though not exclusively, in how it pertains to children and young people.

Notes

1. Note though that there is much ambiguity about the use of the term 'children' or 'youth', especially in relation to 15–18 years old where according to international age-based definitions both labels apply. Yet, the choice of term matters. A study framed in terms of gang youth suggests a very different research problem than a study on street children even though the subjects may well be the same young people.
2. Note here too a recently launched Collaborative Research Network on 'life course' between the Association for Anthropology and Gerontology, the Anthropology of Aging and the Life Course Interest Group (AALCIG) and the Anthropology of Children and Youth Interest Group, see: https://lists.capalon.com/lists/list-info/acyig_lifecourse
3. Note that *Facebook* requires one to enter a date of birth when setting up an account and uses 13 as the minimum age for opening an account.
4. In the Korean age system (co-existing in Korea with a chronological system based on calendar years from birth), a newborn baby is con-

sidered one year of age at birth and turns two on the first day of the New Year (Gregorian calendar).

5. Age is an important marker of seniority, but at times this may be overruled by other markers of rank such as religious status, kinship relations, class or nationality.

6. Virginia Morrow (2013: 152) refers in this respect to the idea of 'functional age'.

7. The idea of generation as life phase has several points of overlap with the notion of social age discussed above. Yet, what sets the two apart is that the idea of life phase implies the larger framework of the life course. Social age, on the other hand, does not necessarily mobilise such a larger generational order as it foregrounds subjectivities and performativity.

8. Note here also the branding of cohorts into generational identities for commercial purposes, as is illustrated by the frequent use of terms like 'generation X', 'generation Y', etc., in the marketing literature.

9. The term 'generationing' has been defined by Mayall (2002: 27) as 'the relational process whereby people come to be known as children, and whereby children and childhood acquire certain characteristics'. Clearly, the idea of generationing is by no means limited to children and youth.

References

Alanen, L. (2001). Explorations in generational analysis. In L. Alanen & B. Mayall (Eds.), *Conceptualizing child-adult relations* (pp. 11–22). London/New York: RoutledgeFalmer.

Alderson, P., & Morrow, V. (2004). *Ethics, social research and consulting with children and young people*. Ilford/Essex: Barnardo's.

Alexander, P. (2014). Learning to act your age: 'Age imaginaries' and media consumption in an English secondary school. In D. Buckingham, S. Bragg, & M. J. Kehily (Eds.), *Youth cultures in the age of global media* (pp. 136–149). Basingstoke/New York: Palgrave Macmillan.

Amit-Talai, V., & Wulff, H. (Eds.) (1995). *Youth cultures: A crosscultural perspective*. London/New York: Routledge.

Ansell, N. (2005). *Children, youth and development*. London/New York: Routledge.

Ansell, N. (2009). Childhood and the politics of scale: Descaling children's geographies? *Progress in Human Geography, 33*(2), 190–109.

Appadurai, A. (1996). *Modernity at large: cultural dimensions of globalization.* Minneapolis/London: University of Minnesota Press.

Ariès, P. (1962). *Centuries of childhood: A social history of family life.* Vintage Books/Random House: New York.

Balagopalan, S. (2014). *Inhabiting 'childhood': Children, labour and schooling in postcolonial India.* Basingstoke/New York: Palgrave Macmillan.

Barendregt, B. (2008). Sex, cannibals, and the language of cool: Indonesian tales of the phone and modernity. *The Information Society, 24*(3), 160–170.

Beazley, H., & Chakraborty, K. (2008). Cool consumption: Rasta, punk and Bollywood on the streets of Yogyakarta, Indonesia and Kolkata, India. In U. M. Rodrigues & B. Smaill (Eds.), *Youth, media and culture in the Asia Pacific region* (pp. 195–214). Newcastle: Cambridge Scholars Publishing.

Boellstorff, T. (2008). *Coming of age in second life: An anthropologist explores the virtually human.* Princeton/Oxford: Princeton University Press.

Bourdillon, M. F. C., White, B., & Myers, W. E. (2009). Re-assessing minimum age standards for children's work. *International Journal of Sociology and Social Policy, 29*(3/4).

Boyden, J., & Zharkevich, I. (forthcoming). The impact of development on children. In H. Callan (Ed.), *International encyclopedia of anthropology: Anthropology beyond text.* New York: Wiley Blackwell.

Boyden, J., Dercon, S., & Singh, A. (2015). Child development in a changing world: Risks and opportunities. *The World Bank Research Observer, 30*(2), 193–219.

Buckingham, D., Bragg, S., & Kehily, M. J. (Eds.) (2014). *Youth cultures in the age of global media.* Basingstoke/New York: Palgrave Macmillan.

Camfield, L. (2011). Editorial: Young lives in transition: From school to adulthood? *European Journal of Development Research, 23*(5), 669–678.

Carsten, J. (2004). *After Kinship.* Cambridge: Cambridge University Press.

Christensen, P., & James, A. (Eds.) (2000). *Research with children: Perspectives and practices.* London/New York: RoutledgeFalmer.

Christie, R. (2015). Millennium Development Goals (MDGs) and indigenous peoples' literacy in Cambodia: Erosion of sovereignty? *Nations and Nationalism, 21*(2), 250–269.

Clark-Kazak, C. R. (2009). Towards a working definition and application of social age in international development studies. *Journal of International Development, 45*(8), 1307–1324.

Cole, J., & Durham, D. (Eds.) (2007). *Generations and globalization: Youth, age, and family in the new world economy.* Bloomington: Indiana University Press.

Cole, J., & Durham, D. (2008). Globalization and the temporality of children and youth. In J. Cole & D. Durham (Eds.), *Figuring the future: Globalization and the temporalities of children and youth* (pp. 3–23). Santa Fe: School for Advanced Research Press.

Corsten, M. (1999). The time of generations. *Time & Society, 8*(2-3), 249–272.

Côté, J. E. (2014). Towards a new political economy of youth. *Journal of Youth Studies, 17*(4), 527–543.

Edmunds, J., & Turner, B. S. (2005). Global generations: Social change in the twentieth century. *The British Journal of Sociology, 56*(4), 559–577.

Elder, S. (2014). *Labour market transitions of young women and men in Asia and the Pacific, Work4Youth publication series no. 19.* Geneva: International Labour Office, Mastercard Foundation.

Enfield, N. J. (2007). Meaning of the unmarked: How 'default' person reference does more than just refer. In N. J. Enfield & T. Stivers (Eds.), *Person reference in interaction: Linguistic, cultural and social perspectives* (pp. 97–120). Cambridge: Cambridge University Press.

Evans, G. (1998). *The politics of ritual and remembrance: Laos since 1975.* Chiang Mai: Silkworm Books.

Evans, R. (2015). Negotiating intergenerational relations and care in diverse African contexts. In R. Vanderbeck & N. Worth (Eds.), *Intergenerational space* (pp. 199–213). London/New York: Routledge.

Ezbawy, Y. A. (2012). The role of youth's new protest movements in the January 25th revolution. *IDS Bulletin, 43*(1), 26–36.

Gerber, N., & Huijsmans, R. (2016). From access to post-access concerns: Rethinking inclusion in education through children's everyday school attendance in rural Malaysia. In C. Hunner-Kreisel & S. Bohne (Eds.), *Childhood, youth and migration: Connecting global and local perspectives* (pp. 203–221). Dordrecht: Springer.

Gigengack, R. (2014). 'Beyond discourse and competence: Science and subjugated knowledge in street children studies.' *the European Journal of Development Research* 26(2): 264–282.

Goddard, V., & White, B. (1982). Special issue: Child workers and capitalist development. *Development & Change, 13*(4), 465–652.

Gottlieb, A. (2004). *The afterlife is where we come from: The culture of infancy in western Africa.* Chicago/London: University of Chicago Press.

Grieg, B. (1994). Invisible hands: The political economy of child labour in colonial Zimbabwe, 1890-1930. *Journal of Southern African Studies, 20*(1), 27–52.

Hanson, K., & Nieuwenhuys, O. (Eds.) (2013). *Reconceptualizing children's rights in international development: Living rights, social justice, translations.* Cambridge: Cambridge University Press.

Hart, J. (2008). *Business as usual? The global political economy of childhood poverty, Young lives technical note no. 13.* Oxford: Young Lives, Department of International Development, University of Oxford.

Heinonen, P. (2013). *Youth gangs & street children: Culture, nurture and masculinity in Ethiopia.* New York/Oxford: Berghahn.

Herrera, L. (2006). What's new about youth? *Development & Change, 37*(6), 1425–1434.

Herrera, L., & Bayat, A. (Eds.) (2010). *Being young and Muslim: New cultural politics in the global south and north.* Oxford/New York: Oxford University Press.

Hoang, L. A., & Yeoh, B. S. A. (2015). Children's agency and its contradictions in the context of transnational labour migration from Vietnam. *Global Networks, 15*(2), 180–197.

Hoddinott, J. (1992). Rotten kids or manipulative parents: Are children old age security in western Kenya? *Economic Development & Cultural Change, 40*(3), 545–565.

Honwana, A., & De Boeck, F. (Eds.) (2005). *Makers and breakers: Children and youth in postcolonial Africa.* London: James Currey.

Hopkins, P., & Hill, M. (2010). Contested bodies of asylum-seeking children. In K. Hörschelmann & R. Colls (Eds.), *Contested bodies of childhood and youth* (pp. 136–147). Basingstoke/New York: Palgrave Macmillan.

Hopkins, P., & Pain, R. (2007). Geographies of age: Thinking relationally. *Area, 39*(3), 287–294.

Howard, N. (2014). Teenage labor migration and antitrafficking policy in West Africa. *The ANNALS of the American Academy of Political and Social Science, 653*(1), 124–140.

Huijsmans, R.B.C. (2010). *Migrating children, households, and the post-socialist state: An ethnographic study of migration and non-migration by children and youth in an ethnic Lao village.' Department of Geography.* Unpublished PhD thesis. Durham, Durham University.

Huijsmans, R. (2011). The theatre of human trafficking: A global discourse on Lao stages. *International Journal of Social Quality, 1*(2), 66–84.

Huijsmans, R. (2013). Doing gendered age': Older mothers and migrant daughters negotiating care work in rural Lao PDR and Thailand. *Third World Quarterly, 34*(10), 1896–1910.

Huijsmans, R. (2014a). Becoming a young migrant or stayer seen through the lens of 'householding': Households 'in flux' and the intersection of relations of gender and seniority. *Geoforum, 51,* 294–304.

Huijsmans, R. (2014b). Gender, masculinity, and safety in the changing Lao-Thai migration landscape. In T.-D. Truong, D. Gasper, J. Handmaker, & S. I. Bergh (Eds.), *Migration, gender and social justice: Perspectives on human security* (pp. 333–349). Heidelberg/New York/Dordrecht/London: Springer.

Huijsmans, R. (2015a). Children and young people in migration: A relational approach. In C. N. Laoire, A. White, & T. Skelton (Eds.), *Movement, mobilities and journeys* (p. 6). Singapore: Springer.

Huijsmans, R. (2015b). Youth, phones and companies: Impressions from Southeast Asia. *8th conference of the European Association for Southeast Asian Studies (EuroSEAS).* Vienna, 11–14 August.

Huijsmans, R. (2016). Critical geopolitics of child and youth migration in (post) socialist laos. In M. C. Benwell & P. Hopkins (Eds.), *Children, young people and critical geopolitics* (pp. 139–154). Farnham: Ashgate.

Huijsmans, R., & Baker, S. (2012). Child trafficking: 'Worst Form' of child labour, or worst approach to young migrants? *Development and Change, 43*(4), 919–946.

Huijsmans, R., & Lan, T. T. H. (2015). Enacting nationalism through youthful mobilities? Youth, mobile phones and digital capitalism in a Lao-Vietnamese borderland. *Nations and Nationalism, 21*(2), 209–229.

Huijsmans, R., George, S., Gigengack, R., & Evers, S. J. T. M. (2014). Introduction. Theorising age and generation in development: A relational approach. *European Journal of Development Research, 26*(2), 163–174.

Izzi, V. (2013). Just keeping them busy? youth employment projects as a peace-building tool. *International Development Planning Review, 35*(2), 103–117.

Jeffrey, C. (2010). *Timepass: Youth, class, and the politics of waiting in India.* Stanford: Stanford University Press.

Jeffrey, C., Jeffery, P., & Jeffery, R. (2008). *Degrees without freedom: Education, masculinities and unemployment in North India.* Stanford: Stanford University Press.

Johnson-Hanks, J. (2002). On the limits of life stages in ethnography: Toward a theory of vital conjunctions. *American Anthropologist, 104*(3), 865–880.

Jones, M. (2009). Phase space: Geography, relational thinking, and beyond. *Progress in Human Geography, 33*(4), 487–506.

Kabeer, N. (2000). Intergenerational-contracts, demographic transitions, and the 'quantity-quality' tradeoff: Parents, children and investing in the future. *Journal of International Development, 12*(4), 463–482.

Katz, C. (2004). *Growing up global: Economic restructuring and children's every-day lives.* Minneapolis/London: University of Minnesota Press.

Kierkegaard, S. (2008). Cybering, online grooming and ageplay. *Computer Law & Security Review, 24*(1), 41–55.

Kolk, A., Rivera-Santos, M., & Rufín, C. (2013). Reviewing a decade of research on the "Base/Bottom of the Pyramid" (BOP) concept. *Business & Society, 53,* 338–377.

Koning, J. (1997). Generations of change: A Javanese village in the 1990s. *Faculteit der Politieke en Sociaal-Culturele Wetenschappen.* PhD thesis. Amsterdam, University of Amsterdam.

Kraftl, P. (2013). Beyond 'voice', beyond 'agency', beyond 'politics'? Hybrid childhoods and some critical reflections on children's emotional geographies. *Emotion, Space and Society, 9,* 13–23.

La Fontaine, J. S. (Ed.) (1978). *Sex and age as principles of social differentiation.* London/New York/San Francisco: Academic.

Lall, M., & Vickers, E. (Eds.) (2009). *Education as a political tool in Asia.* London/New York: Routledge.

Laz, C. (1998). Act your age. *Sociological Forum, 13*(1), 85–113.

Liebel, M. (2004). *A will of their own: Cross-cultural perspectives on working children*. London/New York: Zed Books.

Lukose, R. (2005). Consuming globalization: Youth and gender in Kerala, India. *Journal of Social History, 38*(4), 915–935.

MacDonald, R. (2011). Youth transitions, unemployment and underemployment: Plus ça change, plus c'est la même chose. *Journal of Sociology, 47*(4), 427–444.

Maconachie, R., & Hilson, G. (2016). Rethinking the child labor 'problem' in rural Sub-Saharan Africa: The case of Sierra Leone's half shovels. *World Development, 78*, 136–147.

Maira, S., & Soep, E. (Eds.) (2005). *Youthscapes: The popular, the national, the global*. University of Pennsylvania Press: Philadelphia.

Mannheim, K. (1952). *Essays on the sociology of knowledge*. London: RKP.

Mayall, B. (2002). *Towards a sociology for childhood: Thinking from children's lives*. Maidenhead: Open University Press.

Mazzucato, V., & Schans, D. (2011). Transnational families and the well-being of children: Conceptual and methodological challenges. *Journal of Marriage and Family, 73*(4), 704–712.

Mazzucato, V., Kabki, M., & Smith, L. (2006). Transnational migration and the economy of funerals: Changing practices in Ghana. *Development and Change, 37*(5), 1047–1072.

McMichael, P. (2004). *Development as social change: A global perspective* (3rd ed.). London: Sage.

McNamee, S., & Seymour, J. (2013). Towards a sociology of 10–12 year olds? Emerging methodological issues in the 'new' social studies of childhood. *Childhood, 20*(2), 156–168.

Mead, M. (2001 [1928]). *Coming of age in Samoa: A psychological study of primitive youth for western civilisation*. New York: Perennial Classics.

Meek, D. (2012). YouTube and social movements: A phenomenological analysis of participation, events and cyberspace. *Antipode, 44*(4), 1429–1448.

Melchiorre, A. (2004). *At what age?...are school-children employed, married and taken to court?*. Right to Education Project.

Mesch, G. S., & Talmud, I. (2010). *Wired youth: The social world of adolescence in the information age*. Hove/New York: Routledge.

Mills, M. B. (1999). *Thai women in the global labor force: Consuming desires, contested selves*. New Brunswick/London: Rutgers University Press.

Montgomery, H. (2007). Working with child prostitutes in Thailand: Problems of practice and interpretation. *Childhood, 14*(4), 415–430.

Morrison, H. (2015). *Childhood and colonial modernity in Egypt*. Basingstoke/New York: Palgrave Macmillan.

Morrow, V. (2013). What's in a number? Unsettling the boundaries of age. *Childhood, 20*(2), 151–155.

Mosse, D. (2005). *Cultivating development: An ethnography of aid policy and practice*. London/Ann Arbor: Pluto Press.

Mosse, D. (2010). A relational approach to durable poverty, inequality and power. *Journal of Development Studies, 46*(7), 1156–1178.

Myers, W., & Bourdillon, M. (2012). Introduction: Development, children, and protection. *Development in Practice, 22*(4), 437–447.

Naafs, S., & White, B. (2012). Intermediate generations: Reflections on Indonesian youth studies. *The Asia Pacific Journal of Anthropology, 13*(1), 3–20.

Närvänen, A.-L., & Näsman, E. (2004). Childhood as generation or life phase? *Young, 12*(1), 71–91.

Nayak, A., & Kehily, M. J. (2013). *Gender, youth & culture: Global masculinities & femininities* (2nd ed.). Basingstoke: Palgrave MacMillan.

Nieuwenhuys, O. (1994). *Children's lifeworlds: Gender, welfare and labour in the developing world*. London: Routledge.

O'Connell Davidson, J. (2005). *Children in the global sex trade*. Cambridge/Malden: Polity Press.

Piot, C. (1999). *Remotely global: Village modernity in West Africa*. Chicago/London: The University of Chicago Press.

Proctor, T. M. (2009). *Scouting for girls: A century of girl guides and girl scouts*. Santa Barbara: Greenwood Publishing Group.

Punch, S. (2002a). Research with children: The same or different from research with adults? *Childhood, 9*(3), 321–341.

Punch, S. (2002b). Youth transitions and interdependent adult-child relations in rural Bolivia. *Journal of Rural Studies, 18*(2), 123–133.

Punch, S. (2007). Negotiating migrant identities: Young people in Bolivia and Argentina. *Children's Geographies, 5*(1), 95–112.

Punch, S. (2015). Youth transitions and migration: Negotiated and constrained interdependencies within and across generations. *Journal of Youth Studies, 18*(2), 262–276.

Punch, S. (2016). Exploring children's agency across majority and minority world contexts. In F. Esser, M. S. Baader, T. Betz, & B. Hungerland (Eds.), *Reconceptualising agency and childhood: New perspectives in childhood studies* (pp. 183–196). London: Routledge.

Rigg, J. (2007). *An everyday geography of the global South*. Abingdon/New York: Routledge.

Robson, E., Panelli, R., & Punch, S. (Eds.) (2007). *Global perspectives on rural childhood and youth: Young rural lives*. New York: Taylor & Francis Group.

Scott, J. C. (1998). *Seeing like a state: How certain schemes to improve the human condition have failed*. New Haven/London: Yale University Press.

Semedi, P. (2016). Pramuka: Scouting days of fun. In K. Robinson (Ed.), *Youth identities and social transformations in Modern Indonesia* (pp. 113–129). Leiden/Boston: Brill.

Shah, N., & Abraham, S. (2009). *Digital natives with a cause? A knowledge survey and framework*. Hivos Knowledge Programme Report. The Hague, Bangalore, Humanist Institute for Cooperation with Developing Countries (HIVOS), Centre for Internet and Society.

Sinha-Kerkhoff, K. (2011). Seeing the state through youth policy formation: The case of the state of Jharkhand. *Africa Development, XXXVI*(3&4), 67–88.

Smith, S. H. (2013). In the heart, there's nothing': Unruly youth, generational vertigo and territory. *Transactions of the Institute of British Geographers, 38*(4), 572–585.

Spyrou, S. (2011). The limits of children's voices: From authenticity to critical, reflexive representation. *Childhood, 18*(2), 151–165.

Streuli, N. (2012). *Children's experiences of Juntos, a conditional cash transfer scheme in Peru, Working paper no. 78*. Oxford: Young Lives, Oxford Department of International Development, University of Oxford.

Szymańska-Matusiewicz, G. (2014). The researcher as 'older sister', 'younger sister' and 'niece': Playing the roles defined by the Vietnamese pronominal reference system. *Qualitative Research, 14*(1), 95–111.

Thelen, T., Vetters, L., & Von Benda-Beckmann, K. (2014). Introduction to stategraphy: Toward a relational anthropology of the state. *Social Analysis, 58*(3), 1–19.

Thomas, A. (2000). Meanings and views of development. In T. Allen & A. Thomas (Eds.), *Poverty and development: Into the 21st century* (pp. 23–48). Oxford: Open University Press with Oxford University Press.

Thorne, B. (2004). Editorial: Theorizing age and other differences. *Childhood, 11*(4), 403–408.

Tisdall, E. K. M., & Punch, S. (2012). Not so 'new'? Looking critically at childhood studies. *Children's Geographies, 10*(3), 249–264.

Twum-Danso Imoh, A., & Ansell, N. (Eds.) (2013). *Children's lives in the era of children's rights: The progress of the convention on the rights of the child in Africa*. London: Routledge.

United Nations. (2016). *Sustainabledevelopment knowledge platform*. Retrieved February 21, 2016, from https://sustainabledevelopment.un.org/?menu=1300

Uprichard, E. (2008). Children as 'being and becomings': Children, childhood and temporality. *Children & Society, 22*(4), 303–313.

Utrata, J. (2011). Youth privilege: Doing age and gender in Russia's single-mother families. *Gender & Society, 25*(5), 616–641.

Valentin, K. (2007). Mass mobilization and the struggle over the youth: The role of Ho Chi Minh Communist youth Union in urban Vietnam. *Young, 15*(3), 299–315.

Van Bueren, G. (1995). *The international law on the rights of the child*. The Hague/Boston/London: Save the Children & Martinus Nijhoff Publishers.

Vanderbeck, R. M., & Worth, N. (2015). Introduction. In R. M. Vanderbeck & N. Worth (Eds.), *Intergenerational space* (pp. 1–14). London/New York: Routledge.

Vigh, H. (2006). *Navigating terrains of war: Youth and soldiering in Guinea-Bissau*. Oxford: Berghahn Books.

Vigh, H. (2009). Motion squared: A second look at the concept of social navigation. *Anthropological Theory, 9*(4), 419–438.

Wells, K. (2009). *Childhood in a global perspective*. Cambridge/Malden: Polity Press.

White, B. (1996). Globalization and the child labour problem. *Journal of International Development, 8*(6), 829–839.

White, B. (2012). Agriculture and the generation problem: Rural youth, employment and the future of farming. *IDS Bulletin, 43*(6), 9–19.

Whitehead, A., Hashim, I. M., &Iversen, V. (2007). *Child migration, child agency, and inter-generational relations in Africa and South Asia* (Working paper T24). Brighton, Development Research Centre on Migration, Globalisation & Poverty, Sussex University.

Willis, P. E. (1981). *Learning to labour: How working class kids get working class jobs*. Hampshire: Gower Publishing Company Ltd.

Wilson, H., & Huntington, A. (2006). Deviant (M)others: The construction of teenage motherhood in contemporary discourse. *Journal of Social Policy, 35*(01), 59–76.

World Bank. (2006). *World development report 2007. Development and the next generation*. Washington, DC: The International Bank for Reconstruction and Development/The World Bank.

Woronov, T. E. (2016). *Class work: Vocational schools and China's urban youth*. Stanford: Stanford University Press.

Worth, N. (2014). Youth, relationality, and space: Conceptual resources for youth studies from critical human geography. In J. Wyn & H. Cahill (Eds.), *Handbook of children and youth studies*. Singapore: Springer.

Wyn, J., & White, R. (1997). *Rethinking youth*. London/Thousand Oaks/New Delhi: Sage.

Xu, Q. (2015). One roof, different dreams. In R. M. Vanderbeck & N. Worth (Eds.), *Intergenerational space* (pp. 183–196). London/New York: Routledge.

Young, M. E. (Ed.) (2007). *Child development from measurement to action: A priority for growth and equity*. Washinghton, DC: The International Bank for Reconstruction and Development/The World Bank.

Young Lives. Young lives: An international study of childhood poverty. From http://www.younglives.org.uk/

Zetter, R. (1991). Labelling refugees: Forming and transforming a bureaucratic identity. *Journal of Refugee Studies, 4*(1), 39–62.

Theorising Age and Generation in Young Lives

Locating Young Refugees Historically: Attending to Age Position in Humanitarianism

Jason Hart

Of the estimated 59.5 million forced migrants globally (UNHCR 2015) countless numbers have been displaced for several years or decades. While some have experienced flight first-hand, there are also many who have been born into a setting of displacement and may themselves have become parents or even grandparents to children who inherit refugee status. Sahrawi people in Algeria, Somalis, Congolese, and Sudanese in the camps of East Africa, Afghans in Pakistan and Iran, Palestinians dispersed across the various countries of the Fertile Crescent, Bhutanese in Nepal, Rohingya in Bangladesh, and the Karen in Thailand are only some of the world's long-term displaced populations. The wave of displacement from Iraq that began with the US-led invasion and removal of Saddam Hussein

---

This chapter is based largely on an article under the same title that appeared in the European Journal of Development Research (2014) Vol. 26(2): 219–232.

J. Hart (✉)
Department of Social and Policy Sciences, University of Bath,
Claverton Down, BA1 7AY Bath, Somerset, UK

R. Huijsmans (ed.), *Generationing Development*,
DOI 10.1057/978-1-137-55623-3_2

has created a new, long-term displaced population. The Iraqi refugees have been joined in countries of the Middle East region and in efforts to relocate to Europe and beyond by huge numbers of Syrians. Neither population group looks likely to 'return' to their country of origin in the foreseeable future.

Reflecting the typically high proportion of young people amongst the world's long-term displaced, sociological attention to refugee children and youth has grown in recent years (e.g. Boyden and de Berry 2004; Hart 2008a; Chatty 2010) However, consideration of the relational dynamics of age is still at an early stage: some way behind that given to gender (e.g. Indra 1998; Turner 1999; Nolin 2006). This chapter is motivated by the conviction that attention to the young as 'aged' (as well as 'gendered') social beings is vital to enhance understanding of the lived experience of long-term displacement (Clark-Kazak 2009).

Over recent years, even humanitarian organisations that are not focused specifically on the young have developed projects that target this section of the population. There is a tendency in such work to focus upon the 'challenges and priorities' of young people (Evans and Lo Forte 2013: 12) without necessary consideration of the ways in which these challenges and priorities are informed by what Christina Clark-Kazak (2009) refers to as 'social age' or what I refer to here as 'age position'. Thus when working with young people in their teens for example, there is an underlying assumption that the 'challenges and priorities' that they articulate are simply an expression of generic (albeit gendered) experience particular to their chronological age. Although important, this is only one aspect of a young person's age position. It is also necessary to consider how the needs and aspirations that they voice might be shaped by (1) communal experience; (2) kinship relations—particularly between parents and children; and (3) wider societal processes of change. Together with life phase, these are all aspects of the framework that I suggest for producing a necessarily multi-faceted understanding of the age position of young people. This framework utilises the notion of 'generation' to illuminate and bring together these different aspects.

Employment of generation as a central principle not only enables understanding of the age position of young people, it also offers a framework for learning about processes of social change and the ways that these impact different sections of a refugee population. In recent years, the United Nations High Commission for Refugees (UNHCR) has introduced the category of 'Protracted Refugee Situations' (PRS): a label applied to refugees 'for 5 years or more after their initial displacement, without immediate prospects for implementation of durable solutions' (UNHCR 2009: preamble). Yet, the categorisation of all populations displaced for five years or longer uniformly as 'PRS' collapses time and diverts attention from the ongoing dynamics of change as manifest, for example, in social organisation, family composition, gendered and intergenerational relations, as well as the link between such change and wider historical events. As I seek to explain, 'generations', in its various meanings, offer a conceptual basis for considering change in a fluid and open-ended manner. Young people, like others in the refugee population, are affected by and involved in such change in ways that reflect their age (as well as gender, class, etc.) position. Attending to such specificity would be significant for humanitarian efforts, not least in the search for viable long-term solutions: solutions that must be enacted at a particular historical moment and that will have different implications for different sections of a displaced population.

The generational framework for exploring the age position of young displacees and the changing context of their lives is here illustrated by material produced through ethnographic fieldwork in a Palestinian refugee camp in Amman, Jordan. Hussein Camp was established in the wake of the 1948 Arab–Israeli War. During the period of my research in the late 1990s and early 2000s, it was home to approximately 50,000 Palestinian refugees, the majority of whom had never seen the territory from which their elders had originally fled. In this paper, I draw particularly upon my interactions with young men in the age range 10–20. I begin, however, by arguing for the importance of attending to the young in historical terms.

THE YOUNG AS HISTORICAL ACTORS

In an influential and much-cited article, anthropologist Liisa Malkki notes the 'effect of the bureaucratized humanitarian interventions that are set in motion by large population displacements...to leach out the histories and the politics of specific refugees' circumstances' (1996:178). In her view, the nature of such interventions makes it difficult 'for people in the refugee category to be approached as historical actors rather than simply as mute victims' (Ibid). There is a *governmental* dimension to such an effect in the form of technocratic processes that construct displaced people and their complex experiences as homogenised 'cases' in accordance with 'bureaucratic dictates' (Zetter 1991:47). However, meaningful engagement with the long-term displaced as historical actors also entails two distinct but inter-related *conceptual* challenges. The first concerns the agency of refugees, while the second relates to the connection between the forcibly displaced and historical processes. Each of these in respect of the young is discussed in turn.

The Agency of the Young

The latter decades of the twentieth century witnessed the emergence of the field of childhood studies informed by the work of scholars in the disciplines of sociology, social policy, anthropology, human geography, philosophy, and history, amongst others. This field partly came into being as a result of dissatisfaction with the hitherto dominant view of 'socialisation' that took the child to be a passive object of adult instruction. Scholars identified with this emerging field have insisted that the young be considered as 'active in the construction and determination of their own social lives' (Prout and James 1997:8). Such an argument, now widely taken as normative amongst practitioners as well as academics, entails assertion of the child as a social actor able to exercise agency in transforming his or her circumstances. To some extent, this view is evident in the approach to programmatic interventions enacted by organisations working with the long-term displaced. The current vogue for 'child/youth participation' in humanitarian projects is usually surrounded by rhetoric about the young as 'agents' (White and Choudhury 2007; Percy-Smith and Burns 2013; Plan International 2015). Yet, closer inspection reveals that organisations' acknowledgement of agency is often mediated by their own mandate, values, or strategic interests. Thus, for example, young refugees under the age of 18 are commonly seen as agents when engaged in peacebuilding activities but as exploited victims when they engage with military groups (Save the Children 2008; McEvoy-Levy 2011; McGill and O'Kane 2015). Clarity about the ways that the young seek to transform their circumstances requires us to be more reflexive about the constraints of our own moral worldview and/or institutional position.

Young People Within Historical Process

While those categorised as 'children' are seen, in some senses and contexts, as social actors and thus as makers of history, less consideration has been given to the ways that the lives of the young might be located within the historical trajectory of a society. Such enquiry is distinct from that pursued by authors such as Phillipe Ariès, Harry Hendrick, and Hugh Cunningham into the construction of childhood as a social institution over time. The issue that I am raising relates not only to the pre-existing conditions that the young must negotiate but also to the ways in which their outlook and aspirations are shaped within a particular historical moment, mediated by personal experience and the experiences of those around—family, community members, and peers.

The relatively scant attention given to the historicity of young people's lives is in sharp contrast to the common focus upon their future. That the young become productive adult citizens who ensure the nation's prosperity has been a central concern of policy-makers and political leaders since at least the latter part of the nineteenth century in Europe and North America (e.g. Kent 1991). This concern has been taken up by development practitioners and rights activists who have advocated investment in children in the global South, principally in the form of Western-style education, as a means to achieve future social and economic development (e.g. World Bank 2006; Tembon and Fort 2008; Plan International 2008).

Scholars within the field of childhood studies have questioned the dominant focus upon children's futures, insisting that we remain attentive to the young as social actors in the present (Uprichard 2008). The argument has been made for viewing the young as human 'beings' rather than as human 'becomings' (Qvortrup 1991). Yet, as Emma Uprichard has noted, this dichotomy is misleading, since 'it does not account for any future constructions of the child' (2008: 306). In other words, what the young may become is an issue of reflection and daily activity for both themselves and those around them in the present.

Undoubtedly, in order to understand young people's lives and actions in the present, we need to consider the impact of imaginings of the future. It is also vital, I would argue, that attention is paid to the ways that the past informs the lives of the young in terms of their present and with regard to their imaginings of and aspirations for the future. To the notion of the child as 'being' and 'becoming', we might add the idea of 'having been'.

Within popular discussion and in the accounts of philosophers, there is a tendency to view the child as a blank slate upon which knowledge is gradually written through experience (see also Morarji, this volume). Assumptions of this kind are prevalent in the programming of development and humanitarian organisations. This is evidenced, for example, in peacebuilding and peace education projects that are usually predicated on the belief that young people's experiences register only at a superficial level. Personal contact with the 'enemy' and/or a sound peace education curriculum are seen as capable of over-riding such experience, leading to the aspiration for co-existence. Detailed assessments of such projects cast doubt on the thinking of implementing organisations (e.g. Bekerman and Maoz 2005; Niens and Cairns 2005; Salomon 2006).

As Marilyn Strathern has argued, there exists no realm 'logically prior' to society (1996: 64), rather we are all 'already embedded in relations' (Ibid: 94). This perspective replaces the commonly assumed dichotomy of 'individual' versus 'society' with a view of 'sociality… as intrinsic to the definition of personhood'. (Ibid: 64). Strathern's argument is consonant with the critique of conventional views of socialisation as a process during which 'the adult…offers directions' and 'the child…responds accordingly and is finally rewarded by becoming "social", by becoming adult' (Prout and James 1997: 13). Reconceptualising the 'child' as inherently social renders as untenable assumptions that the young are blank slates at any point separable from their socio-historical context.

One further conceptual obstacle to acknowledgement that young refugees are fully implicated in historical processes remains—namely a view found in some quarters that long-term camp dwellers exist in a state of limbo, isolated from wider society. It is certainly true that many encamped populations are formally obliged to remain within the confines of a camp. This is not the reality for all refugees, however. Notwithstanding the efforts commonly instigated by governments to contain migrants and inhibit their movement, displaced people find ways to move in and out of camps, operating within the informal economy and accessing services officially denied to them (e.g. Kaiser 2006: 608). Thus, there are grounds to question the assumption that refugees are 'warehoused': to use a term found in some of the writing about the long-term displaced (e.g. Smith 2004).[1] The assumed state of separation and limbo indicated by this term has led some scholars to suggest that within refugee camps collective processes of change—both material and discursive—are suspended. Marc Augé, for example, has argued that refugee camps are, like airport terminals and shopping malls, 'non-places' which are simply 'there to be passed through' (1995: 104) and in which residents fail to invest meaning. The work of Liisa Malkki offers an opposed view. Her account of Burundian Hutus displaced to Tanzania illustrated that life in the confines of the camp was 'enabling and nurturing an elaborate and self-conscious historicity among its refugee inhabitants'. (1995: 52). How we are to explore and make sense of young people's role in and relationship to such historical processes is the challenge that I now seek to take up.

EMPLOYING THE NOTION OF 'GENERATION'

Generation as Cohort and as Historical Period

Across the sociological literature, the notion of 'generation' has been commonly used as if the phenomenon to which it refers is self-evident. Yet, closer examination reveals that authors have utilised the term in diverse and often contradictory ways. According to a review by David Kertzer, 'generation' has been employed to signify four distinct phenomena: 'cohort', 'historical period', 'life stage', and 'kinship descent' (1983).

'Generation' in its cohort aspect has been typically used by scholars in order to group together people born during anything from a single year to a decade or more. To invoke 'generation' in this way does not necessarily imply any sense of commonality subjectively experienced or the existence of a shared 'frame of interpretation' (Corsten 2003:48). In Karl Mannheim's highly influential thesis about the 'problem of generations' (1952[1928]), the objectively determined category of 'cohort' is referred to as 'generation location'. When those within an age cohort share some sense of commonality they become, in Mannheim's terms, 'generation as actuality'. For this to happen, he deemed it necessary to 'experience the same historical problems' (Ibid: 304). Various authors have taken up Mannheim's enquiry into the ways that cohorts of children, younger than the 'youth' in which he was especially interested, become self-conscious groupings (e.g. Corsten 2003; Hengst 2009). It is in this latter, subjective sense of 'generation as actuality' that I employ 'cohort' in the schema suggested below.

In the refugee and migration literatures, generation is often invoked with reference to either the moment of departure or of settlement in a new locale. Thus, we find frequent discussion of differences between 'first' and 'second' (etc) generation migrants/refugees. Such usage can be misleading, however. While it may, in some respects, indicate age differences as, for example, in use of the term 'Generation 1.5' to indicate children who arrived in a country at age 12 or less (Rumbaut 2004: 1162), it also commonly groups together people of very different chronological ages and at diverse stages in the life course. The particular time that a large number of people were forced to flee or when they reached a new country might be deemed to constitute a clear historical period. However, age and life phase, amongst other factors, will inevitably mediate experience of integration or resettlement. Thus, it is important to attend to both the point of exile as a historical moment or period as well as cohort objectively determined by chronological age in order to understand experience without conflating the two through unreflexive use of terms such as 'first generation refugee'.

Generation as Life Stage and in Kinship Descent

The two remaining uses of generation amongst the four that Kertzer enumerated (op. cit.) invoke 'life stage' and 'kinship descent' respectively. The first of these refers to phases such as 'youth', 'middle age', or 'post-retirement'. Each of these entails different entitlements and obligations as determined by local cultural and political-economic conditions.

As Peter Loizos has pointed out, position in the life course can have an important bearing upon how displacement is experienced (2007). In his study of Greek Cypriots forced to flee to the south of the island by the events of 1974, he observed the differences between younger people without caring duties 'who might be free to consider their options'; elders (60 years plus) 'who have discharged their major lifetime responsibilities' and would therefore 'not be faced with the tasks of provision for dependents'; and those in middle adulthood (34–44 years old) who carried 'multiple responsibilities for others' and who were, therefore, 'likely to experience displacement as hugely unsettling' (2007: 207–208). These observations illustrate the effects of being displaced at a particular point in the life cycle as differentiated from the so-called 'cohort effect' when a group of peers, through their interaction, develop a common reaction. Both are important to understanding age position and the impact of events but they are not the same.

The fourth major way in which 'generation' is employed, according to Kertzer, is to denote the distinction between kin (op. cit. 126). This brings to mind images of family trees in which parent–child connections constitute the vertical axis and sibling and conjugal relationships the horizontal. Much of the migration literature utilises 'generation' in this sense within studies that seek to ascertain differences between parents and children in values, knowledge, class position and—specifically in relation to migrants and refugees—with regard to processes of integration (Hirschman 1994; Rumbaut 2004; Zhou 1997).

The parent–child dynamic has been an important theme in the consideration of generation within childhood studies. Leena Alanen, in particular, has drawn attention to the 'generational order': likening the mutual constitution of the generations of 'children' and 'adults', respectively, to the gendered ordering of relations between 'men' and 'women' (2009). Alanen is interested in the role of children in reproducing such an order, observing that scholars have tended to look at this from the sole perspective of adults/parents and the actions associated with 'parenting'. Citing Berry Mayall (1996), she suggests that we should also pay attention to processes of 'childing' (2001:135). The observations of Rachel Hinton about the actions of Bhutanese refugee children in the camps of Nepal (2000) provide a helpful illustration of this point. Hinton cites the example of five-year-old Kamal to suggest the ways that the young 'encouraged care-givers to define themselves as supportive parents' (p. 209) in a situation of long-term displacement where many adults struggled with depression and 'feelings of abandonment' (p. 200):

> Frequently in the private forum of his own home he resorted to breastfeeding and behaviour patterns regarded as immature within his culture for a child of his age… He emphasized and even created dependency and in so doing made salient his parent's value. (p. 207)

Amongst a displaced population being a 'good child' can also entail demonstration of loyalty to the homeland or to cultural origins (e.g. Miller et al. 2008:77) Such demonstrations are produced by and serve to reproduce the 'generational order' indicated by Alanen (2009). I take this point up below when discussing how, in Hussein Camp, young people negotiate the expectations of adults with regard to knowledge of and feeling for the Palestinian homeland.

EXPLORING THE AGE POSITION IN HUSSEIN CAMP

Young Palestinian Refugees as Historical Actors: Milk-kinship

Hussein Camp in Amman was one of four camps established in Jordan to house Palestinians fleeing their homes as a result of the Arab–Israeli War of 1948. The extended family and village/town of origin have both constituted key principles of social organisation in the camp. Over the years, however, the neighbourhood—consisting of around 30 houses on one street of the camp—has also gained significance in terms of everyday relations of mutual support and in the choice of marriage partners. In the development of neighbourhood identity and cohesion, and in the social change that this represents children play an important role from infancy: their bodies are the vehicles through which 'community' is reproduced.

According to Islamic law, a child who feeds from a woman's breast would thereby establish a relationship with her of milk kin (*rid'aa*) (Altorki 1980). Otherwise unrelated infants who breastfeed from the same woman therefore become 'milk siblings'. In the case of male and female milk siblings, there would be a consequent relaxation of the distancing otherwise customary from around the time of puberty. There would also be a prohibition upon them marrying one another. In Hussein Camp, such relationships of milk kin were both effect and cause of close physical proximity and social solidarity. Partly through milk-kinship, the camp evolved from an emergency facility housing groups of refugees differentiated along lines of family/clan and location of origin into a community made up of self-conscious neighbourhoods. As the vehicle for milk kin relationships, the young were thus implicated from birth in the ongoing development of social relations within the space of the camp: their bodies objects and subjects of processes of change that are thoroughly historical.

Generations in Hussein Camp

In keeping with the assumptions extant within the literature noted above, residents of Hussein Camp frequently invoked the notion of 'generation' in relation to the moment of exile. Those who directly experienced displacement were commonly referred to as 'first generation', their children born in the camp become 'second generation', and so on. However, those who fled from Palestine in 1948 were inevitably of very different chronological ages. In addition, in most families, it was common for two or three generations—in kinship descent terms—to flee from their villages together. Thus, while the notion of 'first generation refugee', etc., was heard in the camp and noteworthy from a rhetorical point of view, it is not helpful in understanding age position. Suffice to say that the young people with whom I conducted fieldwork had all been born in Hussein Camp. For the most part, this was also true for their parents.

More relevant here are the kinship and cohort aspects of generations. The dynamics between children and their parents/grandparents at the individual level should be considered as an aspect of the objectification of the young in popular political discourse. The notion of 'generation' (in Arabic *jeel*) was invoked explicitly in rhetorics of redemption of the community-in-exile. Thus, in Hussein Camp, adults spoke in formal gatherings about young people (implicitly male) as *jeel al-awdeh* ('generation of return') and as *jeel al-aqsa* ('generation of al-Aqsa'). The first of these was part of the nationalist, broadly secular, project of return to former homes and homeland. The latter term employs an explicitly Islamic symbol—al-Aqsa mosque: the third holiest shrine in Islam. This term was in keeping with the discourse—promoted by Islamists—of Palestine as holy Muslim land that needed to be redeemed, rather than as a place that held specific importance for the families and communities displaced from there. Although the two terms were often used interchangeably, the difference between them is illustrative of broader differences within the community of Hussein Camp at that time, with the increasing prominence of the Islamist movement in many of the institutions of the camp, including the youth club (see Hart 2004).

The public discourse that positioned teenage males as agents of collective redemption illustrates one way in which the generational order was reproduced in Hussein Camp in the late 1990s. Young men (and women) in the youth centres and schools would engage in organised activities such as folklore performances and recitations intended to demonstrate and affirm their connection to Palestine and willingness to play the role identified for them by adults. Within the family and neighbourhood, the reproduction of the generational order was overlaid by the dynamics of kin relations. On countless occasions in homes and in casual conversations sitting in the narrow streets of the camp parents, relatives or older neighbours would ask children to tell me about Palestine. The young people would always respond with seriousness, reciting information about the town or village from which the family or neighbourhood members came, together with information about the fertile land, the sea, and so on. While these small performances were ostensibly for my benefit, I came to understand that they were also demonstrations of loyalty to adults significant in those young people's lives. They signalled awareness of adult authority and of the duty to demonstrate respect to parents, grandparents, and older people in the neighbourhood.

Amongst young males, such gestures of respect and public displays of loyalty were often mixed with private expression of unease about the project of 'return' to Palestine. In the case of teenage males in Hussein Camp, the prospect of subsistence farming was far from the ambitions shaped by life in Amman and a classroom-based education (see Turner 2001:163). Some expressed to me explicit antipathy towards the project of 'return' due to specific experience within the family. In several of the households that I visited regularly men in their forties or older who had once been involved as *fedayi* (freedom fighters) with one or other faction and had been injured or imprisoned and tortured, served as exemplars to their sons and nephews of the failure of the nationalist project of return. These men were often unable to function in their expected role within the family and community. Moreover, reports commonly circulated that the monthly pension payable to the former *fedayi* or their families by the PLO was being received spasmodically, if at all. It was noticeable that amongst the young male relatives of such men interest in and engagement with the collective project of redeeming Palestine held diminished attraction. This is illustrative of an intersection between the events of a particular moment (generation as historical period) and the formation of a cohort specific disposition.

Many males in their early teens spoke to me of their ambitions to join one of the professions in Jordan. However, by age 16 or 17, such talk began to be replaced by discussion of migration in search of a better life. Sat together in the streets of the neighbourhood or during trips out of town conversation would often turn to the viability and relative merits of different destination countries. They swapped information about men who had migrated and returned as visitors bearing symbols of their apparent success. Such discussions may be seen as one aspect of the production of a cohort specific perception of the refugees' situation and prospects. Also important to note was the phase of life of these young men: a point at which the transition to (gendered) social adulthood became an issue of increasing concern.

In the foregoing discussion I have sought, in general terms, to indicate ways in which the different notions of 'generation' found across the literature and distinguished by Kertzer (1983) may be applied to the setting of Hussein Camp. I now move to give this discussion more detail through consideration of a particular individual and the changes that I witnessed in him from early teens to age 18.

Qusay

The research that I conducted in Hussein Camp was focused on the ways that Palestinian refugees in the second decade of life described a relationship to 'Palestine'. This was a place that none of them had seen first-hand but about which they had heard a great deal from different sources—the family, school, mosque, and youth club to name only the most obvious. Most of the 50 or so young people with whom I engaged— as researcher, teacher, neighbour, and friend—were full Jordanian citizens as well as refugees registered with the United Nations Relief and Works Agency (UNRWA).

One of the most articulate and outspoken of my young interlocutors was a young man whom I shall call 'Qusay'. He took pride in his impressive knowledge about his family's village in Palestine and displayed the greatest awareness of Palestinian folklore of all the young people with whom I engaged. Qusay was 12 when we first met through my involvement as a volunteer English teacher in the local UN school. About six months later, a football championship was held for nations throughout the region. Palestinian and Jordanian teams were amongst those competing. There seemed to be support for both amongst the young people in Hussein Camp. In the days leading up to a match between the two, I asked several of them which of the two teams they would be supporting and why. Qusay was one of my respondents. I had fully expected him to say that he was behind the Palestinian team given the evident pride with which he had spoken about Palestine on several occasions previously. He had also expressed stout support for the *Wihdat* football team in the Jordanian national league: a team that, due to its association with the other main refugee camp in Amman, was considered 'Palestinian'. However, to my great surprise, he told me that he would be supporting the Jordanian team. When I asked him about the reason for this, he replied:

> Look, Palestine is the country of my forefathers and my father but I was born here, I eat and drink from Jordan and I am clothed from here. So it is my country and I must support it.

In 2003, I returned to Hussein Camp. By this time, Qusay was 18 years old. A few months earlier, he had completed the *Tawjihi* high school matriculation exam. A good overall score in this exam is vital for students hoping to pursue higher education. Given the intelligence, energy, and academic aptitude, he had displayed as a 12 and 13 year old, I anticipated that Qusay would have done very well in the *Tawjihi*. When I asked him about this, however, he surprised me again. It transpired that he had achieved a poor result—certainly not high enough to secure a place at a university or college of any standing. In the course of our subsequent meetings, we spoke at some length about this result and about his experience over the years since my initial time in Hussein Camp. At one point, he said:

> I cry when I think of my life as a child. We only thought about tomorrow, about playing.
>
> When I was in tenth grade [15-16 years old] I began to lose hope in the future. I understood that no matter what I do, here in Jordan I am a Palestinian refugee from a poor family. I can't succeed. After that I wasn't interested in school. I lost my ambition.

During my original fieldwork, I had witnessed many young men in Hussein Camp begin to lose their enthusiasm for study around the age of 13. Through inspection of school registers, I had noted the common spike in the dropout rate around this age and in the successive years. Most of those young men I had known who had dropped out around the age of 13 were not especially academic and often they or their parents affirmed that a long-term livelihood might be better achieved through some form of apprenticeship. On the other hand, there were young men in the camp who had done well at school, gone on to university, and were pursuing employment in various professional fields both in Amman and overseas, as a consequence of talent, single-minded determination, and perhaps some measure of good fortune or, at least, helpful connections.

Given his energy, entrepreneurial skills, and keen intelligence, I had anticipated that Qusay would be one of those who would continue with and succeed in their studies. However, through our further discussions, I learned from him about particular experiences that had discouraged him. It transpired that Qusay's father had lost his job working for a government-owned corporation a couple of years earlier and had struggled since to find regular employment. Qusay's eldest brother had taken on responsibility as the main breadwinner working overseas, but his earnings were insufficient. Qusay spoke bitterly about his father's redundancy claiming that when the company made cuts they had targeted employees of Palestinian origin. It seemed that this single experience, more than any other, had sharpened within him a sense of marginality inflected both by class and by origin. Examples of successful and very wealthy Palestinians were abundant in Amman, but such people were commonly as distant to Qusay and many of his peers as the 'pure Jordanians' who, in their view, ran the government and army and who, according to general perception in Hussein Camp, discriminated in access to higher education and public employment against the Palestinians.

Qusay's surprising failure in the *Tawjihi* examination and his sense of despondency prompted me to think further about the ways that young people may be situated historically. The notion of 'generation', with the four dimensions of (1) kinship descent; (2) cohort; (3) life stage; (4) historical period seemed especially salient as a heuristic for comprehending this.

In a later conversation with Qusay, he told me about various male friends of his age who had gone to fight against the allied forces in Iraq (this was a few months after the March 2003 invasion by the USA, UK, and allied forces). He shared his own thoughts about following in their footsteps and becoming a 'martyr'. Although this was a plan that he ultimately did not put into practice, his evident interest in doing so gives some indication of an important shift in thinking between young men of his cohort and that of fathers and grandfathers—as supporters of the secular nationalist movement—at a similar stage in their lives. This entailed a refocusing of collective identification: the concern with 'Palestine' as an ancestral homeland from which all had a familial connection was giving way to a sense of membership in a pan-Islamic community. Rather than fighting for the liberation of specific villages and towns lost to Israel in 1948 and 1967, the goal appeared to be shifting for young men of Qusay's cohort to undertake *jihad* against an alien power that threatened part of the Islamic *ummah*—whether in Palestine or elsewhere in the region. This change is indicated in the move from the term *jeel al-awdeh* ('generation of return') to *jeel al-aqsa* ('generation of al-aqsa') discussed above.

The new focus was part of the vision offered by the Islamists who had become a powerful presence within Hussein Camp—an historical change significant for young people who attended the youth club and other institutions of the camp. The Islamists offered an ideology distinctly different from that of the PLO—various factions of which had, until the late 1990s, run the youth club in the camp. The vision of the Islamists stressed the importance of faith as an essential element of the struggle for liberation. Furthermore, they suggested that the failure of previous generations—understood in kinship terms—could be explained by lack of such faith. Thus, an important element of change was discernible in their outlook and in the means of pursuing redemption from a position of exile. The attraction expressed by Qusay and others in his cohort to the project of liberating Islamic land that rejected the secular Palestinian nationalism of parents and grandparents can be located at the intersection of generation in the aspects of historical period and kinship, respectively.

While all young men aged 18 in 2003 might, at one level, be considered members of the same cohort (Mannheim's 'generation location'), as already mentioned not all young men of Qusay's chronological age responded like him to the political events unfolding at that moment. Those that did, shared also his sense of alienation from Jordanian society for the perceived discrimination against Palestinian refugees. Together these young men might be considered to constitute Mannheim's 'generation as actuality'. This cohort aspect of generation illustrated by Qusay and his friends was commonly reinforced by intense social interaction amongst boys from an early age. The neighbourhood of the camp provided a forum wherein knowledge was imparted and constructed, attitudes formed, and collaborative action undertaken (see Hart 2008b). As a group, young men participated in activities organised by Islamists. Through the youth club, they participated in trips, sports events, and cultural evenings. They also joined afterschool classes focused on study of the Quran. Through these various activities, young men strengthened the bond between them while engaging with a particular religious-political discourse often very different from that espoused by parents and grandparents within the domestic realm.

To understand Qusay's educational trajectory and his views at age 18, it is also helpful to consider the life phase aspect of generation. Through the teenage years, young men typically became increasingly aware and reflective about the longer-term prospects for securing a viable livelihood. This was not a matter of economy alone but had important implications for social standing. Marriage was a critical rite of passage towards achievement of respected male adult status. However in order to get married a young man needed to be in a position to pay the *mahr* (brideprice), provide accommodation and clothing for the couple and fund the wedding celebrations themselves. The consequences of failing to marry by one's mid or late twenties were made evident by the awkward position of unmarried males in the camp. No longer boys but not yet heads of their own households with children of their own, such males often kept a low profile (Hart 2008b). The prospect of such a fate was clear to Qusay and, like several of his peers, was attributed to the political-economic marginality of Palestinian refugees in Jordan: something that they could see no direct means to overcome.

Qusay's experience of life between the ages of 12 and 18 had occurred within a set of political-economic events that were, inevitably, historically specific, contributing to the distinctiveness of the teenage years of him and his cohort from that of parents. Key features of this period from 1997 to 2003 that had particular salience for Qusay and his cohort included the worsening economic situation in Jordan for those at the lower end of the socio-economic ladder. While prices rose, partly as a consequence of the removal of subsidies on basic goods by the government, wages improved little. The job market had grown progressively more crowded during the 1990s as a consequence of the expulsion of Palestinians from several Gulf states following the Iraqi invasion of Kuwait and subsequent war, and the very limited opportunities for employment in that region thereafter. Moreover, increasingly stringent restrictions on immigration introduced by many European states, Canada, Australia, and the United States had made it far harder for young men like Qusay to follow the path of men in previous decades who had sought education or gainful employment abroad. The stories of success, real or imagined, told by relatives and neighbours returning from overseas contrasted sharply with young men's experiences of standing in long queues outside Western embassies in the futile quest for a visa.

The prospects for 'return' to Palestine during this period were dimmer than ever. The Oslo Peace Process instigated in 1994 had, by the late 1990s, come to a virtual halt. In any event, this process offered no obvious prospect of return for Palestinians living outside the occupied territory of the West Bank, Gaza, and East Jerusalem. The Palestine Liberation Organisation (PLO), under the leadership of Yasser Arafat, which had negotiated with Israel on behalf of the Palestinian people was, by the late 1990s, considered by many I spoke with in the camp to have abandoned them.

Two years after the 1995 signing of the Jordan–Israel peace treaty, the authorities began to demolish homes in one part of Hussein Camp in order to construct a new highway through the city. Hundreds of families were displaced as a consequence. For many young people, as well as their parents and grandparents, this was interpreted as evidence of the Jordanian authorities' determination to thin out areas where large numbers of Palestinian refugees lived in close proximity as part of its project of alignment with Israel and western interests.

Throughout this same period, the Islamists had grown in strength and numbers both within Hussein Camp and more widely in Jordanian society. I have already suggested key ways in which their vision differed from that of Palestinian nationalism as espoused by the PLO that had failed to deliver on its promises or compensate for sacrifices made.

I have here mentioned a few of the historical events and processes that most obviously impacted the lives of Qusay and his peers. It was these events that were discussed as part of everyday interaction. The impact of such events and their interpretation were always mediated by the cohort, and by the relationship between parents and children (generation in kinship terms), as well as by gender. Thus, for example, the dwindling support offered to the refugees by the PLO compounded the sense amongst young men that the nationalist movement had failed and that the sacrifices of older generations had been for nothing. For their part, parents and grandparents could offer little to counter this view. The appeal of the Islamists' vision for Qusay and other young men in his cohort is comprehensible from a perspective that invokes generation in the four distinct ways suggested by Kertzer.

CONCLUSION

As governments, specialist organisations and civil society across Europe (and elsewhere) engage with unprecedented numbers of desperate people seeking sanctuary, further standardisation of various aspects of humanitarian interventions is likely. In relation to young people, the use of categories based upon chronological age such as 'child' (0–18), 'adolescent' (10–19), and 'youth' (15–24) will continue to inform programmatic responses across diverse contexts. Projects focused on participation and on reproductive health with 'adolescents' or on livelihoods with 'youth' are examples of this link between chronological age and certain forms of intervention. While such age-based standardisation ensures a degree of visibility and inclusion for sections of the population once largely ignored within humanitarian intervention it also risks reducing the complexities of age position to a simple number.

This paper has explored the need and means to attend to age position in a more complex and multiple manner. This is important not only in order to comprehend the particular needs and challenges of individuals but also to make sense of the differential impact of larger historical processes. I have discussed four dimensions of age position utilising the principal sociological uses of the term 'generation' identified by Kertzer: as 'cohort', 'historical period', 'kinship descent', and 'life stage'. Discussion of one young man, Qusay, was offered to illustrate the dynamics of age position in the ambiguous and marginal setting of a camp for long-term refugees.

Over the period that I engaged with him, important changes occurred in Qusay's age position—from that of a 12-year-old boy focused on schoolwork, sport, and music in a fairly narrow spatial domain to an 18-year-old young man looking towards the prospects of attaining social adulthood possessed of a wider sense of his social, economic, and political environment and aware of societal expectations. By this point in his life, feelings of alienation and marginality had replaced those of loyalty to the country of residence. Were I to engage with Qusay 20 years later—at the age of 38—no doubt his views would take a different shape. Understanding the aetiology of these views might entail consideration of the impact of wider historical changes; the experiences of his cohort of friends and acquaintances; the obligations towards his elderly kin; and the expectations and entitlements associated with his likely role as a father or, failing that, his predicament as an adult (in terms of chronological age at least) who had not thus far perpetuated the family line. Conversely, consideration of the views of a young male growing up in Hussein Camp today would need to take cognizance of current historical changes. This would likely include the emergence of social media and ease of access to the Internet, as well as wider political developments such as the rise of 'Islamic State', the massive influx to Jordan of refugees from across the region, and the upsurge in violence in the occupied Palestinian territories.

I have developed my argument through focusing on one specific young man and one particular displaced population. Nevertheless, the need for attention to age position is surely vital in efforts to support other displaced populations, including refugees from Syria and Iraq currently on the move across the Middle East and Europe. Imagine, for example, a 16-year-old young man from Syria migrating in the company of peers. A standard response from authorities in many European countries is to provide some form of mental health support to a person who would be labelled by the authorities as an 'unaccompanied asylum seeking child' (UASC). Such a response is bound up with assumptions of traumatisation and the inherent vulnerability of those deemed 'children'. Behind this are normative ideas around chronological age and the nature and function of family. Considering age position in the four dimensions of 'generation' described above may yield a more empowering institutional response. Attending to this young man's cohort-informed ideas, to his sense of loyalty to parents and other kin (whether living or deceased), to his life experience thus far, and to the trajectory he perceives towards (male) social adulthood could enable a richer understanding of needs and aspirations, as well as of the forces that have shaped these.

Along with concern for the immediate needs of forced migrants, humanitarian response entails the search for long-term solutions. In the Palestinian case, this remains elusive. However, if the moment arrives when the obstacles to a viable solution become surmountable an understanding of the history of exile will be vital. This history can be told at many levels: from the national narrative to the specific and dynamic histories of individuals. Each of those individual histories will inform the response of Palestinians to any proposed solution and all will be mediated by factors of class, gender, and, in its various dimensions, age as well.

NOTE

1. This is by no means to deny or downplay the enormous obstacles or the violations of basic human rights that many refugee camp dwellers globally experience.

REFERENCES

Alanen, L. (2001). Childhood as a generational condition: Children's daily lives in a central Finland town. In L. Alanen & B. Mayall (Eds.), *Conceptualizing child-adult relations* (pp. 129–143). RoutledgeFalmer: London.

Alanen, L. (2009). Generational order. In J. Qvortrup, W. Corsaro, & M.-E. Honig (Eds.), *The Palgrave handbook of childhood studies* (pp. 159–174). Basingstoke: Palgrave Macmillan.

Altorki, S. (1980). Milk kinship in Arab society: An unexplored problem in the ethnography of marriage. *Ethnology, 19*(2), 233–244.

Augé, M. (1995). *Non-places: introduction to an anthropology of supermodernity.* London: Verso.

Bekerman, Z., & Maoz, I. (2005). Troubles with identity: Obstacles to coexistence education in conflict ridden societies. *Identity, 5*(4), 341–357.

Boyden, J., & de Berry, J. (Eds.) (2004). *Children and youth on the Frontline: Ethnography, armed conflict and displacement.* Oxford: Berghahn Books.

Chatty, D. (Ed.) (2010). *Deterritorialized youth: Sahrawi and Afghan refugees at the margins of the Middle East.* Oxford: Berghahn Books.

Clark-Kazak, C. (2009). Towards a working definition and application of social age in international development studies. *Journal of Development Studies, 45*(8), 1307–1324.

Corsten, M. (2003). Biographical revisions and the coherence of generation. In B. Mayall & H. Zeiher (Eds.), op. cit. (pp. 46–70).

Evans, R., & Lo Forte, C. (2013). *UNHCR's engagement with displaced youth: A global review.* Geneva: UNHCR. http://www.unhcr.org/513f37bb9.html. Accessed 21 Oct 2013.

Hart, J. (2004). Beyond struggle and aid: Children's identities in a Palestinian refugee camp in Jordan. In J. Boyden & J. de Berry (Eds.), op. cit.

Hart, J. (Ed.) (2008a). *Years of conflict: Adolescence, political violence and displacement.* Oxford: Berghahn Books.

Hart, J. (2008b). Dislocated masculinity: Adolescence and the Palestinian Nation-in-exile. *Journal of Refugee Studies, 21*(1), 64–81.

Hengst, H. (2009). Collective identities. In J. Qvortrup, W. Corsaro, & M-E. Honig (Eds.), op. cit. (pp. 202–214).

Henriques, J., Hollway, W., Urwin, C., Venn, C., & Walkerdine, V. (1984). *Changing the subject: Psychology, social regulation and subjectivity.* London: Routledge.

Hinton, R. (2000). Seen but not heard: Refugee children and models for intervention. In P. C. & M. T. Smith (Eds.), *Abandoned children* (pp. 199–212). Cambridge: Cambridge University Press.

Hirschman, C. (1994). Problems and prospects of studying immigrant adaptation from the 1990 population census: From generational comparisons to the process of 'Becoming American'. *International Migration Review, 28*(Winter), 690–713.

Indra, D. (Ed.) (1998). *Engendering forced migration: Theory and practice.* Oxford: Berghahn Books.

Kaiser, T. (2006). Between a camp and a hard place: Rights, livelihood and experiences of the local settlement system for long term refugees in Uganda. *Journal of Modern African Studies, 44*(4), 597–621.

Kent, G. (1991). Our children, our future. *Futures, 23*(1), 32–50.

Kertzer, D. (1983). Generation as a sociological problem. *Annual Review of Sociology, 9*, 125–149.

Loizos, P. (2007). 'Generations' in forced migration: Towards greater clarity. *Journal of Refugee Studies, 20*(2), 193–209.

Malkki, L. (1995). *Purity and exile: Violence, memory and national cosmology among Hutu refugees in Tanzania.* Chicago: University of Chicago Press.

Malkki, L. (1996). Speechless emissaries: Refugees, humanitarianism, and dehistoricization. *Cultural Anthropology, 11*(3), 377–404.

Mannheim, K. (1952). The problem of generations. In K. Mannheim (Ed.), *Essays in the sociology of knowledge*. London: Routledge and Kegan Paul.

Mayall, B. (1996). *Children, health and the social order*. Buckingham: Open University Press.

McEvoy-Levy, S. (2011). Children, youth and peacebuilding. In T. Maytok, J. Senehi, & S. Byrne (Eds.), *Critical issues in peace and conflict studies*. New York: Lexington Books.

McGill, M., & O'Kane, C. (2015). *Evaluation of child and youth participation in peacebuilding*. Global Partnership for Children and Youth in Peacebuilding. https://www.sfcg.org/wp-content/uploads/2014/11/2015July_Eval-of-ChildYouth-Peacebuilding-Colombia-Nepal-DRC.pdf. Accessed 27 Jan 2016.

Miller, K.E., Kushner, H., McCall, J., Martell, Z., & Kulkarni, M.S. (2008). Growing up in exile: Psychosocial challenges facing refugee youth in the United States. In J. Hart (Ed.), op. cit. (pp. 58–88).

Niens, U., & Cairns, E. (2005). Conflict, contact, and education. *Theory into Practice, 44*(4), 337–344.

Nolin, C. (2006). *Transnational ruptures: Gender and forced migration*. Aldershot: Ashgate.

Percy-Smith, B., & Burns, D. (2013). Exploring the role of children and young people as agents of change in sustainable community development. *Local Environment, 18*(3), 323–339.

Plan International. (2008). Paying the price: The economic cost of failing to educate girls. http://plan-international.org/girls/reports-and-publications/paying-the-price-the-economic-cost-of-failing-to-educate-girls.php?lang=en. Accessed 31 Oct 2013.

Plan International. (2015). Children will be critical agents of change in the implementation of the Sustainable Development Goals. https://plan-international.org/blog/2015/08/five-reasons-success-sdgs-depends-youth-engagement. Accessed 27 Jan 2016.

Prout, A., & James, A. (1997). A new paradigm for the sociology of childhood?: Provenance, promise and problems. In: A. James & A. Prout (Eds.), *Constructing and reconstructing childhood: Contemporary issues in the sociological study of childhood* (2nd ed., pp. 7–33). London: Falmer Press.

Qvortrup, J. (1991). Childhood as a social phenomenon—An introduction to a series of national reports (*Eurosocial Report No. 36*). Vienna: European Centre for Social Welfare Policy and Research.

Rumbaut, R. (2004). Ages, life stages, and generational cohorts: Decomposing the immigrant first and second generations in the United States. *International Migration Review, 38*(3), 1160–1205.

Salomon, G. (2006). Does peace education *really* make a difference? *Peace and Conflict, 12*(1), 37–48.

Save the Children. (2008). Global report on 'children's participation in armed conflict, post conflict and peace building: Adult's War and Young Generation's Peace'. http://www.essex.ac.uk/armedcon/story_id/000835.pdf. Accessed 27 Jan 2016.

Smith, M. (2004). Warehousing refugees: A denial of rights, a waste of humanity. In *World refugee survey 2004* (pp. 38–56). Washington, DC: US Committee for Refugees and Immigrants.

Strathern, M. (1996). The concept of society is theoretically obsolete. In T. Ingold (Ed.), *Key debates in anthropology* (pp. 60–66). London: Routledge.

Tembon, M., & Fort, L. (Eds.) (2008). *Girls' education in the 21st century.* Washington, DC: The World Bank http://siteresources.worldbank.org/ EDUCATION/Resources/278200-1099079877269/547664-1099080014368/ DID_Girls_edu.pdf. Accessed 7 Sept 2013.

Turner, S. (1999). Angry young men in camps: Gender, age and class relations among Burundian refugees in Tanzania. *New issues in refugee research* (Working paper no.9). Geneva: UNHCR.

Turner, S. (2001). *The barriers of innocence: Humanitarian intervention and political imagination in a refugee camp for Burundians in Tanzania.* PhD thesis, Roskilde University.

UNHCR. (2015). Mid-year trends 2015. http://www.unhcr.org/56701b969. html. Accessed 27 Jan 2016.

UNHCR, ExCom. (2009). Conclusion on Protracted Refugee Situations. No. 109 (LXI).

Uprichard, E. (2008). Children as 'beings and becomings': Children,childhood and temporality. *Children & Society, 22*(4), 303–313.

White, S. C., & Choudhury, S. (2007). The politics of child participation in international development: The dilemma of agency. *The European Journal of Development Research, 19*(4), 529–550.

World Bank. (2006). *World development report 2007. Development and the next generation.* Washington, DC: The International Bank for Reconstruction and Development/The World Bank.

Zhou, M. (1997). Growing up American: The challenge confronting immigrant children and children of immigrants. *Annual Review of Sociology, 23*, 63–95.

CHAPTER 3

Bodies, Brains, and Age: Unpacking the Age Question in the Dutch Sex Work Debate

Sara Vida Coumans

MOVING BEYOND AGE AS A GIVEN

Introduction: Age, Bodies and Sex

A common question asked to children in the Netherlands is: *How old are you?* As the case in many other places, Dutch children learn that age is not only a date that belongs to them; it is also a key principle which organises their place in society (Melchiorre 2004). The precise number of our age is not physically marked on our body. Yet, age is embodied. Our bodies age. This gives age a corporeal dimension and renders bodies markers of generational identities (Huijsmans 2010: 122; Hörschelmann and Colls 2010). But bodies are also illusive sites of chronological age. Social conditions and individual biological properties lead our bodies to age at different

This chapter is based on Coumans, S.V. (2014) 'How Age Matters: Exploring contemporary Dutch debates on age and sex work.' ISS Working Paper No. 588. The Hague: International Institute of Social Studies. I would like to acknowledge the support and encouragement I have received from Wendy Harcourt and Loes Keysers when doing the research on which this paper is based.

S.V. Coumans (✉)
Independent Researcher, London, United Kingdom

R. Huijsmans (ed.), *Generationing Development,*
DOI 10.1057/978-1-137-55623-3_3

paces. In addition, we also perform age, amongst other things through our bodily presentations and always in a manner that is intertwined with other dimensions of identity (Woodward 2006; Utrata 2011; Huijsmans 2013; Laz 1998: 91).

Sex work brings together various dimensions and effects of age. In contexts where it is legal, sex work is typically regulated by policies hinging on the measure of chronological age. However, age as a relation of power is not only manifest in a static sense through age-based regulation of sex work, but also in a relation manner in both discourse and practice. This is most vividly illustrated in instances where there is a significant difference in age between partners (Montgomery 2008: 183), especially if this concerns sexual relations between people occupying different age-based identities such as children and adults.

In a phenomenological sense, age constitutes an element in sexual fantasies, desires, and performances. Age is not only mobilised through advertisements and images that are part and parcel of the commodification of sex, but also performed through bodily presentations of sex workers ('O Connell Davidson 2005: 102). Further, age affects the moral evaluation of sex work. Even the most forceful proponent of legalising sex work would probably exclude children from participating in it, because, as O'Connell Davidson (2005: 23) explains, the figure of the child prostitute ruptures 'the imagined boundaries that serve to ring-fence both 'childhood' and 'commercial sex'.' Yet, Montgomery (2001: 48) argues that such boundaries necessarily shatter in actual practice due to the ways in which age operates in the bodily economies of sex work:

> In a job that requires beauty, which is often synonymous with youth, prostitutes will invariably be young, and if children are defined as anyone under the age of eighteen, then rates of child prostitution will always be high.

Recent debates in the Netherlands about increasing the minimum age of prostitution from 18 to 21 constitute a fertile field for studying the various ways in which age, bodies, and sex interact and the social logics which give age its prominence, both in contemporary debates on sex work as well as in sex work as a site of practice. Furthermore, I posit that the Dutch debate is of relevance beyond its particular context. Due to its long history of 'prostitution policy'[1], Dutch debates are frequently cited in studies on sex work. The Dutch case is also of interest from a generational perspective. Several anthropologists have argued that the construct of childhood globalised through international frameworks like the United Nations Convention on the Rights of the Child are in origin highly particular:

> The child envisaged by the Convention is an individual, autonomous being, an inheritor of the liberal, humanist ideals of the Enlightenment... (Montgomery, 2008: 6)

Such claims have lead scores of scholars to study alternative conceptualisations of childhood in non-western contexts, yet remarkably few have taken a closer look at the logics underpinning the use of chronological age in demarcating age-based identities in so-called liberal societies. In addition, the Dutch debate over the minimum age also helpfully illustrates two further features that are of relevance beyond the Dutch context. First, the establishment of any minimum age is always necessarily arbitrary and captures social phenomena only in a highly partial manner. Second, the Dutch case is reflective of the general pattern of a gradual increase of minimum ages delimiting young people's involvement in various dimensions of what is considered adult life. This lengthens the time of dependency. Yet, is in deep tension which a simultaneous development in which market forces in particular increasingly target young people as (independent) consumers at an ever younger age (Nayak and Kehily 2013).

The chapter is organised as follows. In the next section, I briefly introduce the historical developments in the Dutch sex work debate and account for the knowledge production that has informed this chapter. Next, I present an analysis of interview material with a range of different actors related to the Dutch sex work debate to uncover the dominant logic underpinning the increase in minimum age. In this regard, I highlight the influence of recent neuroscientific research, which enters the debate through the Dutch language concept of *weerbaarheid*. I argue that brain research has come to eclipse much of the discussion on sex work, the subsequent section highlights how in sex work as practice the ways in which age operates through the body is of far greater importance. In the concluding section I, thus, flag some problems of the prominence of the chronological conceptualisation of age in debating the generational dimension of sex work.

Researching the Dutch Sex Work Debate

Prostitution policy has a long history in the Netherlands. While sex workers have been portrayed as victims of poverty, 'fallen' or 'sinful' women or as 'psychiatrically disturbed' in the 1950s and 1960s—sex workers have never been criminalised under Dutch law (Outshoorn 2012: 234). In the 1980s and the 1990s, sex work was increasingly framed as a profession, in line with the liberal discourse at the time. In those days, sex workers were also increasingly represented as modern and emancipated. This eventually led the Netherlands to become one of the first countries to legalise sex work in 1999 (ibid, 2012: 232, 242).

From 2000 onwards discourses around sex work changed, much in relation to shifts in the Dutch political climate exemplified by the growth of right-wing populist parties that called for a tighter regulation of law, order, and migration. Simultaneously, extensive publicity on young female victims of trafficking and the 'lover boy panic'[2] contributed much to changes in the public opinion on sex work and have done so in a generational way. This has led to a 'renewed discourse about young female victims that eclipsed the image of the modern [adult] consenting sex worker' (Outshoorn 2012: 242). Despite these changes, the Dutch sex work debate also shows some continuity. For example, it has remained remarkably heteronormative. Male and trans* sex workers have largely remained excluded from public debates about sex work (Van Gelder 2011).

The sensationalist media reporting on young women trafficked into prostitution and the failure of the legalisation of sex work as a means to eliminate exploitation in the sector accumulated in a proposed amendment to the regulation of sex work in the Netherlands. This amendment has been proposed in Dutch Parliament in 2009 (Wagenaar and Altink 2012: 285) and is to date (January 2016) still under discussion.[3] While at the national level the regulation has not been approved yet, Amsterdam has already increased the minimum age to 21 in August 2015.[4]

Increasing the legal minimum age for sex workers from 18 to 21 is seen as a prime measure to address the various problems that continue to exist in the sex work sector despite legalisation and regularisation. The key argument put forth by proponents of the amendment is that young people of 21 years of age are *meer weerbaar* (literally: more able to defend themselves) than those of 18 years of age (Dutch Government 2013: 15). This is countered by the argument that a change in the minimum age is unlikely to remove young people below 21 years of age from sex work, but likely to make these young sex workers even harder to reach by social workers, health professionals, and other support structures.

Data Sources and Positionality

The substantial part of the research presented in this chapter relies on qualitative, semi-structured interviews. I conducted the interviews myself between June and September 2013. A total of 15 interviews were completed. The interviewees were selected through a method of snowball sampling, a sampling technique in which the initial interviewees refer the researcher to further interviewees. The interviewees related to the Dutch sex work debate came from a range of personal and professional angles. Among the interviewees was a policy maker, an academic, an awareness-raiser, sex trafficking survivors, an owner of a high-class escort service, former sex workers, a member of a sex workers association, and several social workers who provided different types of care to sex workers including medical care, psychosocial assistance, legal assistance, and pastoral support through everyday, casual conversation.

While I have interviewed some former and current sex workers, none were under the age of 21 at the time of interview (the proposed legal minimum age for sex workers). I recognise that this could be seen as a limitation; however, the focus of this research is analysing discourse created and reproduced by those who are engage with the policy making process, less with its material effects on the policy subjects.

All interviews were conducted in Dutch language which all interviewees spoke fluently. The interviews were recorded and transcribed *ad verbum*. The transcripts have been shared for review with the interviewees prior to finalisation and interviewees have given informed consent to use the materials for research purposes and academic publications. In order to have a broader understanding of the context in which the primary materials are located, I also used secondary data. The secondary data drawn on for this chapter can be roughly categorised into: academic literature, government and NGO documentation, and Dutch newspaper articles, which were published within the period from January 1, 2013 to October 1, 2013. It is further important to note that I conducted the research on which this chapter is based as a young Dutch female student working on an MA degree in Development Studies specialising in Children and Youth Studies. The Children and Youth Studies background heightened my sensitivity towards age-related issues, whilst the development studies literature introduced me to feminist approaches to development and sex work. On top of that, I had been involved for many years in sexual and reproductive rights youth movement, including being a member of the

Youth Coalition for Sexual and Reproductive Rights. Without a doubt, my political standpoint related to the sexual and reproductive rights of young people has influenced the process of knowledge production underpinning this chapter.

AGE, *WEERBAARHEID*, AND THE BRAIN

Policies are typically informed by the chronological conceptualisation of age even though alternative conceptualisations such as 'social age' (Clark-Kazak 2009) and 'relative age' (Huijsmans 2014) may well be more important in structuring everyday social life. In simple terms, in its chronological conceptualisation, age is treated 'as an objective fact defined by the number of years a person has lived' (Laz 1998: 91–2). The growing (global) importance attached to this particular conceptualisation has been related to the 'development of modern industrial society' (ibid, 92) and the idea of 'modernity' more broadly (Scott 1998; Ariès 1962).

Employed in a categorising fashion, chronological age makes legible fluid age-related groupings such as childhood, youth, and old age. The inevitable consequence of such a simplification of generational social landscapes is that 'persons on the neighbouring edges of two classes are likely to be more similar to each other than they are to members of their own class at its other extreme' (Baxter and Almagor 1978: 163). This remains the case wherever the cut-off age is placed. However, one of the arguments for increasing the minimum age for legal employment in prostitution from 18 to 21 was to minimise possible negative effects of the arbitrariness of chronological age-based categories as well as the possibilities of error.

In her Dutch language social history of childhood, Dasberg (2001: 34) argues that the conceptual lens of chronological age always leads to a distorted view of reality as it emphasises *leeftijd* (age) over *leefsituatie* (living condition). Through numerous historical examples, she illuminates the importance of class as shaping the lived experience of being young as far more profound than chronological age. A benign view on the centrality of chronological age in (inter)national law, on the other hand, would emphasise its emancipatory objective: seeking to establish minimum standards, which are lifted constantly through the increase of minimum ages, across an otherwise socially diverse population. Yet, in the various interviews about the proposed increase of the minimum age of prostitution, a different logic was articulated:

> Well, the moment that you are an adult and independent, you will have more life experience and take decisions in a more convinced manner. That is when you know, this is what I want and this is what I do not want. And, this will automatically make you more *weerbaar* (Peter, male Senior Policy Advisor at the Ministry of Security and Justice, The Hague). [5]
>
> *Weerbaarheid* means being able to make choices and define your own limits [...] You have to be able to assess the consequences of your actions, you need to be able to do this very well. So, you need to have a little power and life experience, to know that if you take step A, that you can foresee what step B will look like. You have to know what the potential consequences are and you have to be able to smell danger (Fabienne, female former sex worker, Amsterdam).
>
> At that point [the age of 18], I think that people are just not *weerbaar* enough. I think that at that stage people have not had the opportunities yet to discover their own weaknesses. I think people are just too young (Michelle, female Project Manager Center Child & Human Trafficking, Leeuwarden).

The aforementioned responses speak to a central argument underpinning the proposed increase in the minimum age, which is that young people at the age of 21 are assumed to be more *weerbaar* than those at age of 18 (Dutch Government 2013: 15).

The Dutch term *weerbaar* is at times translated into the English 'resilient' (and *weerbaarheid* translated into 'resilience'). However, the literal meaning of *weerbaar* is 'the ability to defend oneself, to resist', thus, the opposite of the English word 'vulnerable/vulnerability'[6]. This contrasts with 'resilien(t)(ce)'. Resilience refers to the ability to recover from misfortune and to return to an original shape. *Weerbaarheid*, on the other hand, refers to the capacity to fend off such misfortune in the first place. Hence, whilst both terms imply agency they refer to very different manifestations of agency. In addition, as Mizen and Ofosu-Kuzi (2013) argue a lack of *weerbaarheid* may well lead young people to exercise agency. This turns upside down the idea that *weerbaarheid* is a pre-condition of agency as the interview excerpts suggest. The five political parties[7] that from the start were in favour of the increase of the minimum age explain that *weerbaarheid* encompasses the following: skills to protect oneself based on life experience and the possibility to be economically independent (Dutch

Government 2012). *Weerbaarheid* is further framed as a result of a process of becoming an adult with the associated qualities of an ability to assess risks and its longer term consequences as well as social skills required for communication among adults (ibid). The association of *weerbaarheid* with maturity and adulthood is indeed also reflected in the three quotes above. However, deepening the discussion about the concept took it beyond its social connotations to assumed biological prerequisites:

> Your brains have only fully matured at the age of 22 or 23, which means fully overseeing things—you simply cannot do that [doing sex work] before that stage yet. I think your age matters because you have not fully matured physically and mentally yet. Even if you ask a teenager, would you like to do this or that the day after tomorrow, then this is simply difficult. Maybe you would like to do something different that day. It's just difficult to plan (Sofie, female social worker, Utrecht).
>
> Recently we know that this assumption is correct [that young people cannot oversee the long-term implications of certain choices]. This has to do with their brain development; that the brains of young people are only fully developed between the ages of 23-25. It is only at that point that the brains have matured sufficiently to oversee the long-term implications of certain choices. For me this is the most essential difference as to why minors need more protection than adults (Iris, female programme manager Sexual Violence, Utrecht).
>
> If they could make a CT scan for everybody and tell us with the results: 'okay your brains are ready', then that would work for me as well. But well, that is obviously not possible. If we have to link it to an age anyway and research indicates the age of 23, well, then, we have to keep ourselves to that I guess (Anna, female sex trafficking survivor).

It was striking how interviewees from very different professional backgrounds presented a largely consistent and almost unanimous argument about the biological requirements for the social condition of *weerbaarheid*. In these interviews, the book *Puberbrein* ('Adolescent Brain') (2009) was referred to by some of my interviewees. *Puberbrein* is a popular title written by Huub Nelis and Yvonne van Sark from Young Works, a Dutch organisation focussed on youth communication and youth culture. The authors summarise the main message of their work as follows:

> We have written this book because we think that adults overestimate young people, as if they know everything through the Internet about sex, alcohol and drugs—and from the age of 12 we expect young people to deal with

this by themselves. We think that young people need more structure and support. (Yvonne van Sark, YouTube 2009)

Books like *Puberbrein* and the discussion of the concept of *weerbaarheid* in relation to the development of the human brain are reflective of the growing influence of neuroscience on social policies and programmes—not just in the Netherlands. Global actors increasingly argue for interventions in early childhood on the basis of economic and neuroscientific research (Young 2007; Cole and Durham 2007: 8), and much the same holds true for conditional cash transfer programmes targeting early and middle childhood (Palacio this volume).

In specific relation to adolescents and young adults, recent work in the field of neuroscience has overthrown the long-standing idea that the human brain has largely matured by the age of 18:

> The frontal lobes, home to key components of the neural circuity underlying "executive functions" such as planning, working memory, and impulse control, are among the last areas of the brain to mature; they may not be fully developed until halfway through the third decade of life. (Johnson et al. 2009: 216)

Policy makers have been quick to draw on this emerging body of research. It is seen as hard evidence despite the subjective dimension of neuroimaging, the empirical gap between 'behaviour in the real world and…performance *in the scanner*' (Johnson et al. 2009: 219), and the continuing debate between social explanations of adolescent behaviour versus neuroscientific ones (Males 2009). In relation to adolescents, new neuroscientific findings have given justification to the increase in minimum ages in relation to various things based on two arguments. First, some behaviour has become more strictly policed in terms of age (e.g. drinking) because it is harmful for the still maturing brain. Second, other behaviour (e.g. smoking, but also sex work) has seen renewed age-based interventions because of its potential impacts which young people, whose brains are not yet fully matured, are said to not completely oversee and because their behaviour is said to be so often impulse driven. The second argument effectively reassesses agency in relation to youth. That young people exercise agency is not questioned, yet, their ability to make sound judgements is. Raising the minimum age thus becomes a protective measure. It takes away those options that are considered to have a dramatic impact on young people's (later) lives based on the idea that young people do not oversee the consequences of their choices.

At the same time, minimum age debates are not applied in any consistent manner across the board. For example, a minimum age for clients of sex workers is not stipulated in Dutch law and neither is the matter part of public discussions. Since the age of sexual consent is 16, it may be assumed that this is also the minimum age of clients. Furthermore, in the Netherlands, young people are allowed to join the army from the age of 17 and may join armed military missions from the age of 18. As military employment can also be considered high risk work, the contradiction of subjecting sex work to more stringent minimum age regulations and not other types of bodily work was also observed by the co-owner of an escort service:

> In any case, the one 18 year old is not the same as the other 18 year old. I think it differs a lot from person to person. One time I had a girl who was 25, who I thought was incredibly naïve. Whereas, I also had a girl once who was 19 and I thought she was incredibly sophisticated. Look, I do not really mind that the minimum age went to 21 and for my business it does not really matter. But I do find it a bit strange that you are expected to make every other decision about your life. Apparently your brains are developed enough to decide what you will study, to go on a mission with the army, to enter the police force and all that stuff. Apparently, you are old and wise enough for all those aspects – but when it comes to prostitution, then, you are not mature enough. Well, I think that this is a bit odd (Gabriella, female co-owner *The Courtesan Club*, Amsterdam).

Again in other interviews the relation between chronological age and *weerbaarheid* in the context of sex work was challenged on fundamental grounds:

> More *weerbaar*? Will you be more *weerbaar* at 21 than at 18, against the power of prostitution? No. I do not think so. [...] You know, I was 21 when I was a prostitute, was I *weerbaar*? No. I believe that if you are 26 you will not be *weerbaar* when you are beaten up" (Laura, female sex trafficking survivor, Rotterdam).

Sex Work, Gender, and Age Beyond Its Chronological Form

An inordinate passion for pleasure is the secret of remaining young[8]

This quote from Oscar Wilde welcomes visitors to the website of *The Courtesan Club*, a high-class escort service in Amsterdam. The quote speaks to the desire for remaining young in contemporary society. It also frames sex as pleasure and its central place on an escort services website suggests a relation between (sexual) pleasure and staying young.

Since it is mostly young people who are selling sex it is also worthwhile to briefly pause to consider age-related qualities that are important in commercial sex other than the chronological age of the sex worker. A former sex worker who entered the business when she was around 30 years old is well placed to comment on this especially because her body lacked the youthful qualities of many of her younger colleagues' bodies:

> I had many colleagues who were much younger and who presented themselves in a way that men always find very sexy: with good boobs and round buttocks. They were sexy according to this classical model of the female body. And they were younger than I was. They had much nicer hair and a beautiful skin. I had neither of those. Those are all key qualities that make a person stand out more (Fabienne, female former sex worker, Amsterdam).

Fabienne emphasises the importance of the youthful female body as a site of attraction in commercial sex work. Age, in this sense, is a corporeal quality and something that is staged and even performed in a distinctly gendered manner. A young, well-shaped female body also carries connotations of good health and is associated with fertility. However, the co-owner of an Amsterdam-based escort club was quick to observe that the staging of the young female body is not something exclusive to the sex industry:

> Well, I do not think that this is something that relates to only sex workers, I think that many women make an effort to have a young appearance. Yes, I think that this is not any different with sex workers. Well, maybe not to only make an effort to have a young appearance but just to make sure you do not age too much, maybe it is more related to that: to erase the signs of ageing. But well, with escort services and sex work in general, you will be judged on your physical appearance, you can have a great character but if you look on the websites you will not be judged on your character but based on a picture – so on what do you select? Clients select based on an appearance that they find attractive (Gabriella, female co-owner *The Courtesan Club*, Amsterdam).

Beyond appearance, youthful female bodies also eroticise in other ways. For some male clients, it suggests purity. For others, it evokes ideas of innocence or (sexual) inexperience (Doezema 2010: 49). Indeed, sexual fantasies revolve to a large extent around the interplay between gender and generation (at times race also enters in), something which the commercial sex industry has long recognised and acted upon ('O Connell Davidson 2005: 102).

However, in the sex sector, even young bodies can 'expire' quickly. The following quote from a female trafficking survivor who first got involved in sex work at the age of 20 suggests that this has less to do with bodily changes and more with a constant desire for 'new' bodies amongst, at least, part of the male clientele:

> Well, in the beginning I did not have to do much to attract clients as clients feast on new meat. You simply don't have to do much if you are new. You just need to stand there and, in any case, your curtains will close very often. The clients that go there often are simply waiting for you (Laura, female sex trafficking survivor, Rotterdam).

Nonetheless, a fading youthfulness of the female body poses a serious challenge to most female sex workers:

> Then [by age 35 or so] you will have to look for your success elsewhere, but you will not find it through your body, you will have to find it through another career. Or you need to become famous or write a book (Fabienne, female former sex worker, Amsterdam).

Even so, the bold claim that 'an old prostitute is a redundant prostitute' (Ennew 1986: 11, in Montgomery 2001: 48) was contested. A female sex trafficking survivor I interviewed explained that some clients prefer to stick to the same sex worker even though her body may, over time, lose some of its youthful qualities, whilst there are also some male clients whose sexual fantasies lead them to older female sex workers whose bodies are distinct from the stereotypical youthful female body.

So far, the discussion has focused on female sex workers and has assumed heterosexual relations. However, the sex industry is a highly diverse sexual landscape (Van Gelder 2011). Moreover, I learnt that age, in its many facets, works in different ways in relation to sex workers with different gender identities. Several of the people with whom I spoke explained that while there is a large market for both female and male young sex workers; the desire for youthful bodies is especially high in relation to young male sex workers:

Well, there is a market for young women and young men. Especially for young men! The 'expiry date' for men in the business is very near. Young boys are simply very attractive. Young boys are quite popular in homosexual contacts (Fabienne, female former sex worker, Amsterdam).

Male sex workers, I learnt, have mostly lost their commercial attraction in sex work already by the age of 30 or so. In the Netherlands, trans* sex workers, on the other hand, are generally speaking somewhat older as they take more time to develop their gender identity (female social worker, Utrecht). Most trans* sex workers in the Netherlands are male to female sex workers. Like female sex workers, also trans* sex workers have much longer career possibilities in the sex industry than male sex workers. Reflecting on these differences led me to consider how gendered domination interacts with age as a relation of power within the practice of commercial sex.

For this it is important to appreciate that masculinity is not necessarily specific to the male body. Masculinity is 'an identity expressed through sexual discourses and practices that indicate dominance and control' (Pascoe 2007: 13). Kulíck builds on this notion of masculinity and describes the relevance of the act of penetration for understanding how gender is performed:

> The locus of gender difference is the act of penetration – if one only penetrates, one is a 'man', if one gets penetrated, one is something other than a man – one is either a viado, a faggot; or a mulher, a woman. (Kulíck 1998: 227)

In the context of sex work, Pascoe's and Kulíck's understanding of masculinity shed some light on the variation in career lengths as well as starting ages between the different groups of sex workers.

In normative heterosexual relations, sex workers in a female body are usually imagined as the dominated and powerless. Age nuances this relation but generally does not unsettle it. This is more complex in cases where both sex workers and their clients have male bodies. Following Kulíck (1998), I suggest that here the act of penetration becomes far more important in marking dominance (see also Lyttleton 2008). In this context, I would hypothesise that age potentially unsettles the fragile production of dominance and that the apparent widespread preference for young

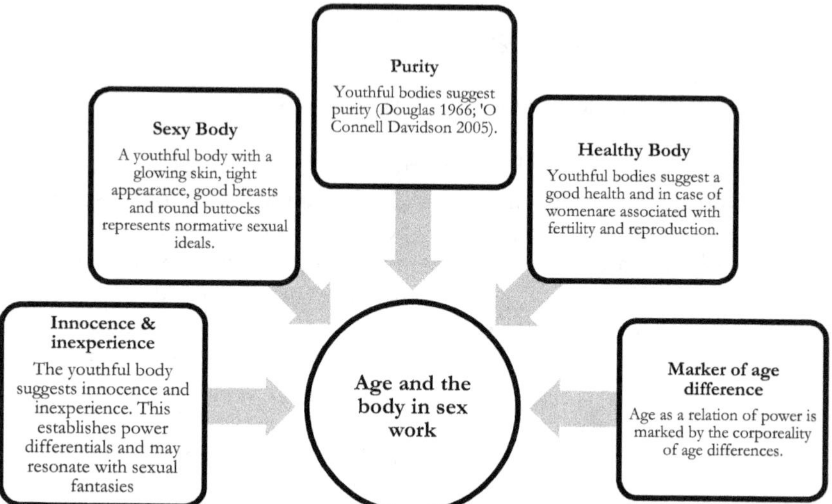

Fig. 3.1   The various ways in which age operates through the body in sex work

male sex workers needs to be seen in this light as through distinct corporeal age difference some necessary further power difference is achieved.

Figure 3.1 summarises the various ways in which age operates through the body. However, the aforementioned discussion has illustrated that age works in myriad ways and always intersects with gender.

Concluding Thoughts

In this chapter, I have used the Dutch debate on the increase of the minimum age of legal employment in the sex industry as a starting point to unravel the various ways in which understandings of the body and concepts of age interact and inform debates about prostitution policy. Chronological age is widely recognised as a state simplification (Scott 1998), employed to make populations legible. In this sense, chronological age must be recognised as something that is made important, amongst other things, through social protection policies (Laz 1998).

I have furthered these debates on chronological age by arguing that in the Dutch discussion on the minimum age of prostitution advances in neuroscientific research have attributed renewed signficance to the measure of chronological age. Neuroimaging techniques have shown that the human brain is only fully developed around half way through the third decade of life. This has sparked renewed interest in the 'maturity of judgment' (Johnson et al. 2009: 216)—especially in relation to policies concerning adolescents and youth. The idea of the maturity of judgement shapes the Dutch debate on the increase of the minimum age of employment in the sex sector through the notion of *weerbaarheid*. *Weerbaarheid* refers to the ability to fend off misfortunes and to resist. Yet in discussions with various actors, it was also found to be understood as an ability to fully oversee the consequences of one's actions, including its longer-term consequences. *Weerbaarheid*, in this sense, is thus about agency and how to value the agency exercised by young people.

However, the relation between brain development and the minimum age is problematic for a number of reasons. First, a central concern with the maturity of judgement risks reducing debates on sex work to rational choice arguments based on essentialised, age-based assumptions. Indeed, chronological age, thus, comes in the way of appreciating the social conditions that increase the likelihood of certain groups of people to enter sex work at a young age (Dasberg 2001: 34; Montgomery 2001; Males 2009). Second, a focus on the brain obfuscates the various ways in which age operates through the body. In this chapter, I have not more than skimmed the surface and phenomenological research will have to further the significance of the various ways in which the body is perceived and experienced as an age-related phenomenon in the context of sex work. Even so, the interview material and observations presented indicate that the corporeality of age, and its myriad intersections with gender (and no doubt race too), is of far greater importance for understanding sex work than the chronological conceptualisation of age that dominates policy discussions.

NOTES

1. In this chapter I use the term 'prostitution policy' when referring to the Dutch policy context as this is the term used in this debate. In other instances I use the term 'sex work'.
2. The English term 'lover boy' is used within the Dutch context and refers to 'young men forcing vulnerable young girls into prostitution, giving rise to new welfare projects to "save" them' (Outshoorn 2012: 238).
3. The proposed prostitution law is titled 'Rules related to the regulation of prostitution and combating abuses in the sex industry' (per-

sonal translation from the Dutch 'Wet regulering prostitutie en bestrijding misstanden seksbranche').

4. Website Amsterdam Municipality. Accessed January 17 2016: https://www.amsterdam.nl/zorg-welzijn/overig/prostitutie/nieuws-media/persbericht/

5. To conceal the identity and protect confidentiality of individuals who have been interviewed pseudonyms have been used for all the quotes in this chapter.

6. Van Dale online Dutch language dictionary, accessed at www.vandale.nl on 6 January 2016.

7. These five political parties are: CDA, VVD, PVV, ChristenUnie, and SGP.

8. Website *The Courtesan Club* 2013. Accessed September 10 2013: http://www.thecourtesanclub.com/index.php?option=com_content&view=article&id=14

References

Ariès, P. (1962). *Centuries of childhood: A social history of family life*. New York: Vintage Books/Random House.

Baxter, P. T. W., & Almagor, U. (1978). Observations about Generations. In J. S. La Fontaine (Ed.), *Sex and age as principles of social differentiation* (pp. 159–181). London/New York/San Francisco: Academic.

Clark-Kazak, C. R. (2009). Towards a working definition and application of social age in international development studies. *The journal of development studies, 45*(8), 1307–1324.

Cole, J., & Durham, D. L. (2007). *Generations and globalization: Youth, age, and family in the new world economy*. Bloomington: Indiana University Press.

Dasberg, L. (2001). *Grootbrengen door Kleinhouden als Historisch Verschijnsel (personal translation: Bringing up by keeping small as an historic phenomenon)* (16th ed.). Amsterdam/Meppel: Boom.

Doezema, J. (2010). *Sex slaves and discourse masters: The construction of trafficking/Jo Doezema*. London: Zed Books.

Douglas, M. (1966). *Purity and danger: An analysis of concepts of pollution and taboo*. London: Routledge.

Dutch Government. (2012). Regels betreffende de regulering van prostitutie en betreffende het bestrijden van misstanden in de seksbranche (Wet regulering prostitutie en bestrijding misstanden seksbranche) (a webpage of Overheid.nl). https://zoek.officielebekendmakingen.nl/dossier/32211/kst-32211-E?resultIndex=42&sorttype=1&sortorder=4. Accessed 26 Sept 2015.

Dutch Government. (2013). Memorie van Toelichting; bijlage van Wetsvoorstel Regulering prostitutie en bestrijding misstanden seksbranche (a webpage of Rijksoverheid). http://www.rijksoverheid.nl/onderwerpen/prostitutie/documenten-en-publicaties/kamerstukken/2009/11/11/memorie-van-toelichting.html. Accessed 7 May 2013.

Ennew, J. (1986). *The sexual exploitation of children*. Cambridge: Polity Press.

Hörschelmann, K., & Colls, R. (Eds.) (2010). *Contested bodies of childhood and youth*. Basingstoke/New York: Palgrave Macmillan.

Huijsmans, R. (2010). *Migrating children, households, and the post-socialist state: An ethnographic study of migration and non-migration by children and youth in an ethnic Lao village*. Department of Geography. Unpublished PhD thesis. Durham, Durham University.

Huijsmans, R. (2013). Doing gendered age': Older mothers and migrant daughters negotiating care work in rural Lao PDR and Thailand. *Third World Quarterly, 34*(10), 1896–1910.

Huijsmans, R. (2014). Becoming a young migrant or stayer seen through the lens of 'householding': Households 'in flux' and the intersection of relations of gender and seniority. *Geoforum, 51*, 294–304.

Johnson, S. B., Blum, R. W., & Giedd, J. N. (2009). Adolescent maturity and the brain: The promise and pitfalls of neuroscience research in adolescent health policy. *Journal of Adolescent Health, 45*(3), 216–221.

Kulick, D. (1998). *Travesti: Sex, gender and culture among Brazilian transgendered prostitutes*. Chicago: The University of Chicago Press.

Laz, C. (1998). Act your age. *Sociological Forum, 13*(1), 85–113.

Lyttleton, C. (2008). *Mekong erotics: Men loving/pleasuring/using men in Lao PDR*. Bangkok: UNESCO.

Males, M. (2009). Does the adolescent brain make risk taking inevitable? A skeptical appraisal. *Journal of Adolescent Research, 24*(1), 3–20.

Melchiorre, A. (2004). At what age? Are school-children employed, married and taken to court?. Right to Education Project. Accessible from: http://www.right-to-education.org/resource/what-age-%E2%80%A6are-school-children-employed-married-and-taken-court-2nd-edition.

Mizen, P., & Ofosu-Kusi, Y. (2013). Agency as vulnerability: Accounting for children's movement to the streets of Accra. *The Sociological Review, 61*(2), 363–382.

Montgomery, H. (2001). *Modern babylon? Prostituting children in Thailand*. New York/Oxford: Berghahn Books.

Montgomery, H. (2008). *An introduction to childhood: Anthropological perspectives on children's lives*. Chichester: Wiley-Blackwell.

Nayak, A., & Kehily, M. J. (2013). *Gender, youth & culture: Global masculinities & femininities* (2nd ed.). Basingstoke: Palgrave MacMillan.

Nelis, H. & Sark, Y. (2009) *Puberbrein*. Kosmos Uitgevers.

O'Connell-Davidson, J. (2005). *Children in the global sex trade*. Cambridge/ Malden: Polity Press.

Outshoorn, J. (2012). Policy change in prostitution in The Netherlands: From legalization to strict control. *Sexuality Research and Social Policy, 9*(3), 233–243.

Pascoe, C. J. (2007). *Dude, you're a fag: Masculinity and sexuality in high school*. Berkeley: University of California Press.

Scott, J. C. (1998). *Seeing like a state: How certain schemes to improve the human condition have failed*. New Haven: Yale University Press.

Utrata, J. (2011). Youth privilege: Doing age and gender in Russia's single-mother families. *Gender & Society, 25*(5), 616–641.

Van Gelder, P. (2011). Seksuele Dienstverlening Door Mannen in Den Haag: Ontwikkelingen Op Het Internet. *Journal of Social Intervention: Theory and Practice, 20*(3), 41–58.

Wagenaar, H., & Altink, S. (2012). Prostitution as morality politics or why it is exceedingly difficult to design and sustain effective prostitution policy. *Sexuality Research and Social Policy, 9*, 279–292.

Woodward, K. M. (2006). Performing age, performing gender. *NWSA Journal, 18*(1), 162–189.

Young, M. E. (Ed.) (2007). *Child development from measurement to action: A priority for growth and equity*. Washington, DC: The International Bank for Reconstruction and Development/The World Bank.

YouTube. (2009) Introductie Puberbrein Binnenstebuiten. *Puberbrein Website*. http://www.puberbrein.nl/_index.php?parentId=3. Accessed 10 Sept 2013.

CHAPTER 4

The Impact of 'Age-Class' on Becoming a Young Farmer in an Industrialised Agricultural Sector: Insights from Nova Scotia, Canada

Elyse N. Mills

INTRODUCTION: YOUNG FARMERS AND AGRARIAN FUTURES

In the past few years, the widespread departure of youth from rural areas has sparked concern about the future of agriculture, drawing attention from both scholars and policymakers worldwide. Various studies have shed light on reasons *why* rural youth appear uninterested in rural and agrarian futures (see Rigg 2006; Tadele and Gella 2012; White 2012), and a range of actors have now become vocal about halting this trend (see Bennell 2007; Proctor and Lucchesi 2012; FAO et al. 2014). Young people's disinterest in farming and departure from rural areas are issues often discussed in relation to concerns about youth un(der)employment, the growing dominance of large-scale commercial agriculture, food security, and the emergence of food sovereignty movements.

E.N. Mills (✉)
International Institute of Social Studies of Erasmus University Rotterdam, Kortenaerkade 12, 2518 AX The Hague, Netherlands

© The Author(s) 2016
R. Huijsmans (ed.), *Generationing Development*,
DOI 10.1057/978-1-137-55623-3_4

This chapter aims to build upon both the rural youth and agrarian studies literature, by expanding the focus to include a group of young people that has thus far attracted very minimal scholarly attention (Temudo and Abrantis 2015 is an exception): those who still choose to become farmers despite significant obstacles. Of particular interest are those who are not from farming families, termed 'newcomers' by Monllor (2012). These youth are confronted with additional barriers in setting up farming futures, as they will not inherit the resources, property or knowledge that many young people from farming backgrounds ('continuers') benefit from.

Focusing on the case of Nova Scotia, Canada, this chapter explores *why* these youth are still interested in rural and agrarian futures and *how* are they able to overcome obstacles in becoming farmers. In doing so, I propose a relational perspective that is particularly attentive to the generational dimension of becoming a young farmer.[1] I introduce the concept of 'age-class', which draws attention to the shared, generational position of young people aspiring to become farmers, while also expanding this horizontal perspective by highlighting important socioeconomic differences between them. Highlighting the interplay between generation, life phase and class also contextualises this chapter's analysis of one's agency in becoming a young farmer—illustrating how groups of young people are affected differently by Canada's agricultural policies, and how this has caused some groups to create their own spaces through which to influence rural and agricultural development.

Methodologically, this research combines a theoretical and conceptual discussion with a more concrete exploration of young farmers' experiences and involvement in decision-making processes. It draws on data obtained from government documents, academic journals, and project reports. This is complemented with material obtained from interviews (conducted in 2013) with key informants (see Table 4.1), which sheds further light on the role of young farmers' organisations in Nova Scotia and helps to frame the Nova Scotian context within a global perspective.

This chapter is structured as follows: First, a global contextualisation of how contemporary agriculture is becoming generationally unbalanced. The second section conceptualises 'age-class' and how it can be used to frame the analysis of young farmers, their opportunities, and the obstacles they face when beginning their careers. The third section examines the industrial agricultural system in Canada and the ways in which it creates an exclusionary environment for farmers of particular age-classes. The

Table 4.1 Overview of respondents

Name	Organisation	Note
Rebecca Sooksom	Nova Scotia Department of Agriculture (Agricultural Transition Officer)	Resource Coordinator for ThinkFARM, a programme that supports initiatives to attract new entrepreneurs into the agricultural sector
Brad McCallum	Nova Scotia Young Farmers (coordinating member)	Executive Director of the Agri-Commodity Management Association (ACMA) and recipient of the 'Outstanding Young (under 35) Agrologist Award' for 2014
Blain Snipstal	La Vía Campesina Youth (member)	A young (male, under 35) farmer in Maryland and a member of the USA-based Rural Coalition
Morgan Ody	La Vía Campesina Youth (member)	A young (female, under 35) farmer in Bretagne and a member of the Confederation of Farmers in France

All information presented here, such as age and position, pertains to 2013

fourth section then narrows its focus on Nova Scotia, highlighting how the trajectories of young farmers in the province offer a unique perspective in juxtaposition to the rest of Canada. Building on this, the fifth section points out how socio-political factors in rural Nova Scotia have been crucial in facilitating the collective agency of young farmers and the formation of their organisations. In the sixth section, the importance and impact of this mobilisation is then emphasised via the subsequent development of new provincial agricultural policies, which aim to facilitate smoother entry for more young people into the sector. In the final section some concluding remarks are offered.

THE GENERATIONAL PROBLEM IN CONTEMPORARY AGRICULTURE: A GLOBAL PERSPECTIVE

The number of young people working in agriculture is decreasing drastically worldwide, with particularly illustrative statistics emerging from countries in the Global North. In Canada for instance, the proportion of young farmers (under 35) within the total farming population dropped from 11.5 to 9 per cent between 2001 and 2006. Similarly, across the European Union (EU) Member States, the percentage dropped from 9 to 6 between 1990 and 2012 (European Commission 2012: 3; RGC 2000:

2). And this trend is certainly not limited to Northern countries—reports from various countries in the Global South show comparable data on ageing farmer populations and declining numbers of young people (see Ghosh 2015; Anyidoho et al. 2012; Sumberg et al. 2012; Tadele and Gella 2012).

It is commonly assumed that younger generations today are disinterested in farming. In most societies it is perceived as an occupation requiring continuous hard work for little economic gain (Rigg 2006: 191). Mills' (1999) research further suggests that the many rural youth in rapidly changing societies, such as Thailand, consider the countryside backward and prefer to exchange it for an urban life that they consider more 'modern'. White attributes this to 'an assault on rural culture', which occurs partially through modern schooling, and partially 'through global consumerism and media of all kinds' (2012: 12). In addition, gerontocratic rural societies create a difficult environment for young people to feel valued for who they are. However, it is not just youth themselves who appear to be keen to leave the countryside—parents (including those who are farmers themselves) often encourage their children to do so, in the hope that urban areas will offer them better educational opportunities and chances of finding 'valued' forms of work. Nugin's (2014: 62) research in rural Estonia further illustrates how even rural youth workers, despite concerns about the phenomenon, 'promote' such out-migration as a move 'forward', and 'a means of self realisation' for rural youth. In the European context, the exodus by rural youth is considered as an important force behind the 'dejuvenation' of rural areas (Thissen et al. 2010).

Such conditions have left many retiring farmers with no successors, usually forcing them to sell their land. Large agri-businesses and investment companies have been keen buyers, setting into motion a domino effect in which the growing prevalence of large industrialised farms increases both the demand for and price of land. High land prices make it virtually impossible for most young farmers to purchase property (Chinsinga and Chasukwa 2012)—particularly in highly industrialised countries of the Global North, such as Canada (Lerohl and Unterschultz 2000; Carbone and Subioli 2008). These dynamics add to the generational divide between (young) urban and (old) rural areas, complicating intergenerational knowledge exchange, impacting property and asset inheritance, weakening familial relationships, and causing urban areas to continue expanding while rural areas are deserted.

Next to the intergenerational dynamics that contribute to these problems, young people are also disadvantaged due to their generational positions as youth or young adults. For instance, in countries such as Canada, the highly mechanised organisation of the agricultural sector makes it extremely capital intensive, and most young farmers do not have the assets required either for start-up or to be competitive afterward. In addition, fewer farmworkers are required to maintain large production outputs, and those with prior experience who need less initial training are considered more employable (Pouliot 2011; Bennell 2007; RGC 2000). Farming also stands apart from other types of employment in that it can be better understood as a lifestyle rather than simply a job, due to the time, labour, and dedication it demands. It is a highly time-intensive and place-based occupation, which stands at odds with the images of youth represented through consumer culture emphasising flexibility, mobility, and urbanity.

Despite global concerns about the future of agriculture, governments have been reluctant to implement policies that support young farmers. Where such policies *are* in place, they typically work in an exclusionary manner by targeting only a specific subgroup of young farmers. In the Canadian context, which is discussed in more detail below, the policy focus is on those young farmers pursuing industrialised methods of agriculture, as this fits with dominant ideas of agrarian development in Canada. Since most young farmers involved in industrialised farming come from advantaged backgrounds, policies favouring them deepen the already significant divide between 'continuers' and 'newcomers', as the latter group typically lacks access to the familial resources needed to attain capital, land, training, and education, and yet are typically not eligible for government support. This is especially true for those newcomers interested in alternative agricultural methods, such as small-scale and/or organic farming (Pouliot 2011; AGRI 2010).

The generational problem in agriculture has been picked up by several organisations and incorporated into on-going agrarian struggles, such as those over land, food sovereignty, and indigenous rights. This includes organisations like La Vía Campesina (LVC) Youth and Nova Scotia Young Farmers (NSYF), which are both highlighted in this chapter. La Vía Campesina Youth is an international network with local chapters, whereas NSYF is a provincial organisation. Importantly, both are youth led and are composed of members under the age of 35. Although these two organisations have different histories, goals, and member bases, they share a common concern about the lack of recognition and acknowledgement for the particular obstacles young farmers face due to their generational position (see NSYF 2013; La Vía Campesina 2013; AGRI 2010).

These organisations illustrate the agency of young farmers and rural youth, and their bold intentions to change the future of agriculture globally. The theme of agency has received much attention in the youth studies literature, yet less so in relation to collective forms of agency as exemplified by these organisations. Arguably, however, such collective forms of agency potentially have a much greater impact on development processes. Yet, such a functional approach to agency should not obscure the *individual* agency exercised by members of such organisations, which may illuminate important dimensions silenced by the institutional discourses of organisations. Through their activities and engagement with other (policy) actors, young farmers' organisations also give meaning to the construct of 'young farmers'. This is done in a generational fashion, by defining 'young farmers' in relation to age, and also by drawing upon their particular youthfulness. As Lanza points out:

> The fact that young people participated in specific instances of mass politics does not imply that that politics was framed under the category of 'youth,' nor that their politicization (the process of becoming political) was argued, justified, and expressed through their 'youthfulness'. (2012: 33)

LVC seeks to attribute their youth network with a degree of youthfulness, which can be illustrated by the use of an exclamation mark ('Youth!') in reference to their youth network (see La Vía Campesina Youth 2014). An exclamation mark signals energy, urgency, loudness, and emotions—qualities that contribute to giving LVC's youth network a youthful political identity.

Analysing 'Age-Class': Bridging Youth and Agrarian Studies

Much of the policy literature on youth employs a horizontal understanding of youth. Youth, in this sense, is defined in terms of chronological age. However, as White and Wyn argue:

> Young people do not constitute a homogenous social group any more than adults do. Growing up is a gendered, classed and 'raced' experience, in which the outcomes are far from equal... it is vital for the sociological study

of youth to provide both an analytical framework in which young people's lives are situated and contextualised within unequal social structures, and to offer a political perspective that offers the basis for challenging those structures. (1998: 318–9).

In agrarian studies, on the other hand, dynamics of social differentiation have long been central in analyses. Class, and to a lesser extent gender, are recognised as important social relations shaping agrarian dynamics. However, until recently this literature had little to say about generation, and how age-based positions interact with other relations of social differentiation—impacting young people's chances of becoming a farmer (see Archambault 2014; Berckmoes and White, this volume). Further, where class is employed in the contemporary youth studies literature, it is often in relation to youth subcultures and identities, with relatively little attention to its classical, material, understanding in relation to the means of production (Furlong and Cartmel 2007 is a notable exception). Seeking to address this gap, I propose the concept of 'age-class', which weaves together a twofold horizontal perspective (combining life phase and a Mannheimian understanding of generation) with a vertical perspective (material understanding of class). I employ this concept in order to shed light on how the interplay between this binary understanding of generation, interacts with the structural role of class, and how this impacts choices, agency, and capabilities in young people's (aspirational) agricultural careers.

In social analysis, class is conventionally determined by 'the social relations of production between classes of producers (labour) and non-producers' (Bernstein 2010: 124). As a concept, it has been employed to illuminate inequalities in social structures and access to material resources (Wright 2000). Through class analysis, researchers seek to gain a better understanding of the social lives, political orientations, life experiences, and behavioural patterns of other people (White and Wyn 1998; Veltmeyer 1986). Class, in this sense, is understood as a structural context within which agency must be contextualised and understood (White and Wyn 1998). A class-based framework directs debates on why young people are turning away from the agricultural sector, to the structural relations preventing some from establishing themselves as farmers, as well as to how young people seek to redress these inequalities through collective action (which contributes to shaping them into a Mannheimian generation) (Boreham et al. 1989).

When class analysis is used in youth studies, there is a common tendency to categorise young people on the basis of the socioeconomic position of their parents, based on the assumption that they are not financially independent (Furlong and Cartmel 2007). However, Mannheim's (1952) work on generation posits that cohorts, based on their shared 'coming of age' experience in a particular historical time, may develop a generational identity that is distinct from their parents' generation, despite sharing similar class-based positions. In combination, a life phase understanding of generation further complicates the silencing of generation in class-based analyses. Based on a shared position in the life course, there is a degree of commonality between young people, in terms of the objectives they have, and the problems they face in achieving social adulthood. The concept of age-class is cognisant of these two intersecting generational dynamics and combines this with a material understanding of class. On this basis, I propose the following typology:

1) The *large-scale industrial farmer class* includes (prospective) young farmers from wealthy, well-established farming families who are able to inherit their family's farm or purchase a piece of land and the necessary start-up capital to integrate relatively easily into the agricultural sector. This group can be understood in relation to the 'rich peasants' class: emergent capitalist farmers who are able to accumulate assets and expand their production (Bernstein 2010). These young farmers likely do not need loans or grants from the government, but if they do need extra start-up money, their families can use their assets as collateral. Young farmers in this category have also received a good agricultural education, either at a post-secondary institution or through practical experience working on their family's farm. Thus, they have all the opportunities and privileges to ensure they face few obstacles during the beginning stages of their careers.

2) The *small- to medium-scale farmer class* includes (aspiring) young farmers who do not necessarily come from farming families, and those who do. The latter generally come from small- to medium-scale farms and may not inherit land from their parents. There are a few reasons for this—their family may only have enough land to pass on to one of their children, or their parents may not be able to retire due to financial difficulties. This group can be understood in relation to the 'middle peasants' class: those who are able to reproduce their capital at the same rate as production, and their labour at the

same rate as consumption (Bernstein 2010). These young farmers must pursue financial assistance from the government or banks for start-up costs, but could also be eligible for grants if they already have a significant amount of agricultural education or work experience. They face countless obstacles when entering the sector, namely because they are not always able to acquire the necessary funds and the cost of farmland has become quite high due to increasing demand. Those who do not come from farming backgrounds are further limited by their lack of experience, which may cast them as less advantageous investments for governments.

3) The *farmworker/wageworker class* includes (aspiring) young farmers who come either from non-farming backgrounds or from small-scale farming families and are unable to rent or buy a piece of land because they do not qualify for grants and have no collateral to use for loans. This group can be understood in relation to the 'poor peasants' class: those who struggle to reproduce both their capital and their labour via farming (Bernstein 2010). Thus, these young farmers often end up as wageworkers on other people's farms, usually with the hope of saving enough money to eventually become an independent farmer (see Table 4.2).

Building upon the definition for 'young farmers' noted earlier, an 'aspiring young farmer' (categories C, D, E, and F) is one who wishes to work in agriculture but has not been able to fully integrate into, or become fully employed by the sector for various reasons. These reasons include being unable to acquire the funds required to purchase or rent a piece of land, or being unable to acquire the training (via formal education or an apprenticeship) required to start and operate a farm. This includes people from both non-farming and farming backgrounds, but *does not* include those who have been able, or are expected to establish themselves easily in the sector as the result of family connections or wealth ('prospective young farmers')—in other words, those from well-established farming families (category A) or upper-class non-farming families (category B).

Aspiring young farmers from categories C and D are an anomaly in that they face similar obstacles in obtaining land as those from categories E and F, yet instead of becoming wageworkers on someone else's land, they often still manage to own land and become successful small business owners. Of particular interest here are those who come from non-farming families (category D) but decide by their own volition to pursue a career

Table 4.2   Typology of young farmers

Familial background	'Prospective Young Farmers'	'Aspiring Young Farmers'	
	large-scale industrial farmers	*small- to medium-scale farmers*	*Farmworkers/wageworkers*
Farming ('Continuers')	(A) From wealthy, well-established farming families with large-scale farms	(C) From families with small- to medium-scale farms and average wealth	(E) From families with small-scale farms and very little wealth
	→ Can inherit land, knowledge and networks	→ Unlikely to inherit land (probably must buy/rent land), can inherit knowledge and networks	→ Cannot inherit land (must work on someone else's land), may inherit knowledge and networks
Non-farming ('Newcomers')	(B) From non-farming family upper-class families	(D) From non-farming middle-class families	(F) From non-farming lower-class families
	→ Must buy their own land, will not inherit knowledge or networks	→ Must buy/rent land, will not inherit knowledge or networks	→ Must work on someone else's land, will not inherit knowledge or networks

Source: Author's own construction

in farming, often due to the belief that alternative agricultural methods (non-industrial) are possible. This raises questions of how they are able to acquire land, through which pathways they have established themselves in the sector, and how the economic context of a particular region is consequential in this. Since young farmers generally have not acquired enough credit history or savings to rent or buy their own piece of land, they often must first find work on someone else's farm or seek off-farm employment.

YOUNG FARMERS AND INDUSTRIALISED AGRICULTURE: THE CANADIAN CONTEXT

In most Canadian provinces—especially those with ample farmland (Ontario, Manitoba, Saskatchewan, and Alberta)—a few wealthy families or corporations dominate the agricultural sector through the operation of large-scale industrial farms (which in Canada refers to farms with gross revenues above CAD 250,000). Due to the competitiveness of the agricultural market, there are few young small-scale farmers thriving in these provinces, with most young people in the region working on large-scale farms owned by their families (Statistics Canada 2012a, b).

Lower- and middle-class young farmers (age-class categories C, D, E, and F) find themselves in a particularly difficult situation, as they are usually without the means to set up their own farm, and often depend on being hired as farmworkers. Yet, given their relative lack of work experience and undeveloped professional networks, the chances of succeeding in doing so in a large-scale industrialised farming system are slim (Carbone and Subioli 2008; Bollman 1999). Decades of farm mechanisation have made established farmers more selective regarding who they hire, usually favouring older, more experienced individuals, and excluding those who are younger. Young farmers with little work experience are often forced to seek off-farm employment far from home, or to accept wages considerably lower than their older co-workers, with little chance of ever having their own farms (Pouliot 2011).

A desire to work on the land, frustrated by the difficulties most young people face in finding a place in the industrial agricultural system, has contributed to some young people in Canada (and globally)—including those from non-farming backgrounds—practicing and advocating for alternative methods of farming by starting small, organic, less mechanised farms, or establishing cooperatives that produce food for local communities. In Canada, this is especially notable in the eastern province of Nova Scotia (see Fig. 4.1), an economically weak region located within a wealthy industrialised country, which is facing many of the same rural development issues as countries in the Global South.

Between 2006 and 2011, Nova Scotia was the only Canadian province to *increase* its number of farms (3795–3905), total area of farmland (403,044–412,000 ha), and number of farm operators (5095–5225), and was one of the only provinces to *decrease* its average farm size (106–105 ha) (Mascovitch 2012; Statistics Canada 2012a, b). Putting these contemporary patterns into an historical context is important, as Nova Scotia has long been a more supportive environment of young farmers than other provinces. For instance, in the late-1800s, at a time when universities seemed designed to convince young people that farming was not a viable career, several organisations, including the Nova Scotia Farmers Association (NSFA), lobbied for the creation of the Nova Scotia Agricultural College (NSAC), which opened in 1905. Today this college,

Fig. 4.1 Provincial map of Canada (Source: Agriculture in the classroom (http://www.aitc.sk.ca/))

known as the Dalhousie University Agricultural Campus, hosts many workshops and conferences, which offer important spaces for agricultural networking among young farmers (Brent 2002: 195).

Most of the young farmers in the Nova Scotian context can be categorised as 'aspiring young farmers' (age-class categories C, D, E, and F). While they come from many different familial, social and experiential backgrounds, there are common threads uniting them, which also link them with young farmers from other parts of Canada and across the globe. The ideological dimension is an important uniting force, as these young farmers are not only frustrated with the exclusionary generational effects of the industrialised farming system; they also firmly believe that current industrialised methods of farming must change if global food production is going to be sustainable. In the Canadian agrarian context, which is dominated by large-scale wheat and dairy farmers, these 'alternative' young farmers certainly standout; their personal strategies and paths are unique, while simultaneously reflecting similarities that link them together—framing them within a particular age-class that encapsulates both their individual dreams for the future and the issues they collectively face.

PERSONAL TRAJECTORIES: YOUNG FARMERS GAINING GROUND IN NOVA SCOTIA

A study conducted by Haalboom (2013) in Nova Scotia from 2012 to 2013 presents particularly illuminating data on eight young 'newcomer' farmers' personal experiences. Six women[2] and two men were interviewed about their motivations for pursuing careers in the agricultural sector, the challenges they faced, and what they hoped to gain from farming. All of the interviewees were between the ages of 25 and 40 and all came from non-farming families (age-class categories D and F), growing up in both rural and urban environments across Canada. Although Haalboom did not comment on the class position of her respondents, many of them had acquired a university-level education and had managed to buy or rent their own piece of land, rather than becoming wageworkers on someone else's. This indicates that they likely had middle-class upbringings (age-class category D). The respondents indicate that despite having no parental influence in their decision to become farmers, they all became interested in the sector at a young age, generally in their teenage years (Haalboom 2013: 24–33). Haalboom's interview material stresses the lack of start-up support they received from the Canadian government, but also highlights the supportive atmosphere of Nova Scotia's farming communities and the affordability of its land—compared, for example, with the western provinces (Mascovitch 2012). This makes Nova Scotia compelling because it is more conducive to the entrance of young farmers. As one interviewee noted, '[H]ere in Nova Scotia, a person like me of no fabulous wealth has the opportunity to own a beautiful piece of property that can be productive, and something that is permanent' (Haalboom 2013: 29).

As the second largest country in the world, Canada is commonly assumed to be land abundant. However, a vast amount of its land is not suitable for agriculture, particularly in the cold northern regions and rocky coastal areas. Furthermore, the majority of farming takes place in the central Prairie Provinces, where there are concentrated areas of flatlands and little spatial limitations, making it relatively easy for farms to expand. This land is generally targeted by large agri-businesses, and the high demand also increases prices in the region, thus finding farmland that is not only available but also affordable for young farmers is becoming increasingly more challenging (MIJARC et al. 2012; Pouliot 2011). Therefore, as highlighted by Haalboom's research, land ownership in Canada is a critical aspect in realising young people's 'farm dream'—similar to what is being reported in research in the Global South (MIJARC et al. 2012: 8) and Europe (Borras et al. 2013).

Next to the availability of relatively affordable land, it must also be noted that Nova Scotia has a proportionately larger rural population than most other provinces and existing farming communities have been well established for many generations. Such cultural factors matter, as one of Haalboom's interviewees illustrated, noting that '[Nova Scotia] seems to have a very forward-thinking population that is supportive of small farms and eating local. [Nova Scotian] culture is very strong even in its rural communities,' while another called making a living on a small farm a 'really Nova Scotian thing to do' (Haalboom 2013: 35–6). Additionally, all of the interviewees stated that they engaged in styles of marketing that directly connected them to the people who eat their food, seeing this as a form of activism or social justice that seeks both to provide more ethical, wholesome food to their communities, while also protecting the environment:

> I realized farming was the ultimate form of activism to counteract the damage caused by an industrialized, global food system. Farming—providing quality food for local communities—could contribute to the sort of revolution I wanted to see in agriculture, one that deconstructs corporate monopolies and brings people back to supporting direct connections between consumers and farmers, preserving the existence of small-scale and diversified organic agriculture. (Haalboom 2013: 32)

Several of the interviewees were originally attracted to farming with the hope of achieving an independent lifestyle with the freedom to determine their own schedules and career goals. Yet, this is a luxury rarely afforded to young people who are just beginning their careers—particularly in farming, where a significant amount of start-up labour is required. High financial investment during start-up is another important issue for young farmers, as highlighted by Blain Snipstal (La Vía Campesina Youth): 'There are several major barriers that young people face when transitioning into the agrarian sector: access to land, access to capital, access to markets, access to infrastructure, and access to knowledge' (Interview 2013).

All of Haalboom's interviewees echoed this concern, noting that they had to either generate savings for a few years prior to start-up, or work part-time elsewhere while establishing their farms. These young farmers had all accepted that it would take many years before they are able to make a stable living off of their farms. These young 'newcomers' also acknowledged that in the Canadian context, they represent a minority, as most young farmers are 'continuers' (87 per cent of all female farmers and 71 per cent of all male farmers) who come from farming families and experience a much smoother transition into the sector (Haalboom 2013: 5). The latter is especially true for young farmers who come from large-scale industrial farming backgrounds (age-class category A).

The interviewees also highlighted the importance of continued agricultural training and education. This is often acquired by attending conferences and workshops organised by the Nova Scotia Federation of Agriculture, ThinkFARM, and the Dalhousie Agricultural Campus. These events are however not just a mechanism of knowledge transfer—they are also important for networking purposes, as this is where young farmers meet, share experiences, and develop professional and social networks (Haalboom 2013). Such face-to-face meetings are especially important for young farmers. The spatiality of farming means that many young farmers live and work in relatively isolated rural areas with limited opportunities for meeting a wide range of farming peers. Such events also have political potential, as they help generate a collective identity, help illuminate shared concerns, and can lead to the formulation of collective strategies. Thus, these spaces have likely been a key factor in facilitating the formation of young farmers' organisations, in Nova Scotia and globally—leading young farmers to become active participants, seeking to influence rural development processes and policies.

Collective Agency: The Emergence of Young Farmers' Organisations

Farmers' unions and organisations have been an important part of the rural social fabric of Canada for decades, playing a key role in the development of the country's agricultural regions. In the past, farmers would have been members of these organisations regardless of their age; however, as concerns about the future of agriculture have increased, young farmers have formed organisations of their own. These organisations can be seen as a form of collective agency, which here refers to intentional human actions occurring within evolving social contexts. The collective agency exercised by young farmers through their organisations illustrates a reactive and deeply political form of agency responding to the constraints of social structures (Sanderson 1999). By exercising such forms of collective agency, structural positions also become more visible, as participating in such organisations contributes to the formation of an age-class consciousness (which I illustrate below). This is reminiscent of the way in which Mannheim (1952) discussed the emergence of generational units among groups of individuals within, what he termed, an 'actual generation'.

The NSYF, established in 2001, has quickly been gaining prominence in decision-making processes in the province. Brad McCallum, a coordinating member of the NSYF, described the organisation's functions as providing networking, educational and development opportunities, as well as a voice for young Nova Scotian farmers. Due to its formal connection to the Nova Scotia Federation of Agriculture, the NSYF is able to participate in provincial policy discussions, and is also very active in agricultural awareness, educating the public about who produces the food they eat (Interview 2013). The NSYF aims to identify the obstacles facing young farmers, promote collaboration, exchange solutions that can be applied in both Canada and abroad, facilitate knowledge exchange, support farm transfers from older to younger farmers, and prepare young farmers to be more actively involved in both provincial and federal organisations (NSYF 2013).

At a national level, the Canadian Young Farmers' Forum (CYFF), established in 1997, plays a crucial role in supporting organisations provincially (including the NSYF), both financially and through the facilitation of various conferences and workshops. The CYFF aims to provide multifaceted developmental opportunities for young farmers and facilitates young farmers' networks, recognising the importance of knowledge and information exchange (CYFF 2013). The CYFF highlighted that, despite Canada's main agricultural policy being called 'Growing Forward' (introduced in 2007), young farmers were not addressed anywhere in the document. The Forum was able to participate in the development of the 'Growing Forward II' policy, after putting steady pressure on the federal government to allow some of its members to be present in policy revision discussions. This revised policy was introduced in 2013, and more specifically acknowledges the crucial role young farmers' innovation plays in the future of agriculture by highlighting the issues which members of CYFF brought to the discussions (Haalboom 2013; AGRI 2010). The updated policy proposes a 'renewal strategy' that refocuses funding and responds to the various needs of beginning farmers, while also addressing market forces that increase the price of farmland, and introducing more mentorship and agricultural education opportunities to increase young farmers' skills (AAFC 2013; Pouliot 2011).

Young farmers' organisations communicate officially with the federal government via the National Future Farmers' Network (NFFN), which met for the first time in 2010, bringing together 45 participants from various segments of the Canadian agricultural sector. It was created by the Ministry of State-Agriculture, which from 2006 to 2011 was led by Jean-Pierre Blackburn—a Minister who was quite devoted to increasing the 'youth lens' in development policies and programmes (AAFC 2010). The NFFN focuses specifically on assisting *young* farmers (rather than on all beginning farmers), in order to address the lack of governmental resources being allocated to them, and link them directly to the Department of Agriculture and Agri-Food (Pouliot 2011).

The establishment of these organisations has been an important step for young farmers toward functioning as a cohesive network, and illustrates that individual differences—such as geographical location or type of agricultural producer—can be of lesser importance than the commonality of belonging to the same age-class. This highlights age-class consciousness as a pivotal factor in uniting groups of individuals who face similar inequalities when accessing resources, and who also hold the same position in relation to the means of production (Wright 2000). It is also demonstrative of young people 'negotiating contemporary economic and social change through new and diverse ways' by 'exercising their collective power and asserting their collective voices on issues of wider social importance' (Wyn and White 2000: 167, 179). Blain Snipstal (La Vía Campesina Youth) aptly captures just how critical unity among young farmers is

> It's an historical moment that we're in, particularly for us in the Global North, but really everywhere, as the capitalist model of agriculture expands and we're seeing different reverberations facing youth in particular... there's an international aspect where we need to recognise that from the Global South a lot of this inspiration has been developed by our comrades and partners there. However, we need to also recognise and cherish that here in the [North] we also have a historical legacy of resistance and building a foundation of revolutionary pedagogy and thought. (Food First 2013)

Both formal young farmers' organisations and more informal, individual action, such as engaging in alternative modes of agriculture, can be conceptualised as overlapping forms of the expression of agency that emerge as a result of intersecting factors (such as age and class). In Nova Scotia, young farmers have different goals in regard to political action and how they engage with the government varies based on their individual interests. However, despite the diversity of their backgrounds and issues they face in operating their own farms, they have managed to become an organised and cohesive unit. White and Wyn (1998) highlight this type of agency as a collective project in which young farmers are using organised actions to change policies, gain more access to resources, and demonstrate their willingness to modify the existing social order. Discussions of this nature can often be abstract and not always rooted in real-life change; however, in this case, there has indeed been a visible impact on agricultural policies in Nova Scotia, and in Canada more generally.

Agricultural Policies and the Potential of Generational Renewal

Since 2010, the Canadian government has implemented a few policies intended to support young farmers during the difficult start-up phase, yet applying for things like installation aid programmes has very specific requirements that exclude large groups of young farmers—particularly those from poorer backgrounds and non-farming families (age-class categories D, E, and F). For example, in the 'Growing Forward' (I) programme, young farmers must possess a certain level of education and work experience in order to qualify for loans and grants (Statistics Canada 2002). Additionally, mentorship programmes have been designed to pair young farmers with wealthy large-scale farmers who have a vested interest in promoting the benefits of industrial agriculture, and thus teach their mentees business management skills related specifically to this model (Statistics Canada 2002).

However, in Nova Scotia, more inclusive policies and programmes have emerged as a result of the concerted effort of organisations like NYSF. As noted above, Nova Scotia has historically been more supportive than other provinces of young farmers. For instance, the Dalhousie University Agricultural Campus hosts many workshops and conferences, intended to encourage the maintenance of strong rural communities by fostering networking among young farmers. The Nova Scotia Department of Agriculture (NSDA) also supports the promotion of both formal educational opportunities and informal knowledge sharing (Haalboom 2013, Interview with Rebecca Sooksom 2013). Additionally, Farm Credit Canada (FCC) offers loans of up to CAD 500,000 to beginning farmers under the age of 40, regardless of whether they have minimal credit history, provided they present a solid business plan. Such programmes are particularly important for those from families that are (likely) unable to pass on land to them (age-class categories C, D, E, and F). These loans offer low interest rates, no processing fees, flexible repayment plans, and allow young farmers to begin building credit history (FCC 2013).

The NSDA is making great strides in policy implementation through its ten-year strategy 'Homegrown Success', which promotes local food production and consumption and intends to increase the number of local farms by five per cent over the next seven years. This strategy recognises that the demographic of young farmers in the province is unique and requires a wider range of projects and programmes. For example, beginning in 2009, the ThinkFARM Working Group Initiative (an extension of 'Growing Forward II') released the second edition of its 'Guide for Beginning Farmers in Nova Scotia' in 2012, which discusses everything from making business plans and locating available resources, to finding the right piece of land. There is also information on the FarmNEXT programme, which offers funding of up to CAD 30,000 through the Nova Scotia Farm Loan Board for new farmers (for both start-up and succession costs), as well as tips for finding a mentor and the types of mentorship offered (NSDA 2012, Interview with Rebecca Sooksom 2013). While there is no data to directly connect the establishment of programmes like ThinkFARM to an increase in the number of farms and operators in Nova Scotia over the past five years, it is probable that the province's increasing attention to supporting young farmers—particularly those from non-farming backgrounds (age-class categories D and F)—has made an important impact on the accessibility of the sector.

Nova Scotia certainly appears to be embracing its reputation of being a welcoming place for young and small-scale farmers, both economically and socially, due to its supportive community atmosphere. In 2013, the province even introduced a new licence plate containing the phrase 'Buy Local', as a strategy for promoting the purchase of locally grown produce (CBC 2013). Certainly, Nova Scotia is not without limitations, and the high unemployment rate must not be overlooked, as this is likely a major factor lowering the value of land, and some may argue is forcing young people into farming out of necessity. However, there has been no research published that supports this argument, and while most of the young farmers interviewed by Haalboom stated that they are seeking alternatives to the current global food system, none cited job scarcity as a reason for pursuing an agricultural career. Their choice to farm has been fuelled by their own personal desires to do so, while also collectively challenging the existing structure of the agricultural system (Haalboom 2013). This kind of political action demonstrates the importance of one's age-class position in unifying people around a common cause and reiterates that today, expanded perspectives on class remain important tools for understanding life experiences, social structures, and inequalities. These expanded perspectives are not only useful in 'modernising' social theories, making them more relevant to current contexts, they are also multifunctional in that they can be applied to different fields of study—such as youth and agrarian studies—bridging gaps between particular theoretical perspectives.

Concluding Remarks

This chapter has sought to illuminate the ways in which structural factors impact young farmers' abilities to gain access to land, resources, and employment in the agricultural sector. In so doing, it has examined how agricultural policies are implicated in this, as well as how the collective agency demonstrated by young farmers has contributed to changes in policymaking spaces. The mobilisation of young farmers' organisations has also contributed to the formation of a generational identity revolving around questions of: who will be the next generation of farmers? and what types of agriculture will they be engaged in? Both the conceptual discussion and empirical case study data presented here demonstrate that the current industrial agricultural model has exclusionary characteristics that provide unequal opportunities to different groups in society, of which the declining number of young farmers acts as a vivid illustration. This points to the structural inequalities that plague not only the agricultural economy, but also the entire global capitalist system that it is a part of—particularly in regard to the labour market and access to productive resources. This inequality is framed by the dual concept of age-class, which acts as a common thread linking the various aspects of this discussion—as well as the multiple characteristics that determine both young farmers' social positions and their generationally distinct forms of (collective) agency.

Institutionally, governments play the most prominent role in addressing the obstacles facing young farmers; however, they have yet to fully embrace this responsibility in a manner that sufficiently addresses young people from various backgrounds. Most young people are abandoning the countryside to pursue employment in the cities due to the precariousness and perceptions of rural livelihoods. Rural unemployment levels are high and young farmers from lower- to middle-class families (age-class categories C, D, E, and F) are the most vulnerable to job insecurity, generally due to fewer opportunities to access education and learn new skills. Increasing the interest of young people in farming should be at the core of rural development plans in countries around the world, but they should also focus on offering more support to those who have remained and are already trying to make a living in agriculture—including the youthful collectives representing them. Prioritising young farmers' assistance programmes is crucial for the survival of local and domestic agricultural sectors.

Voices of farmers—both young and old—are calling for a radical transformation in the structure of the agricultural system worldwide, one that allows small-scale farms and farmers to thrive, through the production of natural foods and more direct connections to markets and consumers (see La Vía Campesina 2013). As long as young farmers continue exercising their agency, structural changes are possible, as the perpetual tension between the two allows for continuous social transition. Opening doors for young farmers to inherit or start their own farms is pivotal, and this includes the provisioning of more loans and grants to support the purchase or rental of land. Certainly, access to land is the most important factor for young people to be able to farm, and yet it is also the biggest obstacle they face. In order for effective changes to be made, the structural issues creating inequalities in land ownership must be better understood, thus academics and policymakers alike must focus more on exploring these structures.

The intention of this chapter is that it serves as a platform from which to draw more attention to the fact that there *are* young people who still pursue farming careers and they are visibly committed, not only to making a living in agriculture, but also to demonstrating their agency and political engagement. These young farmers are mobilised, organised, and involved in their communities and are creating networks both at home and abroad. Provincial organisations are making connections across Canada and international organisations do so around the world. Future research should delve deeper into the structure of these organisations, and could even use class analysis to examine relations between the individual young farmers within them. Additionally, although gender and ethnicity have not played an analytical role in this chapter, these social relations should be thoroughly addressed in subsequent research, especially in terms of their interplay with class and the role they play in the lives of young farmers.

NOTES

1. The conceptualisation of 'young farmers' as it is intended here draws on the definitions used by the Canadian Young Farmers' Forum (CYFF) and the Federation of Young Farmers of Quebec (FRAQ), which is someone between the ages of 18 and 35 who works in, or wishes to work in, the agricultural sector (Haalboom 2013: 6; AGRI 2010: 6).
2. Interestingly, although six out of eight of the young farmers in Haalboom's study were women, the study does not suggest that any of them have faced particular gender-based obstacles. Further, the gender composition of Haalboom's sample does not appear to reflect a Canadian-wide trend. Statistics Canada reports that just 26 per cent of Canadian farmers are women (maintaining roughly the same percentage since 1991), and that the number of female farm operators under the age of 35 has decreased by more than 50 per cent since 1991.

REFERENCES

Agriculture and Agri-Food Canada (AAFC). (2010). Minister Blackburn invites young farmers to the National Future Farmers Network. http://www.market wired.com/press-release/minister-blackburn-invites-young-farmers-to-the-national-future-farmers-network-1336554.htm. Accessed Oct 2015.

Agriculture and Agri-Food Canada (AAFC). (2013). *What is growing forward?* Government of Canada. http://www4.agr.gc.ca/AAFC-AAC/display-afficher.do?id=1200344086309&lang=eng#q1. Accessed June 2013.

Anyidoho, N. A., Leavy, J., & Asenso-Okyere, K. (2012). Perceptions and aspirations: A case study of young people in Ghana's cocoa sector. *IDS Bulletin, 43*(6), 20–32.

Archambault, C. (2014). Young perspectives on pastoral rangeland privatization: Intimate exclusions at the intersection of youth identities. *European Journal of Development Research, 26*(2), 204–218.

Bennell, P. (2007). *Promoting livelihood opportunities for rural youth*. Rome: Knowledge and Skills for Development, International Fund for Agricultural Development (IFAD).

Bernstein, H. (2010). *Class dynamics of Agrarian change*. Halifax: Fernwood Publishing.

Bollman, R. (1999). *The age old phenomenon of the aging farmer*. Vista on the Agri-Food Industry and the Farm Community (pp. 1–12). Ottawa: Statistics Canada.

Boreham, P. R., Clegg, S. R., Emmison, J. M., Marks, G. M., & Western, J. S. (1989). Semi-peripheries or particular pathways: The case of Australia, New Zealand and Canada as class formations. *International Sociology, 4*(1), 67–90.

Borras, S., Franco, J., & van der Ploeg, J. D. (2013). Introduction: Land concentration, land concentration and people's struggles in Europe. In J. Franco & S. Borras Jr. (Eds.), *Land concentration, land grabbing and people's struggles in Europe* (pp. 6–32). Amsterdam: Transnational Institute.

Brent, D. (2002). *Going forward: Agricultural modernity in Nova Scotia, 1933–1956*. Ottawa: Library and Archives Canada, Published Heritage Branch.

Canadian Broadcasting Corporation (CBC). (2013). *Buy local movement coming to N.S. Licence Plates*. Halifax: CBC News. http://www.cbc.ca/news/canada/nova-scotia/story/2013/08/27/ns-buy-local-licence-plate.html. Accessed Aug 2013.

Canadian Young Farmers' Forum (CYFF). (2013). *About CYFF: Educate, energize, empower*. http://cyff.ca/cyff/. Accessed June 2013.

Carbone, A., & Subioli, G. (2008). *The generational turnover in agriculture: The ageing dynamics and the EU support policies to young farmers*. Paper presented at the 109th European Association of Agricultural Economics Seminar, Viterbo (Italy), 20–21 November, 2008.

Chinsinga, B., & Chasukwa, M. (2012). Youth, agriculture and land grabs in Malawi. *IDS Bulletin, 43*(6), 67–77.

Committee on Agriculture and Agri-Food (AGRI). (2010). *Young farmers: The future of agriculture*.' Report of the standing committee, 40th Parliament, 3rd Session. Ottawa: House of Commons Canada.

European Commission. (2012). Generational renewal in EU agriculture: Statistical background. *EU Agricultural Economic Briefs*, Brief Number 6, June 2012.

FAO, IFAD and CTA. (2014). Youth and agriculture: Key challenges and concrete solutions. Rome, Wageningen, Food and Agricultural Organization of the United Nations (FAO), International Fund for Agricultural Development (IFAD), Technical Centre for Agricultural and Rural Cooperation (CTA).

Farm Credit Canada (FCC). (2013). *Young farmers' loan*. Regina: Farm Credit Canada. http://www.fcc-fac.ca/en/products/lending/Young_Farmer_loan_e.asp. Accessed Aug 2013.

Food First. (2013). Video interview with Blain Snipstal published on September 23, 2013. http://www.youtube.com/watch?v=vVbX00QdgZk. Accessed Nov 2013.

Furlong, A., & Cartmel, F. (2007). *Young people and social change: New perspectives* (2nd ed.). Berkshire: Open University Press.

Ghosh, N. (2015). Empty rice bowl looms as Thai farmers grow older. *Strait Times*. Singapore, 15 August 2015.

Haalboom, S. (2013). *Young Agrarian culture in Nova Scotia: The initial and ongoing motivations for young farmers from non-agricultural backgrounds.* Halifax: Dalhousie University.

La Vía Campesina. (2013). *Together, peasant youth can move forward.* http://via-campesina.org/en/index.php/our-conferences-mainmenu-28/6-jakarta-2013/1422-together-peasant-youth-can-move-forward. Accessed Aug 2013.

La Vía Campesina Youth. (2014). *Youth and agriculture.* http://viacampesina.org/en/index.php/main-issues-mainmenu-27/youth-mainmenu-66. Accessed Oct 2015.

Lanza, F. (2012). Springtime and morning suns: "Youth" as a political category in twentieth-century China. *The Journal of the History of Childhood and Youth, 5*(1), 31–51.

Lerohl, M., & Unterschultz, J. (2000). *Agriculture in Canada: Who will grow the food?* Presented at the Western Agricultural Economics Association Annual Meetings, Vancouver, British Columbia, June 29–July 1.

Mannheim, K. (1952). The problem of generations. In *Essays in the sociology of knowledge*. London: RKP.

Mascovitch, P. (2012). Number of Nova Scotia farms increasing. *FCC express*. Regina: Farm Credit Canada.

Mills, M. B. (1999). *Thai women in the global labor force: Consuming desires, contested selves.* New Brunswick /London: Rutgers University Press.

MIJARC, FAO and IFAD. (2012). Summary of the findings of the project implemented by MIJARC in collaboration with FAO and IFAD: Facilitating access of rural youth to agricultural activities. The Farmers' Forum Youth Session, 18 February, (2012).

Monllor, N. (2012). Farm entry: A comparative analysis of young farmers, their pathways, attitudes and practices in Ontario (Canada) and Catalunya (Spain), final report. Accessed through http://www.accesstoland.eu/IMG/pdf/monllor_farm_entry_report_2012.pdf

Nova Scotia Department of Agriculture (NSDA). (2012). *ThinkFarm: Guide for beginning farmers in Nova Scotia* (2nd ed.). Halifax: Nova Scotia Department of Agriculture.

Nova Scotia Young Farmers (NSYF). (2013). *About Nova Scotia young farmers.* Bible Hill: Nova Scotia Federation of Agriculture. http://www.nsyoungfarmers.ca/about/. Accessed Aug 2013.

Nugin, R. (2014). "I think that they should go. Let them see something". The context of rural youth's out-migration in post-socialist Estonia. *Journal of Rural Studies, 34,* 51–64.

Pouliot, S. (2011). The beginning farmers' problem in Canada (working paper). Structure and Performance of Agriculture and Agri-Products Industry Network (SPAAN), Iowa State University.

Proctor, F., & Lucchesi, V. (2012). *Small-scale farming and youth in an area of rapid rural change*. London /The Hague: International Institute for Environment and Development (IIED), Hivos.

Rigg, J. (2006). Land, farming, livelihoods and poverty: Rethinking the links in the rural South. *World Development, 34*(1), 180–202.

Ross Gordon Consultants (RGC). (2000). *The future of young farmers in the European Union: Working paper, Agriculture, forestry and rural development series*. Luxembourg: European Parliament.

Sanderson, S. (1999). *Social transformations: A general theory of historical development, expanded edition*. Oxford: Rowman & Littlefields Publishers, Inc..

Statistics Canada. (2002). *Perspectives on labour and tncome, 3:2, Minister of Industry*. Ottawa: Statistics Canada.

Statistics Canada. (2012a). *More farms in Nova Scotia*. Ottawa: Statistics Canada. http://www.statcan.gc.ca/pub/95-640-x/2012002/prov/12-eng.htm#Farm_operators. Accessed July 2013.

Statistics Canada. (2012b). *Snapshot of Canadian agriculture*. Ottawa: Statistics Canada. http://www.statcan.gc.ca/pub/95-640-x/2012002/00-eng.htm. Accessed July 2013.

Sumberg, J., Anyidoho, N. A., Leavy, J., te Lintelo, D. J. H., & Wellard, K. (2012). Introduction: The young people and agriculture 'problem' in Africa. *IDS Bulletin, 43*(6), 1–8.

Tadele, G., & Gella, A. A. (2012). A last resort and often not an option at all: Farming and young people in ethiopia. *IDS Bulletin, 43*(6), 33–43.

Temudo, M., & Abrantes, M. (2015). The pen and the plough: Balanta young men in Guinea-Bissau. *Development and Change, 46*(3), 464–485.

Thissen, F., Droogleever Fortuijn, J., Strijker, D., & Haartsen, T. (2010). Migration intentions of rural youth in the Westhoek, Flanders, Belgium and the Veenkoloniën, The Netherlands. *Journal of Rural Studies, 26*(4), 428–436.

Veltmeyer, H. (1986). *Canadian Class Structure*. Toronto: Garamond Press.

White, B. (2012). Agriculture and the generation problem: Rural youth, employment and the future of farming. *IDS Bulletin, 43*(6), 9–19.

White, R., & Wyn, J. (1998). Youth agency and the social context. *Journal of Sociology, 34*(3), 314–327.

Wright, E. O. (2000). *Class counts: Comparative studies in class analysis*. Cambridge: Cambridge University Press.

Wyn, J., & White, R. (2000). Negotiating social change: The Paradox of youth. *Youth and Society, 32*(2), 165–183.

CHAPTER 5

Mainstreaming Social Age in the Sustainable Development Goals: Progress, Pitfalls, and Prospects

Christina Clark-Kazak

INTRODUCTION

This chapter presents the results of a comprehensive quantitative and qualitative textual analysis of the Sustainable Development Goals (SDGs) and the corresponding United Nations (UN, 2015) Resolution A/RES/70 with a view to understanding the degree to which social age has been mainstreamed into the SDGs. The SDGs are an important policy framework for contemporary aid programming. This chapter analyses the ways in which different age groups, categories, and familial relationships are constructed within the SDGs and the UN resolution adopting them, and the implications for development practice. While the SDGs are more age sensitive than the preceding Millennium Development Goals (MDGs), as discussed below, they still present age primarily in terms of categories of exception, and pay little attention to the ways in which intergenerational power relations operate in development contexts. Therefore, I conclude

C. Clark-Kazak (✉)
International Studies, Glendon College, York University,
2275, Bayview Avenue, M4N 3M6 Toronto, ON, Canada

© The Author(s) 2016
R. Huijsmans (ed.), *Generationing Development*,
DOI 10.1057/978-1-137-55623-3_5

this chapter with some recommendations for future work to more fully mainstream social age within development policy and programming.

Theoretical and Methodological Framework

This chapter takes social age as its conceptual point of departure. Social age refers to socially constructed definitions and attributes ascribed to different age groups, as well as generational power relations (Clark-Kazak 2009b; 2011). Social age provides a complementary theoretical and definitional approach to the dominant focus on chronological age underpinning international and domestic law, such as the United Nations Convention on the Rights of the Child. While chronological age is used in development policy and programming as an ostensibly "neutral" administrative tool to determine eligibility for particular projects, it is actually itself socially constructed within particular historical and cultural contexts in which the chronological passage of time is perceived of as a marker of biological development (Laz 1998; Ennew 2011; Clark-Kazak 2009b). Piaget's age-based stages of early childhood have been widely influential in education programming, while biological assessments are standard practice in medical monitoring of children in Western countries. However, this focus on chronological age and standardised physical, cognitive, and social development measurements has been critiqued from within the education, psychological, and medical communities and literature (Boyden 2001). At the other end of the ageing spectrum, gerontologists, such as Sir John Grimley Evans (2003) also question chronological age-based assumptions. In order to understand "true ageing," Grimley Evans contends that we need to understand complex interactions between extrinsic (environmental and lifestyle) and intrinsic (genetic) factors that occasion differential capacities and experiences of adaptability as time passes. The social age framework acknowledges that chronological age can be a convenient—if imperfect—proxy for biological development and thus administratively useful, but maintains that chronology is an insufficient lens through which to understand complex generational power relations.

Social age places intra- and intergenerational relationships squarely at the centre of analysis. It is therefore aligned with the generationing framework developed by Huijsmans in the introduction to this book (see also: Huijsmans et al. 2014). In particular, it resonates with the introductory chapter's focus on relationships, thereby allowing attention to the ways in which social age intersects with other power relations, with particular attention in this chapter to gender. I have chosen to maintain the conceptual framework of "social age" because it is broader than generation. While social age pays attention to the latter, it also allows for a focus on the ways in which specific age categories are constructed and made meaningful in particular development contexts. In this way, the chapter analyses both how age categories are represented and constructed, and also the generational relationships in which they are embedded. Moreover, while Huijsmans (this volume: 6–7) argues for the need to "work across age boundaries," he and other authors in this book still focus mainly on children and youth. Indeed, Mayall's (2002: 27) definition of "generationing" is child-specific: "the relational process whereby people come to be known as children, and whereby children and childhood acquire certain characteristics." Huijsmans rightly points out that "generationing" is not limited to children and young people, but still focuses mainly on the intersection between childhood studies and development studies. In contrast, social age pays attention to the whole age spectrum, from birth to old age, thereby allowing for a more expansive analysis that contextualises socially constructed age categories in relation to each other, and within intergenerational power relations. This inclusive approach, as well as attention to generational relationships, counteracts a problematic "children-in-development" approach that ghettoises and marginalises age issues, as explained below. The development of social age as a theoretical framework is partially intended as a way to facilitate mainstreaming of social age issues into development discourse, policy, and programming (Clark-Kazak 2009b).

Mainstreaming refers to the integration of "an equity perspective throughout the policy-making process, from conception to implementation to review, and all stages in between" (Donaghy 2004: 393). While most often associated with "gender mainstreaming," development researchers, practitioners, and policy-makers are increasingly considering "diversity mainstreaming" to reflect the intersection of gender with age, race, class, etc. (Hankivsky 2005; Kabeer 2005) in development programming. However, research indicates uneven success in the implementation of mainstreaming, which requires a comprehensive shift in approach and behaviour (Moser 2005). Most relevant to this analysis of the SDGs, "although intended to effect organisational change (Hartsock 1981), mainstreaming may actually de-politicise radical agendas by incorporating 'language' into technocratic planning and programming without changing the reality on the ground" (Clark-Kazak 2009a: 1312). In other words, instead of transforming the approach by problematising the norm—as mainstreaming is intended to do—the inclusion of particular buzzwords glosses over deeply rooted power relations that reinforce inequality. "The solution is not to 'integrate' them [oppressed people] into the structure of oppression, but to transform that structure so that they can become 'beings for themselves'." (Freire 1972: 48)

As a step towards transforming these structural power relations, I have advocated for comprehensive social age analysis (Clark-Kazak 2009b). The first step in social age mainstreaming is to generate and analyse age-disaggregated data for the population as a whole, as well as for the particular issue under study. This underscores my point that both chronological and social age markers are important to development programming. The SDGs do contain a progressive provision for the collection of data disaggregated by age (Target 17.18). Social age mainstreaming thus involves an understanding of both age-related demographic information and social relationships and power structures within which human beings engage in development. Therefore, it also includes an analysis of the aged division of labour; dynamic intra- and intergenerational power relations; and socially constructed roles and norms attributed to different age groups (see Clark-Kazak 2009b for a detailed description of the steps in social age mainstreaming).

In this chapter, I focus explicitly on the language that is used to describe age categories and relationships. I use the terms "age-specific" and "age-inclusive" when language about chronological or social age is used in relation to both age categories and age relationships. However, the presence of such age-specific language does not necessarily indicate age sensitivity (an attention to differential roles in, and impacts of, development initiatives due to social age), nor social age mainstreaming. Indeed, if age-specific language reinforces negative age stereotypes or age-normative (Huijsmans et al. 2014) power relations, it can be counterproductive to the equity perspective underlying social age mainstreaming.

Through a comprehensive quantitative and qualitative textual analysis, this chapter therefore assesses the degree to which social age has been mainstreamed into the discourse of the SDGs and the corresponding UN resolution A/RES/70, which adopted *Transforming Our World—the 2030 Agenda for Sustainable Development*. These SDGs goals and policy documents frame development programming and priorities (Sachs 2012) and are thus important reference points in the international development landscape. Progress on the SDGs will be reported annually and development agencies will justify their programming on the basis of these goals (Alkire and Samman 2014). Age-specific language within the SDGs therefore not only (re)produces meanings ascribed to particular age categories and relationships but also has the potential to translate into real development outcomes. As the UN resolution states, "The new Goals and targets will come into effect on 1 January 2016 and will *guide the decisions we take over the next 15 years*" (A/RES/70/1, paragraph 21, my emphasis).

The SDGs and corresponding UN resolution are therefore both discursively and policy relevant. Discourse "governs the way that a topic can be meaningfully talked about and reasoned about" (Hall 1997: 44). The ways in which age categories and relationships are represented in the text provide insights not only into social age but also into the ways in which this knowledge is constructed: "the discursive approach provides us not only with insights on 'how' the 'other' is represented but also 'by whom' and for 'what reasons'" (Lamers 2005: 44). Here, it is important to recognise the SDGs as an attempt to create a "universal" (UN resolution A/RES/70, paragraph 2) commitment to specific development goals and targets to follow up and improve on the MDGs. The UN resolution itself acknowledges that the MDGs were only partially completed (preamble, paragraph 3) and that the SDGs are an attempt "to address [the MDGs'] unfinished business" (Declaration, paragraph 2).[1]

The SDGs also build on international legal and normative frameworks for which there is broad political consensus. Paragraphs 10, 11, and 12 specifically reference the UN Charter, the Universal Declaration of Human Rights, international human rights treaties, and various summits and declarations. It is clear that some of the language in the SDGs reproduces and reaffirms commitments made in these other documents and fora. Some could thus argue that there is an inherent tension between the universality of the SDGs and the context specificity implied by social age (Harris-Short 2003). However, I argue in the conclusion of this chapter that, by ensuring age-specific language is relational rather than categorical, universal documents like the SDGs can provide an inclusive framework within which social age can be mainstreamed into locally meaningful policies and programs. In other words, the transformative potential of social age is that it includes—but analytically distinguishes among—biological development, chronology, and socially constructed power relations. Proponents of social age mainstreaming can thus build on age-specific language within existing national and international laws, norms, and standards, but progressively move towards a more holistic, relational approach.

Findings presented in this chapter are based on a three-phased social age analysis of UN resolution A/RES/70, with particular attention to the SDGs. First, content analysis was undertaken to determine the frequency and location of the following age-related terms: baby/babies, infant, newborn, birth, child/children/childhood, minor, young, youth, adolescent, teenage(r), parent, father, mother, grandparent, grandfather, grandmother, adult, elder, elderly, old, older, senior, family/lies, partner, spouse, year old, age, and generation.[2] These terms were chosen based on an initial reading of the documents, as well as my previous age-based discourse analysis (Clark-Kazak 2009a, 2014, 2016, Forthcoming). The purpose of this quantitative analysis was to determine the relative discursive presence of different age categories, relationships, and issues within the documents. Second, grounded theory—in particular, the construction of "analytic codes and categories from data" (Charmaz 2014: 7)—was used to inductively identify the main themes associated with age categories, relationships, and issues. This qualitative analysis informed understandings of socially constructed norms and attributes ascribed to age and generation. A close reading of the document also allowed for an identification of where social age was absent, most noticeably when other categories of "difference"—such as gender and/or ability—were mentioned. A third phase of analysis involved returning to the quantitative analysis to add the frequency with which age-related terms were associated with particular themes. This allowed for quantitative and qualitative measurement of the significance of age-related terms.

A Step Towards Social Age Mainstreaming

It is important to acknowledge that the SDGs and UN resolution A/RES/70 do adopt age-inclusive language in certain areas. This is within the context of a document that explicitly recognises problems of inequality (SDG 10) and the need to promote inclusion (SDG 9, 11, 16) and development "for all" (SDG 3, 4, 6, 7, 8, 16). The UN resolution presents the SDGs as "an Agenda of the people, by the people and for the people" (paragraph 52) with goals and targets that are intended to be "people-centred," "universal," and "transformative" (paragraph 2).

Two of the SDGs explicitly reference age in such a way as to make social age mainstreaming possible. SDG3 is to "Ensure healthy lives and promote well-being *for all at all ages*" (my emphasis), and SDG4 is to "Ensure inclusive and equitable quality education and promote *lifelong learning opportunities for all*" (my emphasis). By using language that includes "all ages" and "lifelong … opportunities," these SDGs allow for an understanding of age that goes beyond rigid, bounded age categories. In translating these SDGs into concrete development programming, both the letter and spirit of these goals favour age-inclusive and age-sensitive approaches. For example, education in development contexts has historically been associated with formal education for primary-school-aged children, with some attention to secondary and tertiary education (Chabbott 2003; Boyden 2013). The MDGs (2016) reinforced this focus on formal primary education with MDG2: "Achieve universal primary education" and its associated Target 2A: "Ensure that, by 2015, children everywhere, boys and girls alike, will be able to complete a full course of primary schooling." In comparison, the SDG language of "lifelong learning opportunities for all" expands the discussion of education from one specific age category (children) to learning across the lifespan.

In contrast, SDG5 on gender equality explicitly mentions girls. While this could be considered to be an acknowledgement of the intersection of social age and gender, by focusing on one-gendered age category—girl(s)—this goal and its associated targets conflate gender with females and age with children, thereby reinforcing gender and age-normativity, as will be discussed below (cf Kabeer 2005). Of the 169 targets, 22 have social and/or chronological age-specific references in relation to poverty reduction, food security, education, gender equality water and sanitation, employment, and justice.[3] These targets will be analysed in greater detail in relation to specific themes in the next sections.

The frequency and quality of age-specific references in the SDGs and UN resolution indicate that social age has been "mainstreamed" to a certain degree within the SDGs. In comparison, the MDGs, which preceded the SDGs, had two goals with an implicit and explicit focus on children (respectively, MDG 3 "Universal Primary Education" and MDG 4: "Reduce Child Mortality"). Only three targets implicitly and explicitly mentioned children and young people (Target 1B, "Achieve full and productive employment and decent work for all, including women and young people," Target 2A, referenced above, and Target 3A, "Eliminate gender disparity in primary and secondary education"). The age-specific references in the MDGs were categorical, rather than relational and focused almost exclusively on children and young people, with other age groups much less visible. Not only do the SDGs contain more age-specific and age-sensitive language but also include more generational categories, although there are still some limitations at both ends of the age spectrum, as discussed below. This indicates that there has been some progress towards social age mainstreaming within the SDGs, especially in comparison to the MDGs.

DISCURSIVE CONSTRUCTION OF AGE CATEGORIES

Despite these attempts to recognise social age within development processes, the SDGs and broader UN resolution unevenly represent particular age categories and relationships. Table 5.1 illustrates this quantitatively.[4] I have disaggregated the goals and targets from the whole UN resolution (which includes these goals and targets) because of the discursive and policy importance of the SDGs and their targets.

Infants and older people are rarely explicitly mentioned in the UN resolution as a whole and even less in the SDGs and targets. All references to infants are in relation to health issues, with a particular emphasis on preventing hunger and mortality (three of the four references). The document thus presents only a partial understanding of infants in terms of their biological development needs, with little attention to social relationships (Gottlieb 2004). This is not to deny the very real nutritional needs in the early stages of life (Dercon and Krishnan 2009), but rather to point out that textual references to children in the SDGs are exclusively focused on biological development, rather than broader social age issues. At the other end of the age spectrum, older people are similarly invisible. They are only mentioned four times in the whole document, including three times in

Table 5.1   Age categories and relationships in the SDGs

Age category or relationship	Frequency: whole UN resolution	Frequency: goals and targets
Infant	5	3
Child	45 (child = 24; girl(s) = 16; boy(s) = 5)	24 (child = 13; girl(s) = 9; boy(s) = 2)
Young person	15	7
Adult	42 (adult = 2; man/men = 8; woman/women = 32)	27 (adult = 2; man/men = 5; woman/women = 20)
Older person	4	3
Parent	4	1
Family	5	3
Generation	9	1

the targets themselves. In these references, older people are listed with other groups of people and are presented as "vulnerable" (para 23; Target 11.2) and having particular needs in relation to nutrition (Target 2.2) and accessing "green and public spaces" (Target 11.7). There is no recognition of older people's positive contributions to development, nor of their roles as community leaders and in social age-based hierarchies.

In the SDGs and UN resolution, children are most often associated with education, health, and protection needs. The educational focus is on early childhood (Target 4.2), primary and secondary (Target 4.1) education. Children are explicitly *not* mentioned in relation to technical and vocational education (Targets 4.3 and 4.4). This is consistent with their exclusion from discussions of labour, as discussed below. However, it contradicts research that shows that working children would like to combine labour with education (Liebel 2004; Woodhead 1999: 43), and advocacy by organisations of working children (Kundapur declaration, 1996) and researchers with a diversity of experiences (Open Letter to members of the UN Committee on the Rights of the Child, CRC, 2016). In terms of health, children—especially those under the age of five—are mentioned in relation to nutrition (Target 2.2) and "preventable deaths" (Target 3.2). Finally, in some cases, children as a whole or particular groups of children are constructed as vulnerable (Target, 4.5, Target 11.2) and in need of protection against child labour, violence, and torture (Target 16.2).

Children are explicitly *dis*associated with employment. Indeed, the document contains specific language signalling a commitment to "end child labour in all its forms" (paragraph 27; see also Target 8.7). This reproduces international legal commitments found in International Labour Organization (ILO) Convention 138, which sets the minimum age for admission to employment and work. However, the nuances found in the Convention on the Rights of the Child and ILO Convention 182 on the worst forms of child labour are not replicated in the SDGs. There is little distinction between forms and aspects of work that are detrimental to children and young people, and forms and aspects of work that can be beneficial to their development and, in some cases, essential to their integration into labour markets later in life (Ennew et al. 2005; Bourdillon et al. 2010). In the document, children are discursively absent in any areas relating to work, thereby rendering invisible their important economic contributions to families and households (Nieuwenhuys 1994; Heissler and Porter 2013). Similarly, children are missing from discussions of economic resources, as in target 1.4: "By 2030, ensure that all men and women, in particular the poor and the vulnerable, have equal rights to economic resources." In many of the gender equality targets, the language of "women and girls" is used, but girls are *not* mentioned along with women in some of the gender equality targets in relation to "decision-making in political, economic and public life" (Target 5.5), economic resources (Target 5.a) and technology (Target 5.b). In other words, children are constructed as economically unproductive and non-participants in public spheres of decision-making (Levison 2000).

In contrast to children, youth are explicitly referenced in relation to employment (paragraph 14; paragraph 27; Target 8.5, Target 8.6) and young people's need for technical and vocational training (Targets 4.3 and 4.4), sometimes immediately following discussion of child labour. This indicates that the documents discursively construct young people as workers, where labour is beneficial to their development and should be prioritised. Ansell (2005: chapter 6) similarly underscores this socially constructed difference between children and young people by juxtaposing concerns for child labour with "the problem" of youth unemployment.

Implicitly and explicitly in the UN resolution and SDGs, children are often constructed as "human becomings" (Qvortrup 2009) who are important in relation to *future* development, rather than development actors in the present. This is illustrated by the following citation: "We will strive to provide children and youth with a nurturing environment for the full realization of their *rights and capabilities*, helping out countries *reap the demographic dividend*, including through *safe schools* and *cohesive communities and families*" (paragraph 25, my emphasis). While there is some recognition of children's rights and capacities, these are assumed to not yet be "fully realized." Therefore, the "World" must "invest in its children" (para 8) in the present, to benefit in a future "free from violence and exploitation" (compare with Palacio, this volume; see also Jauhola 2011). The language of "investment" and "capabilities" also demonstrates the influence of social capital theory and the capabilities approach in development discourse (Fukuda-Parr 2003; Stewart and Deneulin 2002).

Girls are mentioned 16 times, while boys are referenced only five times. In many cases, the document groups "women and girls" together in relation to gender equality and "empowerment." Girls are also mentioned in relation to health, such as the "nutritional needs of adolescent girls" (Target 2.2) and sanitation (Target 6.2). Boys are only ever mentioned in relation to others—such as "both boys and girls" (para 15; Targets 4.1 and 4.2) and "men and boys" (para 20 × 2). In some cases, girls and boys are placed in opposition to each other, such as "All forms of discrimination and violence against women and girls will be eliminated, including through the engagement of men and boys" (para 20). This implies that boys (and men) are not themselves subject to gender violence and that they are included as part of the solution because of an assumption that they are primarily responsible for the problem.

While a comprehensive gender analysis is beyond the scope of this paper, two additional points merit mention here. First, females are much more discursively visible than males and are often presented in terms of specific needs. This relative "visibility," however, serves to reinforce males as the "norm" because females are cited as cases of exception. This is implied, for example, in Target 4.6: "By 2030, ensure that all youth and a substantial proportion of *adults, both men and women*, achieve literacy and numeracy" (my emphasis). The fact that "men and women" have to be explicitly mentioned after "adults" highlights gender normativity. Second, there is a heteronormative bias in the document. People who identify as neither male nor female are not included and sexual orientation is not mentioned as a marker of "difference." These cursory findings indicate that the desire for a "systematic mainstreaming of a gender perspective in the implementation of the Agenda" will not be possible because the SDGs and resolution do not themselves fully integrate a gender mainstreaming perspective.

Limited Attention to Intergenerational Relationships

Similarly, social age mainstreaming is hampered by limited attention to intergenerational relationships in the SDGs. There is only one reference to mother in the UN resolution: "We affirm that planet Earth and its ecosystems are our common home and that 'Mother Earth' is a common expression in a number of countries and regions" (paragraph 59). The only other references to parental relations are biological, as they relate to maternal health (paragraphs 16 and 26; Target 3.1). Parental roles, as described in the document, are thus explicitly gendered, with no reference to fathers (Hoang and Yeoh 2011). Moreover, motherhood is constructed in "natural" ways in relation to the environment and/or health. In the SDGs, human mothers are only visible in their biological reproductive roles—"walking wombs" as Tiessen (2014: 204) has quoted one of her interviewees in a different context. There is no recognition that parents and grandparents have social relationships with their children, nor that intergenerational relationships intersect with other power relations, such as gender (Huijsmans 2013; Bastia 2009; Nyland et al. 2009; King and Vullnetari 2009; McKay 2007).

References to family are limited (five in total). Two pertain to family planning (paragraph 26; Target 3.7), thereby discursively constructing the family in biological terms. The other three references are relational: promoting "shared responsibility within the household and the family" (Target 5.4), focusing on doubling productivity and incomes of "family farmers, pastoralists and fishers" (Target 2.3), and underscoring the importance of "cohesive communities and families" (paragraph 25). These latter three relational references are a positive development, but are not quantitatively nor qualitatively present enough to adequately recognise the role of reciprocal intergenerational relationships in both individual and collective human development (Douglass 2006; Kofman 2004).

"Generation" is referenced throughout the text, but only in its most generalised conceptualisation in terms of humanity as a whole today in relation to people collectively in the future. This is most evident in the last section—"A call for action to change our world"—of the Declaration. Three paragraphs merit extensive citation here:

> 49. Seventy years ago, an earlier generation of world leaders came together to create the United Nations. [...]
>
> 50. Today we are also taking a decision of great historic significance. We resolve to build a better future for all people, including the millions who have been denied the chance to lead decent, dignified and rewarding lives and to achieve their full human potential. We can be the first generation to succeed in ending poverty; just as we may be the last to have a chance of saving the planet. [...]
>
> 53. The future of humanity and our planet lies in our hands. It lies also in the hands of today's younger generation who will pass the torch to future generations.

These citations exemplify the ways in which generation is portrayed throughout the document—in relation to a collective responsibility for human development, as emphasised by the universalising language of "we" and "our." The use of first person plural problematically implies that there is a current global cohort of "adults" who share common values and responsibilities in relation to a current global cohort of "children and young people." The homogeneity implied by such binary oppositions problematically overlooks power hierarchies within and across generations and their intersectionality with class, gender, birth order, age sets, etc. (Clark-Kazak 2009b: 1310–1311; Bettelheim 1963; Braungart and Braungart 1986; Spencer 1990; Arnaut 2005, Stewart 1977; Baxter and Almagor 1978a, b). This idea of a "global generation" within the UN resolution glosses over power differences within and between generations in families and communities and how these are related to development.

The inattention to intergenerational and familial relationships is problematic. Despite the frequency of references to children, as mentioned above, all of these instances pertain to children as a categorical stage of human development, rather than in intergenerational relationships. As I have argued elsewhere (Clark-Kazak 2009a, b, 2014), thinking about people in terms of static age categories divorced from broader social structures contributes to a "children-in-development" approach that repeats some of the mistakes of the "women-in-development" (WID) approach of the 1970s. While WID was rightly criticised for focusing attention exclusively on women, rather than on gender norms and relationships (Rathgeber 1990; Kabeer 1994), current age programming too often emphasises specific chronological age categories, rather than thinking about social age within the context of families, households, communities, and states. Huijmans and colleagues (2014) have similarly advocated for a relational analysis in contrast to categorising individuals in static chronological age terms. I will return to this point in the conclusion. A "children-in-development" approach also problematically conflates age with children, just as gender is too often associated only with females (Clark-Kazak 2009b).

Finally, while adults are only mentioned twice, the document references women 32 times and men 8 times. As mentioned above, this reinforces a gendered and aged "norm," while a growing list of "Other" categories needs particular attention. For example, paragraph 23 of the UN resolution states, "People who are vulnerable must be empowered. Those whose needs are reflected in the Agenda include all children, youth, persons with disabilities (of whom more than 80 per cent live in poverty), people living with HIV/AIDS, older persons, indigenous peoples, refugees and internally displaced persons and migrants." This list is likely motivated by a desire to be inclusive, as emphasised in the "for all" language throughout the SDGs and UN resolution more broadly. However, it implicitly constructs those mentioned as exceptional—even problematic—categories that deviate from "normal" development. This age-normativity (and gender normativity, explored in more detail in relation to references to boys vs girls above) is quantitatively and qualitatively more present in the document than the inclusive language of *"for all at all ages"* (my emphasis) found in SDG 3.

CONCLUSIONS AND RECOMMENDATIONS FOR GREATER AGE SENSITIVITY

Age-sensitive references in SDGs 3 and 4 ("lifelong learning opportunities for all") are promising points of departure for those interested in social age mainstreaming in development. This language opens up the possibility of understanding age in a relational sense, as an identity issue that affects power relations and access to opportunities and resources. As such, the SDGs are an important step forward from the MDGs. However, the continued construction of essentialised age categories limits the "transformative" potential of the SDGs.

In future documents, it is recommended to build on age-inclusive language which is relational, rather than category specific. For example, goal 10.2 is to "empower and promote the social, economic and political inclusion of all, irrespective of age, sex, disability, race, ethnicity, origin, religion or economic or other status." This goal places the emphasis on inequities embedded in power relations and status and allows for the possibility of intersectionality of these relationships. In contrast, goal 11.2 calls for the expansion of public transport "with special attention to the needs of those in vulnerable situations, women, children, persons with disabilities and older persons." This latter categorisation approach essentialises particular groups of people as "vulnerable" and provides more rigid, compartmentalised understandings of barriers to transportation access. Such essentialised categorisation is problematic for two reasons. "Firstly, it overlooks heterogeneity; assumed vulnerable characteristics do not necessarily hold true for all members of the categories at all times in all circumstances. Secondly, it implies a fixed state of being, thereby losing the contextual and relational aspects of vulnerability and hence conceptually ruling out a change of circumstances." (Clark 2007: 285) Such language could be rewritten in future documents as "with special attention to vulnerability in relation to gender, age and ability." This proposed revision recognises that vulnerability exists and needs to be addressed by the SDGs and development programming, but avoids the pitfall of stigmatising heterogeneous groups of people as inherently "vulnerable" categories. Focusing on power relations also moves beyond a problematic conflation of gender with females and age with children.

Careful attention should be paid to language that implicitly or explicitly "others" particular groups. For example, the following quote contains an unfortunate combination of relational and categorical language which reinforces age-, gender-, and other normative language: "All people, irrespective of sex, age, race or ethnicity, and persons with disabilities, migrants, indigenous peoples, children and youth, especially those in vulnerable situations [...]" (para 25). The first part is relational and focuses on intersecting power relations; the second part (starting with "persons with disabilities ...") discursively constructs particular identity categories that are perceived to be different.

Development scholars, practitioners, and policy-makers need to recognise intergenerational relationships as both sources of support and as sites of power relations. The UN resolution and SDGs are an improvement on the MDGs by explicitly recognising problems of inequality. However, as argued above, they do not go far enough to acknowledge and address power relations within and between generations. Instead, they alternate between very expansive, collective notions of humanity as "generations" and particular attention to individuals in fixed age categories in isolation without regard for social relationships. There is a resulting lack of attention to the meso levels of families and communities and the intergenerational relationships within them.

It is at this local level where the SDGs and their targets will ultimately be implemented—or not. While this chapter has focused on age-specific language within the UN resolution and SDGs, this discursive and normative framework will be translated into action in varying social, political, economic, and cultural contexts. It is within these specific contexts where social age analysis has the potential to transform the ways in which age is perceived and taken into account within development programming. As argued above, there is no contradiction between universal frameworks and socially constructed local understandings of age, if the former construct age not only in terms of fixed chronological age categories, but also as relational and intersectional with other power relations. This chapter has demonstrated that the SDGs discursively do both. Those interested in social age mainstreaming can thus build on the progressive language of equity and inclusion to advocate for social change at national and international levels.

NOTES

1. There is a large literature analysing progress towards the MDGs; for example: Waage et al. (2010), Bourguignon et al. (2010), Vandemoortele (2009), Fukuda-Parr et al. (2013).
2. I gratefully acknowledge Emily Leahy's research assistance with the content analysis.
3. See Appendix 1.
4. The following terms were counted as belonging to each age category; only words used in an age context were included in the quantitative analysis. For example, "premature death" was not counted as "infant" because the context made it clear that reference was being made to death at a later stage in life.

> Infant: baby/ies, infant, newborn, neonatal, premature.
> Child: child/ren, childhood, girl, boy, minor (sometimes used to indicate individuals under legal voting age).
> Young person: Youth, young, adolescent, teenage(r).
> Adult: adult, man/men, woman/women
> Older person: elder(ly), old(er), senior
> Parent: grand/parent, grand/mother, grand/father, maternal

APPENDIX 1: AGE-SPECIFIC REFERENCES IN TARGETS

Target 1.2: "By 2030, reduce at least by half the proportion of *men, women and children of all ages* living in poverty [...]"

Target 2.1: "By 2030, end hunger and ensure access by all people, in particular the poor and people in vulnerable situations, *including infants*, to safe, nutritious and sufficient food all year around."

Target 2.2: "By 2030, end all forms of malnutrition, including achieving, by 2025, the internationally agreed targets on stunting and wasting in *children under 5 years of age*, and address the nutritional needs of *adolescent girls*, pregnant and lactating women and *older persons*."

Target 3.2 "By 2030, end preventable deaths of *newborns and children under 5 years of age*, with all countries aiming to reduce *neonatal mortality* to at least as low as 12 per 1000 live births and *under-5 mortality* to at least as low as 25 per 1000 live births."

Target 4.1 "By 2030, ensure that *all girls and boys* complete free, equitable and quality primary and secondary education leading to relevant and effective learning outcomes."

Target 4.2: "By 2030, ensure that *all girls and boys* have access to quality *early childhood development*, care and pre-primary education so that they are ready for primary education."

Target 4.4: "By 2030, substantially increase the number of *youth* and adults who have relevant skills, including technical and vocational skills, for employment, decent jobs and entrepreneurship."

Target 4.5: "By 2030, eliminate gender disparities in education and ensure equal access to all levels of education and vocational training for the vulnerable, including persons with disabilities, indigenous peoples and *children in vulnerable situations*."

Target 4.a: "Build and upgrade education facilities that are *child*, disability and gender sensitive and provide safe, non-violent, inclusive and effective learning environments for all."

Target 5.1: "End all forms of discrimination against all women and *girls* everywhere."

Target 5.2: "Eliminate all forms of violence against all women and *girls* in the public and private spheres, including trafficking and sexual and other types of exploitation."

Target 5.3: "Eliminate all harmful practices, such as *child, early and forced marriage* and female genital mutilation."

Target 5.c: "Adopt and strengthen sound policies and enforceable legislation for the promotion of gender equality and the empowerment of all women and *girls* at all levels."

Target 6.2: "By 2030, achieve access to adequate and equitable sanitation and hygiene for all and end open defecation, paying special attention to the needs of women and *girls* and those in vulnerable situations."

Target 8.5: "By 2030, achieve full and productive employment and decent work for all women and men, including for *young people* and persons with disabilities, and equal pay for work of equal value."

Target 8.6: "By 2020, substantially reduce the proportion of *youth* not in employment, education or training."

Target 8.7: "Take immediate and effective measures to eradicate forced labour, end modern slavery and human trafficking and secure the prohibition *and elimination of the worst forms of child labour, including recruitment and use of child soldiers, and by 2025 end child labour in all its forms*."

Target 10.2: "By 2030, empower and promote the social, economic and political inclusion of all, irrespective of *age*, sex, disability, race, ethnicity, origin, religion or economic or other status."

Target 11.2: "By 2030, provide access to safe, affordable, accessible and sustainable transport systems for all, improving road safety, notably by expanding public transport, with special attention to the needs of those in vulnerable situations, women, *children,* persons with disabilities and *older persons.*"

Target 11.7: "By 2030, provide universal access to safe, inclusive and accessible, green and public spaces, in particular for women and *children, older persons* and persons with disabilities."

Target 16.2: "End abuse, exploitation, trafficking and all forms of violence against and torture of *children.*"

Target 17.18: "By 2020, enhance capacity-building support to developing countries, including for least developed countries and small island developing States, to increase significantly the availability of high-quality, timely and reliable data disaggregated by income, gender, *age,* race, ethnicity, migratory status, disability, geographic location and other characteristics relevant in national contexts."

References

Alkire, S., & Samman, E. (2014). *Mobilising the household data required to progress toward the SDGs* (OPHI working paper 72). Oxford: Oxford University.

Ansell, N. (2005). *Children, youth and development.* London/New York: Routledge.

Arnaut, K. (2005). Re-generating the nation: Youth, revolution and politics of history in Cote d'Ivoire. In J. Abbink & I. Van Kessel (Eds.), *Vanguard or vandals: Youth, politics and conflict in Africa.* Leiden: Brill.

Bastia, T. (2009). Women's migration and the crisis of care: Grandmothers caring for grandchildren in urban Bolivia. *Gender & Development, 17*(3), 389–401.

Baxter, P. T. W., & Almagor, U. (1978a). Introduction. In P. T. W. Baxter & U. Almagor (Eds.), *Age, generation and time: Some features of East African age organisations* (pp. 1–36). London: C. Hurst & Co.

Baxter, P. T. W., & Almagor, U. (1978b). Observations about generations. In J. La Fontaine (Ed.), *Sex and age as principles of social differentiation* (pp. 159–181). London: Academic.

Bettelheim, B. (1963). The problem of generations. In E. Erikson (Ed.), *Youth: Change and challenge* (pp. 76–119). New York: Basic.

Bourdillon, M., Levison, D., Myers, W., & White, B. (2010). *The rights and wrongs of children's work.* New Brunswick/London: Rutgers University Press.

Bourguignon, F., Bénassy-Quéré, A., Dercon, S., Estache, A., Gunning, J. W., et al. (2010). The millennium development goals: An assessment. In R. Kanbur

& M. Spence (Eds.), *Equity and growth in a globalizing world* (pp. 17–40). New York: World Bank.

Boyden, J. (2001). Some reflections on scientific conceptualisations of childhood and youth. In S. Tremayne (Ed.), *Managing reproductive life: Cross-cultural themes in fertility and sexuality* (pp. 175–193). Oxford: Berghahn Books.

Boyden, J. (2013). 'We're not going to suffer like this in the mud': Educational aspirations, social mobility and independent child migration among populations living in poverty. *Compare: A Journal of Comparative and International Education, 43*(5), 580–600.

Braungart, R., & Braungart, M. (1986). Life-course and generational politics. *Annual Review of Sociology, 12*, 205–231.

Chabbott, C. (2003). *Constructing education for development: International organizations and education for all.* New York: Falmer.

Charmaz, K. (2014). *Constructing grounded theory.* New York: Sage.

Clark, C. (2007). Understanding vulnerability: From categories to experiences of congolese young people in Uganda. *Children & Society., 21*(4), 284–296.

Clark-Kazak, C. (2009a). Representing refugees in the life cycle: A social age analysis of United Nations High Commissioner for Refugee annual reports and appeals, 2000–2008. *Journal of Refugee Studies, 22*(3), 302–322.

Clark-Kazak, C. (2009b). Towards a working definition and application of social age in international development studies. *Journal of Development Studies, 45*(8), 1–18.

Clark-Kazak, C. (2011). *Recounting migration: Political narratives of Congolese young people in Uganda.* Montreal: McGill-Queen's University Press.

Clark-Kazak, C. (2014, 2016 [second edition]). 'From "children-in-development" to social age mainstreaming in Canada's development policy and programming? Practice, prospects and proposals.' In S. Brown, M. den Heyer, & D. Black (eds) *Rethinking canadian aid* (pp. 211-226). Ottawa: University of Ottawa Press.

Clark-Kazak, C. (Forthcoming). *Age, generation and migration: A social age analysis of Canada's immigration policy and practice.* Montreal/Kingston: McGill-Queen's University Press.

Dercon, S., & Krishnan, P. (2009). Poverty and the psychosocial competencies of children: Evidence from the young lives sample in four developing countries. *Children Youth and Environments, 19*(2), 138–163.

Donaghy, T. B. (2004). Applications of mainstreaming in Australia and Northern Ireland. *International Political Science Review, 25*(4), 393–410.

Douglass, M. (2006). Global householding in Pacific Asia. *International Development Planning Review, 28*(4), 421–445.

Ennew, J. (2011). Has research improved the human rights of children? Or have the information needs of the CRC improved data about children. In A. Invernizzi & J. Williams (Eds.), *The human rights of children: From visions to implementation* (pp. 133–158). London: Routledge.

Ennew, J., Myers, W. E., & Plateau, D. P. (2005). Defining child labor as if human rights really matter. In B. H. Weston (Ed.), *Child labor and human rights: Making children matter* (pp. 27–54). Boulder: Lynne Rienner Publishers.

Freire, P. (1972). *Pedagogy of the oppressed* (trans: Ramos, M. B.). Harmondsworth: Penguin.

Fukuda-Parr, S. (2003). The human development paradigm: Operationalizing Sen's ideas on capabilities. *Feminist economics, 9*(2-3), 301–317.

Fukuda-Parr, S., Greenstein, J., & Stewart, D. (2013). How should MDG success and failure be judged: Faster progress or achieving the targets? *World Development, 41*, 19–30.

Gimley Evans, J. (2003). Age discrimination: Implications of the ageing process. In S. Fredman & S. Spencer (Eds.), *Age as an equality issue* (pp. 11–20). Oxford/Portland: Hart Publishing.

Gottlieb, A. (2004). *The afterlife is where we come from.* Chicago: University of Chicago Press.

Hall, S. (1997). The work of representation. In S. Hall (Ed.), *Representation: Cultural representations and signifying practices* (pp. 13–74). London: Sage.

Hankivsky, O. (2005). Gender vs. diversity mainstreaming: A preliminary examination of the role and transformative potential of feminist theory. *Canadian Journal of Political Science, 38*(4), 977–1001.

Harris-Short, S. (2003). International human rights law: imperialist, inept and ineffective? Cultural relativism and the UN Convention on the Rights of the Child. *Human rights quarterly, 25*(1), 130–181.

Hartsock, N. (1981). 'Political change: Two perspectives on power. In N. Benevento (Ed.), *Building feminist theory: Essays from quest* (pp. 3–19). New York/London: Longman.

Heissler, K., & Porter, C. (2013). Know your place: Ethiopian children's contributions to the household economy. *European Journal of Development Research, 25*, 600–620.

Hoang, L. A., & Yeoh, B. S. A. (2011). Breadwinning wives and "left-behind" husbands: Men and masculinities in the Vietnamese transnational family. *Gender & Society, 25*(6), 717–739.

Huijsmans, R. (2013). Doing gendered age': Older mothers and migrant daughters negotiating care work in rural Lao PDR and Thailand. *Third World Quarterly, 34*(10), 1896–1910.

Huijsmans, R., George, S., Gigengack, R., & Evers, S. J. T. M. (2014). Theorising age and generation in development: A relational approach. *European Journal of Development Research, 26*(2), 163–174.

Jauhola, M. (2011). The girl child of today is the woman of tomorrow': Fantasizing the adolescent girl as the future hope in post-tsunami reconstruction efforts in Aceh, Indonesia. *Rhizomes 22*, http://www.rhizomes.net/issue22/jauhola/

Kabeer, N. (1994). *Reversed realities: Gender hierarchies in development thought.* London: Verso.

Kabeer, N. (2005). 'Gender equality and women's empowerment: A critical analysis of the third millennium development goal 1. *Gender & Development, 13*(1), 13–24.

King, R., & Vullnetari, J. (2009). The intersections of gender and generation in Albanian migration, remittances and transnational care. *Geografiska Annaler: Series B, Human Geography, 91*(1), 19–38.

Kofman, E. (2004). Family related migration: A critical review of European Studies. *Journal of Ethnic and Migration Studies, 30*(2), 243–262.

Kundapur declaration. (1996). http://www.concernedforworkingchildren.org/empowering-children/childrens-unions/the-kundapur-declaration/.Accessed 3 Mar 2016.

Lammers, M. (2005). Representing poverty, impoverishing representation? A discursive analysis of NGOs' fundraising posters. *Graduate Journal of Social Science, 2*, 37–74.

Laz, C. (1998). Act your age. *Sociological Forum, 13*(1), 85–113.

Open Letter to members of the UN Committee on the Convention of [sic] the Rights of the Child. January 20, 2016. Accessible here: https://www.opendemocracy.net/open-letter-better-approach-to-child-work

Levison, D. (2000). Children as economic agents. *Feminist Economics, 6*(1), 125–134.

Liebel, M. (2004). *A will of their own: Cross-cultural perspectives on working children.* London/New York: Zed Books.

Mayall, B. (2002). *Towards a sociology for childhood: Thinking from children's lives.* Maidenhead: Open University Press.

McKay, D. (2007). Sending dollars shows feeling' – Emotions and economies in Filipino migration. *Mobilities, 2*(2), 175–194.

Moser, C. (2005). Has gender mainstreaming failed? *International Feminist Journal of Politics, 7*(4), 576–590.

Nieuwenhuys, O. (1994). *Children's lifeworlds: Gender, welfare and labour in the developing world.* London: Routledge.

Nyland, B., Zeng, X., Nyland, C., & Tran, L. (2009). Grandparents as educators and carers in China. *Journal of Early Childhood Research, 7*(1), 46–57.

Qvortrup, J. (2009). 'Are children human beings or human becomings? A critical assessment of outcome thinking. *Rivista Internazionale di Scienze Sociali, 117*, 631–653.

Rathgeber, E. M. (1990). WID, WAD, GAD: Trends in research and practice. *The Journal of Developing Areas, 24*(4), 489–502.

Sachs, J. D. (2012). From millennium development goals to sustainable development goals. *The Lancet, 379*(9832), 2206–2211.

Spencer, P. (1990). The riddled course: Theories of age and its transformations. In P. Spencer (Ed.), *Anthropology and the Riddle of the Sphinx: Paradoxes of change in the life course* (pp. 1–26). London: Routledge.

Stewart, F. H. (1977). *Fundamentals of age-group systems.* London: Academic.

Stewart, F., & Deneulin, S. (2002). Amartya Sen's contribution to development thinking. *Studies in Comparative International Development, 37*(2), 61–70.

Tiessen, R. (2014). Gender equality and the 'two CIDAs': Successes and setbacks, 1976–2013. In S. Brown, M. den Heyer, & D. Black (Eds.), *Rethinking Canadian aid* (pp. 195–210). Ottawa: University of Ottawa Press.

Millennium Development Goals. http://www.un.org/millenniumgoals/. Accessed 3 Mar 2016.

United Nations Resolution A/RES/70/1, 21. (2015, October). http://www.un.org/ga/search/view_doc.asp?symbol=A/RES/70/1&Lang=E. Accessed 3 Mar 2016.

Vandemoortele, J. (2009). The MDG conundrum: Meeting the targets without missing the point. *Development policy review, 27*(4), 355–371.

Waage, J., Banerji, R., Campbell, O., Chirwa, D., Collender, G., et al. (2010). The millennium development goals: A cross-sectoral analysis and principles for goal setting after 2015. *The Lancet, 376*, 991–1023.

Woodhead, M. (1999). Combatting child labour: Listen to what the children say. *Childhood, 6*(1), 27–49.

PART II

Everyday Relationalities: School, Work and Belonging

Generationing School Bullying: Age-Based Power Relations, the Hidden Curriculum, and Bullying in Northern Vietnamese Schools

Paul Horton

INTRODUCTION

School bullying is nothing new, and has been an issue of interest for some time. However, it was not until the 1970s that sustained focus was placed on the issue, with a number of studies conducted in the UK (Laslett 1977; Lowenstein 1977, 1978) and, perhaps more significantly, in Scandinavia (Heinemann 1972; Olweus 1978). While research into school bullying is now being conducted in many corners of the globe (Cluver and Orkin 2009; Fleming and Jacobsen 2009; Jimerson and Huai 2010; Owusu et al. 2011; Pottinger and Stair 2009; Sittichai and Smith 2015), the majority of research continues to focus on wealthier, more developed nations and there has been relatively little focus on bullying in schools in developing countries (Ohsako 1997; Owusu et al. 2011). This is reflective of debates in education and development that have been more concerned with the

P. Horton (✉)
Department of Behavioural Sciences and Learning, Linköping University, SE-58183 Linköping, Sweden

R. Huijsmans (ed.), *Generationing Development*,
DOI 10.1057/978-1-137-55623-3_6

quantity and quality of education than the social experiences of it (Gerber and Huijsmans 2016; Ohsako 1997).

Much of the research that has been conducted into school bullying stems from an individual psychology framework that understands school bullying as a subset of aggression. This research has tended to focus on the aggressive behaviour of children and the negative effects of bullying for the mental health of those subjected to it. This is reflected in the most commonly cited definition of school bullying as formulated by the Swedish psychologist Dan Olweus (2003, p. 9): 'A student is being bullied or victimised when he or she is exposed, repeatedly, and over time to negative actions on the part of one or more other students.' Olweus' definition, and others following it, frames school bullying as a relational practice between *students* (i.e. children who attend school).

There has been less focus on the generational dimension of bullying. This includes the bullying of children by adults, the bullying of adults by children, and the extent to which adults create the conditions within which bullying between children is perpetrated and perpetuated. Nonetheless, research highlights that teachers bully students, that students bully teachers, and that teacher behaviour in class influences the extent to which bullying is likely to occur (Horton 2012; James et al. 2008; Pervin and Turner 1998; Rivers et al. 2007; Yoneyama 1999). Even social ecological approaches to school bullying that have a stated focus on the children's interactions with the broader social context still tend to focus on the bullying behaviour of children and how adults can positively influence that behaviour (Espelage and Swearer 2010; Jimerson and Huai 2010). Indeed, despite the fact that adults are also often involved in school bullying, either directly or indirectly, school bullying is generally seen to be a childhood problem and not a generational one.

Anti-bullying initiatives have tended to focus on changing the behaviour of the children involved; often with adults targeted as the instigators of change. Despite the name, even 'whole school' approaches to school bullying focus on the behaviour of the children involved and downplay the role of adults and the school as an institution in school bullying (Duncan and Rivers 2013; Horton 2012). Rather than questioning the role of adults or the adult-devised and governed context of schooling, emphasis is on getting the whole school community on the same page regarding how to deal with the issue, through the development of school anti-bullying policies, increased surveillance, classroom rules, and the introduction of assertiveness or empathy training into the curriculum (Cross et al. 2011; Heinrichs 2003; Jimerson and Huai 2010; Suckling and Temple 2002; Wong et al. 2011).

Despite calls for more focus on the structural aspects of school bullying (Eriksson et al. 2002; Farrington 1993; Galloway and Roland 2004; Harber 2002; Horton 2011, 2016; Yoneyama and Naito 2003), discussions about the role of the school as institution in school bullying have 'not gone much beyond analysis into such things as school size and location' (Yoneyama and Naito 2003: 318). This is problematic because, as Clive Harber (2002: 15) has noted in relation to school violence more generally, schooling may play a role in 'both creating the problem and making it worse'. In this chapter, I challenge the continued overwhelming focus on children in school bullying research and interventions by approaching the issue of school bullying through the analytical lens of 'generationing' (Alanen 2001, 2003; Eckert 2004; Mayall and Zeiher 2003; Punch 2005). In doing so, I argue that it is not sufficient to approach bullying by simply focusing on the agency of individuals. Rather, it is necessary to understand how school bullying is related to the ways in which power is manifested in the deeply generational organisation of schools and the ways in which both children and adults exercise their agency in relation to this (Ansell 2014; Punch 2005).

There have been numerous approaches to and understandings of generation, with generation discussed in relation to both socio-cultural and socio-structural arenas (Alanen 2001, 2003; Christensen and Prout 2003; Mayall and Zeiher 2003). Here I focus predominantly on the socio-structural arena of schooling, wherein socio-cultural relations of generation have been co-opted by the state and generational groupings have become institutionalised as structural aspects of the education system. As Huijsmans et al. (2014) have pointed out, chronological age is made important in particular contexts, most notably in schools, where the agency of school children is circumscribed by structural restrictions and regulations based on their chronological age. In addressing school bullying, it is thus important to consider the ways in which concepts of age and other generational relations influence school bullying. In this chapter, I argue that anti-bullying initiatives focusing on changing the behaviour of individual children need to be rethought in light of the ways in which school bullying is generationed.

METHODS AND STUDY SITE

The chapter draws on long-term ethnographic fieldwork conducted in 2007–2008 in two secondary schools (here referred to as Pho Chieu School and Du Hang School) in Vietnam's third largest city, Haiphong (see Fig. 6.1). Haiphong is an industrial port city best known for shipping and cement production, which has also recently been attracting a vast amount of foreign direct investment. Pho Chieu School and Du Hang School are located in the same district of Haiphong, and are thus under the jurisdiction of the same Bureau of Education and Training (BOET), yet located in two very different socio-economic areas. Du Hang School is located in a relatively wealthier area near a wide shopping boulevard lined with shops, cafes, and restaurants. Pho Chieu School, in contrast, is located in a poorer area on a narrow market street. The two schools hence reflect increasing disparities in wealth and investment in the city (Horton 2012). At the time of study, Du Hang School had over 2000 students and average class sizes of 45 while Pho Chieu School had a relatively smaller student population with approximately 700 students and average class sizes of 35. In order to accommodate the sheer numbers of students, the school days at both schools were split in half, with eighth-grade and ninth-grade students attending in the mornings and sixth-grade and seventh-grade students attending in the afternoons.

The fieldwork included questionnaires, which also included open-ended questions, answered by 906 students from grades six to nine (i.e. ages 11–15); participant observations conducted in two ninth-grade classrooms (here referred to as Class 9A and Class 9B), on the school playgrounds and inside and outside the school gates; eight individual semi-structured interviews with teachers of the two ninth-grade classes (four teachers at each school); ten semi-structured group interviews with ninth-grade students from those classes (five groups of girls, three groups of boys, and two mixed sex groups); and 30 individual semi-structured interviews with ninth-grade students from those classes (15 girls and 15 boys).

Informed consent was obtained from the schools, teachers and students at the centre of the study and all the informants were told prior to being interviewed that their answers would be treated confidentially and would be anonymised. All informants were assigned pseudonyms and were told that the interview was being recorded solely for research purposes and would not be given to third parties. Informants were also told that they

Fig. 6.1 Administrative map of Vietnam (Source: https://www.cia.gov/library/publications/resources/cia-maps-publications/map-downloads/vietnam-admin.jpg/image.jpg (accessed 15 July, 2015))

could stop the interview at any time. While I offered to stop a number of interviews with students when I felt they were getting upset, the students themselves seemed happy to share their experiences and air their views (Horton 2012).

GENERATIONAL INSTITUTIONALISATION IN VIETNAMESE SCHOOLS

As Nicola Ansell (2014: 285) has noted, formal schooling is a 'key agent of social reproduction' and is often put forward as a route for national development. This is particularly evident in the case of Vietnam. Prior to the proclamation of the Democratic Republic of Vietnam (DRV), formal schooling was largely restricted to those privileged few, mostly male, students who were deemed worthy of an education (London 2011; Marr 1981; Pham 2000). However, large numbers of both males and females were already being prepared for their future roles in a socialist Vietnam by being organised into various groupings according to their chronological age (Salomon and Doan Ket 2009; Valentin 2008). The Communist Party's branches for children and youth, the Young Pioneers (ages 9–15) and the Youth Union (ages 15–28), were used by the Communist Party to forward socialist ideals, because as President Ho Chi Minh would later argue, 'In building socialism, we first need socialist persons' (cited in Pham 1991: 42). As in other socialist contexts, education was seen to be crucial for the development of socialist persons and formal schooling was perceived to be a key arena for political socialisation (London 2011; Salomon and Doan Ket 2009; Stearns 2011; Valentin 2008).

Following the proclamation of the DRV on 2 September 1945, education reforms were thus introduced that saw greater and greater numbers of children, including girls, enter formal schooling according to their chronological age. The first education reform of 1950 made schooling in those areas not under French colonial control increasingly available to children aged six to 15 (i.e. grades one to nine). This reform was implemented in the midst of the on-going war between the DRV and the French and, according to former education minister Pham Minh Hac, was explicitly intended 'to educate the young generations to be citizens loyal to the Fatherland, qualified physically and morally to serve the country' (Pham 1991: 29). A second education reform was introduced in 1956, following the end of French colonialism in 1954, which saw formal schooling in northern Vietnam available to children up to the age of 16 (i.e. grade ten). Once again the intention of the reform was to further govern the development of the young generations into 'good citizens, loyal to the Fatherland' (Pham 1991: 31).

A third reform introduced in 1981 then made formal schooling available for children aged 17–18, with the addition of grades 11 and 12 to schools across the country (Le 2000; London 2011; Pham 1991; Tran 2002). This reform came in the wake of national reunification and was seen as a means of ensuring the political socialisation of young people in the south of the country (Tran 2002). The rapid expansion of mass-education has meant that Vietnamese childhoods are increasingly institutionalised. Whilst much has been said about the nationalist dimension of the institutionalisation of Vietnamese childhoods, much less has been said about its generational structure. Reflecting Communist- and Confucian-inspired generational relations that characterise Vietnamese society, the socio-cultural arena of Vietnamese schools is distinctly generational. Piety and respect for seniority, elders, adult figures, and positions of authority is emphasised.

As Rivers et al. (2007: 44) have noted in the UK context, in schools 'a distinct hierarchy is present with principals, vice-principals, and other professional adults forming the top layers with the youngest children at the very bottom of the chain'. This same hierarchy is present in Vietnamese schools, and both schools studied follow this order, with the school principals at the top of the institutional pyramids. Immediately below the principals are the vice-principals, whose job it is to assist the school principals with administrative and organisational matters but also to work as subject teachers. Beneath the vice-principals are the homeroom teachers who are in charge of the particular classes and have direct contact with their respective principal and vice-principal, and their students' parents. The homeroom teachers are responsible for attendance, grading, and problems relating to the students in their designated classes. Students also have subject teachers who report to the homeroom teachers.

The institutional hierarchy at the schools is also based on a principle of age grading, with ninth graders, eighth graders, seventh graders, and sixth graders distinguished from one another by timetabling, curricular content, scholastic requirements, and separation through grade and class location. In addition, hierarchical relations may also be observed between students of the same age-grade. For example, teachers utilise certain students to help them control and discipline other students in the class. Each class has a class monitor and a vice monitor, whose selection is based on their scholastic ability, their perceived behaviour, and their membership of the Youth Union. To be a member of the Youth Union likewise requires good grades and exemplary behaviour (Horton 2012; Madsen 2008).

While schooling in Vietnam is not compulsory after the primary level, there is immense pressure on students, and their parents, not only to attend school but also to achieve scholastically while there (Bayly 2014; Bélanger and Liu 2004; London 2011; Madsen 2008). Educational enrolment, literacy, and scholastic success are connected with national development, and the government has long emphasised the importance of achievement (Bayly 2014). Annual educational Olympiads were introduced into the educational landscape during the 1962–1963 school year, and those students who were to compete in the Olympiads were those deemed to be particularly 'gifted' (Duggan 2001; Pham 1991; Tran 2002). The designation of 'gifted' students was institutionalised in 1981 as part of the third education reform, which introduced specific classes for 'gifted' and 'disabled' students for the first time (Tran 2002). The demonstration of achievement, however, is reduced to the level of information retention, with students expected to memorise the information that is provided for them by teachers. Despite numerous critiques of rote learning through the years, the 2002 curricular reform that called for a shift from rote learning to 'child-centred learning', and the National Education for All Action Plan 2003–2015, which set out the challenge of moving from quantity to quality of education, rote learning continues to be the go-to method for teaching in Vietnamese schools (Hamano 2008; Horton 2012; Le 2000; Pham 2000; Salomon and Doan Ket 2007, 2009; Socialist Republic of Vietnam 2003; Tran 2002).

Reflecting the Confucian influence on Vietnamese society, teachers in Vietnamese schools are given a decisive role in the moral education of students. They are perceived as moral cultivators who act as role models and 'help to form and nurture the personality, moral qualities and abilities of the citizen' (National Assembly of the Socialist Republic of Vietnam 2005; Socialist Republic of Vietnam 1992; see also Morarji's chapter in this book for a discussion of the moral role of teachers). Teachers are positioned as in loco parentis, and are expected to enforce adherence to institutional regulations and expectations through a number of disciplinary punishments. The punishments that students in the two ninth-grade classes in which I conducted participant observations risked being subjected to included being made to clean the blackboard, sent out of class, made to stand at the back of the room, made to answer questions, having their parents called to school, being fined money, having their Youth Union badge confiscated, and being suspended or expelled.

While the 2005 Education Law explicitly states that teachers may not 'disrespect the honour, dignity of learners, or hurt or abuse them physically' (National Assembly of the Socialist Republic of Vietnam 2005: 32), various forms of corporal punishment were also used, especially by male teachers and especially towards male students (Horton 2012). Vietnamese understandings of masculinity and Taoist-inspired ideas about the distinctions between 'hot' (*nóng*) male- and 'cool' (*lạnh*) female-gendered characters (Horton 2012, 2015; Rydstrøm 2003, 2006) shed light on this gendered manifestation of corporal punishment in Vietnamese schools. This highly gendered and generationed top-down model of behaviour management is important for understanding the bullying that occurs.

In relation to school bullying, teachers in Vietnamese schools are thus contradictory figures. They occupy a position of authority vis-à-vis students, they are granted the status of moral cultivators and entrusted with the power to enforce school rules and regulations, yet some teachers exercise these roles through the practice of bullying. Similar to Rivers et al. (2007: 47) observations in the UK context, Vietnamese teachers model a form of interaction that is based on an 'ethic of controlling subordinates'. As the next section illustrates, students use a similar form of interaction in their relations with peers who are younger, junior, smaller, weaker, or otherwise in a less powerful position.

School Bullying and Relations of Differentiation

In the questionnaires, students were asked to explain the Vietnamese term for school bullying (*bắt nạt*). A number of students described *bắt nạt* as something that is done by adults to children: '*the adult bullies the kids*'. A sixth-grade boy gave an example of '*an adult who is bigger, stronger than me, threatening or hitting me*'; while a sixth-grade girl elaborated that '*the adult relies on their strength and size to bully me*'. Participant observations also highlighted that some teachers bullied students through the use of sarcasm, derision, and physical chastisement (Horton 2012). Occasionally, students would also bully teachers. A teacher at Pho Chieu School told me that '*Many teachers are bullied in Vietnamese classes. Mr Nguyen is bullied by his students. When he is at the blackboard, students throw chalk at him*'.

The security guard at the school also told me that he had intervened to help this particular teacher on at least one occasion (Horton 2012).

Although bullying is done by individuals, a student's ability to exercise power, and hence to bully others, is dependent on how they are positioned within the system of differentiations that is prevalent in that particular context (Foucault 1998). As observed above, one particularly prevalent differentiating technique that is made important in schools is chronological age. A number of students explained that bullying is facilitated by differences in chronological age. They explained that bullying is when the '*older person threatens the younger*', when '*the older bully the younger*', when '*someone relies on their age to bully the younger*', when a '*person who is older hits us*', when older people '*rely on age to bully younger*', and '*rely on age to treat badly and use words to offend others*'. Chronological age was, however, not the only differentiating technique at work. Different positions of power within the generational fabric of Vietnamese schools were also expressed in terms of relative seniority. This is evident from students who described bullying as something that is done '*by senior students*', that '*the seniors bully the juniors*', that '*senior students usually bully by cursing and hitting*', that some students '*rely upon their seniority to bully juniors*', that '*the senior bullies the younger*', and that '*senior students bully junior students*'.

A large number of students did not describe bullying in relation to concepts of age, but rather in relation to bodily development, such as size and strength (see also Duncan 1999). Within the various classes of each grade level, there was notable physical variety amongst the students, and students gave examples of bigger people who '*rely on their size to bully the small*', and who '*rely on their size to bully the weaker ones*'. Some students placed themselves into the descriptions as those doing the bullying, describing how '*[we] rely on our size to bully a person smaller than us*', and how '*[we] rely on our size to bully others and order them to do work for us*'. Other students placed themselves into the description as those being bullied by '*a stronger, bigger person who bullies us*'. Physical strength is closely related to bodily size, and this was also highlighted by several students in their descriptions of *bắt nạt* in examples of students who '*rely on their strength to bully the weak ones*'. Again, some students placed themselves into the 'bully' position, describing bullying as when '*[we] bully a person who is weaker than us*', or when '*[we] use our strength to threaten someone to force them to do our bidding*'. Other students gave examples of stronger people bullying them, describing, '*someone stronger is cursing and hitting me*', '*a stronger person who threatens or hits me*', and being '*hit by someone who is bigger and stronger than us*'.

This discussion above shows that various concepts of age that are made important in the institutional organisation of Vietnamese schools function as relations of social differentiation which facilitate bullying. However, the discussion also shows that for many others it is bodily markers such as size and physical strength that serve to differentiate between students. This is a useful reminder that concepts of age, for example, seldom work in isolation, but rather intersect with other markers of differentiation. Lastly, the example of students bullying teachers serves to demonstrate that markers of social differentiation should not be understood as simple determinants of social practice.

SCHOOL BULLYING AND THE HIDDEN CURRICULUM

The descriptions of *bắt nạt* provided by students and presented in the previous section referred to actions such as teasing, threatening, and hitting. Yet they also alluded to some of the functions of school bullying by describing bullying as '*threatening action that forces others to follow*', as '*forcing someone to do something, if not they will be hit*', as being '*teased by others and made to do their will*', and as '*forcing someone to do something that we don't like*'. These descriptions of bullying have also been supported by research conducted in Vietnam's capital city Hanoi and serve to question the overwhelming focus on individual aggression that has dominated conceptualisations of school bullying (Horton et al. 2015).

A number of teachers and students provided examples of the kinds of things that some students were bullied into doing. This included doing school work for other students, letting other students copy their examination and test answers, letting other students use their books and stationery, and shopping at the school canteen. These explanations suggest that school bullying may not only involve relations between adults and children, older and younger, senior and junior, bigger and smaller, or stronger and weaker students but may also stem from the social organisation of schooling.

As Ansell (2014: 285) points out, while formal schooling may be aimed at generating the 'aspirational subjects' necessary for developing the nation, schooling 'does not always produce the aspirational subjects intended'. Indeed, as Phillip Jackson (1968: 33) has noted, students do not simply learn the official stated curriculum while in school, they also learn lessons from the 'hidden curriculum'. The hidden curriculum can be usefully understood as 'the student learning that takes place within the perimeter of a school that is not recorded or reflected within the official curriculum' (Walton 2005: 18). Thinking about the hidden curriculum in terms of generationing allows for a consideration of the ways in which students learn to navigate the generational organisation of schooling by themselves utilising the generational order to their advantage, as well as the other relations of differentiation that become relevant within the context of the school.

The focus on scholastic achievement in Vietnamese schools ensures that great emphasis is placed on having access to the necessary school supplies and the correct answers to teachers' questions, course work, and examinations and tests. However, while teachers expect students to have the necessary supplies and to learn the correct answers, some students have learnt that they can just as easily bully other students into providing these. One teacher at Du Hang School illustrated this with an example of a girl who was '*forced to lend others her books*'. Similarly, a seventh-grade girl described bullying as when other students '*take stationery*', while a seventh-grade boy described it as when students '*punch, kick, attack and steal stationery*'. Highlighting the importance of distinguishing markers such as size, a ninth-grade girl described bullying as when they '*pull hair, take others' stationery, rely on size to bully those smaller than us*'.

Some teachers and students likewise described bullying as some students getting other students to do their class work for them. For example, a mathematics teacher at Du Hang School told me that some students '*are forced to do calculations*' for other students. A seventh-grade boy likewise described bullying as when students '*rely on size to bully others and order them to do work for us*', while a seventh-grade girl described it as when students '*force someone to do exercises and hit them*'. Another seventh-grade girl described bullying as when students '*force others to do the work that we deliver*'. Some students more specifically referred to examinations and tests. An eighth-grade boy, for example, described bullying as when students '*force someone to let them copy their test*', while a ninth-grade girl described bullying as when someone '*takes our exam or test answers*'.

The school days were highly regulated and if students wanted to go to the school canteen, for example, they had to either wait until the allotted 15-minute break or seek the teacher's permission to leave class on false pretences. There was only one canteen at each school and large numbers of students, meaning that trips to the canteen were generally characterised by queuing. Those who opted to go to the canteen during the break did not have much time left for other activities. Some students got around these institutional constraints by bullying other students into shopping at the canteen for them. At least one student in each class, Class 9A and Class 9B, regularly went to the canteen for other students during their daily 15-minute breaks, and in the questionnaires, a number of students described bullying as being forced to buy things at the canteen. An eighth-grade boy, for example, described bullying as when someone forces another '*to do something, buy this thing, [and] give that thing*', while a seventh-grade boy described it as when someone '*tells us to buy water*'. Likewise, an eighth-grade girl described it as when students '*threaten to hit, [and] force to buy food in the canteen*', while a ninth-grade girl described it as when she and her friends '*order juniors to buy something for us even though they don't want to*'. This girl alludes to the hierarchical relation between seniors and juniors and highlights that this form of bullying takes place not only between classmates but also between students in different grade levels.

These descriptions point to disciplinary techniques utilised in schools, such as teaching methods and timetabling, and suggest that these are implicated in at least some of the school bullying that occurs. The descriptions thus serve to remind us that schools are disciplinary institutions that are imbued with power relations, wherein teachers are afforded positions of power based on a generational order (Foucault 1980, 1991). While officially students are expected to be in possession of the necessary books and stationery, to study diligently and acquiesce to the authority of teachers, from the social experience of schooling students also learn that it is possible to get around such expectations by bullying other students into sharing books and stationery, providing the answers to teachers' questions, tests and examinations, and going to the school canteen, for example. This suggests that bullying cannot be reduced to individual aggression but is at least to some extent also something that is learnt through the social experience of schooling. Recognising that learning to employ one's position of relative power is part of the hidden curriculum of schooling suggests that the social experience of schooling is highly contradictory. While schools are disciplinary environments geared towards realising academic achievement, through the hidden curriculum students come to learn that this may well be achieved through means other than academic labour.

SCHOOL BULLYING AND SILENCING

It seems that those who are most likely to be bullied are those who, for whatever reason, are not in a position to resist and who feel that there is nothing they can do to stop the bullying. As a seventh-grade boy wrote, '*I can't do anything when being teased by others*'. Indeed, part of the intention of the bullying that emerged from student responses included to '*make others scared*', '*to make them scared*', to '*make someone scared, lose self-confidence, and become timid*', and to '*make the person who is bullied feel scared and more timid*'.

Bullying may thus be aimed at making some students timid, or 'meek' (*hiền lành*), in order to ensure that they do things for them that they would not otherwise be willing to do (Horton 2012; Horton et al. 2015). Many students in grades six and seven emphasised that bullying made them feel '*very scared*'. Students also wrote that the differences in size and strength contributed to this. As a sixth-grade boy wrote, for example, '*I am very scared because they are bigger and taller than me*'. A number of students also wrote that they were scared that the bullying could lead to fighting. A sixth-grade girl wrote that '*I feel very scared because it will lead to fighting*'. Another sixth-grade girl wrote that '*I am very scared when bullied by others because I'm afraid of being hit by them*'. Here, these girls allude to a distinction between being bullied and being hit or involved in a fight and highlight that some students may accede to the demands of their peers in order to avoid being hit (Horton et al. 2015). An eighth-grade girl described the purpose of bullying as being '*to make the bullied person lose confidence, lose their rights, and make them scared so they don't talk*'. This explanation shows that instilling fear not only serves to make others do something but also to make them *not* do something, namely to speak out about being bullied.

A number of school bullying researchers have highlighted that students are often reluctant to tell anyone about the bullying they are subjected to, and that this reluctance is more pronounced among older students and boys (Craig et al. 2000; Erling and Hwang 2004; Frisén et al. 2008; Hunter and Boyle 2004; Smith 2011; Smith and Shu 2000). This reluctance has also been highlighted in anti-bullying campaigns in various countries, and common advice provided to students has been to speak out about the bullying, especially to responsible adults such as school principals and teachers (Cybermentors 2011; Friends 2008; National Centre against Bullying 2011). Such policy recommendations are supported by research findings suggesting that teachers are more likely to intervene if students report bullying (Atlas and Pepler 2001; Novick and Isaacs 2010). However, research also suggests that many students believe that telling adults makes the situation worse and is thus counter-productive (Mishna 2004; Rigby and Slee 1999; Yoneyama 1999), and that the likeliness of students telling a teacher is dependent on the students' perceptions of those teachers' willingness or ability to do anything about the bullying (Atlas and Pepler 2001; Craig et al. 2000; James et al. 2008).

In the questionnaires, I asked students to indicate who they would tell if they were being bullied. Across the board, the school principal was the person that students indicated they were least likely to tell. While roughly one per cent of girls across the four grade levels stated that they would tell the school principal, for boys there was a quite marked decline from almost six per cent of sixth-grade boys to no ninth-grade boys indicating that they would report bullying to the school principal. These low percentages are perhaps not surprising when one considers the institutional hierarchy characterising Vietnamese schools and the lack of interaction students have with their school principal.

Students appeared to be more willing to tell their homeroom teacher, that is, the teacher who is officially tasked with dealing with such issues. A total of 23.4 per cent of sixth-grade girls and 15.1 per cent of sixth-grade boys indicated that they would tell their homeroom teacher. However, after the sixth grade, the percentage of students who indicated that they would tell their homeroom teacher decreased significantly and only 2.5 per cent of ninth-grade girls and 2.2 per cent of ninth-grade boys indicated that they would tell their homeroom teacher. A similar pattern can be observed in relation to subject teachers, with 21 per cent of sixth-grade girls indicating they would tell a teacher, but only 2.5 per cent of ninth-grade girls indicating that they would do so. While 16 per cent of sixth-grade boys indicated that they would tell a teacher, only 6.7 per cent of ninth-grade boys indicated that they would do so. These findings support other research findings that students are often reluctant to report school bullying, that this reluctance becomes more pronounced the longer students are at school, and that boys are generally less willing than girls to tell a teacher about bullying. However, the willingness of girls to tell a teacher decreased markedly to reach roughly the same level as boys in grade nine, and even lower in the case of telling a subject teacher.

While some researchers have found that the likelihood of students reporting bullying to a teacher is dependent on the students' perception of the teacher in question, in Du Hang School and Pho Chieu School, it seemed unlikely that students would tell any teacher, especially in grade nine. This pattern suggests that there is more to the hidden curriculum than learning to meet the various demands of schooling by employing one's position of relative power; the hidden curriculum also seems to include learning to keep silent about being bullied or about observing school bullying.

This assertion was confirmed in a group interview with ninth-grade girls. They told me that students who tell the teacher deserve to be bullied, and some students appeared to be bullied because they told the teachers when other students broke adult-imposed rules. Indeed, there appeared to be an unwritten rule in the two classes in which I conducted participant observations that telling the teacher was unacceptable and could result in bullying (Horton 2012). As Yoneyama (1999: 86) has noted in the Japanese context, if students 'want to survive the education system, they must keep quiet. To say nothing is a survival skill'.

While those doing the bullying may seek to silence those who would otherwise speak out, those being bullied may, in turn, opt to remain silent in the knowledge that speaking out will make the situation worse for them, as they will then be perceived as the kind of students who tell. A 'wall of collective silence' is thus constructed by both those doing the bullying and those being bullied (Yoneyama 1999: 181). This wall of silence provides a 'shelter' behind which the power relations involved in bullying can be upheld and reinforced (Foucault 1998: 101).

CONCLUSIONS

Much of the research on school bullying and anti-bullying initiatives have focused on school bullying as a childhood problem involving various types of children and their intentionally aggressive behaviour. This understanding of school bullying has largely been arrived at on the basis of research conducted in wealthy countries, where individual psychological approaches continue to dominate research on school bullying.

Drawing on ethnographic research conducted in two northern Vietnamese schools, I have challenged this understanding and suggested that rather than reducing our understanding of school bullying to one of childhood, we need to approach it as a generational problem. This conclusion I have arrived at through the analytical lens of 'generationing', which Mayall (2002: 27) describes as the 'the relational process whereby people come to be known as children, and whereby children and childhood acquire certain characteristics, linked to local contexts'. Schooling is such a relational process, which is structured around age-based hierarchies whilst also constituting a space in which other markers of difference between students are mobilised in the relations of power that characterise school bullying. These institutional age-based hierarchies not only incorporate various kinds of adults—including principals, vice-principals, homeroom teachers, and subject teachers—but also the students themselves, who are categorised into particular schools, grades, and classes.

The generational order thus created is reflected in the descriptions of bullying provided by students, with students pointing to distinctions between adults and children, older and younger children, and seniors and juniors. That students also point to distinctions between bigger and smaller and stronger and weaker students, highlights that generational relations do not work in isolation but rather interact with other markers of difference; most notably size and physical strength. The descriptions provided by teachers and students also highlight that at least some of the bullying that occurs in schools is directly connected to disciplinary techniques of schooling, such as age-based streaming, timetabling, curricular content, teaching methods, compulsory competition, praise and punishment, grading, and testing.

Rather than understanding bullying solely as an exponent of individual aggression I have suggested that bullying, in part, is also something that students acquire from the social experience of schooling and is thus a relational issue rather than an individual problem. Here the concept of the hidden curriculum is helpful. It underscores that students do not simply draw lessons from the official school curriculum but also learn from the social experience of schooling. These lessons include the following: that competition is a central aspect of schooling that has implications not only for their future prospects but also for their relations with teachers and other students; that it is possible to adjust to adult-imposed demands by getting other students to do things, particularly those in a position to exercise less power; that the use or threat of force is an acceptable means for getting those students to do things; that in order to get other students to do things it is necessary to make them too scared to refuse; that it is not acceptable to tell a teacher or other adult member of staff; and that students who do tell deserve to be bullied.

The generational perspective on school bullying presented in this chapter leads to two conclusions. First, if, as the findings presented above illustrate, bullying is generational and is connected to the actions of adults and the institutional constraints imposed and governed by adults, then it is questionable to what extent focusing on the individual behaviour of children is going to help in reducing the extent or effects of bullying in schools. Rather, it seems pertinent to instead question the ways in which the school as a generational institution provides the conditions for bullying to occur. Second, relating school bullying to the hidden curriculum of schooling and appreciating formal schooling as a key agent of social reproduction raises critical questions about the kind of sociality being cultivated in Vietnamese schools. Not only do students learn that they can employ their position of relative power as a means through which to meet the demands placed upon them by the institution of the school, they also learn to keep silent about this despite understanding that such practices are unjust. This latter point has broader societal implications that go well beyond the institutional boundaries of the school and the wellbeing of children.

Acknowledgements This research was generously funded by the Swedish International Development Cooperation Agency (SIDA) and kindly supported by the Vietnam National Institute for Education Sciences (VNIES). I would like to thank everyone who assisted me with the research, particularly the teachers and students who shared their experiences of bullying.

REFERENCES

Alanen, L. (2001). Explorations in generational analysis. In L. Alanen & B. Mayall (Eds.), *Conceptualizing child-adult relations* (pp. 11–22). London/New York: Routledge/Falmer.

Alanen, L. (2003). Childhoods: The generational ordering of social relations. In B. Mayall & H. Zeiher (Eds.), *Childhood in generational perspective* (pp. 27–45). London: Institute of Education, University of London.

Ansell, N. (2014). Generationing development: A commentary. *European Journal of Development Research, 26*(2), 283–291.

Atlas, R. S., & Pepler, D. J. (2001). Observations of school bullying in the classroom. *The Journal of Educational Research, 92*(2), 86–99.

Bayly, S. (2014). How to forge a creative student-citizen: Achieving the positive in today's Vietnam. *Modern Asian Studies, 48*(3), 493–523.

Bélanger, D., & Liu, J. (2004). Social policy reforms and daughter's schooling in Vietnam. *International Journal of Educational Development, 24*, 23–38.

Christensen, P., & Prout, A. (2003). Children, place, space and generation. In B. Mayall & H. Zeiher (Eds.), *Childhood in generational perspective.* (pp. 133–156). London: Institute of Education, University of London.

Cluver, L., & Orkin, M. (2009). Cumulative risk and AIDS-orphanhood: Interactions of stigma, bullying and poverty on child mental health in South Africa. *Social Science & Medicine, 69,* 1186–1193.

Craig, W., Pepler, D., & Atlas, R. (2000). Observations of bullying in the playground and in the classroom. *School Psychology International, 21,* 22–36.

Cross, D., et al. (2011). Three-year results of the friendly schools whole-of-school intervention on children's bullying behaviour. *British Educational Research Journal, 37*(1), 105–129.

Cybermentors. (2011). You can speak out now. *Cybermentors.* www.youtube.com/watch?v=wklre2_18BU. Accessed 23 May 2011.

Duggan, S. (2001). Educational reform in Viet Nam: A process of change or continuity? *Comparative Education, 37*(2), 193–212.

Duncan, N. (1999). *Sexual bullying: Gender conflict and pupil culture in secondary schools.* London: Routledge.

Duncan, N., & Rivers, I. (2013). Introduction. In I. Rivers & N. Duncan (Eds.), *Bullying: Experiences and discourses of sexuality and gender* (pp. 1–9). London: Routledge.

Eckert, G. (2004). "If I tell them then I can": Ways of relating to adult rules. *Childhood, 11,* 9–26.

Eriksson, B., Lindberg, O., Flygare, E., & Daneback, K. (2002). *Skolan – en arena för mobbning [The school – An Arena for bullying].* Stockholm: Skolverket.

Erling, A., & Hwang, C. P. (2004). Swedish 10-year-old children's perceptions and experiences of bullying. *Journal of School Violence, 3*(1), 33–43.

Espelage, D., & Swearer, S. (2010). A social-ecological model for bullying prevention and intervention: Understanding the impact of adults in the social ecology of youngsters. In S. Jimerson, S. Swearer, & D. Espelage (Eds.), *Handbook of bullying in schools: An international perspective* (pp. 61–72). New York: Routledge.

Farrington, D. P. (1993). Understanding and preventing bullying. *Crime and Justice, 17,* 381–458.

Fleming, L. S., & Jacobsen, K. H. (2009). Bullying and symptoms of depression in Chilean middle school students. *Journal of School Health, 79*(3), 130–137.

Foucault, M. (1980). The eye of power: A conversation with Jean-Pierre Barou and Michelle Perrot. In C. Gordon (Ed.), *Michel Foucault power/knowledge: Selected interviews and other writings 1972–1977 by Michel Foucault* (pp. 146–165). Harlow: Harvester Press.

Foucault, M. (1991). *Discipline and punish: The birth of the prison.* London: Penguin.

Foucault, M. (1998). *The will to knowledge: The history of sexuality volume 1*. London: Penguin.

Friends. (2008). Hålla Käften [Keep Quiet]. *Friends*. www.youtube.com/user/Friendsare2009#p/a/u/l0rqOayETxdQ. Accessed 6 June 2011.

Frisén, A., Holmqvist, K., & Oscarsson, D. (2008). 13-year-old's perception of bullying: Definitions, reasons for victimisation and experience of adults' response. *Educational Studies, 34*(2), 105–117.

Galloway, D., & Roland, E. (2004). Is the direct approach to reducing bullying always the best? In P. K. Smith, D. Pepler, & K. Rigby (Eds.), *Bullying in schools* (pp. 37–53). Cambridge: Cambridge University Press.

Gerber, N., & Huijsmans, R. (2016). From access to post-access concerns: Rethinking inclusion in education through children's everyday school attendance in rural Malaysia. In C. Hunner-Kreisel & S. Bohne (Eds.), *Childhood, youth and migration: Connecting global-local perspectives* (pp. 203–221). Dordrecht: Springer.

Hamano, T. (2008). Educational reform and teacher education in Vietnam. *Journal of Education for Teaching, 34*(4), 397–410.

Harber, C. (2002). Schooling as violence: An exploratory overview. *Educational Review, 54*(1), 7–16.

Heinemann, P. (1972). *Mobbning – gruppvåld bland barn och vuxna [Bullying – Group violence amongst children and adults]*. Stockholm: Natur och Kultur.

Heinrichs, R. R. (2003). A whole-school approach to bullying: Special considerations for children with exceptionalities. *Intervention in School and Clinic, 38*(4), 195–204.

Horton, P. (2011). School bullying and social and moral orders. *Children & Society, 25*, 268–277.

Horton, P. (2012). *Bullied into it: Bullying, power and the conduct of conduct*. Stroud: Ethnography & Education.

Horton, P. (2015). Note passing and gendered discipline in Vietnamese schools. *British Journal of Sociology of Education, 36*(4), 526–541. doi:10.1080/01425692.2013.829743.

Horton, P. (2016). Portraying monsters: Framing school bullying through a macro lens. *Discourse: Studies in the Cultural Politics of Education, 37*(2), 204–214. doi:10.1080/01596306.2014.951833.

Horton, P., Kvist Lindholm, S., & Nguyen, H. (2015). Bullying the meek: A conceptualisation of Vietnamese school bullying. *Research Papers in Education, 30*(5), 635–645. doi:10.1080/02671522.2015.1027728.

Huijsmans, R., George, S., Gigengack, R., & Evers, S. T. J. M. (2014). Theorising age and generation in development: A relational approach. *European Journal of Development Research, 26*(2), 163–174.

Hunter, S. C., & Boyle, J. M. E. (2004). Appraisal and coping strategy use of victims of school bullying. *British Journal of Educational Psychology, 74*, 83–107.

Jackson, P. W. (1968). *Life in classrooms*. New York/London: Columbia University Teachers College Press.

James, D., et al. (2008). Bullying behaviour in secondary schools: What role do teachers play?'. *Child Abuse Review, 17*, 160–173.

Jimerson, S., & Huai, N. (2010). International perspectives on bullying prevention and intervention. In S. Jimerson, S. Swearer, & D. Espelage (Eds.), *Handbook of bullying in schools: An international perspective* (pp. 571–592). New York: Routledge.

Laslett, R. (1977). Disruptive and violent pupils: The facts and the fallacies. *Educational Review, 29*, 152–162.

Le, V. T. (2000, July 24–28). *Inclusive education – A new phase of education in Vietnam*. Paper presented at the International Special Education Congress. University of Manchester.

London, J. (Ed.) (2011). *Education in Vietnam*. Singapore: Institute of Southeast Asian Studies.

Lowenstein, L. F. (1977). Who is the bully? *Home & School, 11*, 3–4.

Lowenstein, L. F. (1978). The bullied and nonbullied child: II. *Home & School, 13*, 3–4.

Madsen, U. A. (2008). Towards eduscapes: Youth and schooling in a global era. In K. T. Hansen (Ed.), *Youth and the city in the global South* (pp. 151–173). Bloomington: Indiana University Press.

Marr, D. G. (1981). *Vietnamese tradition on trial 1920–1945*. Berkeley: University of California Press.

Mayall, B. (2002). *Towards a sociology for childhood: Thinking from children's lives*. Maidenhead: Open University Press.

Mayall, B., & Zeiher, H. (2003). Introduction. In B. Mayall & H. Zeiher (Eds.), *Childhood in generational perspective* (pp. 1–26). London: Institute of Education, University of London.

Mishna, F. (2004). A qualitative study of bullying from multiple perspectives. *Children and Schools, 26*(4), 234–247.

National Assembly of the Socialist Republic of Vietnam. (2005). *Education law*. Hanoi: National Assembly.

National Centre against Bullying. (2011). Top tips for kids. *National Centre against Bullying*. www.ncab.org.au/Page.aspx?ID=192. Accessed 23 May 2011.

Novick, R. M., & Isaacs, J. (2010). Telling is compelling: The impact of student reports on bullying on teacher intervention. *Educational Psychology, 30*(3), 283–296.

Ohsako, T. (1997). Tackling school violence worldwide: A comparative perspective of basic issues and challenges. In T. Ohsako (Ed.), *Violence at school: Global issues and interventions* (pp. 7–19). Paris: UNESCO.

Olweus, D. (1978). *Aggression in the schools: Bullies and whipping boys*. Washington: Hemisphere Publishing Corporation.

Olweus, D. (2003). A profile of bullying. *Educational Leadership, 60*(6), 12–17.

Owusu, A., Hart, P., Oliver, B., & Kang, M. (2011). The association between bullying and psychological health among senior high school students in Ghana, West Africa. *Journal of School Health, 81*(5), 231–238.

Pervin, K., & Turner, A. (1998). 'A study of bullying of teachers by pupils in an inner London school.' *Pastoral Care* 16 (4) December, 4–10.

Pham, M. (1991). *Education in Vietnam 1945–1991.* Hanoi: Ministry of Education and Training of the Socialist Republic of Vietnam.

Pham, M. (2000). *Education for all in Vietnam (1999–2000).* Hanoi: National Committee for Literacy.

Pottinger, A. M., & Stair, A. G. (2009). Bullying of students by teachers and peers and its effects on the psychological well-being of students in Jamaican schools. *Journal of School Violence, 8*(4), 312–327.

Punch, S. (2005). The generationing of power: A comparison of child-parent and sibling relations in Scotland. *Sociological Studies of Children and Youth, 10,* 169–188.

Rigby, K., & Slee, P. (1999). Suicidal ideation among adolescent school children, involvement in bully-victim problems, and perceived social support. *Suicide and Life-Threatening Behaviour, 29*(2), 119–130.

Rivers, I., Duncan, N., & Besag, V. (2007). *Bullying: A handbook for educators and parents.* Westport: Praeger.

Rydstrøm, H. (2003). *Embodying morality – Growing up in rural Northern Vietnam.* Honolulu: University of Hawaii Press.

Rydstrøm, H. (2006). Masculinity and punishment: Men's upbringing of boys in rural Vietnam. *Childhood, 13*(3), 329–348.

Salomon, M., & Doan Ket, V. (2007). Doi moi, education and identity formation in contemporary Vietnam. *Compare, 37*(3), 345–363.

Salomon, M., & Doan Ket, V. (2009). "Đổi mới, education and identity formation in Vietnam'. In M. Lall & E. Vickers (Eds.), *Education as a political tool in Asia* (pp. 139–156). Oxon: Routledge.

Sittichai, R. and P. K. Smith (2015). 'Bullying in South-East Asian countries: A review.' *Aggression and Violent Behaviour* 23: 22-35. http://dx.doi.org/10.1016/j.aub.2015.06.002

Smith, P. K. (2011). Bullying in schools: The research background. In R. Dixon (Ed.), *Rethinking school bullying: Towards an integrated model* (pp. 22–37). Cambridge: Cambridge University Press.

Smith, P. K., & Shu, S. (2000). What good schools can do about bullying: Findings from a survey in English schools after a decade of research and action. *Childhood, 7,* 193–212.

Socialist Republic of Vietnam. (1992). *Constitution of the socialist Republic of Vietnam.* Hanoi: National Assembly.

Socialist Republic of Vietnam. (2003). *National Education For All (EFA) Action Plan 2003–2015*. Hanoi: National Assembly.

Stearns, P. N. (2011). *Childhoods in world history* (2nd ed.). London: Routledge.

Suckling, A., & Temple, C. (2002). *Bullying: A whole-school approach*. London: Jessica Kingsley.

Tran, K. (2002). *Education in Vietnam: Current state and issues*. Hanoi: The Gioi.

Valentin, K. (2008). Politicised leisure in the wake of *Doi Moi*: A study of youth in Hanoi. In K. T. Hansen (Ed.), *Youth and the city in the global South* (pp. 74–97). Bloomington: Indiana University Press.

Walton, G. (2005). The hidden curriculum in schools: Implications for Lesbian, Gay, Bisexual, Transgender, and Queer Youth. *Alternate Routes, 21*, 18–39.

Wong, D. S., et al. (2011). Program effectiveness of a restorative whole-school approach to tackling school bullying in Hong Kong. *International Journal of Offender Therapy and Comparative Criminology, 55*(6), 846–862.

Yoneyama, S. (1999). *The Japanese high school: Silence and resistance*. London: Routledge.

Yoneyama, S., & Naito, A. (2003). Problems with the paradigm: The school as a factor in understanding bullying (with special reference to Japan). *British Journal of Sociology of Education, 24*(3), 315–330.

CHAPTER 7

'Being Small Is Good': A Relational Understanding of Dignity and Vulnerability Among Young Male Shoe-Shiners and Lottery Vendors on the Streets of Addis Ababa, Ethiopia

Degwale G. Belay

INTRODUCTION

In cities across the Global South, the presence of children on the street is highly visible (Thomas de Benítez 2011). Ethiopian cities are no exception as is illustrated by Mains' (2012) observations of street life in the Ethiopian city of Jimma and Heinonen's (2013) work in Addis Ababa:

> The streets are dotted with women selling mangoes, boys with portable scales who weigh customers for a small fee, shoeshiners and children selling lottery tickets (Mains 2012: 38).

D.G. Belay (✉)
School of Governance and Development Studies, Hawassa University,
05 Hawassa, SNNPR, Ethiopia

© The Author(s) 2016
R. Huijsmans (ed.), *Generationing Development*,
DOI 10.1057/978-1-137-55623-3_7

A key argument presented in this chapter is that street-working children are part and parcel of the widespread urban informal economy and urban street life at large. Yet, in scholarly and public discourses, categorising approaches, such as the notion of 'street children', continue to dominate. Categorising approaches tend to delink analyses of children's lives from the environments, relations, and economies they are embedded in, thus glossing over important relational distinctions that various street-based populations work hard to enact and maintain through their everyday street-based practices. Indeed, as Gigengack (2014: 268) observes, categories such as the infamous distinction between 'children on the street' and 'children of the street' often say more about the social logic of organisations, scholars, and social workers concerned about street children than the actual lives of the children these categories seek to refer to.

In line with the general thrust of this book, the analysis presented in this chapter is relational. In doing so, I focus on two widespread street-based occupations: shoe-shining and lottery vending. Both occupations are an integral part of street life in Addis Ababa, Ethiopia's capital city, and, as the chapter illustrates, intrinsically related to society at large. I, thus, view categories such as formal–informal, child–adult, and street–residential as relational constructs which boundaries are highly fluid in everyday practices. The chapter demonstrates that it is not incidental that the street-based occupations of shoe-shining and lottery vending are widely done by young boys. Employing a gender and generational lens illuminates that the qualities necessary for shoe-shining and lottery vending are distinctly generational. In addition, normative ideas about the appropriate place of girls put street-working girls at a very different moral evaluation than their male peers.

As I show in this chapter, the young street-based workers appropriate the occupations of shoe-shining and lottery vending as an entrepreneurial money-making activity. Being successful at it provides them a sense of self-worth and enables them to distinguish themselves socially from other street-based populations. Whilst dignity and pride, thus, emerged as important concepts from the research, achieving this was always fragile and open to contestation. First, realising a degree of dignity through these two street-based occupations is generationally limited to the condition of childhood, and secondly, the young workers are highly vulnerable to exploitation and abuse due to the deeply unequal social organisation of the street-based economy and young workers' structural position within this.

The research on which this chapter is based was conducted in July and August 2014 in the area around Piassa Minilik II square in the centre of Addis Ababa (part of Arada Sub-city). This site was selected since it is well-known for its buzzing street activities and the ethnically diverse characteristics of its street-based working population. A total of 16 shoe-shiners and lottery vendors participated in the research. Most were between 10 and 17 years of age. However, I also interviewed an older shoe-shiner (19 years old) and a former shoe-shiner (39 years old) as well as two older lottery vendors (23 and 80 years old, respectively) to bring out generational perspectives on the occupations. The sample also included a number of other important variations such as young workers who combined work with school and those who worked exclusively, relative newcomers to the job and young people who had been doing the work for some years already, and variation in terms of educational attainment although all young workers had completed at least grade 2 and often more than that (with one having completed grade 12).

I have employed an ethnographic approach, combining participant observation of street-working life with semi-structured interviews. Rapport was relatively easily established with the shoe-shiners but harder to achieve with the lottery vendors. This was partly due to the itinerant nature of lottery vending and also because they initially misunderstood my interest in their working lives as dangerous because many had been robbed by male youth. However, once I had developed good relations with some young shoe-shiners and lottery vendors and they had concluded that despite my youthful appearance I had no bad intentions, others were also more forthcoming.

In addition to spending time with young street-based workers, the ethnographic approach also helped in meeting customers, which allowed me to incorporate their views too. More formal interviews were further conducted with a range of authorities such as the local police and people working for the Ethiopian National Lottery Administration (ENLA). All interviews and conversations for this research were conducted in Amharic language, which all respondents could converse in. Participation in the research was based on full-informed consent, and all names presented in this chapter are pseudonyms for the sake of protection. Moreover, all research material in this chapter, including the photographs, is reproduced here with the participants' full consent. Furthermore, mindful of the fact that my research activities ate into my respondents' working time, I limited interviews to quiet times of the day. In addition, I had my shoes shined regularly and purchased plenty of lottery tickets, partly to build the necessary rapport in the early stages of the research and also to compensate for lost working time. Whilst taking part in the hectic rhythm of urban street life was important for understanding young working lives contextually, I complemented that with casual interviews over shared coffees and meals in order to reflect more deeply on certain observations.

The following section starts with situating children's presence on the street in the context of migration. Then, the social organisation of the two street-based occupations is analysed from a relational perspective, paying particular attention to the generational position of the young workers. The final sections look at street-based working children's constructions of dignity through their street-based occupations in the social landscape of the urban street life, children's vulnerabilities, and their agentic responses.

The Migrant Dimension of Children's Street-Based Work in Addis Ababa

A contemporary feature of the Addis Ababa's street-based economy that has received relatively little attention in the older literature is its migrant dimension. According to a Ministry of Labour and Social Affairs official who was interviewed as part of the research, many of the children working on the streets of Addis Ababa originate from the countryside and have typically come to Addis Ababa without their parents or adult guardians. This migration dimension was also reflected in my study sample: all seven young lottery vendors I interviewed originated from Merawi district, located some 500km north-west of Addis Ababa. Out of the seven young shoe-shiners only two originated from Addis Ababa with the others coming from Hadya zone, nearly 300km south-west of Addis Ababa and one from Wolayta, 390kms from Addis Ababa (see Fig. 7.1).

Migration is often networked, and this is not different among young migrants (Huijsmans 2012). The migrant networks shaping migration into Addis Ababa are typically ethnic in fabric. Consequently, entry into various street-based occupations is shaped by relations of ethnicity, which overlap with place-based relations. Most young people reach Addis Ababa following the footsteps and instructions of older peers and relatives from their villages and home-districts. It is through these connections that young people access shared, rented accommodation and are also socialised into particular street-based occupations. In addition, young street-based

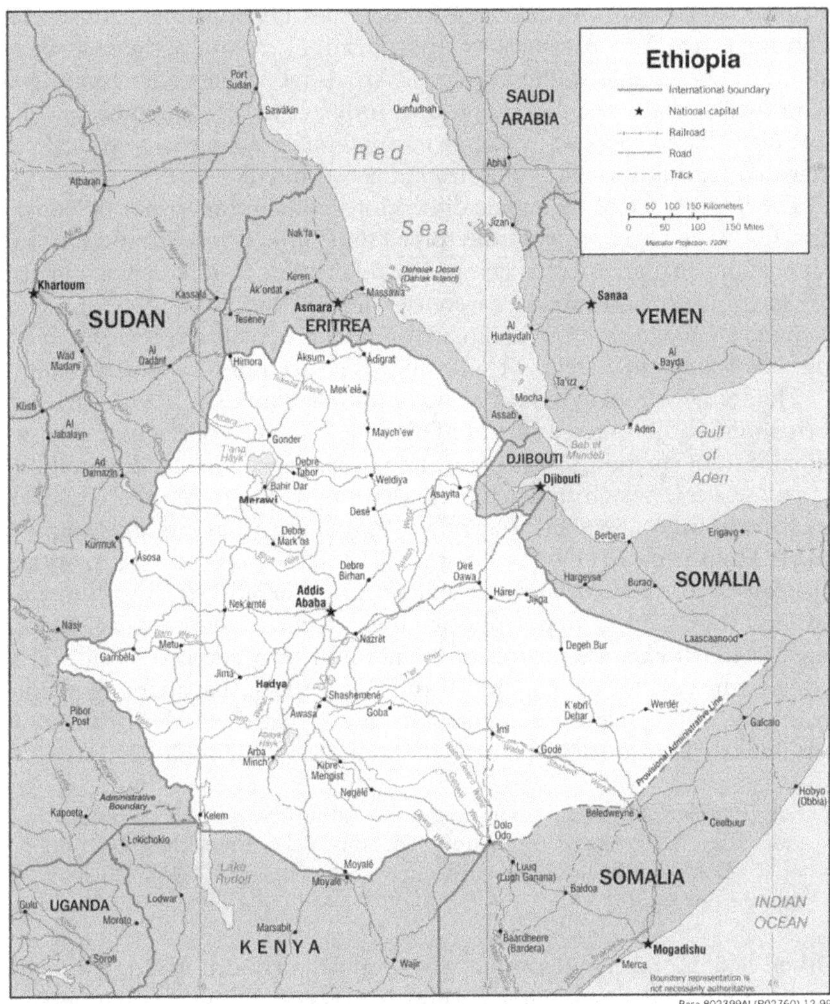

Fig. 7.1 Map of Ethiopia (Reproduced from: https://www.cia.gov/library/publications/resources/cia-maps-publications/)

workers would also set up informal rotating credit schemes (called *Iqub*) with peers with whom they shared ethnicity and/or origin.

For shoe-shining, ethnic relations also affected the type of shoe-shining young boys have access to. Shoe-shining can be done at fixed spots or on an itinerant basis. As discussed in more detail below, there are several advantages to shoe-shining in a fixed location, especially those at busy spots. In the sample studied, only the two shoe-shiners who originated from Addis Ababa were working itinerantly as entry to the more profitable place-based spots was difficult to obtain without access to the ethnic networks through which the profession is organised.

The importance of the ethnic dimension should however not be understood in static terms as over time some ethnic groups move out of certain occupations that are then taken over by others. For example, till about ten years ago, many street vendors were of Gurage ethnicity. At present, however, most Gurage have left the streets for more profitable employment, leaving shoe-shining to people of Hadya and Wolayta ethnicities predominantly.

Children involved in migration without their parents or adult caregivers are commonly considered as 'out of place' and in need of rescue and rehabilitation. An emerging body of research on 'independent child migration' has gone some way to nuance such views by highlighting that children must be seen as constrained agents in migration (Hashim and Thorsen 2011; Huijsmans 2011). Bordonaro (2012: 416–7), in this light, argues that for the Cape Verdean street children, he studied, 'streetward migration' must be seen as 'opportunistic rather than fatalistic' whilst also noting that much like other forms of migration it 'may succeed or fail'. This was also the case for the children I studied in Addis Ababa. Young people from the countryside were increasingly aware that the path of education was unlikely to lead to paid employment (see also: Mains 2012):

> Education is not profitable. The graduates I know in our village do not have jobs. Their hope to get jobs is doomed…this makes them chew *khat*. So, what would have been my fate had I stayed? (Mengistu, 14-year-old shoe-shiner from Hadya)

Others had, however, not given up the promise of education. For them, the long school holidays provided them with an opportunity to earn money in order to continue their studies. Four out of the seven young shoe-shiners and three out of the seven lottery vendors were planning to return home after the school holidays and continue their education. Tewodros' case shows an even more complicated combination of school and work:

> I came to Addis Ababa in April just before the classes ended but I returned home in June to take my final exams. After the exams I came back to town again to continue my work (Tewodros, 12-year-old lottery vendor).

Lastly, for some young workers, the main motivation for leaving for Addis Ababa to work was a necessary household contribution:

> Mom and dad are old and they are unable to work. So it is me who helps them by sending money home (Wogenie, 14-year-old shoe-shiner from Hadya).

Such reasoned motivations to leave rural villages for street-based work in Addis Ababa does not mean that parents were necessarily supportive or even informed about their sons' migration. Dereje, for example, left his home in Merawi district at the age of 15. He explained that he decided to migrate 'without consulting my parents'. He had already quit school after completing primary four and was motivated to leave for Addis Ababa after seeing his peers returning from town with consumption goods and money for their parents. In order to pay for the trip, he had stolen 200 *Birr* (€7.55) from his father's pocket.[1] Once he had arrived in Addis Ababa, he spent 4 *Birr* (€0.15) on a phone call to one of his friends in the village, whom he asked to inform his parents that he was now in the city. He first returned home after five months with 2000 *Birr* (€75.55) for his parents.

WE ARE WORKERS, NOT STREET CHILDREN!

In some cases, coming to Addis Ababa was evidently motivated by hardships in the countryside and little faith in the prospects of education. Yet, this does not preclude it from also being driven by aspirations:

> We also came here for *ketema Mayet* (enjoying the city). As rural children, we always long for the city, especially Addis Ababa the place everybody talks about (Dereje, 17-year-old lottery vendor from Merawi district).

Similar to what Mills (1997) observed among rural Thai adolescent girls, for the boys I worked with, coming to the city must also be understood in terms of self-realisation. Whereas Mills argues that factory-based work in Bangkok allows young Thai women to participate in an urban modernity, rendering these girls 'up-to-date', for the young lottery vendors and shoe-shiners in Addis Ababa it is the dignity they derive from the money-earning dimension of their work that matters.

Work (*sira*) is an integral part of rural Ethiopian childhoods (Abebe 2007: 81–82). *Sira* is socially valued and includes any work that requires mental or physical efforts. It is through *sira* that children and youth demonstrate that they are 'good children'. However, what sets the *sira* done by children in rural communities apart from the work they do on the streets of Addis Ababa is its entrepreneurial and money-generating dimension. This distinction is captured by the term *shikella* which my respondents used in reference to the success of their work. For example, on days when the boys had earned little, they would utter things like:

> *Zare alishekelkum, zare shikella yellem* (I did not make any money today, today there was no *shikella*)

In his research on children's street-based work in Addis Ababa, Abebe (2008) also came across the term *shikella*. He elaborates that

> in Amharic, *shikella* is a collective term for a wide variety of different activities that young people carry out in the informal sector as sources of livelihood. It connotes a great deal of dynamism, agency and entrepreneurial skills as well as the freedom to use the financial resources thus obtained (Abebe 2008: 280).

Whilst some income generating was necessary for the young shoe-shiners and lottery vendors to cover their daily expenses, the capacity to earn (demonstrated through their *shikella*) also indicated that they had achieved a degree of *rasin mechal* (independence). It allowed them to *beteseb magez* (support their family) and to realise *rasin melewot* (self-improvement). These are all highly valued social attributes in the Ethiopian context, which boys seek to mobilise in order to establish themselves as respected young men. Similar to Abebe's findings (2008: 280), *shikella* is also important as a discursive realm through which young street-based workers seek to distinguish themselves from street children, gang youth, and other people present on the street whose activities, such as begging, loitering, pickpocketing, and so on, are neither considered *sira* nor *shikella*. The young shoe-shiners and lottery vendors I worked with would refer to children and youth involved in such activities as *borco*.

Heinonen (2013) explains that the term *borco* has highly negative connotations. It is associated with 'drug addicts, thieves, vagabonds and dangerous criminals' (ibid. 2013: 92). The Ethiopian anthropologist Ephrem Tessema described *borco* as follows: 'One who lives in the streets and is unable to return to a normal way of life. A person who falls victim to addiction and other deviant behaviour' (quoted in Heinonen 2013: 92).

The street-working children I studied derived their dignity from associating themselves with the 'normal way of life'. As Heinonen (2013) also observed in her work with street children and gang youth in Ethiopia, the young shoe-shiners and lottery vendors fully embraced the cultural values of mainstream Ethiopian society. Hence, they strongly insisted that they were not *borco* or street children, and in their everyday practices they sought to disassociate themselves from characteristics attributed to street children. For them, street children were those who slept in the street, didn't want to work, begged for money, were pessimistic about their lives and futures, did not attend to their personal hygiene, ate leftover food (*bule*) as child beggars often do (Abebe 2008: 278), were involved in delinquent behaviour, and had no ambitions.

Thus, in order to maintain their position in the social hierarchy of Ethiopia's street life, the young shoe-shiners and lottery vendors claimed they would not pee in the streets but pay 2 *Birr* (€0.08) to use toilets in small guesthouses and restaurants (even though non-street-working customers, including children, often used these services without being charged) and made it a point to have their meals in small, cheap eating places. However, this self-positioning is always contested. For example, in their everyday interactions with (potential) customers, young street workers are often reminded that they occupy a different, and lower, social position when at the receiving end of abuse and mistreatment.

Shoe-Shining and Lottery Selling Through the Lens of Generation

Both shoe-shining and lottery vending are considered part of the informal economy. Taking a closer look at both street-based occupations shows, however, that they are closely tied to the formal part of the economy. This problematises a categorical understanding of the economy, whilst the generational dimension employed shows the social embeddedness of economic relations.

Lottery Vending and the State

The lottery tickets sold on the streets of Addis Ababa by the young lottery vendors studied are issued by the ENLA. The ENLA falls under the Ethiopian Revenue and Customs Authority and is mandated with the responsibility of printing, issuing, and regulating lottery activities. According to ENLA officials interviewed, its annual revenue is in the range of 700–800 million *Birr* (€26.4–€30.2 mln). The profits generated through this state-organised gambling programme are used to finance socio-economic development (Federal Democratic Republic of Ethiopia 2009).

The ENLA does not sell lottery tickets directly to the public. Instead, outside of Addis Ababa, it sells its tickets to official agents and within the capital city, where there are no official ENLA agents, to vendors directly. Young lottery vendors at times deal directly with ENLA but also purchase their lottery tickets from so-called *Meto-shach*. *Meto* (meaning 100 in Amharic) refers to the largest denomination in Ethiopian currency (100 *Birr*), whilst *shach* means seller. *Meto-shach* are typically adult-aged vendors with the capital to purchase large quantities of lottery tickets from ENLA which they either sell to the public directly or in smaller quantities to other vendors, such as the young people studied here. Many *Meto-shach* are from Merawi district and, thus, relate easily to young vendors from that district.

Obtaining tickets from *Meto-shach* reduces the profit ratio for the young vendors by one per cent. Yet, it also provides them with some important services and security. For example, if young vendors are unable to sell their tickets due to emergencies (e.g. serious illnesses, having to leave Addis Ababa for family emergencies), most *Meto-shach* would buy back the unsold tickets provided they have not passed the drawing date.[2] *Meto-shach* also provide some important additional services such as purchasing tickets on credit, stapling service for purchased tickets, accepting damaged paper money, and at times issuing small loans to young vendors in case of emergencies. Sometimes *Meto-shach* would charge a small fee for such services, but once young vendors have built up a good relation with their *Meto-shach,* these services were often offered at no cost. Hence, the relation between young lottery vendors and *Meto-shach* is much more than a mere commercial relation.

The profit generated from lottery vending is normally divided as follows: ENLA (80 per cent), agents (5 per cent), and vendors (15 per cent). Yet, in the absence of agents, the arrangement is different in Addis Ababa where ENLA takes an 85-per cent share. Young vendors can either purchase directly from ENLA and earn a 15-per cent share (with taking the risk of unsold tickets) or purchase from a *Meto-shach* who takes out 1 per cent, leaving 14 per cent for the lottery vendors. In practice, most young lottery vendors purchased their tickets both from ENLA directly as well as from *Meto-shach*. For them it is important to maintain relations with a

Meto-shach whilst they were also attracted to increase their profit margin by getting their tickets directly from ENLA. In addition, there are also practical constraints. For example, ENLA only sells tickets during office hours (8:30–17:00) and not during weekends and holidays. Young lottery vendors in need for additional tickets outside of office hours, thus, have to rely on *Meto-shach*.

Despite an Ethiopian labour law that prohibits young people below the age of 14 to work, ENLA officials acknowledged that lottery vending by children is widespread. Yet, they did not regard it as ENLA's role to do much about this:

> ENLA is a profit making organization; ...though national laws ban child work below age 15, we cannot prohibit them from buying tickets for vending (ENLA official, 21 July 2014).[3]

Whilst it may indeed be difficult for the ENLA to prohibit *Meto-shach* to sell tickets to under-aged vendors, young lottery vendors made it clear that the ENLA itself was also unconcerned about who was selling their tickets as long as they were sold. When I asked a 12-year-old vendor whether anyone could purchase tickets directly from the ENLA, he responded,

> Why not a dog as long as it brings money? It is business! As far as we pay the price, we can purchase tickets (Tewodros, 12 years).

Earning money from lottery selling is based on the quantities of tickets sold. For this reason, a main quality of vendors is to move swiftly through crowded places, where they try to engage with as many potential buyers as possible. Lottery vendors are, thus, constantly in a hurry, and their pace is always ahead of those of others. Such hurried movements on the street are considered inappropriate for adults, but a cherished quality of children. This was confirmed by Desta, a 23-year-old lottery vendor, who had been doing the work for six years but was, at the time of interview, planning to move on into other work:

> Children are good at lottery vending. They are fast enough to move on the streets and sell tickets.

It should be noted, however, that this refers to boys only. For girls, streets are regarded as a dangerous place, and any girl seen involved in lottery selling is suspect of promiscuity.

Shoe-Shining

In contrast with lottery selling, shoe-shining requires some start-up capital to purchase the necessary inputs. Shoe-shiners typically start with very little and often borrowed equipment. As they start earning money, they gradually expand their accessories as generally the larger the range of accessories, the greater the profitability of the shoe-shining business. For example, during the time of study, the going rate for *KIWI*-based shoe-shining was 3–4 *Birr* (€0.11–0.15) and cream-polishing 7 *Birr* (€0.26). However, the profitability of the business depended ultimately on its location. Shoe-shiners working from a fixed place in a busy area earned considerably more than their itinerant peers. For example, whilst place-based shoe-shiners earned about 70 *Birr* (€2.65) per day, itinerant shoe-shiners (see Photo 7.1) typically earned 30–40 *Birr* per day (€1.13–€1.51).

The difference in earnings is partly explained because for place-based shoe-shiners it is easier to attract regular customers and since they do not have to carry around their ware for the services they offer, their services can be more elaborate and attractive to customers. For example, Photo 7.2 shows that the young shoe-shiners working from a fixed location have set up seating arrangements for their customers, which protect them from the elements. Also, they have several bottles of fluid and plastic containers with water at their disposal, which allows them to offer a more diverse set of services than the average itinerant shoe-shiner who is unable to carry all this in his shoe-shining box (see Photo 7.1).

The place-based shoe-shiners further explained how working together in the same spot meant they had lots of time for making fun together during the quiet times of the day, and they would also watch each other's products, including the 'bank', the wooden box (see Photo 7.2) which functions as both a stand for the customers shoes as well as a safety box in which shoe-shiners keep their earnings. The itinerant shoe-shiners who were interviewed, on the other hand, complained about the difficulty of carrying around their shoe-shining box and how this box was often the focus of an insult and easily stolen if left unattended. For example, when itinerant shoe-shiners request people to shine their shoes, pedestrians not interested in the service would often remark in a derogatory manner: 'The shoe-shine box you carry is bigger than you' (Bereket, 12 years).

Gaining a foothold in a profitable shoe-shining spot depends on the social networks of young shoe-shiners—oftentimes determined by shared ethnicity and place of origin. It is also through such fixed working places

Photo 7.1 Itinerant shoe-shiner (Photo credits: Author 2014)

Photo 7.2   Fixed-place shoe-shining (Photo credits: Author 2014)

that young shoe-shiners are incorporated in the formal part of street life. This is most notably the case through the forced collaboration of some young shoe-shiners with local police stations. In lieu of leaving their illegal businesses undisturbed, local police expect young shoe-shiners to be their eyes and ears on the street. Talking about this with officials at a nearby police station, I was told that collaborating with young shoe-shiners was meant to 'reduce the burden on the police in keeping peace and security

Photo 7.3 Gown worn by fixed-place shoe-shiners (Photo credits: Author 2014)

in Addis Ababa'. In some cases, this collaboration was evidently displayed. Photo 7.3 shows a folded gown worn by young shoe-shiners. Mengistu, a 14-year-old shoe-shine boy, explained that he was obliged to purchase the gown from the local police for 50 *Birr* (€1.87) in order to have his working place secured. The gown displays on the backside in Amharic language the slogan, 'Let's Fight Crime Together' and includes both the address and the telephone number of the local police station.

Once shoe-shiners have occupied a certain place and are registered with the local police, the police does not allow them to change their workplace. Yet, working without collaborating with the police is even trickier as young shoe-shiners risk being accused of working as a secret agent who is undermining the regime. Beyond their relation with the police, shoe-shiners also participate in the formal part of street life when they purchase their inputs and services from nearby shops, cafeterias, and restaurants. This includes leaving their shoe-shine boxes in the care of shops at the end of a working day at the cost of 3 *Birr* (€0.11).

In the Ethiopian context, shoe-shining is considered a low-prestige occupation and therefore shunned by most adults. However, the work is considered appropriate for children because it is considered light and not very difficult. It is for this reason that the ten-years-old Belayneh does not consider shoe-shining work to constitute a form of 'child labour'. 'Child labour' (*yehitsanat gulbet bizbeba*), he explained, refers to work in which a child is forced to work beyond his/her physical capacity. Zelalem, a 19-year-old shoe-shiner who has completed grade 12, further commented that

> 10 to 15 years of age is a good period for shoe-shining because it is a time of no shame. Education also makes one more shameful to be a shoe-shiner. If I were illiterate I could work as a shoe-shiner even as an adult.

Zelalem emphasises the generational dimension of street-based work. Similar to lottery vending, the work of shoe-shining is fully compatible with (male) childhoods and even an opportunity to demonstrate oneself as a 'good child'. Yet, it is work that is best avoided if one wants to be taken seriously as a social adult:

> Being small is good when shoe-shining. The big ones [i.e. adults] are hopeless. They cannot change their future anymore. But when you are a kid, you have hope because you have much time to change yourself (Belayneh, 10-year-old shoe-shiner).
>
> I have exited from shoe-shining because I got married (Abebaw, 39-year-old former shoe-shiner who left the job after seven years at age 23).

The older shoe-shiners I interviewed were, thus, either considering leaving the business or remained reluctantly involved for lack of other options. The generational dynamics of shoe-shining were not, however, only caused by the diminishing social value of the work in relation to the age of the worker. There is also a material factor: physically strong young adults can have higher earnings through casual day labour than through street-based jobs.

INSISTING ON AGENCY

> I personally respect other street works. However, for me lottery vending is the best street work, because I think it generates more money. But, I do not have full information to say this; it is what I think (Tewodros, 12-year-old lottery vendor).

It would be wrong to say that migrant children from the Ethiopian countryside choose to enter lottery vending or shoe-shining even though their migration is relatively unmediated by parents or other adults. The notion of choice wrongly implies a flat urban social landscape in which a range of occupations are open for migrant children. Above I have emphasised the importance of migrant networks, which are often ethnic and origin based, in shaping migrant trajectories and elaborated on the importance of generation as a structuring relation. Despite a reality in which choice is highly structured, young street-working migrants were keen to emphasise their occupation as a positive choice rather than socially determined. As Table 7.1 illustrates, young shoe-shiners evaluated their work positively in relation to lottery vending whilst lottery vendors did precisely the same in relation to shoe-shining.

Woodhead (1999) reports similar findings based on a Swedish *Save the Children* multi-country study on 'Children's perspectives on their working lives'. With the exception of children working in occupations that are the source of 'cultural stigma and personal shame' (sex work being the case in point), working children evaluated their work in positive terms 'even when it is hazardous and exploitative' (ibid. 1999: 33). Woodhead explains this paradox as 'an indicator of personal and cultural investment in coping with a familiar situation' (ibid.). Although this coping strategy cannot be denied on the basis of my research in Addis Ababa, it is important to also recognise the positive self-evaluation of one's work as an agentive act of meaning making, a discursive and also material practice through which street-working children position themselves favourably in the social landscape of the Addis Ababa's streets. This self-positioning is highly relational, and the excerpts presented in Table 7.1 illustrate that it serves firstly to reify themselves as workers (doing *sira*) as opposed to 'street children' and 'gang youth', who they associate with destructive and illegal activities such as drug addiction and gambling. Secondly, the main argument used to evaluate their own work more positively than the given alternative is the claim that it is not just work (*sira*) but that it offers more scope for realising entrepreneurial money-making objectives (*shikella*), which we have seen above is a highly valued quality among the young male migrants. The cases of Desta and Gizachew illustrate that the young workers were not merely telling tall tales when making these comparisons. Desta's six years of lottery vending provided him with the capital to construct his own house and a grinding mill in his home town. Gizachew, on the other hand, had achieved much less after five years of shoe-shining.

Table 7.1   Which work is best? Shoe-shiners and lottery vendors evaluating their work

Shoe-shiners' evaluation of their own work relative to lottery vending	*Lottery vendors' evaluation of their own work relative to shoe-shining*
It requires less starting capital	We do not need many working materials, unlike shoe-shining
We have a fixed working place	
The work is easy to learn	We enjoy moving on the streets
We can receive tips	We earn a better income
We can have regular customers	
We earn a better income	
Shoe-shiners' evaluation of lottery vending relative to their own work	*Lottery vendors' evaluation of shoe-shining relative to their own work*
A 15-per cent commission is insignificant	The work cannot generate much profit
The work is tiresome especially for physically weaker workers	It takes a long time to earn enough money to move out of the work and enter better jobs because of its low profit margin
It is gambling and open to fraud by both sellers and buyers	Shoe-shiners are exposed to addiction due to peer pressure since they spent the day in groups

Although he was able to send home regularly products like soap, sugar, oil and small amounts of money, his earnings had not been sufficient to move into a new occupation like Desta had realised.

The centrality of *shikella* in young people's self-evaluation of their street-based occupations resonates with Abebe's findings (2008) among child beggars. Also for the shoe-shiners and lottery vendors studied here, constructing their activities in terms of *shikella* needs to be understood as an effort to 'reconstruct a positive self-identity that is free from stigma… In doing so, they also *defend* their activity as legitimate and productive that generates money based on effort' (Abebe 2008: 280, original emphasis).

Structural Vulnerabilities, Children's Responses, and its Social Effects: Profits, Safety, Fraud, and Violence

For street-working children, the discursive and material work of positioning themselves as workers involved in entrepreneurial activities is an important form of agency. Yet, the sense of dignity these young workers may thus realise is a vulnerable one. It is constantly under challenge because of their structural position in the urban social landscape. For example, in everyday interactions with the (adult) public, young street-based workers are frequently reminded of the low social position they occupy in the eyes of most urbanites, typically through insults and derogatory remarks:

> Some people demoralise us by saying, '*Yesew chama tashetalachihu*' [You are always smelling others' shoes] (Bereket, 12-year-old shoe-shiner).

> *Sidib* [insult] is our major challenge, nothing else! Some people do not respect us (Belayneh, 10-year-old shoe-shiner).

> People call us *shebelaw* and *komiche* which refers to being *fara* [illiterate], ignorant rural people (Minilik, 14-year-old lottery vendor).[4]

Carrying cash and selling services in an informal manner also render young street-based workers vulnerable. For example, customers may refuse paying the appropriate payment for their services, or even worse, some street youth may steal these young street workers' earnings. In such cases, the young street workers have to take their loss. Threatened by the physical size of adult customers or gang youth and without much support to fall back upon, their vulnerable position in the Addis Ababa streets is easily exploited.

Working in groups on fixed locations, as many young shoe-shiners do, may be understood as a collective response to some of these vulnerabilities. Yet, this is not an attractive option for lottery vendors for whom the chance of entrepreneurial success, but also their vulnerability, increases the more independent they operate and the more risky places they venture into. For example, when selling tickets in bars, young people are vulnerable to abuse, yet may also have a chance to make additional profits:

> Sometimes drunkards become fuddled and, by mistake, give us extra money when they pay for the tickets (Belachew, 17-year-old lottery vendor).

Lottery sellers, thus, constantly face a trade-off between profits and safety. During the day when safety is generally less of an issue, they typically work on their own, whilst at night and in dangerous places, they would typically work in pairs or in small groups.

Another attraction of working in risky places like bars is that these are good places to meet customers who are new to the lottery system. In such cases, young vendors would not shy away from some petty fraud by explaining the lottery system wrongly or paying out lower cash prizes than the customers had actually won. As Habtamu, a 13-year-old lottery vendor, explains,

> We consider fraud as luck. It is about being smart, and to counteract the tricks and abuse others mete out on us.

Fraud must thus be understood as a form of agency. Yet, through this exercise of agency, young lottery vendors reinforce the widespread idea that lottery vendors are fraudsters and gamblers and cannot be trusted. In the already deeply unequal urban social landscape, such discourses may be mobilised as a justification to abuse or exploit young lottery vendors as the encounter below illustrates:

> I was chatting with some shoe-shiners. Across the street some older youth were hanging out. One of them was washing cars and others were chewing *khat*. They called out to a young lottery vendor and started scratching his tickets. After a few minutes, I observed a dispute and one of the youth started beating the young lottery vendor. When I approached them and asked what was happening, the youth responded: '*These vendors are gamblers; they collect their income at the expense of unlucky people. I scratched 20 tickets but I got nothing. So I got angry.*' The young vendor was crying and replied: '*It is ENLA that printed the lottery tickets. It is not my fault. Please pay me.*' The youth argued that they would only pay if they would first win a prize and demanded to scratch more tickets.

The vignette above illustrates two other sources of vulnerability specific to lottery vendors. The first is created by the young lottery vendors themselves in their efforts to succeed in *shikella*. This leads young vendors to encourage customers to continue scratching tickets till they win a prize by emphasising that the tickets are not very expensive (1–3 *Birr* per ticket). Importantly, the scratching is done before any payment is made, and money is only received when the transaction is completed in full. This money-making strategy is the source of plenty of disputes, especially since lottery vendors are often-times dealing with several customers at the same time, making it very easy for customers to cheat the young vendors. Some customers refuse to pay for the number of tickets they have actually scratched, claiming that they have scratched fewer. Others would indeed refuse to pay at all if no prizes are won.

A second source of vulnerability is structural and integral to the lottery system. ENLA regulations (see Photo 7.4) stipulate that small prizes of up

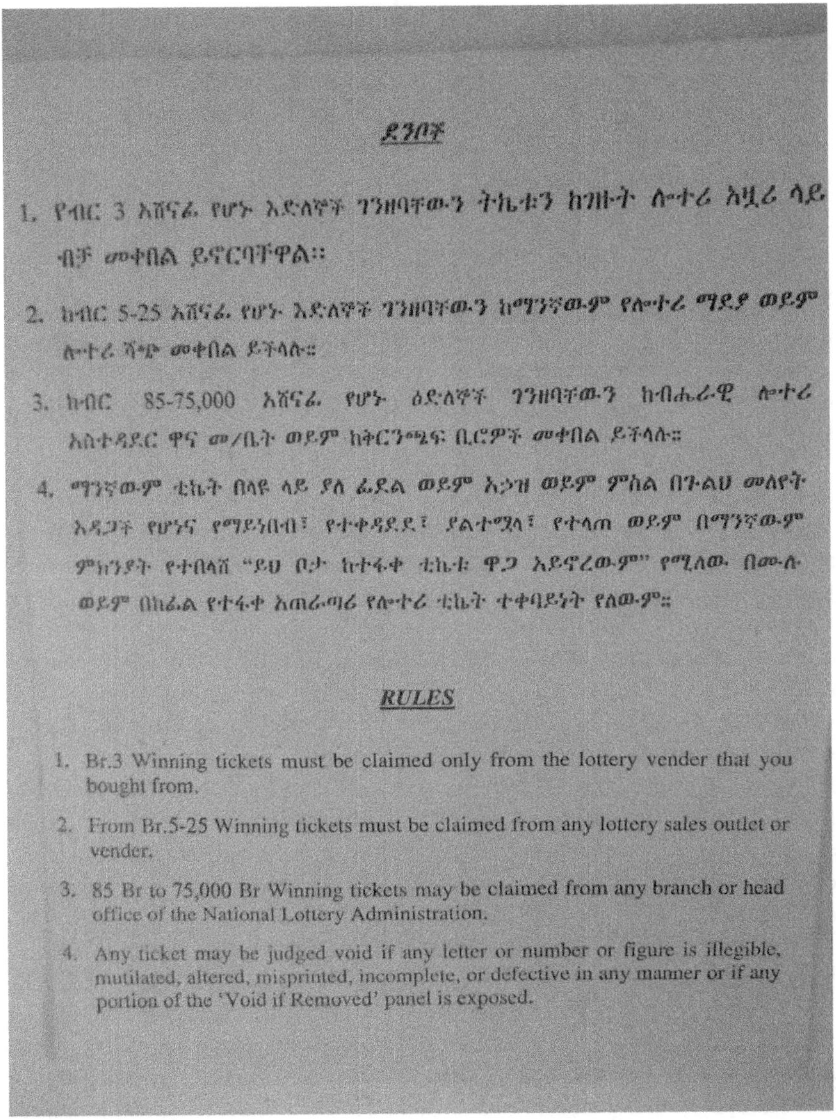

<u>ደንቦች</u>

1. የብር 3 አሸናፊ የሆኑ እድለኞች ገንዘባቸውን ትኬቱን ከገዙት ሎተሪ አዟሪ ላይ ብቻ መቀበል ይኖርባቸዋል፡፡

2. ከብር 5-25 አሸናፊ የሆኑ እድለኞች ገንዘባቸውን ከማንኛውም የሎተሪ ማደያ ወይም ሎተሪ ሻጭ መቀበል ይችላሉ፡፡

3. ከብር 85-75,000 አሸናፊ የሆኑ ዕድለኞች ገንዘባቸውን ከብሔራዊ ሎተሪ አስተዳደር ዋና መ/ቤት ወይም ከቅርንጫፍ ቢሮዎች መቀበል ይችላሉ፡፡

4. ማንኛውም ቲኬት በላዩ ላይ ያለ ፊደል ወይም አኃዝ ወይም ምስል በጉልህ መለየት እዳጋች የሆነና የማይነበብ፣ የተቀዳደደ፣ ያልተሟላ፣ የተላጠ ወይም በማንኛውም ምክንያት የተበላሸ "ይህ ቦታ ከተፋቀ ቲኬቱ ዋጋ አይኖረውም" የሚለው በሙሉ ወይም በከፊል የተፋቀ አጠራጣሪ የሎተሪ ቲኬት ተቀባይነት የለውም፡፡

<u>RULES</u>

1. Br.3 Winning tickets must be claimed only from the lottery vender that you bought from.

2. From Br.5-25 Winning tickets must be claimed from any lottery sales outlet or vender.

3. 85 Br to 75,000 Br Winning tickets may be claimed from any branch or head office of the National Lottery Administration.

4. Any ticket may be judged void if any letter or number or figure is illegible, mutilated, altered, misprinted, incomplete, or defective in any manner or if any portion of the 'Void if Removed' panel is exposed.

Photo 7.4 Lottery ticket—backside of a 3-*Birr* scratch ticket (Photo credits: Author 2014)

to 25 *Birr* (just under €1.-) may be claimed directly from the vendor (and prizes of 3 *Birr* must be claimed from the vendor directly). The young vendor must, then, retain the winning ticket and return it to the ENLA office in order to reclaim the prize money. This, indeed, means that it is the young lottery vendor who is vulnerable to a considerable financial risk in case winning tickets get lost, stolen, or damaged.

CONCLUSION

Based on a review of international research on street children published between 2000 and 2010, Thomas de Benítez (2011: ix) highlights as one of the 'top four gaps in street children research' that it is 'not systematic' in the sense that 'street children's experiences are disassociated from the laws, policies, interventions and environments that affect them'.

The relational approach employed in this chapter went some way to redress this void by studying young street-working lives in connection to the urban social landscape of which they are part and parcel. I have done so with a special focus on the generational and gendered fabric of street-based work, how this shapes children's social position in street-based economies, and how this is key to understand young people's sense of dignity in relation to street-based work. As the title of this chapter indicates, generational identities matter. Despite the low value associated with street-based work in general, the young male migrants appropriate shoe-shining and lottery selling with a sense of dignity. They insist viewing their activities as work (*sira*) and an opportunity for doing *shikella* (entrepreneurial money-generating activity). By appropriating these socially valued qualities, young street-based workers distinguish themselves from street children and gang youth, whom they claim have no dignity and hope in their lives.

The sense of dignity achieved through such relational self-positioning in everyday street-based working practices is, however, fragile and generationally limited. Whilst 'being small is good' in the sense that it allows young people to mobilise the childhood space for appropriating their street-based work in socially valued terms, it also means that older street-based workers are subject to very different moral evaluations which are hard to rework from the generational position of young adulthood.

In addition, 'being small' also renders young street-based workers vulnerable to abuse and exploitation. Their limited physical strength makes them an easy target for youth and adults who are after their cash. However, it would be wrong to see vulnerability as a mere function of physical size and age. Vulnerability is not just generational. It is in part also structural as well as produced through young workers agency. This is particularly evident in the case of lottery vending, where young vendors' location in the economic relations comprising the business is one of structural vulnerability which can only be partially mediated by working together with *Meto-shach*. Furthermore, in their quest for *shikella,* young lottery vendors engage in risky sales strategies which render them vulnerable to abuse and exploitation but also reinforce stereotypes of young lottery vendors as fraudsters. The latter feeding discourses the urban public may draw upon in order to legitimise unfair treatment of young street-based workers, thus perpetuating the justification of everyday generational violence.

Notes

1. During the research period the Euro:*Birr* exchange rate fluctuated around €1:26.5 *Birr*.
2. Note that the ENLA as of 1974 stopped taking back any unsold tickets from vendors, thus placing the financing risk solely on the shoulders of the vendors.
3. The Ethiopian labour law stipulates 14 as the minimum age of employment; yet, the ENLA official interviewed here misquoted it as 15.
4. *Komiche* and *Shebelaw* refers to styles of dress and general conduct signalling someone's rural origins. *Komiche* refers to shorts traditionally worn by the Amhara ethnic group in Northern Ethiopia, whilst *shebelaw* emphasises one's rurality.

References

Abebe, T. (2007). Changing livelihoods, changing childhoods: Patterns of children's work in rural Southern Ethiopia. *Children's Geographies, 5*(1/2), 77–93.

Abebe, T. (2008). Earning a living on the margins: Begging, street work and the socio-spatial experiences of children in Addis Ababa. *Geografiska Annaler: Series B, Human Geography, 90*(3), 271–284.

Bordonaro, L. I. (2012). Agency does not mean freedom: Cape Verdean street children and the politics of children's agency. *Children's Geographies, 10*(4), 413–426.

Federal Democratic Republic of Ethiopia. (2009). National lottery administration re-establishment. Federal Neraarit Gazeta. Regulation No. 160/2009. Regulation No. 160/2009.

Gigengack, R. (2014). Beyond discourse and competence: Science and subjugated knowledge in street children studies. *The European Journal of Development Research, 26*(2), 264–282.

Hashim, I., & Thorsen, D. (2011). *Child migration in Africa*. Uppsala/London/New York: The Nordic Africa Institute & Zed Books.

Heinonen, P. (2013). *Youth gangs & street children: Culture, nurture and masculinity in Ethiopia*. New York/Oxford: Berghahn.

Huijsmans, R. (2011). Child migration and questions of agency. *Development & Change, 42*(5), 1307–1321.

Huijsmans, R. (2012). Beyond compartmentalization: A relational approach towards agency and vulnerability of young migrants. *New Directions for Child and Adolescent Development*, (136), 29–45.

Mains, D. (2012). *Hope is cut: Youth, unemployment and the future in urban Ethiopia*. Philadelphia: Temple University Press.

Mills, M. B. (1997). Contesting the margins of modernity: Women, migration, and consumption in Thailand. *American Ethnologist, 24*(1), 37–61.

Thomas de Benítez, S. (2011). *State of the world's street children: Research*. London: Consortium for Street Children.

Woodhead, M. (1999). Combatting child labour: Listen to what the children say. *Childhood, 6*(1), 27–49.

CHAPTER 8

'We Don't Even Use Our Older Children': Young Children Accompanying Blind Adult Beggars in Tamale, Ghana

Wedadu Sayibu

INTRODUCTION

It is Friday morning at the traffic junction near Tamale Central Mosque. The green light for pedestrians switches on. A boy of about seven years old hurriedly crosses the street, accompanying a blind adult woman of about 50 years old. He carries a small plastic bowl in one hand and with the other he holds the blind woman. A line of cars queues up for the traffic light. In a fast pace, the boy guides the older woman past the line of cars. He briefly stops at every car, raising his plastic bowl above his head and tapping it gently against the car window of the driver's seat. At every stop, the older woman starts chanting words of prayers. Some people open their windows and put some money in the boy's bowl, then, the couple pauses a bit longer and the older woman continues her words of prayers asking for Allah's mercies and blessings for the driver before the young boy guides her to the next car.

Scenes like the above are commonly observed in Tamale, the largest city in the North of Ghana. Upon first impression, one might think these chil-

W. Sayibu (✉)
Regional Advisory Information and Network Systems (RAINS),
Tamale, Northern Region, Ghana

R. Huijsmans (ed.), *Generationing Development*,
DOI 10.1057/978-1-137-55623-3_8

dren are helping their disabled parents. Whilst this is indeed true in some cases, in many other instances this is not the case. Some of the children have entered the arrangement through the institution of fostering whilst others' entry into the world of begging in Tamale can best be described in terms of migration

Despite the variations in the arrangement of young children accompanying blind adult beggars, there are also some common questions. For example, why is it that we typically see only young children accompanying disabled adult beggars, blind adult beggars in particular, and seldom older children? What is the role of these children in the arrangement? And what does the presence of a child do to the moral evaluation of begging in a context in which it is an illegal activity according to law, a stigmatised activity according to societal perceptions yet also widely practiced and extremely visible? Addressing these questions requires approaching the involvement of children in begging from a relational perspective. That is, in relation to socio-economic conditions in which the practice is situated and in relation to the socio-cultural, religious and legal frameworks from which begging derives its meaning. Such a relational approach needs to incorporate a generational perspective as the arrangement itself is inter-generational.

Concentrating on inter-generational begging arrangements comprising adult beggars accompanied by young children also contributes to research on begging. Despite some notable exceptions (e.g. Swanson 2007; Bop and Truong 2014), the begging literature is typically divided between research taking a non-generation specific approach which oftentimes results in a focus on adults (e.g. Weiss 2007; Kassah 2008) and research focusing on specific age groupings of beggars such as child beggars (e.g. Abebe 2008; Delap 2009). Studying both the adult beggars and their young companions offers much scope for a generational analysis. Begging is in this chapter, thus, conceptualised as a 'relational process whereby people come to be known as children, and whereby children and childhood acquire certain characteristics' (Mayall 2002: 27).

In the next section I briefly introduce the research setting: Tamale and its position in Ghana. I continue with a description of the research process that has informed this chapter before situating the phenomenon of begging into the socio-cultural, economic, and religious context of northern Ghana. The remainder of the chapter concentrates on the generational dimensions and dynamics of children accompanying blind adult beggars on the streets of Tamale. I do so by discussing why it is only young children who act as companions, what the presence of a child does to the moral evaluation of begging, the variations observed in the relational arrangements, and the gendered exit and entry dynamics of young child companions.

CONTEXT: TAMALE AND THE NORTHERN REGIONS

The research on which this chapter is based was conducted between July and September 2014 in the city of Tamale (see Fig. 8.1). Tamale is the administrative capital of the Northern region of Ghana and the largest city in the North of Ghana. It is a relatively new city established in 1908 by the British to serve as an administrative centre for the then Northern Territories of the Gold Coast. It is the second largest city by area size in Ghana, and as per the 2010 Housing and Population Census, it has a total population of 371,351. Tamale is inhabited predominantly by people of Dagomba ethnicity. They constitute around 80 per cent of the Tamale population and most of them (about 90 per cent) are Muslim.

The city of Tamale serves as a hub for all administrative and commercial activities of the entire Northern region and functions as the political, economic, and financial capital of the region. The city also serves as a converging zone and commercial capital of the three regions comprising the north of the country (Northern, Upper East, and Upper West regions).

As Weiss (2007: 12) argues, in Ghana 'socio-economic inequality is also a regional factor, closely linked with the 'North-South' divide of the country' in which the northern parts are those that are less developed, more marginalised and, thus, often stigmatised as the 'backward' part of Ghana. The socio-economic divide in Ghana has ethnic, religious, and historical geographies too. Whilst prior to colonisation the Muslim population in the North of Ghana was comparatively wealthy, due to its relation with the colonial state, its non-integration in the modernising project of the colonial state and because of the economic policies pursued by the colonial state, the Muslim population found itself in a marginalised socio-economic position towards the end of the colonial era (Weiss 2007: 14). These relations of inequality have arguably only been reinforced by structural adjustment programmes and policies of economic liberalisation implemented in the postcolonial era. Kwankye (2012: 535) refers in this respect to a Ghana's 'spatial imbalance in development' with the Northern regions consistently scoring poorest in contemporary poverty indicators and living standard surveys. Economic inequalities have triggered considerable migration flows within Ghana. In this migration landscape, Tamale

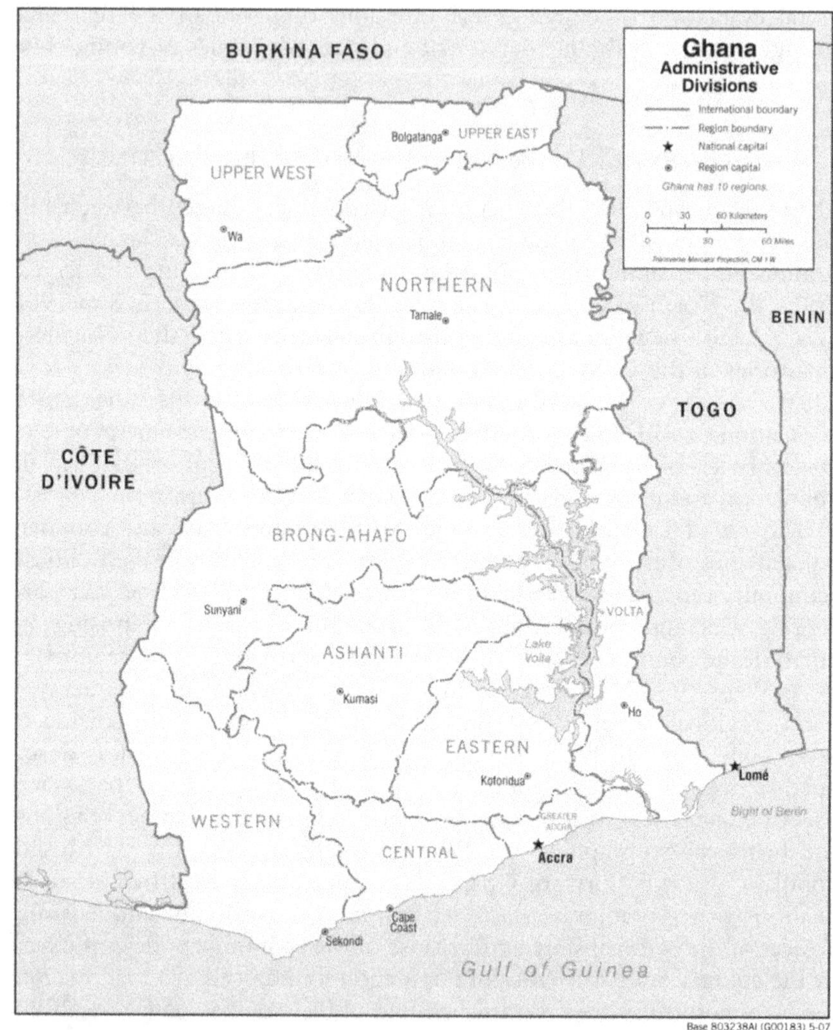

Fig. 8.1 Administrative map of Ghana (*Source*: https://www.cia.gov/library/publications/resources/cia-maps-publications/map-downloads/ghana_admin.jpg/image.jpg Accessed 5 June 2015)

is both an important site of departure as well as destination for migrants (Hashim and Thorsen 2011), including child migrants and disabled people (Kwankye et al. 2007; Weiss 2007).

RESEARCHING CHILDREN ACCOMPANYING ADULT DISABLED BEGGARS

The study on which this chapter is based adopted a qualitative methodology. According to O' Leary (2010: 114), qualitative research '...works at delving into social complexities in order to truly explore and understand the interactions of processes, lived experience and belief systems that are a part of individuals, institutions, cultural groups, and even the everyday'.

The chapter brings together voices of blind adult beggars, their young child companions as well as voices from the almsgiving public and officials. Yet, the central focus is on the experiences of the children involved in this activity, which is contrasted with adults' reasons for involving children into the work of begging. To this end, a total of 33 people participated in the study. This included 15 children who accompanied adult beggars (8 girls and 7 boys) and five adult beggars (3 females and 2 males). Out of the 15 children I worked with, 5 were not related to the adult beggars whom they accompanied, whilst ten were. Out of the ten kin-related children, three were biological offspring from the adult beggars and seven were fostered.

In addition, I interviewed three officials from respectively: the Tamale department of social welfare, the Tamale Metropolitan Assembly, and the children's department in Tamale. These officials were interviewed to gain a better understanding of the legal and policy context in which begging in Tamale needs to be understood. Here, my personal connections, as an employee at a local NGO, were very helpful in terms of accessing these informants. On top of that, I also interviewed ten members of the general public (five women, five men) who are confronted with the sight of children accompanying adult disabled beggars on a daily basis in order to gain insight into the moral evaluation of the practice.

In-depth interviews and participant observation were the main techniques comprising the qualitative methodology employed. Given the unequal power relations between children and the adult beggars, I made it a point to interview children and their adult partners separately in order to allow especially the children to speak freely (see also Notermans 2008).

Interviews lasted between 30 and 45 minutes and were conducted in an informal, semi-structured manner in locations where they would normally do their work. This allowed the participants to feel at ease and allowed me to point at things happening in the streets to trigger the conversation. Adult respondents were interviewed once with the exception of two blind women whom I interviewed twice. For the children, the interview was divided into two sessions (spread across two different days). Thus, each child was interviewed twice, which allowed for follow-up questions and helped in developing a better level of rapport.

Observation was also employed and this proved a very useful tool in generating data about the mundane activities of the children and their adult partners as well as their interactions with members of the public. The locations where the in-depth interviews were conducted were the same spots at which the observations were carried out. Similarly, the interviews with the officials were conducted at their offices and mostly in English. I have employed several strategies to gain access to and build rapport with the adult beggars and their child companions. As a native from Tamale and speaking the local Dagbani language, I initially approached the beggars on the streets directly and explained in a personal manner the purpose of my research and my intention to work with them and their child companions. Only very few accepted to grant me the interviews on such first encounters. With some others, I made an appointment for an interview at a later date. Yet, this was even less successful as many refused the interview when I returned. This difficulty in establishing a research relation changed when some adult beggars suggested I should first seek permission from the Ghana Federation of the Disabled. This is an umbrella organisation working on behalf of all disabled persons in Ghana, including the disabled beggars I intended to work with. Once this organisation had granted research permission and informed their members about my work, the initial suspicion quickly faded and more people volunteered to participate in the research than I could accommodate.

Consent was sought from the children and their parents or guardians and was preceded by an explanation of the purpose of the research. Being a native of the area also facilitated the rapport-building process. The local language was used where possible and the English language in other cases. For all conversations, both manual note taking and tape recording were used to aid the capturing of information.

To work with the children, I first asked the adult beggars for their consent to interview the children separately. They initially proposed that I could interview them in their presence. Some even argued that the information I would gather from the adults represents the views of the children as well. Eventually, I succeeded in convincing them of the need to interview the children separately and alone. Once the adult permission was given, I then proceeded to seek consent from the children directly, which included explaining that I would treat their information confidentially. Whilst some (about four) children were confident to interact with me right from the beginning, the rest looked very shy and timid. But as the discussions continued and with the introduction of some jokes, they gradually opened up. By incidence, I also learnt that many of the children accompanying blind adult beggars were very interested in the music and videos I had on my phone for my own children. I decided to use this in my interview strategy. If children appeared shy and timid, I suggested we first watch some videos together on my phone which made them feel more comfortable and eased them into the interview. For sake of confidentiality, all names of both adult and child respondents that I use in this chapter are pseudonyms.

Although research ethics state that one should ideally avoid the use of money to entice research participants, I felt this general principle needed some adjustment when working with people who rely on being giving money for their daily subsistence. After all, my research time was their working time and I felt ethically obliged to compensate for that in terms of some token money for their lunch or breakfast. Also, doing participant observation about begging naturally includes almsgiving. Each participant (both adult and children) I gave Ghc 2.00 for lunch or breakfast depending on the time of interview.[1]

BEGGING IN GHANA: ILLEGAL YET LICIT

> If one so much as scratches the surface of begging as a distinctive phenomenon, it reveals a steam of symbolic meanings and moral conundrums that is as perplexing as it is rich. (Dean 1999: 1)

Kassah (2008: 163) describes begging as 'a vibrant informal economic activity in many cities in Ghana...practiced by both disabled and non-disabled Ghanaians and refugees from neighboring politically unstable countries'. At the same time, begging constitutes a criminal act that is punishable under the 1969 National Liberation Decree 392. According to Kassah (2008: 163), these are not just empty words as 'attempts were for example made by the government in 1991 to forcibly get rid of disabled beggars on the streets of Accra, using social workers and law enforcement agents'.

On the streets of Tamale, the beggars and almsgivers I spoke with were not aware, however, that begging and destitution are criminal offences under Ghanaian law. Interviews with officials in Tamale confirmed that the law was indeed not strictly implemented and beggars were mostly left alone by the authorities as long as they stayed away from the prime locations of the city:

> We have never arrested any beggar as the law stipulates. These are extremely vulnerable persons and prosecuting them will only increase their woes. Though the law exists, there is always a human face to the law. We have however occasionally driven them off the streets because it is risky for them. Their presence on the streets is a nuisance and an eyesore to visitors. They can beg around the public mosques, but not on the major streets. (Excerpt from interview with the public relations officer of the Tamale Metropolitan Assembly)

Van Schendel (2006) makes the point that distinctions between what is 'legal' and 'illegal' can be usefully complemented by attending to the distinction between 'licit' and 'illicit'. Whereas legality refers to the realm of the state, (il)licitness describes whether activities are considered right or wrong according to societal perceptions. Weiss (2007: 19) confirms the licitness of begging in Ghana by pointing out that in both Christian and Muslim societies 'the act of giving alms is regarded as a recommended, if not obligatory, form of piety'.

In Islam, a normative distinction is made between obligatory (*zakāt*) and voluntary (*sadaqa*) almsgiving. *Sadaqa* refers to almsgiving as 'an individual, pious act and never has any collective connotations' as is the case with *zakāt* (Weiss 2007: 20). The giving of alms is thus an intrinsic element of Islam, even though asking for alms is not permitted. However, almsgiving only constitutes a pious act if the receiver is a 'deserving' poor. The Qur'ān identifies 'the poor' and 'the needy' as two of the eight categories that are eligible recipients of alms, yet does not give precise definitions of these terms (Weiss 2007: 29). Disabled beggars are by the Ghanaian public generally considered appropriate recipients of alms even though Islam forbid the practice of begging (ibid. 2007: 30):

> As for me, I don't give *sadaqa* to strong and non-disabled persons. When they approach me, I tell them to go and search for something productive

to do. These days it is difficult to actually know who really deserves *sadaqa* according to what the religion teaches us. So, I have decided to only give to the disabled because they are very poor and cannot generate income themselves. (Alhasaan Mustapah, a 45-year-old male almsgiver)

However, almsgiving is not exclusively motivated by religious beliefs. Oftentimes, motivations to give alms are rooted in different, yet interwoven frames of logic of which religion is just one. This is explained by a 51-year-old male almsgiver, Karimu Mahamadu:

Some people give to beggars to solve their own problem. I for instance, when I have a problem or wish to get something I usually consult my *Mallam* [Islamic teacher who might also do fortune telling]. He will ask me to give such and such to so and so a person. He can ask me to give, say, GHC 20.00 or pieces of white and red cola nuts or a mixture of rice, millet, corn, etc. to, say, a blind woman, or a mother with male twins,[2] etc. Once I do that, my problem may be solved or my wish may be granted.

Almsgiving and alms-seeking although closely related are subject to very different moral evaluations. Almsgiving is generally considered virtuous; it is praised by the religious and cultural ethos of the society. Alms-seeking in the form of begging is perceived; however, very differently. It is a punishable offence under Ghanaian law and also prohibited according to Islamic teaching. Apart from it being illegal, begging is also considered by many Ghanaians as unacceptable, stigmatising, and devaluing (Kassah 2008: 163). At the same time, disabled beggars are generally considered appropriate recipients of Islamic charity. They are considered the most destitute, and in the absence of any welfare programmes[3] or other means to realise an income their begging is socially sanctioned and, thus, becomes a vehicle through which other Ghanaians can enact their moral virtue.

CHILDREN ACCOMPANYING BLING ADULT BEGGARS IN TAMALE: SETTING THE SCENE

In Tamale, the work of begging is structured by the secular and religious rhythm of the day. Beggars start their work in the morning rush hour, typically around 8 am and continue begging till well into lunch time (1 pm). From 1 pm through to about 3:30 pm the beggars converge in a number of central places in Tamale. This period of the day coincides with two of the five daily Muslim obligatory prayers which the beggars observe. One such place where beggars congregate has for this reason become known as 'Barimansi line' (meaning 'beggars line').

Whilst the adult beggars pray, rest, and use their lunch, their child companions can be seen running errands for their adult partners such as fetching water, buying food, and accompanying them to toilets or urinals and to the mosques. Immediately after the second afternoon obligatory prayers, the beggars and their young companions move back onto the street where they continue begging till around 6:00 pm. By that time, the night sets in and afternoon rush hour has come to a close.

The beggars work every day of the week and their begging takes both passive as well as active forms (Dean 1999). It is particularly in the active forms of begging that child guides are essential. Children guide their blind adult partner from one vehicle to the other, who then prays for God's blessings on the potential donor, both before and after the receipt of money or other forms of support (see also: Kassah 2008: 165).

Despite begging being a stigmatised activity in Ghana, for the adult beggars it is one of the few ways to socialise with other people sharing their conditions:

> I am out here every day so that people will see my situation and support me. From the proceeds of begging I can buy food and clothes as well as support my children. Also, as I come out here, I see my colleagues in similar situations and this gives me hope and consolation. I have been doing this for more than 20 years now…I can't stop begging because I earn a living from it and it also provides me with a sense of hope and belonging. (Abibata Dokurugu, a 51-year-old female blind beggar)

The children accompanying blind adult beggars were also seen playing together during the afternoon hours, yet this social dimension of the activity was never emphasised in their oral accounts. Instead, and in contrast with the adult beggars, virtually all child companions stressed the demeaning and stigmatising nature of the activity (compare with Belay, this volume, for other forms of street based work):

> Begging is very difficult. Sometimes you go to stand in front of people and they just ignore you and some even shout at you and insult you. Sometime you will walk for hours without anybody giving you anything. I wish my grandmother had stopped this activity. I can't ask her to stop because she says if we stop we can't get food to eat. (Asana Yakubu, 10-year-old girl)

I don't like begging. I get tired everyday walking around the streets with the beggar. Some people insult us and some will just ignore us. Sometimes I feel discouraged and ashamed but I have to continue because, through this, I get money to support myself. We also send money and foodstuff to my parents every month to help support the family. I chose to come to Tamale with him [adult beggar]. I come from Bongo in the Upper East Region. When he was looking for a child to guide him, I told my parents I could go with him so as to support them and my younger siblings. (Samuel Martin, 12-year-old male)

Reliable estimates on the proceeds of begging are rare. Kassah (2008: 165) argues that in Accra beggars 'could earn an average of 40,000 Ghanaian cedi daily, which is far above the minimum daily wage of 19,000 cedis'. In my research in Tamale, the beggars estimated their daily earnings at about Ghc 10.00. On good days, their earning could go up to Ghc 20.00, whereas on bad days it might be as little as Ghc 6.00 or 7.00, which is still on par with the minimum wage (Ghc 6.00 per day). The purchasing power of these figures is broadly in line with Kassah's, noting the redenomination exercise of the 'new cedi' into the 'Ghana cedi' in 2007 (at an exchange rate of 1:10,000) and inflation.

All the money earned through begging goes to the adult partner. All adult beggars interviewed claimed they gave their child companions some money to purchase their own lunch (typically around Ghc 1.00), whilst two adult beggars also gave their child companions some additional money (around Ghc 1.00–2.00 depending on the day's earnings) for saving. These figures were confirmed by the 15 children I interviewed; indeed all received lunch money whilst only three out of 15 received some additional money. In addition, in virtually all cases, money and foodstuffs are periodically sent directly to the immediate families of the children.

BEGGING AND THE CONDITION OF CHILDHOOD: WHY IS IT CHILDREN WHO ACCOMPANY BLIND ADULT BEGGARS?

Weiss's (2007: 74) research suggests that most beggars on the street of Tamale do not originate from Tamale. My research confirms this finding as is illustrated by Mejida Yidana, a 45-year-old male beggar:

As a blind man, there is only little I can do for a living. I largely lived at the mercy of my family members when I was growing up. But now that I have a wife (who is also blind) and children, the support we get from family members cannot sustain all of us. These days, everybody looks after their children and wives alone. They expect us to also fend for ourselves which we can only do through begging. But I feel ashamed begging in my own village where everybody knows who I am. In this city [Tamale] I can stand in front of anybody to beg freely because nobody knows me.

In Ghana, families detest having their relatives begging for alms because the stigma attached to begging extends to the larger family (Kassah 2008: 164). Hence, most families will try to support their needy and disadvantaged relatives but the increasing hardships, poverty, and unemployment situations have greatly challenged families' commitments to this kinship principle of solidarity. Begging needs, thus, be seen as a last resort for poor people and an activity they are unlikely to engage in in their places of origin.

In Tamale, it is typically blind adult beggars who are accompanied by young children. The presence of child companions in begging is not unique to Ghana. In her research in Ecuador, Swanson (2007) also observed the presence of children among indigenous Calhuaseñas beggars. Interestingly, she discusses the very different understandings of the involvement of children in begging. Especially, if adult beggars were not accompanied by their own children, the presence of children was highly contested. Ecuadorian social workers, urban planners, and religious leaders would in such cases talk about 'child renting' because they would understand the practice as a commercial transaction through which adult beggars would acquire the presence of a child with the aim of invoking greater public sympathy. Such a reading was reinforced by the observation that 'women must return with 50% of the child's earning and provide the child with a new set of clothing' (ibid. 2007: 714). Indigenous women, however, viewed the arrangement differently. They would talk about 'lending' or 'sending' children, and 'by sending young children to the city with their relatives, indigenous women believe they are allowing children to get to know the city, which is considered a benefit for the child' (ibid. 2007: 715). In addition, Swanson (2007: 715) notes that the presence of child companionship in begging is also 'tied to an economy of organized caring'. This way, parents are temporarily relieved from some childcare responsibilities.

In the context of Tamale, the presence of children in begging is equally contested, yet also underpinned by a social logic. In Tamale, child companions are usually 4–14 years old, and may be girls or boys. To be sure, children's involvement in begging is prohibited. The International Labour Organisation (ILO) considers it one of the worst forms of child labour and the African Charter on Rights and Welfare of the Child also prohibits against using children in all forms of begging (Article 29). However, these international norms coexist with local norms which construct children's involvement in begging as compatible with local understandings of being a 'good child'. This is illustrated by the following response of Wuni Abibatu, a 53-year-old blind woman who begs as a livelihood:

> Children have the kind of work expected of them and adult have theirs. I cannot ask my husband to accompany me. I cannot even contemplate it. We don't even use our older children because they are strong enough to do proper work. Begging is not a type of work for strong looking people.

The quote also illustrates another factor. Blind beggars obviously need sighted companions. They need a set of eyes to guide them through the traffic and help them make contact with potential almsgivers. However, the moment these set of eyes belong to an adult or an older child, the moral evaluation of their activity changes dramatically:

> It looks abnormal for adults who look strong to accompany us for begging. People will not give us anything as they expect him or her to go and work and look after us. So it is good for my wife to stay and look after the home and the youngest children whilst we [himself and his 13-year-old male guide] work to bring money home. (Issahaku Zakaria, 48-year-old male blind beggar)

> I give alms in order that Allah will have mercy on me. He enjoins us to show mercy to the poor so that He will also show us mercy. I don't give to any beggar I see on the street because most of them especially the non-disabled are not genuine. I look out for the poor. Mostly I give to the blind or the very aged. If I even see that the blind is accompanied by a grown child I don't give to them. The child needs to be encouraged to go to school or work otherwise when the one he is accompanying is no more he may turn into a beggar himself. (Amshawu Alhassan, 35-year-old female almsgiver)

The interview excerpts show that the presence of able-bodied partners changes the moral evaluation of begging by blind people from worthy of almsgiving to that of lazy people unworthy of any support. The exception is the presence of a young child who is seen as not yet capable of earning an independent income. This particular condition of childhood leaves the moral evaluation of begging by blind adult people in tact as one that is a worthy recipient of alms. In fact, it reinforces it as a young, small child elicits public sympathy (see also Swanson 2007: 714) and the notion of childhood innocence underpins the general belief among Muslims in northern Ghana that showing mercy, in whatever form, to a child, means that one will receive a multitude of mercy and reward from Allah. In addition, it is also noteworthy that it is believed that a child's prayer is answered faster because children are seen as innocent, especially those who have not yet reached adolescence. Next to the question why it is young children that accompany blind adult beggars, my research also lead to another question: why did I not encounter any disabled children begging on the streets of Tamale? In all fairness, in my research people told me about two disabled children who beg yet I failed to locate them. The absence of disabled children from begging can also be explained by the condition of childhood. When disabled people are still children, they are often hidden from public view. Visibility would mean that the stigma associated to disability would become attached to the entire family, with all its negative consequences (Kassah 1998: 70). In addition, as children, disabled people generally elicit the moral support of family members and also tend to subject themselves to such care. This often changes when disabled people grow up into adults, especially when they start forming relations themselves and establish their own families. In combination with economic hardships, these disabled adults often have to, and at times want to, fend for themselves with begging one of the few livelihood opportunities available to them (Weiss 2007; Kassah 2008).

Variations in Child Guides–Adult Beggar Arrangements

The previous section has illustrated that young children are the perfect guides for blind adult beggars as they enhance the sympathy on which begging relies and they do not disturb the image of a 'deserving poor' worthy of *sadaqa*. Even so, different arrangements can be observed of children accompanying adult beggars. Some blind adult beggars work with the company of their own offspring, and others are accompanied by children of relatives, whilst again others roam the streets in the company of non-related children. Similar to Swanson's research in Ecuador, also in Tamale, each arrangement is informed by its own social and cultural logic.

Children Accompanying Their Own Parents

Most disabled beggars I spoke to were married or had been married and had children from these marriages. Yet, only few (3 out of 15) were accompanied by their own children. Adult beggars explained that their own children were not suitable for begging because they had already reached adolescence, and in other cases, they were not available because the children were no longer staying with their disabled parents following a divorce. For those who were accompanied by their own offspring, often-times both parents were blind and involved in begging and the children were socialised into their parents' only source of livelihood:

> The father of the child who guides me is also blind. He also begs and you can find him at the other traffic junction near the bank. He is guided by the elder sister of this child [estimated to be 9 years old, and the elder sister 12 years old]. We both beg because that is the only thing we can do for a living. Our children understand our situation because we are blind but we gave birth to them. We do not get any support from our extended family or the state, so if they do not support us to beg, there will be no food for all of us. We use our own children because they understand our situation. If you use a child from outside, the child may steal some of the proceeds. (Meimunatu Sulemana, a 40-year-old female blind beggar)

In cases like the above, children have either never been to school or have dropped out early and are socialised into the work with very little scope for alternatives. They typically start accompanying their parents from the age of four onwards. By the time they have matured physically (around the age of 12), they are mostly replaced by a younger sibling or another child as the work of begging is incompatible with the presence of an older able-bodied child but also because by that age other work opportunities become available to these children.

The excerpt above also highlights the importance of morality that is attributed to the relationship between parents and their own offspring. Non-related children are seen as a possible risk as they might prioritise their own interests above those of the blind adult beggar and his/her family. In addition, morality may also underpin the motivation of own offspring to become involved in begging despite the stigma attached to it:

> I was staying with my mother in her village and attending school. I was doing very well as my class teachers used to tell me. But when news got to

me that my blind father no longer has any child to guide him, I voluntarily decided to withdraw from school and to offer my support to him. We are saving the money we get from begging and very soon we will use it to do farming and animal rearing. With this my father will no longer have to beg and I can also go back to school. I can combine the farming activities with my education. As for begging, nobody likes to be associated with it if not compelled. People look down on you as a beggar. (Abdul Razak Amidu, 12-year-old boy)

Child Fostering and Begging

The child was given to me by my younger brother and his wife to take care of me as I cannot see. She guides me wherever I go… to the toilet, to the mosque, and any place that I must go. She is my eye. I use to be in the village and receive support from family members. These days farming which is their main occupation is no longer good. I can no longer solely depend on them. So I was advised to come to the city where I can solicit help from people. My brother gave me one of his children to support me. As we get money and foodstuffs we also send part of it to support them in the village. (Hawa Ibrahim, 55-year-old female blind beggar)

In part because own children age out of begging, most blind beggars are not accompanied by their own children but by children of kin or fictive kin. The relationship is in such cases rooted in the social institution of child fosterage which has a long history in much of West Africa and is still very much alive today (Goody 1972; Kuyini et al. 2009). The institution of fostering is often characterised as a risk coping mechanism employed by Ghanaian families to compensate for some form of economic and/ or demographic hardship and to take advantage of resources through the extended family and other social networks (Kuyini et al. 2009). The arrangement revolves around a system of reciprocity—where the children on the one hand serve as guides for disabled beggars whom in turn are responsible for their daily needs and may provide these children with some income or other material support from the proceeds of the activity as well as an informal settlement packages when they reach adolescence. These benefits may also extend to the immediate families of the children. For example, food and some proportion of money may be periodically sent to the parents of these children.

One reading of the fostering arrangement underpinning begging is that children serve as instrumental agents through which blind adults are transformed from care burdens into productive members of the family by involvement in the highly stigmatised activity of begging. Decisions about such arrangements are made through layers of consultations among family members including kin and fictive kin. However, children themselves are seldom actively included in such consultation processes and mostly just informed about the final outcome:

> I used to stay in the village with my parents. There I was attending school but the quality is not good. One day the old man came looking for a child to assist him to beg in Tamale. He is from our village but moved to Tamale to do begging. He used to be guided by another boy who left for Accra. My parents convinced me to accompany him as the schools in Tamale are better than the one in the village, so I did. But he has not yet sent me to school. He says we will have to work and save to buy school uniforms and books before he enrolls me. I have been here for more than a years now. Sometimes he sends money and foodstuffs to my parents in the village. (Faiza Umar, 10-year-old girl)

EDUCATION, ASPIRATIONS AND CHILD MIGRATION

Conventional interpretations of the fostering system leave very little space for children's agency. Indeed, as argued in the previous section, it is tempting to view children as instrumental agents and it is true that their opinions are seldom sought in the consultation processes. However, even though fostering is largely an adult-centred institution, that doesn't render children passive. For example, children also expressed their own aspirations in relation to leaving the village and becoming a guide to a blind adult beggar in the city of Tamale. These aspirations typically revolved around accessing better quality education than the substandard education available in rural villages:

> I am accompanying this woman because of my education. My parents asked me to follow her to Tamale to guide her to beg so that I can continue my education. Though my parents also benefit from this, the main reason for engaging in the activity is my education. I am planning to quit the activity and go into other activities with the little savings I am making now. I can't continue to guide her to beg forever. (Farouk Abdul Majid, 13-year-old boy)

Unfortunately, however, such educational aspirations were seldom realised. Some children never entered school despite this being a key motivation for them to leave the village and become involved in begging. This was the case for Faiza Umar (10 years old). Farouk Abdul Majid, who is quoted above, did attend school but complained that he frequently misses classes because of his begging work. Indeed, their work on the streets of Tamale often turned out to be incompatible with studying:

> I wish I could perform better than I am currently doing. But I don't get time to study after school hours. Very early in the morning, I bring the old man to the spot behind Picorna hotel where he begs while waiting for me to return from school so that we can roam around. Long hours of walking during the day make me very tired in the night. So I sleep very early without even opening my books to revise. I wish my parents could afford my educational expenses so that I wouldn't have to do this work and will be able to learn like my other colleagues are doing. (Mohammed Fatawu, 11-year-old boy)

Although the gendered dynamics underpinning school attendance were not explored in detail it is noteworthy that the two boys referred to above both ensured that the promise to send them to school was delivered. Farouk Abdul Majid achieved this by threatening the adult beggar he accompanied to run back to his village if he was not sent to school. Faiza Umar, on the other hand, just resigned to her fate to the discretion of her adult partner.

Highlighting children's own aspirations in relation to fostering serves to show that fostering may for some children be an institution through which their migratory ambitions can be realised from within their social position of children living in conditions of poverty (Hashim 2007; Whitehead et al. 2007). In addition, the relational fabric of child movement through the social institution of fostering differs from that of children guiding their own parents. This point is also illustrated by the quote of Farouk Abdul Majid above who actively contemplates leaving the arrangement for a different occupation, something that is much more delicate to realise in arrangements in which blind beggars are accompanied by their own offspring (for a more general argument about this in relation to child migration see Huijsmans 2012).

In some cases, children realise their migratory aspirations outside the licit social institution of fostering. One example constitutes a 14-year-old boy who explains he had learnt about the possibility of becoming a guide of an adult beggar in Tamale through an older friend who was about to quit the arrangement. Enticed by the gifts and money with which this friend had returned to the village he decided to leave the village without informing his parents:

> When I started guiding the blind man, my parents didn't know. I was first introduced to him by a friend who used to guide him. When my parents got to know that I was guiding him to beg, they asked me to stop. But I couldn't stop because they don't have money to support me in school. As I continue to take care of my needs and also support them from the proceeds I get, they later approved of my engagement in the activity. (14-year-old boy)

In those cases in which children have entered the world of begging through their own migration, it is the children themselves who negotiate the conditions of the arrangements, albeit often from a highly constrained position due to poverty and the absence of alternative options.

Age and Gender in Entry and Exit into Accompanying Blind Adult Beggars

As explained above, children's entry and exit into accompanying blind adult beggars is shaped by the condition of childhood. Conceptions of childhood relate to the measure of chronological age. Yet, on the streets of Tamale, it is primarily social age that shapes children's entry and exit into begging. The concept of 'social age' draws attention to the 'socially constructed meanings applied to physical development' (Clark-Kazak 2009: 1310) and to the responsibilities assigned to, and obligations towards people occupying particular life phases such as infants, children, youth, adults, and elderly (Huijsmans 2013).

On the streets of Tamale, social age necessarily mattered more than chronological age because most children (and adults) I interviewed did not know their date of birth and thus their precise chronological age. Consequentially, maturity and its social attributes were mostly related to physical manifestations of human development such as bodily changes and the onset of menstruation for girls. When girls started to develop breasts and started having their first menstruation they typically stopped guiding blind adult beggars. Boys tended to continue the work a bit longer and exited when their physical development meant they were no longer seen as children who evoke sympathy, but as youth who are considered strong enough to take on the responsibility of earning a living through labour.

Chronological age I could in most cases only determine by approximation. Asking the children about the number of younger siblings gave in some cases a good idea of their chronological age, whilst in those cases I also interviewed their parents or knowledgeable adults I estimated children's chronological age by inquiring about major events that happened at the time of the child's birth. With this strategy the ages of the children who were interviewed were estimated to be in the age bracket of four to 16 years with majority of them in the 8–14 years bracket. Their adult partners on the other hand ranged from 35 to 60 years.

Interviews with the adult beggars revealed that on average they had changed about four to six guides since they started begging with the exit point of children in this activity being around 10–12 years for girls and 12–14 years for boys. Girls did exit earlier not only because of differences in the tempo of physical maturation between girls and boys but also because for girls the involvement in begging was said to have a greater effect on their marriage prospects than for boys. If girls were still involved in the begging activity when reaching puberty, their chances of finding a respectable marriage partner was believed to greatly decline.

Given the perpetual turnover in child companions and the fact that blind beggars could not go without them, young children were apprenticed into the work in order to allow for a smooth transition. From the age of four, young children would be brought into the work and act as 'shadow guides' whilst older children would then gradually ease out of the work. Hence, it was not uncommon to see two to three children accompanying one blind adult beggar either at the same time or interchangeably (at different times of the day). Those who plan to exit would then already get involved in other economic activities whilst still providing guidance to those preparing to come in (the shadow guides). Importantly, the shadow guides are mostly used at less busy hours and at areas that are considered safe while those who prepare to exit come in during the peak hours and may also accompany the blind adult beggar into areas considered more risky.

Similar arrangements could be observed in case some of the child companions combined their involvement in begging with school attendance. Typically, it is only the older child who is enrolled in school with the young(er) child working as a 'shadow guide'. With this arrangement, the older child guides the blind beggar and the younger child to the street in the morning before going to school. The younger child and their partner then beg at areas considered safe, awaiting the return of the older one to takeover. In case there is only one child companion and this child is attending school, the blind adult beggar would be left in a fixed location to beg till school closes at around 12 noon after which the child companion would continue guiding the blind beggar.

Conclusions

In Tamale, begging is generally considered a stigmatised practice and constitutes a punishable offence by law. Yet, disabled beggars, blind persons included, mostly evade this legal and societal assessment. In the absence of any state support, it is generally accepted that for the disabled, begging constitutes a last resort. This renders them 'deserving poor' and turns their begging into a licit activity. That is, they are considered worthy of receiving *sadaqa* as well as appropriate recipients of non-religiously motivated almsgiving.

The discussion on child companions presented in this chapter illuminated the contested nature of begging and its generational dynamics. Whilst blind adult beggars require a set of eyes to guide them through the streets of Tamale and enable them to realise a livelihood, such set of eyes could only belong to a young child. The condition of childhood which is associated with vulnerability, helplessness, and one that evokes public sympathy is embodied by the young child most undisputedly. Such young children, thus, leave the licitness of the begging activity in tact whilst also reinforcing the enhancement of sympathy on which begging relies as an income-generating activity. This dramatically changes once the child companion has grown into a young youth. This has less to do with reaching a certain chronological age, and all with being associated with a different social age. These generational dynamics intersect with gender. Hence, girls tend to exit begging at an earlier age than boys. Blind adult beggars, thus, regularly need to change their child companions, which also mean that they cannot rely on their own offspring solely and sometimes not at all.

Due to these generational dynamics, a range of different arrangements between child companions and blind adult beggars can be observed. Whilst the relational fabric underpinning these arrangements differs with some effect on the scope for agency of the young companions concerned (see also Huijsmans 2012), it must be emphasised that children's involvement in the highly stigmatised work of begging was across the different arrangement always the result of conditions of poverty and the lack of accessible alternatives (see also Mizen and Ofosu-Kusi 2013). Following Ansell (2009), the latter illustrates that a relational analysis cannot be limited to the micro scale of the inter-generational relationship between the blind adult beggar and the child companion. Although unravelling the social fabric of this relationship is important for understanding children's experiences and their scope for influencing these, a relational analysis must also include broader structures of meaning and relations of inequality that both shape children's everyday experiences in the world of begging and which they constantly negotiate. Furthermore, bringing into conversation the voices of blind adult beggars and their young companions has shown the importance of generation. Despite sharing the same socio-economic position, the social stigma associated with begging, and the closeness in the moral perception of the condition of disability and that of (early) childhood, their different generational locations mean that their respective involvement in the work of begging is experienced and understood in different ways between the blind adult beggars and their young companions. This has important ramification for policy and practice as common approaches to address the fate of disabled adult beggars and their young partners are typically coming from a children's rights perspective or a disability perspective. The latter translates into an approach that is commonly adult-centred whilst the former tends to pay insufficient attention to the adult beggars with whom young companions' lives are intimately connected. Bridging this gap, I would suggest, requires working with both adults and children and attending to the generational dynamics shaping the practice and conditions that bind them together.

Notes

1. At the time of research, the exchange rate was €1 = Ghc 4.1 and $1 = 3.1.
2. In the Ghana and other West African countries, there is the long-standing belief that children of multiple births want to be sent out begging and that these children's wishes must be respected to avoid misfortune (including the death of these children) (Igbinovia 1991). For this reason, mothers with twins or triplets are often seen begging.
3. Up until 2006, Ghana did not have a comprehensive law or policies on disability. Despite the passing of the Disability Act in 2006, still very little state support is in place for people with disabilities.

REFERENCES

Abebe, T. (2008). Earning a living on the margins: Begging, street work and the socio-spatial experiences of children in Addis Ababa. *Geografiska Annaler: Series B, Human Geography, 90*(3), 271–284.

Ansell, N. (2009). Childhood and the politics of scale: Descaling children's geographies? *Progress in Human Geography, 33*(2), 190–109.

Bop, C., & Truong, T.-D. (2014). Complexity of gender and age in precarious lives: Malian men, women, and girls in communities of blind beggars in Senegal. In T.-D. Truong, D. Gasper, J. Handmaker, & S. I. Bergh (Eds.), *Migration, gender and social justice* (Vol. 9, pp. 265–278). Berlin/Heidelberg: Springer.

Clark-Kazak, C. R. (2009). Towards a working definition and application of social age in international development studies. *Journal of International Development, 45*(8), 1307–1324.

Dean, H. (1999). Introduction. In H. Dean (Ed.), *Begging questions: Street-level economic activity and social policy failure* (pp. 1–11). Bristol: The Policy Press.

Delap, E. (2009). *Begging for change: Research findings and recommendations on forced child begging in Albania/Greece, India and Senegal*. London: Anti-Slavery International.

Goody, E. (1972). Kinship fostering in Gonja: Deprivation or advantage? In P. Mayer (Ed.), *Socialization: The approach from social anthropology* (pp. 51–74). London: Tavistock Publications.

Hashim, I. (2007). Independent child migration and education in Ghana. *Development & Change, 38*(5), 911–931.

Hashim, I., & Thorsen, D. (2011). *Child migration in Africa*. Uppsala/London/New York: The Nordic Africa Institute & Zed Books.

Huijsmans, R. (2012). Beyond compartmentalization: A relational approach towards agency and vulnerability of young migrants. *New Directions for Child and Adolescent Development*, (136), 29–45.

Huijsmans, R. (2013). "Doing gendered age': Older mothers and migrant daughters negotiating care work in rural Lao PDR and Thailand. *Third World Quarterly, 34*(10), 1896–1910.

Igbinovia, P. E. (1991). Begging in Nigeria. *International Journal of Offender Therapy and Comparative Criminology, 35*(1), 21–33.

Kassah, A. K. (1998). Community-based rehabilitation and stigma management by physically disabled people in Ghana. *Disability and Rehabilitation, 20*(2), 66–73.

Kassah, A. K. (2008). Begging as work: A study of people with mobility difficulties in Accra, Ghana. *Disability & Society, 23*(2), 163–170.

Kuyini, A. B., Alhassan, A., Tollerud, I., Weld., H., & Haruna, I. (2009). Traditional kinship forster care in northern Ghana: The experiences and views of children, carers and adults in Tamale. *Child & Family Social Work, 14*, 440–449.

Kwankye, S. O. (2012). Independent North–South child migration as a parental investment in Northern Ghana. *Population, Space and Place, 18*(5), 535–550.

Kwankye, S. O., Anarfi, J. K., Tagoe, C. A., & Castaldo, A. (2007). Coping strategies of independent child migrants from Northern Ghana to Southern Cities. Working paper. Brighton, Development Research Centre on Migration, Globalisation, and Poverty, University of Sussex. Retrieved T-23.

Mayall, B. (2002). *Towards a sociology for childhood: Thinking from children's lives.* Maidenhead: Open University Press.

Mizen, P., & Ofosu-Kusi, Y. (2013). Agency as vulnerability: Accounting for children's movement to the streets of Accra. *The Sociological Review, 61*(2), 363–382.

Notermans, C. (2008). The emotional world of Kinship: Children's experiences of fosterage in East Cameroon. *Childhood, 15*(3), 355–377.

O'Leary, Z. (2010). *The essential guide to doing your research project.* London: Sage publications.

Swanson, K. (2007). 'Bad mothers' and 'Delinquent children': Unravelling anti-begging rhetoric in the Ecuadorian Andes. *Gender, Place & Culture, 14*(6), 703–720.

Van Schendel, W. (2006). The Borderlands of legality. *IIAS Newsletter*, 3.

Weiss, H. (2007). *Begging and almsgiving in Ghana: Muslim positions towards poverty and distress, Research Report No. 133.* Uppsala: Nordiska Afrikainstitutet.

Whitehead, A., Hashim, I. M., & Iversen, V. (2007). Child migration, child agency, and inter-generational relations in Africa and South Asia. Working paper T24. Brighton, Development Research Centre on Migration, Globalisation & Poverty, Sussex University.

CHAPTER 9

Travelling Identities: Gendered Experiences While Doing Research with Young *Allochtoon* Dutch Muslims

Mahardhika Sjamsoeoed Sadjad

INTRODUCTION

In 2015, as part of my studies, I conducted an individual research that aimed to understand how Dutch-Muslim youth coming from families with migrant backgrounds give meaning to and position themselves within Dutch society. My research discussed the intersections of race, ethnicity, class, life phase, and religion through my participants' lived experiences of growing up in the Netherlands (Sadjad 2016). My participants' life narratives were situated in the margins of elite discourses of 'the Muslim other' in the West (Hoodfar 1993; Scott 2007) that are often based on hegemonic gender constructs of the aggressive Muslim man and the oppressed Muslim woman.

This chapter, written two months after the completion of my study, explores the relationality of doing research with young people. I pursue this exercise by reflecting back on how gender identities were expressed, manoeuvred, and reproduced during the course

M.S. Sadjad (✉)
International Institute of Social Studies of Erasmus University Rotterdam, Kortenaerkade 12, 2518 AX The Hague, Netherlands

R. Huijsmans (ed.), *Generationing Development*,
DOI 10.1057/978-1-137-55623-3_9

of my research. In doing so, I draw loosely on Thelen et al.'s (2014) framework for relational anthropological research (see Huijsmans, this volume). In my research with Dutch Muslims of migrant descent I traversed various intersecting relational modalities, including different 'legitimate Islamic frameworks' (Amir-Moazami 2010: 197–8), friendships, and research–researcher relations. Gender transpired as an overarching theme cutting across these different modalities and therefore requiring constant reflection and negotiation, which Thelen et al. refer to as 'boundary work'.

The central theme of this chapter is how gender identities are expressed in relation to one another. A researcher becomes an embedded actor within the community where she is doing research. Particular gender identities are expressed through the relationships and interactions formed between the researcher, the research participants, and their environment. Since 'masculinities are indeed produced through interactions between men and women, and through relations between men themselves' (De Neve 2004: 65), my presence as a female researcher becomes essential to the exploration of my participants' masculine identities. My male participants' masculinities cannot be detached from my own expressions of femininity, which also co-constitutes other aspects of our identities, such as race, ethnicity, class, life phase, and religion.

Through this chapter, I narrate my personal experiences of doing research, reflecting on the decisions, vulnerabilities, and uncertainties I felt along the way. I start by first situating my research and positioning myself among my research participants. Then, I share three encounters with one research participant, J. I have selected these particular narratives because I believe they best illustrate how fieldwork is a gendered experience where, as I argue in the conclusion, identities travel, are expressed and represented in relation to one another.

SITUATING MY RESEARCH AND POSITIONING MYSELF

My research on young *allochtoon*[1] Dutch Muslims was carried out roughly between February and November 2015. I say 'roughly' because my growing interest on the topic did not really have a clear starting and cut-off date, but also because as I carried out and wrote about my research it became increasingly clear that the insights and instincts I relied upon were accumulated from my own lifelong experiences being raised as a Muslim woman in Indonesia with periods of living in 'The West', particularly the USA and the Netherlands. Like Behar (1996: 33), I approached my research with a need to know others by knowing myself and who has come to know herself by knowing others.

My study involved six young Dutch Muslims who are categorised as *allochtoon*; they were all Dutch citizens and, with the exception of one participant who migrated from Tanzania with his native Dutch mother when he was nine years old, all of them were born and raised in the Netherlands. J, whose interactions with me are central to this chapter, is of Bangladeshi descent. He was born and raised in Scheveningen, the Netherlands, which he calls home. My participants' ages ranged from 19 to 25 and they were attending a form of higher tertiary education, with the exception of one who graduated the year before participating in my research. Their privileged educational background meant that my participants do not represent the entirety of young Dutch Muslims.

It is important to emphasise that my research did not aim for statistical representation and neither was it driven by any intentions of generalisation (Abbott 2007: 217; Hammersley and Atkinson 2007: 32). Instead, the goal was to evoke further conversations on the topic of integration, conversations that are driven by readers' ability to resonate with, rather than be detached from, participants' experiences (Ellis 2004: 22). In order to achieve this, a lot of thought went into decisions on how to engage and represent my participants throughout the process of 'doing' and 'writing' research. This chapter will look back and reflect on some of these decisions and the experiences that followed.

The research activities I conducted included mapping exercises of participants' hometowns, visiting places they identified on their maps as essential to their experience growing up and living in the Netherlands, and a series of semi-structured interviews. The purpose of this was to situate my participants' experiences growing up in the Netherlands, trigger personal narratives by visiting places that were important to them, and observe how participants and other people acted and interacted within these spaces. I engaged participants in discussions about their neighbourhoods, their relationships with their family members and peers, their memories and opinions of events such as the Charlie Hebdo attack in January 2015, their interests, and their academic and extracurricular activities. The interviews and discussions developed gradually in accordance to the quantity and quality of my interactions with my participants. While my research plans were quite elaborate, the execution varied, depending on participants' insights, comfort, and conveniences.

In autoethnographic research, reliability in its conventional sense does not exist (Ellis 1999: 674). Personal narratives of situated locations are inherently subjected to the limits of memory, perceptions, and imagination. Therefore, following Ellis' advice, I arranged for one last round of meetings with my research participants. My participants and I went through my draft research paper (Sadjad) together and they were invited to comment and offer their insights in order to enrich my own. Ensuring room for questions, comfort, and feedback was crucial to this process. Their participation and representation were essential from design to finish.

As a consequence of my research approach, I developed friendly relationships with most of my research participants. These interpersonal relationships were essential to doing my research. Not unlike myself who turned 29 when writing up my research results, they too were experiencing the liminality of youth; a phase between memories of childhood and demands of adulthood, between obtaining independence and being dependent, and between the hopes and risks that come with future aspirations (Comaroff and Comaroff 2005: 21). This adds a specific life phase dimension to the intersection of class, ethnicity, race, gender, and religion that my research unpacked and elaborated on.

Two participants even introduced me to members of their family and closest communities. D, the only female and Muslim convert among my participants invited me to her graduation and introduced me to her family members. Meanwhile, J, who was the only participant that identified as a Muslim Sufi, introduced me to members of his Sufi community. My interactions with people from their environment helped shed light on how I positioned myself and was positioned by my research participants during the course of our interactions.

These interactions were very much gendered experiences. My first interview with D took place on a bright summer day at a park in Tilburg, a city in the south of the Netherlands. Sitting on the grass we spent over an hour talking about her experiences wearing a *hijab* and deciding after a few months to take it off, about the bullying she experienced by two popular girl groups in secondary school, her decisions to marry her boyfriend when the two converted into Islam, about her parents, and about her future ambitions since at the time she just enrolled to continue studying art. When I described our conversations to my supervisor, I told him, 'It just felt like *girl-talk*'. Our engagement felt natural and intimate to me, just like conversations I would have with my female friends.

In contrast, with my male participants I felt the need to make a more conscious effort to ensure that our interactions were also friendly and relaxed. Despite my efforts, I often felt there was a sense of caution at the back of my mind that influenced what and how I said certain things. Based also on my own experiences growing up among Muslim communities, I was cautious that interactions between people of the opposite sex could be a sensitive issue that young people approach differently depending on their perceptions of social interaction within 'legitimate Islamic framework[s]' (Amir-Moazami 2010: 197–8). Knowing very well that these so-called 'legitimate Islamic frameworks' are highly influenced by the society in which we grew up, my first few interactions with my participants, all of which were unmarried, young men, involved a lot of tip-toeing around subjects to test different limits and see what they were comfortable with.

Despite all of us being Muslims, our comfort levels around the opposite sex varied. This meant that conversations on family, relationships, sex, gender roles, or visits to family houses and mosques were at times limited. During a visit to his local mosque, one participant did not feel comfortable to enter the mosque together. He reasoned that it would be pointless since we would have to enter through the segregated male and female areas. I did not insist and we agreed to continue our conversation on a bench at a park near the mosque.

As our interactions increased, I gained a better sense of what they would be willing to discuss, and judging from the mood of the moment, I became more comfortable asking questions that were more personal. When I entered conversations about dating and relationships with my male participants, I often started with a disclaimer such as, 'Feel free to tell me if you are uncomfortable in answering any of my questions.' I did not do this with D. In doing so, I realised that I was not only anticipating my male participants' discomfort, I was actually acting upon my own. I've never found this disclaimer to be necessary since none of my participants shied away from the topic. Looking back, perhaps I was the one who felt the need of the disclaimer to reposition myself as the researcher and emphasise that I am asking for the sake of my research.

Deconstructing the Singular Narrative of Muslim Masculinities

I first met J on 17 September 2015. He was introduced to me through R who I had approached via email. R invited J to come along and participate in our first meeting. All three male participants who I approached directly to take part in my research, brought along a male friend during our first meetings, all of whom, with the exception of one, also became participants.

Prior to our meeting, I had talked to J on the phone to explain briefly about my research. At first J hesitated to participate, 'I've never really felt a strong connection with the Netherlands,' he said. Elaborating on this sentiment, J explained that when he was about 12 years old all of his friends had started to idolise celebrities they saw on television. During the same time, his older brother, who was 18 years old, told him, 'The coolest person is the one who can sacrifice his pleasures for his cause and no one is a better example of this than Prophet Muhammad.' His brother's statement left a big impression on him. J spent most of his teenage years reading about the life of Prophet Muhammad and could not relate to the interests of most of his peers.

This memory contributed to how he positioned himself within Dutch society. When asked to draw his map, unlike my other participants, J did not stick to one town in the Netherlands. Instead, he drew a map of the Netherlands and West Germany, highlighting two specific locations: the Imam's house in The Hague, the Dutch city where he was raised and attends weekly gatherings, and the Sufi centre in Kall, Germany, where he attends monthly retreats.

For J, emulating Prophet Muhammad was an essential part of his religious beliefs. This informed how he dressed during his weekly gatherings and monthly retreats. Following the Sufi traditions of clothing for men, he explained, made him feel 'ornamented' and 'closer to him [Prophet Muhammad]'. J also said that to emulate Prophet Muhammad also meant to be aware of one's daily etiquette and mannerism. He gave the example of the simple act of entering an elevator, when one should invite others to enter first and greet them with a smile. During our discussions, these aspirations to emulate a figure he held as holy were often expressed in contrast to how he believed society perceived him, a Muslim man of colour.

My first meeting with J and R, who was a male participant of Indonesian-Dutch decent, happened at a *halal* Thai restaurant across from the *Hollands Spoor* train station in The Hague. J had chosen the location and seemed to be quite familiar with the location. After ordering a couple of fried appetisers to share along with bubble tea, we started to talk about my research, their interest in participating, and different experiences growing up in The Netherlands.

During the course of our conversation, we discussed experiences of bullying at school. According to R, when he was in primary school, he experienced a lot of bullying and teasing due to his brown skin (compare with Horton, this volume). The bullying he experienced was often directed at his sexuality; questioning his sexual orientation. R, who gave me the impression of someone who is soft-spoken, quick to laughter, thoughtful, and kind, reasoned that the bullying was partially due to his inability to stand up for himself.

In response to this story, J said he never experienced bullying at school. He said jokingly, 'Other kids probably thought I was a gangster'. He then asked whether I would include this statement in my research, emphasising that he was just joking and did not want people to actually think he was a gangster. I joked back, saying if I did include it I will be sure to add this into the context.

A few weeks later, during another conversation with J, I was sitting on rugs in an oriental-styled restaurant at the Sufi Centre in Kall, Germany. With us was another of J's friend, who was of Pakistani descent. The three of us were sharing a piece of cake in celebration of three wedding rituals that the *Syeikh* had officiated earlier that night. J's friend who was born and raised in Rotterdam, had identified himself as a 'Rotterdammer'. Asked what differentiated a Rotterdammer from other Dutch people, he had answered, 'We are more honest, our language is rougher, and we work harder than everyone else.'

As the three of us were sitting enjoying our cake the topic of J's friend being a 'Rotterdammer' came up again. J responded by saying, 'I always say I come from Scheveningen. If you say you come from The Hague and you are coloured, people automatically assume you come from neighbourhoods where a lot of criminality occurs.' According to J, these assumptions stem from social stigmas that associate race, class, and criminality.

While these interactions were mainly part of casual conversations, they shed light on 'aspects of masculinities which men draw upon in particular contexts to construct shifting ideals and masculine practices' (De Neve 2004: 66). R and J spoke to different masculine identities. These were formed through interactions with their peers, most of whom they identified as being white Dutch students, and in relation to particular locations or places that derive their meaning, in part from, class and racial structures. J's friend embraced the dominant gender identity rooted in the stereotypical rough, honest, white hardworking man from Rotterdam. J on the other hand resisted the gender identity associated with men of colour living in The Hague by associating himself with the specific district where he lives, which does not share the same gender, racial, and class imageries.

The masculine identities assigned to them speak to the diverse gender experiences that men of colour face, particularly within predominantly white-Western societies. The bullying that R experienced in many ways echoes stereotypes of the asexual and passive Asian man that dominates Western literature (Ho 2010: 152). Meanwhile, J's views on how he can be perceived as a 'gangster' or 'criminal' speaks to elite discourses that often stigmatise young men of colour coming from particular neighbourhoods as a social problem.

During my research, one participant told me about a scandal that the national *Trouw* newspaper faced after publishing false reports about the Schilderswijk district in The Hague. An article published on 18 May 2013, titled 'If Your District Turns into a Small Caliphate',[2] claimed that Schilderswijk was a '*Sharia* Triangle' dominated by orthodox Muslims that harassed people on the street for not dressing or acting according to *Sharia* law (DutchNews.nl 19 May 2013).

In these reports, a lot of emphasis was given to describe harassment women faced if they did not dress in accordance to *Sharia* law within Schilderswijk. Even though these claims were later found to be fabricated and the newspaper withdrew the article along with others written by the journalist responsible, they successfully reproduced popular imageries of the Muslim man. According to these images, which can be traced to popular Western discourse on the Muslim Orient in the nineteenth century (Hoodfar 1993: 7–8), the manifestation of Muslim masculinity lies in the oppression of women.

Such gender imagery reproduces the monolithic hegemonic masculinity of the domineering Muslim man, which in turn fails to capture the nuanced masculine identities that my participants adopted and expressed in slight contrast to one another. Moreover, the singular narrative of Muslim masculinity assumes that Muslim men's gender identity is solely constructed on the basis of their faith. While religion is undeniably an important influence in one's gender construct, it cannot be put in a vacuum separated from other aspects of identity such as class, race, ethnicity, place, and life phase.

Neither R, J, nor J's friend referred to their religion when sharing stories that reveal parts of their gender identities. Rather, J's desire to emulate Prophet Muhammad was described in mannerisms that contrasted with the dominant, often singular, depiction of the Muslim man within Western imagery. By reflecting on my research as a gendered experience, I became more sensitive of the different masculine identities that my participants were expressing through personal narratives that were important to the construction of their identities. These narratives are also essential for deconstructing the singular masculine identity that is often associated with young Dutch Muslim men of migrant descent.

'FRIEND OR GIRLFRIEND?' EMBEDDING THE RESEARCHER IN THE FIELD

I was standing outside an apartment building in Schilderswijk, The Hague, unsure what to do. J had invited me to celebrate *Eid al-Adha* at his *Imam*'s house. He had identified this location as an essential part of growing up in The Hague because this is where he attended weekly meetings with his Sufi community. I had arrived before J and was instructed to go in and introduce myself as his friend.

I pressed the bell for the apartment number J had given me. 'Hello?' said a woman's voice through the speaker.

I hesitated. Part of me just wanted to go quietly away—what was I doing celebrating *Eid al-Adha* at a stranger's home? Instead, I answered, 'Hi, *Assalamu Alaikum*, I'm a friend of J's.'

'OK', she said and buzzed me in. I walked through the door, thinking how easy that was.

Once I got inside the building I wasn't sure what to do. What and who would I find behind that door? Should I just wait for J on the stairway? But wouldn't the woman who buzzed me in find it weird if I didn't show up? She was probably already wondering why it was taking me so long to climb up the stairs. I felt like I was crashing someone's party—someone I didn't know, whose party was actually a religious gathering on a holy day.

I took a deep breath and scolded myself, 'Dhika, you are here as a researcher. Pull yourself together and trust that your research participant knew what he was talking about when he told you to go in without him.'

So, I did.

I knocked on the door and a young woman with a wide smile welcomed me in. I wasn't sure what to say other than, 'Happy *Eid Mubarak*.' She returned my greetings and embraced me in a warm hug.

She invited me to come in and take a seat. 'I don't speak Dutch,' I said rather awkwardly. 'That's not a problem, we all speak English here!' she replied and introduced me to her mother, who turned out to be the *Imam*'s wife and hostess of the house.

The older lady also greeted me with an embrace. The daughter told her I was a friend of J's, to which the mother responded with a smile on her face and a twinkle in her eye, 'Friend or girlfriend?'

I was taken aback by this question. 'Just friends,' I said as I forced myself to smile back. The personal nature of the question asked by a woman I just met, caught me off guard. I explained I was an Indonesian student doing research in The Hague and J had invited me to come and celebrate *Eid al-Adha* with them. In answering so, I was subconsciously downplaying my identity as a woman, emphasising instead my identity as a foreign student whose gender was not relevant to the invitation extended to me by J, a male research participant.

At this point of my research I had become increasingly sensitive towards how the social interactions I engaged in during the course of my research were influenced by perceptions and norms related to gender, age, and Muslim identities. I also became increasingly aware of how I consciously and/or subconsciously used these perceptions and norms to manoeuver my way through the social interactions that come with doing research, and in doing so possibly contributed to the reproduction of these perceptions and norms.

A few days after *Eid al-Adha*, I confided in my supervisor and told him how my host's question brought mixed feelings. On one hand, I was taken aback. I was not used to having strangers ask me questions I felt were private. However, on the other hand, the frankness of the question brought some relief. The question allowed me the opportunity to clarify the nature of my relationship with J. I realised later that my hesitation when entering the building was partially influenced by my own self-consciousness on how members of J's Sufi community might perceive our relationship. The possibility that they might think we were more than friends did not sit comfortably with me. It made me feel vulnerable, as though I had no control over how they viewed me and my presence.

Similar experiences of vulnerability occurred through other forms during the course of my research. During the earlier stages of designing my research, I told a *Whatsapp* group that consists of my closest friends in Indonesia about my interests and plans. One male friend jokingly said, 'That is brilliant, Dhika! You found the perfect way to meet guys!' I took a mental note of both the sexist nature of the comment and the internal jokes that it was referring to, then let it pass.

In the middle of my research, I had visited R in his caravan, which was a part of the map that he had drawn for me. After our discussion, R took me to the nearest bus stop on his bicycle. I noticed a woman sitting at the bus stop across the street staring at us. I wondered whether she found it strange seeing a woman wearing a veil laughing on the back of a man's bike at 10 pm in the outskirts of Amsterdam. Did she recognise that I was a Muslim and categorised us as acting 'non-conservatively'? Did our image present a challenge towards the dominant narratives of young Muslims in the West?

Perhaps the lady was in fact thinking of something completely unrelated, not making any assumptions about us. But equally possible, perhaps she was and the answer to both questions could be 'yes'. Her stare made me feel very self-conscious and I wrote about this encounter in my research paper. My older sister, after proofreading an early draft of my paper, took a particular interest in this episode and could not help but ask, 'So, did anything happen that night?'

From the beginning, I understood that my own identity as a young, single, female, Muslim, Indonesian researcher would influence how I would do, analyse, and write about my research. Using an ethnographic research orientation, I did not believe that a researcher is immune from or innocent in propagating her paradigmatic presuppositions that construct her version of reality (Hammersley and Atkinson 2007: 11–12). Rather than instructing researchers to distance themselves from their subjectivities, ethnography requires researchers to acknowledge, reflect on, and inform readers about their positionalities vis-à-vis their research participants, the issues at stake, and knowledge production at large.

However, it was not until after my research was completed and I reflected more deeply on the overall process as a gendered experience, was I able to understand what these comments represented. Statements and gestures made by myself, my participants, and people around us, such as those described above, were windows into how identity is co-constituted through the multifaceted meanings of gender (Cupples 2002: 383). A researcher is embedded in the field, '… we are sexualized subjects, we might be viewed as wives, mothers, desirable foreign women, potential sexual partners and these views impinge on the research process in ways that cannot always be predicted' (Ibid.). Despite the strong influence that feminist literature had on my research, I had found it very difficult to reflect on gender. To do so not only required me to think through my participants' masculine identities but also required me to reflect honestly about my own sexuality and feminine identity.

Travelling and Transforming Identities

On 3 October 2015, I was on a train from Cologne to Kall, Germany. The trip took a bit over an hour and I was feeling quite nervous. J had invited me to attend a religious retreat at a Sufi centre in Kall, which he has been attending regularly since he was 14 years old. It had been a day full of train rides for me. Having taken a morning train with three friends from The Hague to Cologne, I then took the 17.21 train from Cologne to Kall. My friends were going to spend the weekend in Cologne while I spend a night 'doing research' in Kall. I would return to them early the next morning and enjoy the rest of the weekend in Cologne. This arrangement seemed to conveniently mix business with pleasure, but was really organised to create a support system for myself who was feeling nervous about the trip.

The opportunity to visit the Sufi centre seemed important for me to understand how J perceived home and positioned himself within the different localities on his map. However, when J first invited me to join him to go on a road trip to Kall with two of his friends, I hesitated. At the time, I had only met J once. I had written an email to my supervisor about this invitation:

> ... I want to make sure I make a wise decision safety-wise. I don't know whether it would be wise to go on a road trip with three guys, one of which I've only met once. J seemed like a genuinely nice guy who knows two of my [other] research participants quite well. They all have given me very positive impressions in terms of behaviour and manners.
>
> So I guess I wanted to run this by you before I make a decision. Is there a risk and is it worth taking? If I were to make this decision in an Indonesian context I would have more confidence in doing so. I guess, Netherlands and Germany being countries where I hardly have any ties and roots, I'm finding it difficult to calculate and manage risks.

In the end, I decided to join the retreat but travelled to Kall by myself with three close friends waiting in Cologne, just in case. Had I known J as well as I do now, these concerns and precautions would have been completely unnecessary.

Reflecting on my decisions, I realise how much my own identity, as a woman and an Indonesian far away from the familiarities of her own home, colour how I also perceive others. My own doubts were mainly aroused by the uneasiness I felt that followed the image of travelling in a car with three men that I did not know well, if not at all. The confinement of the space, the inability to leave at any given moment, and the foreign roads that we would be travelling through all contributed to my fears. This uneasiness was validated by people I consulted, such as my supervisor and my female friends who agreed to join and wait for me in Cologne. Since they never met J, their advices for caution were likely informed by their own gender ideas.

Researchers often reflect on their position vis-à-vis their research participants in order to establish a 'field identity' to engage with how they gather and analyse evidence (Cousin 2010: 11). Similarities between the researcher and participants' identities are often seen as a basis for researchers to build rapport with their participants—indeed an assumption that I also made when designing and conducting my own research. However, we often forget that rapport—or perhaps more specifically trust—is something that needs to be built both ways. Researchers don't start already trusting participants completely. After all, there is a degree of doubt that is healthy when doing research. What perhaps requires more reflection is our own subjectivities that inform these doubts.

While I felt that I could relate with J and my research participants in many ways—we were both raised and continue to identify ourselves as Muslims, we were going through a similar life phase as students and young adults who are living relatively independent lives from our parents, we have dealt with experiences living as part of a minority group within a Western society, and were struggling with the stereotypes associated with Islam and Muslims post-9/11—there were also differences that coloured my perceptions.

One difference between J and I that coloured our Muslim identities was that I was raised in a conventional Sunni tradition while J was a Sufi. As I watched landscapes of German towns and countryside pass by my window, I recalled how little I knew about Sufism. Growing up, my engagement with Sufism was limited to poetry and fiction exported from the Arab world. I didn't realise until later in my adult life that Sufism was a dimension within Islam.

My first exposure to the *Dhikr*[3] rituals within Sufi traditions was when I accepted J's invitation to celebrate *Eid al-Adha* at his *Imam*'s house. The *Dhikr* ritual I experienced that day was energetic, a combination of movements and recitations that were articulated louder and faster during the length of the ritual, all in praise of *Allah*. While I was familiar with some of the recitations and could follow most of the preceding, it was still very different from the quiet, more personal *Dhikr* custom that I was raised into. Due to my limited exposure to Sufism, I was not entirely sure what I would find in Kall and whether it would help provide insight for my research. Moreover, I was not entirely sure whether I was on that train for the purpose of deepening my understanding as a researcher or rather to satisfy my personal curiosity as a Muslim—perhaps the two were one and the same.

When I finally arrived in Kall, I was greeted by its crisp autumn air and a mountain view that took my breath away after months of living in the Netherlands' flat landscape. After waiting for five minutes, I saw J walking towards me in a long loose tunic and a *taqiyah* (cap). He hadn't yet put on the coned turban he had on during the *Eid al-Adha* celebrations. Even without it his attire attracted attention and the group of young people who exited the station as he came in could not help but look his way.

We greeted each other with a *Salam*. J explained that it would have been easier to pick me up by car but he wanted to show me the walking route to The Centre since I would be returning to the station on my own the next morning. We took a small dirt path that followed a stream through the woods and came out in corn fields. The combination of clean air, blue skies, green landscape, and mountain view was astounding. I could understand why this location was selected to set up one of the main Sufi centres in Europe.

As we were walking towards The Centre, J greeted a tall, bearded young man who was putting on his turban with the help of his reflections on his car that was parked outside The Centre. Like J, this young man had also driven all the way from the Netherlands dressed in long loose tunic. I smiled at the contrast between his traditional attire and his black sneakers and red car. I realised this contrast was visible all around me: the green building that was The Centre with the traditional style of the German houses around it, the Muslim couple walking by in their long loose tunics and veils with the white German couple in their casual wear walking their dog. The contrasts made me feel self-conscious, but I felt more at ease after the white German couple returned our greetings with a smile as we passed each other.

Writing about how women in Wanigela, Papua New Guinea, manoeuvre the ever-present power constellations presented by the practices of sorcery, Christianity, and Western medicine, Underhill-Sem (2005: 28) wrote, 'In this way women's bodies are simultaneously constituted by the places they move within and through, as well as by the discourses about these places.' The quote feels apt to describe how I felt that moment as our male and female bodies travelled in the different attires we wore, bringing with us the identities that constitute who we are, yet at the same time allowing ourselves the quietly assigned identities that travelled through the gazes of others.

When we arrived at The Centre, we entered through its side gate, greeted by groups of little children running around, chasing each other in a chaotic game of tag. The Centre was quite large. We had entered the Centre's backyard that was designed to be an outdoor playground with slides, swings, and seesaws. On our left was the entrance to the main building where J said was where prayers, *Dhikr*, and dinner will be held. This was also the location of the oriental-styled restaurant that became the setting of my conversation with J and his friend. J said the restaurant was the place where people usually sit, have tea, and hang out until morning. An outdoor hallway connected the main building to the Centre's kitchen, two large bedrooms with bunkbeds for men and another for women, each with its own public showers and *wudhu* area. J said there was another large bedroom for children on the second floor of the main building and several small rooms for families that had to be booked in advance.

Until now, I find myself struggling to adequately write and capture the experiences that night in the Sufi centre. To write about the experience coldly, sticking solely to the descriptive facts, would fail to describe the mixture of awe and uncertainty that I felt as I tried to manoeuvre my way through the night. Meanwhile, to write about it with the dramatic colours I feel the experience deserves—a story of bearded men, coned turbans, women dressed in varying colours and styles, some veiled while others were not, of prayers and a midnight *Dhikr* full of energy and song and movement, and the silhouette of a man behind a curtain moving in continuous circles—all of these memories make me question my own positionality and gaze. In writing about my experiences at The Centre, would I be guilty of contributing to the exoticism of the Orient?

As Behar (1996: 3) wrote about the struggles of an ethnographer when doing and writing about her fieldwork, 'Loss, mourning, the longing for memory, the desire to enter into the world around you and having no idea how to do it, the fear of observing too coldly or too distractedly or too raggedly, the rage of cowardice, the insight that is always arriving late… are the stopping places along the way.' I felt a strong desire to fit in, but at the same time took refuge in the privileges of the external observer who could quietly go back in a corner and just watch.

The dualism of my position kept coming back to me through memories of that night. Left to my own devices after dinner and before the *Isha* (night-time) prayer, I stood idly looking at brochures and flyers displayed in the hallways. A young man of Pakistani descent, in jeans and a grey sweatshirt, came up to me and introduced himself as J's friend. He then offered me a tour around the complex. I gladly accepted.

While we walked around the complex I learned that he has been going to The Centre with his family since he was a teenager. We chatted about The Centre, his school, and his proud Rotterdammer identity. I was trying to figure out from the glances we received from people passing by, whether it was appropriate for two people of the opposite sex to walk around privately in this religious setting. He seemed relaxed and I decided to follow his lead. In between our chatting, there was the very subtle exchange of smiles and glances that made me wonder but not conclude. I was never one to successfully recognise subtle flirting. Was his comment about me playing with the rose chain around my neck meant to signify something? I could not tell.

At the end of the tour, we stood talking outside the main building near the playground. Children were still running around, enjoying what was perhaps a rare opportunity to play outdoors after dark. One little girl, about nine years old with long dark hair approached J's friend and the two shared a warm embrace. 'She's my little sister!' he told me proudly. I made a rather awkward comment about the age difference between the two:

'How old are you?' he asked.

'I'm 29,' I replied.

'But that's too old!' he claimed with an obvious look of shock on his face.

I smile at this memory every time I think of it. Until now I do not know for certain what I was too old for, although admittedly I think I could make a guess. We laughed at his comment and continued to chat for some time until we heard the *Adzan* or call for *Isha* prayer. We later continued talking together with J and some cake in the comfort of the oriental-style restaurant.

An ethnographer's life phase often influences the way she engages the environment where she does fieldwork. Gille (2012: 120) points out how young ethnographers often benefit from their youth, since they can easily take up the role of someone that is learning from the people around them. In my case, my role as a student allowed me a shared generational identity with my participants. This helped establish the friendly relationships that I cultivated with them. However, once normative ages were identified, this shared generational identity could also be challenged.

Afterwards, I told my friends in Cologne about this encounter. Rather than being strange, it reminded me of experiences as a young teenager hanging out in groups of friends and flirting with boys in the neighbourhood mosque during Ramadhan, the holy month of fasting in Islam. During Ramadhan, every night Muslims pray *Terawih* together in the Mosque after the *Isha* prayer and listen to sermons delivered by local *Imams*. While Ramadhan is a month of restraint and piousness, as teenagers, my friends and I saw it as a rare opportunity to be allowed to hang out until late at night. While sermons were delivered, we would sit, talk, and laugh outside in the mosque's courtyard. While elders often frowned at the noise we made, no one ever stopped us from sitting together in groups of boys and girls, perhaps because of the religious rituals that validated our presence.

In many ways, my experiences in The Centre were new to me. I was clearly an outsider to the community. However, at the same time I felt a sense of comfort and familiarity in the religious settings and some prayer citations and rituals practiced that night. The oxymoron of being a participatory observer in ethnography means one is continuously trying to balance between participating with a sense of familiarity while still observing from a certain distance.

In doing research about young *allochtoon* Dutch Muslims, I too was bringing along my own ideas, perspectives, experiences, instincts, and thoughts as one who was brought up to be an educated, Indonesian Muslim woman. As identities travel, they also simultaneously transform and consolidate. Doing research honestly and vulnerably means that one cannot exclude herself from the process of doing and writing about her research. One's identity is always present through the interactions, responses, and relationships that she develops with the other active participants in her research.

CONCLUSION

This chapter took me over two months to write. During this time, I have developed a romantic relationship with a Muslim man, one who was not involved in my research. After an argument, I was once told by my partner: 'What is so hard for me is that you often react like I'm trying to overpower you. I'm not.' This comment left me with a lot to reflect on in relation to my own constructions of gender relations. On one hand, our actions may lead to the overpowering of the other without us intending to or being aware of doing so. On the other hand, I could also be guilty of projecting the singular narrative of Muslim masculinity onto my partner, which led me to react with a need to resist rather than understand.

It was through this experience that I realised the need to deconstruct singular narratives of masculinities by being more sensitive to the nuanced experiences that inform one's gender identity. It was also through this experience that I realised how expressions of masculinity cannot be detached from the person to whom these expressions are directed.

This chapter has tried to address these two points by looking back and reflecting on research that I did with young *allochtoon* Dutch Muslims, most of whom were Muslim men. By analysing three encounters with one of my research participants, J, I have shown how masculine identities are not homogenous. Instead, they are nuanced, situated, and are given meaning through their association with one's class, race, religion, ethnicity, place, and life phase.

I have gone further to show how research is inherently a gendered experience where the researcher is embedded in the environment where she is doing 'fieldwork'. One cannot completely escape the gender roles that are assigned to her while doing research. Therefore I found it necessary and insightful to reflect on how comments and gestures that were expressed by myself, my participants, and our environment were important windows to understand how gender identities are expressed and negotiated in relation to each other.

Finally, through these collections of my personal narratives I have shown how identities travel, transform, and consolidate in the process of doing and writing research. Even though I was doing research in the Netherlands, I was always informed by experiences, insights, and perceptions constituted through my own experiences growing up as an Indonesian Muslim woman. By reflecting honestly, I have attempted to be transparent on how my identity influenced the assumptions and decisions I made throughout my research.

As the researcher travels, the knowledge she produces is coloured by the footprints of her journeys. As a researcher, by developing a stronger awareness of self, we become more informed in the different ways we perceive and are being perceived by our participants and their environments.

Notes

1. In the Netherlands, integration is often discussed in relation to the two main categories used in the national census, *Autochtoon* (citizens of Dutch birth and ancestry) and *Allochtoon* (citizens of non-Dutch birth and ancestry – including mixed ancestry).
2. Personal translation of Dutch original '*Als je wijk verandert in een "klein kalifaat"*' (*Trouw* Newspaper. 29 December 2014).
3. *Dhikr* is the recitation of short phrases, prayers, or praises to Allah (God) that can be done individually or collectively, loudly or quietly, depending on one's traditions.

References

Abbott, D. (2007). Doing incorrect research: The importance of the subjective and the personal in researching poverty. In A. Thomas & G. Mohan (Eds.), *Research skills for policy and development: How to find out fast* (pp. 208–228). London: Sage.

Amir-Moazami, S. (2010). Avoiding "youthfulness"?: Young Muslims negotiating gender and citizenship in France and Germany. In L. A. Herrera & A. Bayat (Eds.), *Being young and Muslim: New cultural politics in the global south and north* (pp. 189–205). Oxford [etc.]: Oxford University Press.

Behar, R. (1996). *The vulnerable observer: Anthropology that breaks your heart.* Boston: Beacon Press.

Comaroff, J., & Comaroff, J. (2005). Reflections on youth, from the past to the postcolony in Africa. In A. Honwana & F. De Boeck (Eds.), *Makers & breakers: Children and youth in postcolonial Africa* (pp. 19–30). Trenton: Africa Worlds Press.

Cousin, G. (2010). Positioning positionality: The reflexive turn. In M. Savin-Baden & C. H. Major (Eds.), *New approaches to qualitative research: Wisdom and uncertainty* (pp. 9–18). London/New York: Routledge Taylor & Francis Group.

Cupples, J. (2002). The field as a landscape of desire: Sex and sexuality in geographic fieldwork. *Area, 34*(4), 382–390.

De Neve, Geert. (2004). The workplace and the neighborhood: Locating masculinities in the south Indian textile industry. In R. Chopra, C. Osella, & F. Osella (Eds.), *South Asian masculinities. Context of change, sites of continuity* (pp. 60–95). Delhi: Women Unlimited & Kali for Women.

DutchNews.nl. (2013, May 19). Police, locals deny claim part of the Hague is a "sharia triangle". http://www.dutchnews.nl/news/archives/2013/05/police_lo-cals_deny_claim_part/. Accessed 28 Oct 2015.

Ellis, C. (1999). Heartfelt autoethnography. *Qualitative Health Research, 9*(6), 669–683.

Ellis, C. (2004). *The ethnographic I: A methodological novel about autoethnography.* Oxford: AltaMira Press.

Gille, Z. (2012). Global ethnography 2.0: From methodological nationalism to methodological materialism. In A. Amelino, D. D. Nergiz, T. Faist, & N. Glick-Schiller (Eds.), *Beyond methodological nationalism: Research methodologies for cross-border studies* (pp. 91–110). London/New York: Routledge.

Hammersley, M., & Atkinson, P. (2007). *Ethnography: Principles in Practice / Martyn Hammersley and Paul Atkinson* (3 ed.). London [etc.]: Routledge.

Ho, W. (2010). Seeding Asian masculinities in the US landscape: Representations of men's lives in Asian American literature. In R. Emig & A. Rowland (Eds.), *Performing masculinity* (pp. 149–165). London: Palgrave Macmillan.

Hoodfar, H. (1993). The veil in their minds and on our heads: The persistence of colonial images of muslim women. *RDR/DFR, 22*(3/4), 5–18.

Sadjad, M. S. (2016). An autoethnographic study on Dutch society: Narratives of being and belonging from the perspectives of young allochtoon Dutch-Muslims. ISS working paper series/general series no. 613. The Hague: International Institute of Social Studies of Erasmus University (ISS).

Scott, J. (2007). *The politics of the veil.* Princeton: Princeton University Press.

Thelen, T., Vetters, L., & Von Benda-Beckmann, K. (2014). Introduction to stategraphy: Toward a relational anthropology of the state. *Social Analysis, 58*(3), 1–19.

Trouw Newspaper. (Last updated 2014, December 29). Wat Gebeurt Er Met De Artikelen Van Perdiep Ramesar? (a webpage of Trouw Newspaper). http://www.trouw.nl/tr/nl/5133/Media-technologie/article/detail/3819660/2014/12/29/Wat-gebeurt-er-met-de-artikelen-van-Perdiep-Ramesar.dhtml. Accessed 26 Oct 2015.

Underhill-Sem, Y. (2005). Bodies in places, places in bodies. In W. Harcourt & A. Escobar (Eds.), *Women and the politics of place* (pp. 20–31). Bloomfield: Kumarian Press.

PART III

Negotiating Development

Subjects of Development: Teachers, Parents, and Youth Negotiating Education in Rural North India

Karuna Morarji

INTRODUCTION

On a chilly winter morning, I visited the principal of Kempty government inter-college (high school) in his office on the school premises.[1] He was sitting behind a desk in his office, with a small electric heater by his side for warmth. I was immediately offered a seat, and an attendant was called upon to bring tea. After steaming cups of tea were drunk, we chatted about the fragile future prospects of his students in this rural valley in the foothills of the Indian Himalaya. The principal thus reflected on the value of education for his students:

> You can do any job… if you are doing anything, education is a must. For every occupation….Some of the girls are *very* intelligent…But they are feeling the feedback of their house…it is not very good. They are feeling we

This chapter is based largely on an article under the same title that appeared in the *European Journal of Development Research* (2014) Vol. 26(2): 175–189.

K. Morarji (✉)
Centre for Holistic Learning, Hulekal Village, 581336 Taluka Sirsi, Karnataka, India

© The Author(s) 2016
R. Huijsmans (ed.), *Generationing Development*,
DOI 10.1057/978-1-137-55623-3_10

can't do anything else. We will only do tenth and twelfth [grade] and go
and do the farming or something, we can't do anything else. And we are
encouraging them but they are totally dependent on their parents. I am also
trying to motivate them, but they are unable to understand...

The futures of the students, of all students, are not bright... We are trying
to create awareness in the students, but only a few students are following...
The futures of those children is good. But the percentage is very low, at the
most 5%. Some of these students have been selected in jobs, like the air force,
in engineering, and are also doing postgraduation. But the percentage is very
low. Those who are following are working in the forward sectors.

Here, the principal of a rural inter-college sums up the rationale of education as a means to development: that school-based education is essential
for becoming a productive citizen and complete human being; that the
role of teachers and administrators is to 'motivate' and 'create awareness'
among rural students and parents who lack understanding of the benefits
of education; that girls are intelligent and hardworking but constrained
by cultural and familial gender roles; that a future in farming is a sign of
educational failure, and, for five percent of his students, educational success equals securing jobs in 'forward sectors'.

This chapter focuses on negotiations of school education in a mountainous rural valley in north India. The first section demonstrates how
government school teachers articulate their perceived mandate to improve
and develop their wards, thereby reinscribing notions of rural young people and their communities as 'backward' and, as the inter-college principal stressed, largely destined to failure. I examine how teachers thus
negotiate contradictions between the inclusionary mandate of education-
for-development, and boundary-making practices reproducing teachers'
distinction and, for rural students and their communities, 'futures that are
not bright'.

The second and third sections look at how parents and youth in turn
experience and negotiate education-as-development. In this context, what
one young man described as *'naukri ka* craze', the craze for employment—and, conversely, a strong desire for a future without (or at least
with less) agricultural and manual work—drives people's sense of the value
of education as a means of social mobility. A simultaneous expectation
from education is that it should lead to moral improvement of children
and youth. Yet, given the distance between 'schooled ideals' (Balagopalan
2005) and everyday lives in mountain villages, dominant aspirations
around education are often ambiguously experienced. Teachers and par-

ents thus commonly describe children and educated youth as a 'problem' based on their inability to gain desirable employment. Village elders also expressed disappointment with educated youth's individualism and lack of responsibility. Young women and men varyingly negotiate the perceived compromises and failures of education-as-development, as gendered implications for their current and future lives. Thus, I show how narratives about educated youth reflect generational and gendered tensions around both economic and moral aspects of social reproduction.

I argue that a dominant rationale of education-as-development is put into practice through disciplinary and governmental forms of power in ways that re-entrench existing inequalities and boundaries. But my ethnographic research also highlights the limits of government (cf. Li 2007), chronicling how projects such as schooling and development work as contested practices with diverse outcomes (Da Costa 2008; Jeffrey et al. 2008; Morarji 2010). Thus, in the rural north Indian context of my research, parents, and youth negotiate competing notions of individual and social value and productivity, while teachers face contradictions between imperatives of inclusionary development and the maintenance of class- and place-based boundaries. These experiences are shaped by a dominant rationale, but are also produced *relationally* through local social networks (Jeffrey and McDowell 2004), rural conditions (Vasavi 2006), and negotiations of 'tradition' and 'modernity' (Jeffrey et al. 2008; Gold 2009; Lukose 2005). As elsewhere in north India, school education here is thus a highly 'contradictory resource' (Jeffrey et al. 2008: 210), and part of a broader cultural politics of development (cf. Moore 1999; Sivaramakrishnan and Agrawal 2003).[2] Hence, my attention to *subjects of development*—youth *and* adults—and the ways in which they actively experience and negotiate development interventions (cf. Baviskar 2004; Klenk 2010; Mosse 2005; Pigg 1992).

GOVERNMENT SCHOOL TEACHERS AND THE RATIONALE OF EDUCATION AS DEVELOPMENT

Upon hearing that my research had to do with education and development, a village government primary school teacher responded that Jaunpur—a block in Tehri Garhwal district, Uttarakhand—was a good choice as it has been 'one of the most backward areas'. As a hill region that was formerly a marginalized corner of India's largest and most populous state, Uttar Pradesh, this area in the foothills of the Western Himalaya was categorized as culturally and economically 'backward', exploited as a source of labor and raw materials, and bypassed by state development projects such as roads, irrigation, healthcare, and educational facilities.[3] It is largely a rural area, and the majority of households in small village settlements along the slopes of the valley have traditionally been involved in subsistence-oriented, rain-fed agriculture and animal husbandry as a source of income through sale of goats and milk. During the time of my research, most household economies were supplemented by both local and migration-based income-generating employment, primarily by young men.

Twenty years ago, there were few primary schools in the scattered villages of Jaunpur, teacher absenteeism was common, and children had to trek long distances to get to a school. Basic education was not a mass experience. However, the formation of the new hill state brought increased development funding and intervention in the region, including a significant expansion of government school facilities. During my research, the educational landscape in the Aglar valley was defined primarily by government schools, along with a few NGO and private schools. Several villages had primary schools, as well as middle schools within fair proximity, and all the government schools which I visited seemed to be operating with some degree of regularity. Each side of the valley had one government inter-college. The fact that school-based education, at least up to class five (approximately age ten) and increasingly class ten (age sixteen) or twelve (age eighteen) and even college (age eighteen to twenty-one), has become a part of daily life for communities in the Aglar valley in the last ten years, is perceived as a key indicator of increased 'development' of the region.

In this context, government school teachers and administrators posted in schools in Jaunpur see themselves as key agents of development. They are generally legitimated in this mandate based on their cultural capital and political status. Teachers hold much-coveted, stable, well-paid, and respected jobs, usually reside in and commute from urban areas, send their children to private schools, and generally inhabit middle-class lifestyles. As the largest cadre of government officials in the state, school staff are also influential local representatives of the state apparatus, performing multiple roles beyond their appointed schools. For example, in preparation for state-level elections, I found teachers busy distributing voter ID cards to villagers, and later monitoring elections. They also routinely conduct government duties such as administering household surveys, supervising pulse polio vaccination drives, delivering post, etc. Many have positions in village *panchayat* (local governance bodies), and oversee distribution of community development funds from the state government.

Government school teachers repeatedly articulated their mandate to improve rural children—'*bacchon ko aage badhaana hai*', we have to bring children forward—whom they see 'like *kachchii mitti* (raw clay), they can be shaped, and come to school to be shaped'.[4] Framed by the development imperative, teaching is thus a means of conveying institutionalized knowledge and skills, as well as inculcating capacities and conduct associated with a 'development subjectivity' (Gupta 2003: 71). Such notions of being 'developed' are based on an abstract ideal, but are also embodied in teachers, and distinguish them from the rural communities in which they work. Government teachers in rural schools therefore play a key role in producing and maintaining standards of being—implicitly through the habitus of an ideal middle class, as well as explicitly, by articulating a modernist rationale of education-as-development. This rationale invokes the 'problem' of 'backward' or irrelevant local knowledge and experience—or '...an image of a child in school as a child with no history only a future' (Balagopalan 2005: 86).

Teachers such as Sureshi, the headmistress of Bhatoli village government primary school, illustrate this sense of alterity and how it frames interventions in rural communities. Sureshi commutes daily to Bhatoli village from her home in Dehradun, the nearest city, about 45 km away and an arduous hour-and-a-half to two hour ride in a jeep-taxi or bus along a curvy mountain road. Sureshi was in her mid-30s, and when I visited the school along with Shobhan, my research assistant, I always found her similarly dressed in colorful ironed and starched cotton *salwaar-khameez suits* with tight *churidar* pants, and heeled sandals. She wore lipstick as well as jewelry, and her hair loose and cut in a shoulder-length layered style. Sureshi carried a cell phone, on which she received frequent calls during our interactions. She told us about her involvement in the teachers' union, as well as her position as the treasurer of the village panchayat, and stressed the difficulty she had experienced in working with the local community due to 'corruption and lack of interest'.

In the course of an interview with Sureshi, she repeatedly stressed the importance of 'comprehensive development' and development of 'character' and 'behavior' of students. Such concerns signal particular notions of desirable educated subjects. For example, Sureshi told me that many of her former students remember her fondly because she 'makes extra effort'. She went on: 'I met some ex-students in Delhi, they are big and married now. English was not taught then, and I thought English was very necessary for them for when they would go out, so I taught them "*123*", "*ABC*" and some things like that. Like now I teach them things like "*may I come in*".'

Here, Sureshi equates children's character development with the ability to present themselves as having some exposure to English and being able to exhibit polite behavior in English, and assumes these to be of use in a future 'when they go out' to places like Delhi.

Through her appearance, professional positions and emphasis on the importance of knowledge and ways of being for future lives outside of rural agrarian locales, teachers like Sureshi therefore sustain a particular 'type of culture of educated distinction' (Jeffrey et al. 2008: 65) based on being someone else, somewhere else. Thus, a model of education for future export is culturally produced, as: 'Place attachment and local knowledge are precisely what many rural educators struggle to subvert...and what is often called "broadening the horizons" of rural children and youth' (Corbett 2007: 10). While posited as a placeless, universal vision, it is in fact rooted in, and works to reproduce, the cultural and material values of bourgeois modernity. Behaviors, attitudes, and practices of teachers like Sureshi in and outside the school reflect how, in contemporary India, an urban middle-class represents itself as universal.[5] Teachers embody successful models of this vision of education-as-development in their middle-class lifestyles and values, their authority as guardians of seemingly unmarked, universalized forms of knowledge, as state representatives, and in their attainment of much-coveted stable employment. Teachers illustrate how commonsense visions of being and becoming are reproduced and naturalized through structural means—through their location in a political and cultural economy of development—but also how 'Notions of progress through education... *insinuates itself* into people's everyday actions, thoughts and modes of appreciation, for example through the medium of the formal, informal and hidden curriculum within schools...' (Jeffrey et al. 2008: 63).

In expressing middle-class visions of education and development, teachers are not simply reproducing the interests of their class; they are often faced with and negotiate multiple and seemingly contradictory goals (Li 2007). As the principal of the Kempty high school told me, 'A barrier is lying between the students and the teachers', and recognized this as a 'problem' as the maintenance of such 'barriers' works to counter the inclusionary mandates of education-as-development. Hence, as 'trustees' of development but also as subjects occupying particular class positions, teachers reinforce their own status through tropes of alterity and discipline in ways which limits their ability to affect 'development' in the region. Hence, Sureshi's interventions to teach her wards simple English phrases and mannerisms not covered by the syllabus suggest a recognition of the inadequacy of schooling as a passport to other, more developed worlds and lives for young people in Bhatoli and other mountain villages. Schooling is necessary, but given their positions and the kind of education they receive, it is insufficient to gain the cultural capital, or middle-class 'linguistic and aesthetic knowledge and respectability' (Fernandes 2006: 34).

One way in which teachers and administrators attempt to negotiate the contradictions of their mandate through schooling was to articulate a broadened field of intervention for improvement.[6] Teachers attending a training program told me that 'parents are the ones who need training'. And in a meeting with parents, the principal of the Kempty inter-college repeatedly stressed the need to create a more suitable *mahaul,* or atmosphere, in the home for students to study, and laid out detailed instructions for parents to enforce adequate sleep and study time, and limit TV watching and household work. The disciplinary regime of schooling ideally 'dominates family life around the clock' (Donner 2005: 129), indicating how modern schooling in India favors an upper class/caste habitus without manual work. The principal therefore suggested disciplinary practices that are predicated on values of a modern work ethic (cf. Willis 1977), such as time management, emphasis that the 'work' of students is to study, and distinctions between such 'work' and 'play'. Such disciplinary regimes are assumed not just to be necessary, but superior, as they reflect self-sacrifice and genuine care on the part of parents for their children toward an undeniably desirable end: the principal stressed that 'we want *our* kids to succeed'. Teachers thus negotiate the perceived limitations of the school as a site of development of rural youth by asserting that '... the generalized concepts and values inherent in the parent-child relationship are reproduced most successfully in middle-class households' (Donner 2005: 128).

Changing Generational and Community Relationships

In the rural mountain context of my research, families, households, and communities are *not* organized according to an urban, middle-class ideal. Yet the experience of schooling and the construction of young people as 'educated' have significantly impacted familial and generational relationships, particularly since many of the youth I spoke to are first- or second-generation school goers. These changing relationships counter reified notions of 'development', 'youth', as well as 'schooling'. They counter a singular definition of Jaunpuri households as 'backward'. By necessitating a perspective on youth as part of changing generational and community relationships, they also highlight the relational character of age-based categories (Cole and Durham 2007). And they suggest that schooling '...is a mode of becoming and belonging to particular places and times, within particular families and in relation to siblings and parents with dreams of shared or competing futures' (Da Costa 2008: 290). Hence, changes in familial and community relationships, and the negotiations that they entail, are a part of how people encounter education-as-development in their daily lives, but are not accounted for in a dominant rationale of educational success and failure.

Parents regularly articulated their relationships with educated youth in terms of a breakdown in communication and respect, and expressed intense disappointment, even bitterness and anger, with their behavior. One father of three school-going children from the village of Matela told me that 'Parents are disappointed. It is also so difficult to get jobs, there are millions of people with degrees—and even if a job is possible, it is necessary to have connections, money. There are very few parents who are satisfied, who feel like their expectations and dreams are fulfilled. They see their kids as a problem these days.' Narratives of failure and disappointment are therefore largely about the inability of youth, particularly young men, to secure expected employment and income, hence reflecting the gap between expectations and outcomes of education. But elders also routinely complain that educated youth resist contributing to household and farming work. Young educated women were described as 'wearing fancy clothes' and 'not wanting to dirty their hands with cow dung'. And educated young men were perceived as routinely shirking manual work, doing tasks irresponsibly and with a sense of shame. An illiterate male elder in the village of Matela felt that 'educated youth have no time for house work... If they don't get a job at least they should do house work with responsibility, but if they even have an inter education, they refuse—for example if they are to take out the animals, they will wander around all day.'[7]

This framing of educated youth as a 'generational problem' is about failure to contribute to household production, but also a broader moral failing of responsibility, participation, and relationships. Elders spoke of a lack of 'care' among educated youth, an unwillingness to listen and to participate appropriately in community events. Children and youth who attend school are seen as experiencing the world differently than elders; they have different reference points as to what it means to be a young person, how a young person should behave and appear. A local government primary school teacher in the village of Ghed described educated youth as '*VIP*-like' (a 'very important person'), reinforcing the notion that educated people become individualized as 'special'. He went on to explain what he meant by this: 'They don't want to listen to anyone, they look down on people, do everything on their own account…They have their own system of behavior, dress, hair style… They behave differently in weddings. And no matter how many times you say something, they don't respond'. Parents and community elders thus counter hegemonic notions of educated success, for example, by arguing that dress style and behaviors expressing distinction and individuality become means for educated youth to distance themselves from, and at times even disrespect, a local generational order.

Parents identify a link between youth's individualization and their desire for consumer goods, and a concurrent rejection of all things local. For example, I was told that people gather less to sing and dance in village squares during festivals because they have TVs and VCDs to watch in the comfort of their own homes. As a male village elder in Matela put it 'Now everyone wants good food, good clothes, good soap, good shoes… Educated kids don't like the food that we produce here, like *mandua ka aata* (millet flour). If we make (these) *roti* (breads) no one will eat them'. Another elderly man asked '…where will this [the things that they want] come from? They don't think about this. Twenty-four hours they want money…They put their hands in their back pant pockets and wander around, they just come home for food, and that too want special food'. Hence, parents' double disappointments with the inability of educated youth to gain employment or fulfill local economic and moral roles are concretized in these critical comments on youth's attention on fulfilling private desires for consumer goods.

As such, parents' disappointments express 'tensions between models of personhood based on care and inter-generational reciprocity, and liberal individualism' (Cole and Durham 2007: 20) promoted by development policies and projects such as schooling. For example, the collectivist ethic underlying a subsistence agrarian economy is being eroded by educated youth's changing relationships to manual work. Given the mountainous terrain in Jaunpur, agricultural work such as farming and animal husbandry involve strenuous manual labor, and have traditionally depended upon the entire joint family's—and in some tasks even community's—participation. While young people still contribute to household and farm work, they spend less time doing so—illustrated by a sharp drop in ownership of domestic animals which were traditionally grazed by children—and may do so haphazardly and reluctantly. Participation in agricultural work is a means of contributing to household reproduction, but it is also a way of sustaining inter-generational and community relationships (cf. Dyson 2014). Parents in Jaunpur therefore reproduce the abstract ideal that education should lead to jobs and to moral improvement, but their disappointments also reflect negotiated and relational meanings of educational value in the context of changing rural social reproduction.

Youth's Gendered Negotiations

Priya, an 18 year old from a more remote village in the valley but living with family in Kempty to complete her BA in English and to work as a teaching assistant in an NGO school, told me that 'here all girls I know, except a few who are from better off families, want to earn money'. Many young women I spoke to in Jaunpur dreamt of becoming teachers. Some were also investing time and money in tailoring classes, as running a tailor shop is a popular business for women in the region. Neeta, a 16-year-old girl from Kandikhal village studying in class ten, told me that while she dreams of becoming a teacher, 'there are lots of kinds of work in the world'. The growing awareness of, and interest in, employment among young women reflects how middle-class ideals of education for employment—represented by the school teacher and expressed through normative discourses of success and mobility—frame aspirations for these young women.

The imperative to earn income was linked to a desire to contribute to personal expenses (including marriage costs), as well as doing work other than farming. Educated girls and women stressed that they are not being educated in order to continue doing farming. One teenaged girl told me that 'we are even afraid of the word "farming"'. Girls and young women commonly complained about the hardships involved in farming and animal care in a mountainous environ, as they perform most of the routine work like cutting grass, collecting wood, and working in the fields. As one young woman put it, 'women get weak. This is the reason that educated girls want to do jobs. Or at least leave the village'. Another linked the desire for leisure to changing generational expectations: 'This is a difference between our parents and us, they can work hard, but we want some leisure. There is no end to work here.' Young women defined success as 'less work, equal income', citing the example of an 'officer' who puts in less effort but makes more money. In sharing her aspirations, one girl studying in class ten in Kempty inter-college put it bluntly: 'last chance *me kheti karenge*', farming is our last option. Young women therefore embrace ideals of formal employment and social mobility which valorize monetary income, urban lifestyles and leisure, and simultaneously cast farming and manual work as undesirable.

Yet as Meera's narrative will illustrate, young women varyingly experience and negotiate conflicts between the ideal of education for employment and local gendered scripts of social reproduction in a changing agrarian economy. When I met Meera, she was in her early 20s, and married with two young female children. Her husband was successfully employed in the police force outside of the region. She lived in her marital village and not with her husband at his place of employment because her labor was needed in the household, as they had lots of farm work. In her marital village, she described people as 'less educated', 'backward', with 'very few girls in school, and the birth of a boy is celebrated but not that of a girl'. Meera felt strongly that girls should be able to study as far as they want, and stressed that she herself chose not to study on after marriage (she had studied up to class ten) and that it was also not possible to study once she had children. She also anticipated that she would have to move to educate her daughters, maybe to Nainbagh, the closest town to her village, or elsewhere, as there was only a 'useless government school' in her marital village. 'I won't educate my daughters there.'

Meera clearly values education for her daughters (compare with Srinivasan, this volume), yet based on her own experiences, she also asked: 'What is the meaning of education if we cannot do jobs, if we have to work in the house? It is like being uneducated.' Her question about the value of education beyond employment indicates how gender mediates expectations and evaluations for youth, producing varied 'educated' subject positions (Chopra 2005; Da Costa 2008; Jeffery and Jeffery 1994; Jeffrey et al. 2008). I was repeatedly told by school administrators, teachers, and female students that girls take their studies more 'seriously' than boys and routinely perform better in school, despite having to do much more household work. Like the Kempty inter-college principal, young women told me that 'girls are unable to 'do something' with their studies': '...girls get married fast, they can't do what they dreamed of….then they have to listen to their in-laws, and it doesn't matter if they are educated or not. Families don't think that girls can be educated and do something'.

In negotiating gendered social and familial expectations and evaluations of education and their contradictions with dominant aspirations, these young women reproduce governmental framings of the 'problem' of 'lack of awareness' among families about the value of education for girls. Yet their negotiations of multiple expectations also indicate how a dominant discourse around educational success and work is culturally produced. A key effect of formal schooling on these young women's self-positioning is their conception of desirable work, and, conversely, their continued engagements with manual work (Balagopalan 2008). As Meera pointed out, 'while you study you do less work', hence when schoolgirls become married women and are expected to contribute to hard labor, they find it difficult, 'you are not used to it'. Schooling is thus seen as habituating the body to more sedentary forms of work, leading to physical as well as psychological conflicts with the often rigorous manual labor expected of young brides and daughters-in-law in a mountainous agrarian context. Meera's comments thus suggest how the rationale of a 'development subjectivity' insinuates itself into the habits and bodies of rural youth through the daily routines of schooling. This is a subject position experienced as 'difficult' (Klenk 2010), as it conflicts with demands and expectations of local gendered and generational scripts of social reproduction.

For young women, a universalized discourse of education-as-development is therefore actively negotiated through conflicting ideals and experiences of work, family, and identity.[8] For example, most young women I spoke to acknowledged the fact that they will have to do farming, regardless of their education and contrary desires. Changing gendered divisions of labor have meant that household and farming work are increasingly construed as work for girls, women, and uneducated elders, as 'boys are making money'. These roles also involve shifting evaluations of work, where household work is undervalued in relation to cash-earning work, and in which the multiple values women have ascribed to agricultural work in the region, such as relief from the perceived confines of the house and a chance to socialize and develop friendships with peers (Dyson 2010), as well as relationships with ecological environments (Gurarani 2002), become marginalized. In Bhatoli village, a 16-year-old girl studying in class ten said that 'we will do it (farming), but we don't want to be behind'. Her comment suggests that young women's desires for other kinds of work are not simply rejections of manual labor, but rather indicate negotiations of dominant standards of educational success, *and* experiences of an often increased work burden that is economically and culturally devalued.

Young rural women in my research who continue to engage in manual, agrarian work alongside or after schooling emphasized educated subject positions based on self-improvement and personal transformation.[9] A girl studying in class 12 stressed that 'Education will help us have a better life even if we don't get jobs.' Similarly, a young woman in Talogi village felt that: 'Education changes things from within. You get strong, can talk to everyone, you can live in a better way. You can write, you have knowledge. You don't know anything if you are uneducated.' The moral and behavioral benefits of education for girls were often framed in comparison to the uneducated, as well as to educated boys. A common refrain was that while girls get 'improved' by education, boys 'don't get anything from education'. When I asked a group of young women aged between 16 and 24 what they meant by this, they elaborated that 'Educated boys get spoilt, teach uneducated boys bad things, roam... drink and smoke all kinds of things, spend money...They don't study enough to get jobs. If they do get work, they don't get good jobs, *hotel line*, washing dishes. Girls' behavior gets better from education, educated girls talk better, fight less.' Young men were perceived as not getting 'good' jobs *and* behaving badly, while women are not able to pursue employment but at least their behavior improves. Young women therefore embrace educated subject positions defined by self-improvement, as well as negotiations of compromised outcomes.

The discourse of education for development through employment is, in this context, primarily a male narrative presented as universal, yet young men's reflections also center negotiations. Dinesh, a 24-year-old man with some college education currently 'doing interviews' for jobs while manning a relative's shop in Kempty, emphasized that 'Schooling is only for employment. After being educated, living in the village, doing farming is not compatible. If one has to do this, then there was no need for education. When one doesn't get work one also feels disappointment. One also feels that why did I do all this education? It also seems to me that if I had only studied until class eight, I would have earned two to three *lakh* by now.' This young man's comments reflect clearly the key rationale of education-for-development that education is for employment, yet at the same time stresses failure as a key outcome (cf. Mains 2012).

A group discussion with young men, aged 16–25, in Nautha village illustrated how compromised experiences of work frame self-positioning. I was told that in this village, which is at some distance from a motorable road, not a single person had obtained permanent government employment within the last ten years. These young men were engaged in various kinds of temporary wage labor: as cooks or tea-stall employees in nearby towns, and as daily laborers, including in construction work within the village. All of them said that they also contribute to household work. For young men, desirable and appropriate work is linked to but not only evaluated in terms of wages: 'If one asks people who have studied up to inter-college to come for some daily labor work, they say no, they don't want to be seen picking up rocks, they are ashamed of this', reflecting the notion that manual work is not for educated youth. At the same time, these young men were all engaged in wage-employment based on manual labor, and I was told repeatedly that '*private* jobs are the biggest source of improvement, kids who leave and get jobs making 1500–2000, washing dishes etc.' Hence, even outcomes of material improvement through employment are compromised, as young educated men's income is primarily earned through manual work.

Young men also reflected on how a dominant rationale frames the value of different kinds of work, and the implications for moral evaluations and choices. For example, a young man in his early 20s told me that: 'If someone gets a job, they are a good person, if not they are bad. This is the feeling that comes from education. People also come to feel about themselves that if I get work I am OK, if not I am bad.' Another young man stressed that: 'Employment is a pressure. When people do farming for a living, they are self-sufficient, both the problems and successes are due to their own actions. But when people are not doing jobs, they feel useless.' Here, the externalized, disciplinary pressures of employment are contrasted with the self-sufficiency of farming. Other young men indicated how the pressures to earn corrupt young men's choices and visions: 'How to earn money, youth live in tension around this. Sometimes in this tension young people's visions get changed, they have no trouble doing dishonest work. People change from education, and have a desire to do good work…but end up getting spoilt, not able to do anything', linking moral degeneration with a paucity of models for youth in a changing rural social landscape. Hence, while young men share a general desire for non-manual employment, they also counter notions of the moral valorization of an employment-centered regime of social reproduction. Instead, they experience hegemonic aspirations and the conflation of economic success and failure with self-worth as a tension, as exerting 'shame', 'pressure', even compromising moral judgment and action.[10]

The pressure of employment was therefore at times reflected on as a form of injustice, as young men felt they have to shoulder the burden of changing, and at times conflicting, expectations. Some implicated both parents' and teachers' lack of desire or inability to provide support, guidance, and understanding of the difficulties young men face. For example, an educated young man in Nautha village felt that: 'Within a family, everyone should be educated to avoid the problems that the mix of educated and uneducated brings. A lot of problems stem from this.' Others spoke of the lack of 'concern' on the part of teachers—highlighting the distance cultivated by teachers and the perception that 'teachers don't talk to children'. One young man countered elders' narratives about young men's lack of involvement in household work, suggesting that in the hills, young people's focus on family responsibilities is something that 'holds them back'; 'there is not one young person here who has not done house-work before coming here (to this meeting)'. In this context, Dinesh strongly expressed his frustrations with the narrative of young people getting 'ruined': 'People say that young people have become ruined, but there is also a lot of pressure on them from parents and elders. If you are educated and want to stay in the house rather than leave the village, they say what is the point of education, why study if you are just going to do the same thing….' Hence, from a hegemonic perspective, a young educated man's choice to live in a village is not a rational one (cf. Morarji 2010).

Dinesh went on to offer an alternative view: 'It is not necessary for all youth to get a job, out of four to five, one should take care of the home.' When asked how this would work if all five were educated, he responded that 'There should be a limit on jobs, one should be able to do a job for a certain amount of time, or if a brother gets a job, one should be willing to do work in the fields. Four brothers do not all need to get jobs. It's true that the one left behind is seen as inferior, this is a problem… but it is also a fact that the one who stays behind becomes the family head, he has to take care of day to day things, see to things….' Dinesh thus articulated a desire for 'balance', or different ways of organizing and evaluating social reproduction that can meet both changing needs and maintain relationships to rural place and production.

Desires for 'balance' were elaborated on in young women and men's ambivalent reflections on village versus city life. Most young people initially indicated to me that they would prefer a future in a city. They associated urban life with more 'choice' and opportunities for mobility through studies and employment: the city was thus perceived as a space where 'you can work towards a good future, a good life…to grow, get ahead'. The city was also assessed in relation to perceived negatives of village life: for young women above all, as a space of less work—'we would just have to study and take care of our own food, that's it'—but for both women and men equally as an escape from social pressures, restrictions and constraints associated with the village community: 'we can't speak openly, there are always people telling us what to do, telling us we shouldn't laugh, that we speak too much…'

While educated young people aspired to urbanized visions of work, lifestyle, and identity, Neeraj, a man in his late 20s living in Kempty, told me that 'In the context of village and city, the state of youth is one of dilemma. Those youth who have experienced city life are now tired of it. They understand the difficulties of the city. Now most of them are looking for work near their homes. In cities it is often difficult to make ends meet. Those who have stayed back (in the city) are mostly in difficulties.' This 'state of dilemma' captured the co-existence of young people's varied experiences of past and present, as well as aspirations and visions of future life: they want facilities, a 'bank balance', commodities, less work, 'to live openly', but they also want to 'improve society', 'become something', 'be able to distinguish between right and wrong', 'clean air, water and open space', and strengthen collectiveness and unity in their villages. Such varied desires indicate how a generalized discourse of educational value fails to accommodate a range of ambiguities and negotiations that young people in Jaunpur experience. These negotiations necessarily involve multiple subject positions and notions of self-development, as 'becoming something' includes gaining employment, but also encompasses broader values of social reproduction. Hence, while desires for change shape emergent educated subjectivities for youth in Jaunpur, their '…attitudes and actions also point towards potential reconstructions of responsibility in altered social and economic contexts' (Gold 2009: 365).

Conclusion

The power of development as a governmental project is reflected in the 'public appropriation of societal transformation in the name of development' (Sivaramakrishnan and Agrawal 2003: 3), seemingly overdetermining social narratives about present and future lives. Yet through an ethnographic perspective on education-as-development, I have illustrated how this hegemonic construction is also a negotiated experience, often of failure and compromised outcomes. It is a project which reproduces modernization ideology of improvement and mobility, yet is experienced as a 'contradictory resource' in that it fails to provide the necessary cultural capital for mobility *and* disinherits local youth from local forms of cultural and economic capital valued in a rural mountain context. Teachers, parents, and youth agree that schooling should lead to employment and less manual labor, as well as the moral development of individuals, yet these normative developmental ideals are mediated by contextual realities and differentiated by class, generation, gender, and place.[11] School teachers represent developed subject positions based on urban middle-class ideals, yet thereby also work to reproduce notions of rural students and their communities as 'backward' that contradict their perceived mandate of social development. Parents and community elders express disappointment with educated youth, based on their inability to gain desirable employment or contribute to the moral economy of the village, and indicate both as necessary for social reproduction. Educated young women and men in Jaunpur aspire toward non-manual, income-earning work, yet varyingly negotiate the normative experience of continued involvement in manual work and counter notions of moral 'ruin' by articulating how their actions and choices are shaped in relation to compromised outcomes and conflicting expectations. For 'subjects' of development, experiences of education are therefore often about negotiating, and at times critiquing, contradiction, and failure. Such articulations signal the limits of governmentality (Li 2007), as development and education become recognizable as socially constructed sites of power as well as negotiation and struggle (McMichael 2010).

Negotiations of education-as-development highlight contradictions and compromises—but also, I want to suggest, potentials—that arguably delineate the cultural politics of development in contemporary rural India. For example, they indicate how in contexts like Jaunpur 'youth' are relationally framed by a dominant rationale encountered through teachers and schools, local elders' norms of success and respect, as well as gendered negotiations of aspirations and contradictory outcomes. Young women and men aspire to a modern, urban life, but they also suggest a need for ways to 'balance' desires for employment with realities of educational failure, as well as the ongoing 'work' required to sustain rural place, agrarian production, and inter-generational relationships, thereby generating different subject positions through education, development, and social reproduction.

NOTES

1. Kempty is a semirural *qasba* (between a village and town in classification) in the Aglar River valley of Jaunpur block, Tehri Garhwal district of the north Indian hill state of Uttarakhand. In this chapter, I draw on two years (2006–2008) of qualitative research in this region of the western Himalayan foothills. The research was largely conducted in Hindi, which I speak, read, and write at an intermediate level. In Jaunpur, the local Jaunpuri dialect is spoken, but Hindi is the language of public engagements such as education, commerce, and government. Shobhan Singh Negi assisted me with the research drawn on here. He speaks and writes intermediate English, as well as fluent Hindi and Jaunpuri. I was dependent on Shobhan's knowledge of Jaunpuri for conversations with some elders (particularly older women) who only spoke Jaunpuri. In these conversations, Shobhan would intermittently translate orally into Hindi; I interjected questions in Hindi, and jotted notes in a mix of Hindi and English. All of my interactions with youth took place in Hindi; my jotted notes were bilingual, and when needed I consulted with Shobhan for translations while writing up my notes. Most of my conversations with government school teachers and officials were similarly conducted in Hindi, except when my conversation in Hindi was met with replies in English, and on two occasions (with the Kempty inter-college principal and a block level education department officer), Shobhan actually advised me to introduce myself in English to prove my 'credentials' as well as indicate my recognition of their status and knowledge of English. Thus, the following conversation with the Kempty inter-college principal took place in English.

2. Critical school ethnographies have similarly illustrated how contingency and agency—or cultural productions—mediate processes of reproduction as well as transformation in liberal democracies (Levinson and Holland 1996; Willis 1977).

3. Uttarakhand was formed as a new state in 2000 after a protracted struggle for separation from Uttar Pradesh. Demands for secession were based primarily on the economic and cultural marginalization of the hill region.

4. In her research on girls' education elsewhere in rural north India, Gold (2002: 97) noted that teachers routinely asked students to

"forget" everything that they had in their minds before coming to school, 'to erase them like blank slates'.

5. Cf. Fernandes (2006) and Mazzarella (2003) on middle-class formation and assertion in contemporary India.

6. Hence, 'failure' indicates the need for more, better-targeted, or reformed intervention rather than raising fundamental questions about the terms of success and failure, or of inequalities and exclusions which produce such outcomes (cf. Ferguson 1994).

7. 'Inter education' refers to any inter-college, or high school, education.

8. Young women reflected on the value of education almost exclusively in relation to work and self-improvement. Girls' education does affect marriage, as girls with class 8–12 education (though not lower or higher levels of education) will be 'seen' by an enhanced number of prospective grooms, and hence potentially choose from a wider range of offers. Yet given that education for girls is increasingly the norm, other markers of distinction such as class and caste background, and physical appearance are likely to contribute more to mobility through marriage than education per se.

9. See Jeffrey et al. (2008) on how educated, unemployed young men elsewhere in north India similarly emphasize the value of education for self-improvement.

10. See Jackson (1999) on the importance of recognizing how men's relationships to hegemonic gender discourses around work are often contradictory and complex.

11. While caste and religion do matter in the context of my research, relative caste homogeneity in an almost completely Hindu social milieu means that they are less central as differentiators of educational experiences and outcomes than in other parts of rural north India (cf. Jeffrey et al. 2008).

References

Balagopalan, S. (2005). An ideal school and a schooled ideal: Education at the margins. In R. Chopra & P. Jeffery (Eds.), *Educational regimes in contemporary India* (pp. 83–98). New Delhi: Sage.

Balagopalan, S. (2008). Memories of tomorrow: Children, labor, and the panacea of formal schooling. *Journal of the History of Childhood and Youth*, 1(2), 267–285.

Baviskar, A. (2004). Between micro-politics and administrative imperatives: Decentralization and the watershed mission in Madhya Pradesh. *European Journal of Development Research, 16*(1), 26–40.

Chopra, R. (2005). Sisters and brothers: Schooling, family, and migration. In R. Chopra & P. M. Jeffery (Eds.), *Educational regimes in contemporary India* (pp. 299–315). New Delhi: Sage.

Cole, J., & Durham, D. (2007). Introduction: Age, regeneration, and the intimate politics of globalization. In J. Cole & D. Durham (Eds.), *Generations and globalization: Youth, age, and family in the new world economy* (pp. 1–28). Bloomington: Indiana University Press.

Corbett, M. J. (2007). *Learning to leave: The irony of schooling in a coastal community.* Halifax: Fernwood Publications.

Da Costa, D. (2008). "Spoilt sons" and "sincere daughters": Schooling, security, and empowerment in rural West Bengal, India. *Signs: Journal of Women in Culture and Society, 33*(2), 283–308.

Donner, H. (2005). 'Children are capital, grandchildren are interest': Changing educational strategies and parenting in Calcutta's middle-class families. In J. Assayag & C. J. Fuller (Eds.), *Globalizing India: Perspectives from below* (pp. 119–139). London: Anthem Press.

Dyson, J. (2010). Friendship in practice: Girls' work in the Indian Himalayas. *American Ethnologist, 37*(3), 482–498.

Dyson, J. (2014). *Working childhoods: Youth, agency and the environment in India.* Cambridge/New York: Cambridge University Press.

Ferguson, J. (1994). *The anti-politics machine: "Development", depoliticization and bureaucratic power in Lesotho.* Minneapolis: University of Minnesota Press.

Fernandes, L. (2006). *India's new middle class: Democratic politics in an era of economic reform.* Minneapolis: University of Minnesota Press.

Gold, A. G. (2002). New light in the house: Schooling girls in rural North India. In D. P. Mines & S. Lamb (Eds.), *Everyday life in South Asia* (pp. 86–99). Bloomington: Indiana University Press.

Gold, A. G. (2009). Tasteless profits and vexed moralities: Assessments of the present in rural Rajasthan. *The Journal of the Royal Anthropological Institute, 15*(2), 365–385.

Gupta, A. (2003). The transmission of development: Problems of scale and socialization. In K. Sivaramakrishnan & A. Agrawal (Eds.), *Regional modernities: The cultural politics of development in India* (pp. 65–74). New Delhi: Oxford University Press.

Gurarani, S. (2002). Forests of pleasure and pain: Gendered practices of labor and livelihood in the forests of the Kumaon Himalayas, India. *Gender Place and Culture, 9*(3), 229–243.

Jackson, C. (1999). Men's work, masculinities and gender divisions of labor. *Journal of Development Studies, 36*(1), 89–108.

Jeffery, P., & Jeffery, R. (1994). Killing my heart's desire: Education and female autonomy in rural North India. In N. Kumar (Ed.), *Women as subjects: South Asian histories* (pp. 125–171). New Delhi: Shree.

Jeffrey, C., & McDowell, L. (2004). Youth in a comparative perspective: Global change, local lives. *Youth and Society, 36*(2), 131–142.

Jeffrey, C., Jeffery, P., & Jeffery, R. (2008). *Degrees without freedom? Education, masculinities and unemployment in North India.* Stanford: Stanford University Press.

Klenk, R. (2010). *Educating activists: Development and gender in the making of modern Gandhians.* Lanham/Plymouth: Lexington Books/ Rowman & Littlefield.

Levinson, B. A., & Holland, D. (1996). The cultural production of the educated person: An introduction. In B. A. Levinson, D. E. Foley, & D. C. Holland (Eds.), *The cultural production of the educated person: Critical ethnographies of schooling and local practice* (pp. 1–54). Albany: State University of New York Press.

Li, T. (2007). *The will to improve: Governmentality, development, and the practice of politics.* Durham: Duke University Press.

Lukose, R. (2005). Consuming globalization: Youth and gender in Kerala, India. *Journal of Social History, 38*(4), 915–935.

Mains, D. (2012). *Hope is cut: Youth, unemployment and the future in urban Ethiopia.* Philadelphia: Temple University Press.

Mazzarella, W. (2003). *Shoveling smoke: Advertising and globalization in contemporary India.* Durham: Duke University Press.

McMichael, P. (2010). Changing the subject of development. In P. McMichael (Ed.), *Contesting development: Critical struggles for social change* (pp. 1–14). New York: Routledge.

Moore, D. S. (1999). The crucible of cultural politics: Reworking "development" in Zimbabwe's eastern highlands. *American Ethnologist, 26,* 654–689.

Morarji, K. (2010). Where does the rural educated person fit? Development and social reproduction in contemporary India. In P. McMichael (Ed.), *Contesting development: Critical struggles for social change* (pp. 50–63). New York: Routledge.

Mosse, D. (2005). *Cultivating development: An ethnography of aid and practice.* London/Ann Arbor: Pluto Press.

Pigg, S. L. (1992). Constructing social category through place: Social representations and development in Nepal. *Comparative Studies in Society and History, 34,* 491–513.

Sivaramakrishnan, K., & Agrawal, A. (2003). Regional modernities in stories and practices of development. In K. Sivaramakrishnan & A. Agrawal (Eds.), *Regional modernities: The cultural politics of development in India* (pp. 1–61). New Delhi: Oxford University Press.

Vasavi, A. R. (2006). An emergent new reality?: Some reflections from schools. In M. E. John, P. K. Jha, & S. S. Jodhka (Eds.), *Contested transformations: Changing economies and identities in contemporary India* (pp. 95–112). New Delhi: Tulika Books.

Willis, P. (1977). *Learning to labor: How working class kids get working class jobs.* New York: Columbia University Press.

CHAPTER 11

Little People, Big Words: 'Generationating' Conditional Cash Transfers in Urban Ecuador

María Gabriela Palacio

INTRODUCTION

Children occupy a central position in the theory of change underpinning conditional cash transfers (CCTs). In their most common design, it is children who need to fulfil the conditionality of the transfer (e.g. by attending school or regular health checks) whilst their mothers are typically the cash recipients. These cash transfers are seen as providing some immediate relief to cash-strapped households, whilst also preventing them from 'underinvesting' in their children (Fiszbein et al. 2009).

CCTs are designed to intervene in the economic conditions of receiving households and do so in a generational manner. It is for this reason that I concentrate in this chapter on the generational dimension and dynamics of this popular development intervention. This includes teasing out the role of chronological age as a targeting measure, the various ways in which CCTs contribute to the constitution of certain life phases like childhood but also motherhood, as well as how CCTs reshape various sets

M.G. Palacio (✉)
International Institute of Social Studies of Erasmus University Rotterdam, Kortenaerkade 12, 2518 AX The Hague, Netherlands

R. Huijsmans (ed.), *Generationing Development*,
DOI 10.1057/978-1-137-55623-3_11

of relations shaping children's everyday lives as well as children's perceptions of their position in society.

Despite the centrality of children in the mechanics of CCTs, children's voices are largely absent from the burgeoning literature on cash transfers. In employing a generational approach, I have decentred adults' experiences and perspectives in order to create the conceptual space to bring in children. The chapter title *Little People, Big Words* is illustrative of how CCTs reconfigure the relational position of poor children. In Ecuador, where I have conducted the research on which this chapter is based, malnutrition among children has remained prevalent despite increased social investment. According to official estimates (National Statistics Bureau 2015), a quarter of the children in the country are malnourished. Stunting is a bodily marker of malnutrition, and indeed, many of the children included in CCTs I have studied were small in size. Yet, these 'little people' used 'big words' in our discussions on CCTs. For example, recipient children would not hesitate to posit bold claims such as 'we are needy' and 'the president knows about us, the poor' when talking about their experience of CCTs. It is such remarks that hooked my interest in exploring how CCTs reposition their recipients in sets of social relations and, in particular, how children and their mothers both experience and imagine these changes.

This chapter goes against the grain of most research on CCTs which is typically evaluative, quantitative, and concerned with its effect on poverty reduction (de Haan 2014). It contributes to a small and diverse body of literature that explores the social effects of CCTs beyond their stated objectives. This includes work on recipient mothers that problematises the normative constitution of motherhood which informs these interventions (Molyneux 2006). Others have studied how CCTs enhance women's empowerment (Hanlon et al. 2010). Furthermore, CCTs have also attracted scholarly attention in relation to its effects on political participation. In this sub-literature, CCTs are mostly associated with negative electoral effects, and depicted as political machines used to buy 'poor voters' (Sugiyama 2011; Zucco 2011; De La O 2012). However, a minority of authors view CCTs as having a positive impact on political participation and social inclusion (Barrientos and Villa 2014). Yet, also the alternative literature is largely adult-centric, paying scant attention to how CCTs play out in generational landscapes that include non-adults.

This chapter is organised as follows: the first section traces the origins of CCT programmes and how these travelled to Latin American countries. By doing so, I illuminate a common theoretical ground rooted in human capital theory and productivism. The second section explores the multifaceted experiences with social protection in southern Ecuador. The third section contrasts these accounts with mother–child interactions, with particular attention to the changes that occur when a 'recipient daughter' becomes a 'recipient mother'. The chapter concludes by pointing at some of the frictions and the limitations of delivering welfare on the basis of chronological age.

Research Context and Methods

This chapter is based on a larger doctorate research project on social protection and informal employment in Ecuador. Like most research on CCTs, I had not initially attended to children's perspectives and experiences. When interviewing mothers, (their) children were often around and at times volunteered their views on matters. During one such interview with a recipient mother in southern Ecuador, her son, a child of about eight years old, interrupted the conversation and asked why he was not the one being interviewed instead. His mom, he said, was part of the cash transfer programme just because she had children. And well, he was a child, *her child.*

This encounter led to some readjustment in the research design in order to better understand children's experiences and perceptions of CCTs and to unravel the generational dimensions of CCTs as development interventions. Empirically, this meant including children as research participants in addition to my ongoing work with recipient mothers of adult age.

When expanding my research to include children, I did not aim for a statistically representative sample as the case for my work with adult women. Instead, due to various constraints, I settled for a reasonable cross section of recipient children aged between 6 and 12 years (corresponding to primary school age) with whom I could talk about the cash transfer programme.

The material presented in this chapter is limited to responses from a small group of children from one neighbourhood (*barrio*) sprawling along the outskirts of Loja, a city in the Highlands in southern Ecuador. I was introduced to this neighbourhood by Patty, my parents' housekeeper, who resided in this part of Loja. Patty played an important role in the neighbourhood's Sunday school where she taught catechism to children. Since the Ecuadorian population is primarily Catholic (80 per cent) (National Statistics Bureau 2015), Sunday catechism schools are a common sight and especially popular in smaller cities and towns.

With Patty as my gatekeeper, I was introduced to many kids of the *barrio* who attended Sunday class whilst their parents were attending mass. After initial introductions, I drafted together with Patty some guiding questions about children's understanding and experiences of CCTs. Patty put me in touch with the parents concerned to explain to them about the research project and ask for their approval. Parental consent was obtained orally. On my second Sunday in the *barrio*, we stayed with the kids after the Sunday school and started a group conversation among those interested in participating after we had explained the research to them. About half of the kids who attended catechism stayed for the interviews. Most of the older girls refused to participate—I will come back to this point later. We started with a quick round of questions aimed at exploring whether the kids knew about the CCT (officially named the *Bono de Desarrollo Humano* [BDH] programme, or *Bono* [grant] colloquially). Not surprisingly, all of them were familiar with it. Boys were much more talkative and keen to share their opinions, whilst girls were more reluctant to talk. In the end, we approached a total of 12 kids for further individual interviews: 8 boys and 4 girls. The girls were, on average, slightly older (ten years old on average), whilst the boys were younger (aged between seven and nine years).

Next to primary research with children, the chapter also draws on a second series of interviews that took place in public health centres with recipient mothers. The selection of public health centres as a research site follows the programme's logic: health conditionalities require recipient mothers to take the children for periodical medical check-ups. As such, these sites were useful for interviewing mothers in the presence of their children. The public health centre-based interviews offered much scope for a relational approach by discussing the various ways in which gender, age, and constructs such as motherhood and childhood interact. In addition, the research presented in this chapter is also informed by visits to some homes of *Bono* recipients. These visits were conducted in the company of government caseworkers as part of their weekly visits and were particularly insightful for understanding how the conditionalities of the *Bono* were implemented and policed in everyday contexts.

Conditional Cash Transfers: A Southern Revolution?

CCTs are often celebrated as a revolution from the South, an idea originating from Latin America, a 'wave of new thinking' (Barrientos and Hulme 2009; Fiszbein et al. 2009). Yet, Lavinas (2014) offers an alternative account and links it to academic centres further north. This alternative view emphasises that CCTs are informed by conservative ideas and mainstream economic theory (Standing 2011; Lavinas 2014; Saad Filho 2015) despite their radical and empowering reputation. CCTs, in their modern form, concern human capital theory and targeting—as opposed to universal provisioning, partaking of the neoclassical propositions of their time.

In the 1960s, human capital was at the centre of economic theory. The key conviction was that increased investments in health and education would boost human capital formation, increase labour productivity, and, ultimately, contribute to economic growth. By the 1980s, the thesis of human capital had travelled to South America, and CCTs fitted this model perfectly. Moreover, by schooling children and providing cash-strapped adults with some financial support, CCTs worked as a double-edged sword: alleviating poverty whilst building a human capital basis for securing future economic growth.

Targeting entered the academic debate as a practical solution to the problem of the 'free rider'. Targeting restricts access to welfare to those considered needy. The idea of targeted social interventions, which owes much to the Chicago School, travelled from the USA to Chilean universities in the 1960s. Economists trained in Chicago[1] brought these ideas to *Odeplan*,[2] that would later design the *Subsidio Único Familiar* in 1981 (Lavinas 2014), widely acclaimed to be the first conditional safety net in the region. Both ideas took root in Latin America: the banner of 'human capital' justified providing financial support to poor mothers with school-age children, conditional on school attendance. By means of imposing restrictions on recipients—strict means testing, defining children's 'right age' (Fiszbein et al. 2009), or tedious administrative procedures—only the 'poorest' of the poor would be granted access to the fund. At a time in which universal provisioning was considered unaffordable in the Global South, the scheme was indeed well received.

It was not until the 1990s that CCTs were extended on a large scale, first in Mexico, then Brazil, and subsequently in other Latin American countries. The pivotal moment was the severe crisis of the 1980s. States withdrew from universal social provisioning, prompting the development of 'an innovative' safety net. In parallel, academics contributed to the belief in CCTs too by producing numerous studies that provided evidence of CCTs effectiveness, drawing on the impressive amount of data on poor families obtained from surveys collected for targeting purposes.

It should also be noted that the spread of CCTs in Latin America was in no small part due to the influence of the World Bank, the Inter-American

Development Bank, and other development agencies. Under various social risk management frameworks, these development agents appropriated the intervention of cash transfers as the principal component of social safety nets (Tabor 2002). Consequentially, by the late 2000s, 'virtually every country' in Latin America had a CCT scheme (Fiszbein et al. 2009), and by now about 18 CCT programmes are operating in Latin America, reaching approximately 25 million households (20 per cent of the region's population) (Montaño 2013).

CCTs: Expansion and Variation

The CCT recipe was easy to replicate: give poor families small stipends on the condition that their children attend school or visit a doctor regularly. However, its global expansion cannot be reduced to the power of the simplicity of the idea: it is also relatively cheap to run. At least, investing at early stages of the life course, that is in children, is generally considered much cheaper than 'correcting' underinvestment in education and health among adults. Hence, by the 2010s, CCTs had expanded to most countries in the Global South and also to some countries in the wealthy North.

CCTs around the world share some core features. A target population: usually poor mothers with school-age children defined by means testing, geographical targeting, or any other criteria. The target population receives a monthly or bi-monthly stipend subject to conditions. The recipient population is constantly monitored, both to prevent leakage and to check compliance with the programme's requirements. Despite these similarities, some variations on the theme can be observed as well as some change in its design.

In recent years, a gradual shift is noticeable towards unconditional schemes (Ferguson 2015). This is partly due to its more global uptake in recent years. Evaluations have shown that where basic services are already available, there is a low degree of association between CCTs and improved health or education. In such contexts, conditionality becomes little more than an administrative burden.

The global uptake of CCTs has also produced some variation to the theme. For example, CCTs across the world differ in the degree of intrusiveness. Some emphasise recipients' efforts to lift themselves 'out of poverty'. That is the case in Chile, where the programme requires recipients to sign a contract on 'personalised assistance' regarding health, housing, and education, accompanied by regular meetings with social workers. This is reflected in the title of an evaluation paper of the Chilean scheme prepared by the World Bank: 'With their effort and with one opportunity' (Galasso 2006). It is one of the most complex CCT designs in Latin America, including 'psychosocial support' to recipient families and an elaborated scheme for selection, allocation, and retrieval of the transfer. The central government works with municipalities to asses households' needs and prepare a bundle of services tailored to the poorest. Households are only eligible for transfers once their case has been filed by local social workers and have submitted a joint plan to 'exit poverty' (Ibid.).

Others, like a scheme adopted in North India, include a distinct gender focus as a means to increase 'the perceived value of girls' (using the terminology often found in impact evaluation literature) (Kabeer 1998; Sinha and Yoong 2009). The programme *Apni Beti Apna Dhan* (Our Daughter, Our Wealth) operates like a conventional CCT but prioritises girls. It was introduced with the objective of reducing discrimination against girls (one of the many responses devised against 'daughter killing') (see Srinivasan this volume), encouraging later marriage, and increase in investments in girls' human capital (as stated in the World Bank evaluation report by Sinha and Yoong 2009). After the birth of a female child, mothers are entitled to a 'monetary award' to cover post-delivery needs. Within months, the state endows each girl with a long-term monetary investment: a saving bond only accessible to the girls themselves after they have reached the age of 18, completed schooling, and are still unmarried (Ibid.).

It is worth noting that only girls who are the first, second, or third child in the family are eligible. The scheme has been replicated in other parts of India but is not beyond debate. Some argue it has led to more awareness on gender issues (Krishnan et al. 2014). Yet, it can also be seen as reinforcing gendered roles. By providing a monetary incentive to raise girls, it risks reinforcing a view of girls as a kind of liability. Such understanding not only fails in tackling the root causes of gender discrimination but also highly limits as it protects girls only on the basis of their 'future value' (see also Jauhola 2011).

CONDITIONAL CASH TRANSFERS: 'GENERATIONING' THE MAGIC BULLET

CCTs are designed to reward behavioural changes among recipients. Conditionalities, once imposed at the national scale as part of structural adjustment programmes, are now employed at the level of the household in the name of CCTs. Through financial incentives, recipients are incentivised into making the 'right' choices, whilst the policing of conditionalities demonstrates to taxpayers that recipients do not get money 'for free'.

Yet, behavioural changes are not the sole objective of CCTs. Their ultimate goal is alleviating poverty whilst simultaneously fostering economic growth by means of promoting human capital accumulation. CCTs need thus be seen as productivist (Ferguson 2015) and adult-centric. They aim at cultivating children from poor families into a healthier and better-educated adult labour force. The productivist logic is easily lost sight of because the design of CCTs maps onto globalised ideas of a good childhood and normative trajectories of human development.

Proponents of CCTs in Ecuador emphasise how it contributes to the realisation of children's rights in terms of access to education as expressed through increased enrolment rates (Schady and Araujo 2008; Ponce and Bedi 2010), reduction of child labour (Cecchini and Madariaga 2011; Gonzalez-Rozada and Llerena-Pinto 2011), or regarding the use of health services (Paxson and Schady 2007; Rosero 2012; Younger 1999). Since schooling and health are seen as unquestionable goods which are anchored as children's rights in (inter)national legislation, the productivist logic underpinning the conditionalities of CCTs can easily be read as measures to protect children's rights. Yet, a key difference between a rights-based approach and the human capital approach underpinning CCTs is that the former values children in their present condition as children, whereas human capital is shaped by a productivist discourse valuing children for their future role as adult workers.

The strong emphasis on human capital formation during the early years is based on a life course approach to 'returns to investments' (Heckman 2000). Investing in children, as opposed to adults, has more favourable returns because children, in general, have a longer life ahead of them. In addition, neuroscience and human development have produced firm claims in favour of investing in early childhood due to sensitive periods in brain development and the irreversibility of underinvestment in the early years (Young 2007). These claims have rendered children's bodies as sites of investments and adult bodies as sites of production. In contrast with a rights-based approach, this future-oriented, adult-centric view considers childhood merely as a preparatory phase for adulthood, as adults in the making (Uprichard 2008), lacking of intrinsic value in their present condition of children (see Streuli 2012 for a related discussion on the Peruvian case).

Chronological age is the prime measure by which CCTs define life phases such as childhood and motherhood and connect these to particular conditionalities. In some schemes, childhood is set to end at the age of 16, based on the minimum school leaving age and/or minimum age of employment, while others have 'extended' it until 18 in line with the legal age of majority.

Following Laz (1998: 101), CCTs constitute a powerful example in which a particular conceptualisation of age, chronological age, is made important. It is by virtue of their chronological age that children are included in particular activities, particular spaces, and in effect excluded from the adult world (Huijsmans et al. 2014). In some schemes, also the 'right' age for motherhood is established. This, then, amounts to a normative, age-demarcated constitution of gendered life phases which governs 'the right timing of events in an adolescent girl's life' (Jauhola 2011: n.p.), a theme I will return to below.

THE ECUADORIAN EXPERIENCE: *BONO DE DESARROLLO HUMANO*

Thus far, this chapter has discussed the core ideas underpinning CCTs, their generational dimensions, and briefly commented on some variations in CCT schemes the world over. The Ecuadorian CCT, which is the focus of this chapter, shares the characteristics typical of most other CCT schemes: it is informed by human capital theory and is implemented in a targeted fashion.

The *Bono Solidario*, the predecessor of the current *BDH*, was launched in Ecuador towards the end of the 1990s in a bid to cushion income shocks and to compensate poor families for the elimination of gas and electricity subsidies. Electricity and gas subsidies were seen as too expensive and going to those who did not need them. Thus, the subsidies were removed and replaced by a compensatory cash transfer. It started as a yearly subsidy of 1.2 million *sucres* (equivalent to 48 US dollars) distributed in the form of a monthly stipend of 120,000 *sucres*. The *Bono Solidario* was paid to poor mothers with children below the age of 18, whose family income was below 1 million *sucres* (40 US dollars), with none of the parents earning a fixed wage. In 1999, as the crisis deepened, the transfer was increased to 1.8 million *sucres* (150.000 *sucres*, monthly).

Bono Solidario was framed as a self-targeted, unconditional scheme, administrated by the Catholic church (Kingman Garcés 2002). It was upon the parish priest to identify the needy families. Subsequently, the central government took over the administration of the programme. To this end, a technical unit was created under the now extinct Minister for Social Welfare, in charge of collecting household data, assessing poverty profiles, and constructing the selection criteria. Another programme, *Beca Escolar*—a school grant—was introduced as an additional component aimed at incentivising school attendance among children aged between 6 and 15 years. The *Beca Escolar* was conditional on children's enrolment in school and achieving a 90 per cent attendance rate. However, monitoring of the latter was never fully realised.

By 2003, *Bono Solidario* was reformulated under the influence of the Inter-American Development Bank, its main funder, and became a CCT, renamed BDH. It was scaled up to the national level and given a firm institutional base in the Ministry of Social Development. In this new design, mothers were recognised as the 'most qualified household members to whom resources could be efficiently allocated' (BDH rules and regulations RO/142 2003).

Although cash-based social assistance was devised as a temporary response to crisis, BDH is still in operation today. The initial design envisioned households to be part of the programme for no longer than three years. Yet, some recipients interviewed in 2014 had been in the programme since its inception, that is, for more than 15 years. Throughout the years, BDH has become the flagship instrument for poverty alleviation in Ecuador: it reaches over 1.2 million households (in 2015), and Ecuador ranks first in the region in public spending on CCTs (Cecchini and Madariaga 2011).

Before zooming in on the conditional version of the BDH which targets mothers with dependent children, it is important to note that the BDH also has an unconditional component—a non-contributory pension, targeted to families with disabled members—certified by the governmental agency CONADIS, or to adults above 65 years who fall below the poverty line and do not receive a pension. These two groups are included in the programme without needing fulfilment of any condition.

Different from other experiences with cash transfers in the region, there is a sufficient availability and affordability of schools and health care centres in the country due to a sustained investment in the provision of basic services and adequate infrastructure, a major turning point in state capacity that came after 2007. Thus, BDH assumes poverty to be a demand-side problem—a liquidity constraint among the poor.

The stipend has been fixed at 50 US dollars per household. From its inception, the programme allocated only one flat-rate stipend per household despite growing pressure to consider the number of children per household (see Ponce et al. 2013). Indeed, studies have found that households with a larger number of children tend to be poorer (Montaño 2013). This was also expressed by María, a 12-year-old girl, who, when asked whether she knew the reason why her mother received BDH transfers, replied: 'because I have got many [four] siblings and we are poor … the *bono* is not enough for all of us'. María further stressed that the money was not equally spent among the five of them. Yet, conditionalities are being imposed equally among children, regardless of the household size and gender composition. In the programme's design, no difference is made; if the transfer has to be divided by five children or allocated to a lone child, all children have to fulfil the programme's conditions.

Conditionalities and the Reconfiguration of Childhood

Chronological age, next to poverty indicators, determines the inclusion and/or exclusion criteria of the BDH. Only adult mothers with children of the 'right age' are eligible (Fiszbein et al. 2009). In the case of Ecuador, this is children below 16 years of age. Chronological age has to be proven with birth certificates of at least one of the dependent children.

It is worthwhile noting that the age threshold has reduced over time from 18 to 16 years. In Ecuador, 18 is the legal age of majority, and this threshold was used to determine the eligibility for the BDH programme in the 2003 version. In recent years, the emphasis on age of majority is replaced by the age of 16, which is the minimum age of (legal) employment. The lowering of the age threshold has significantly reduced the number of recipients and, thus, the cost of the scheme.

The conditionalities regarding education have been relaxed over time: children aged between 6 and 16 years have to be enrolled in a school and should be attending regularly. Yet there are no specific requirements regarding school performance. Also the stated bi-monthly check on children's school attendance is not carried out in practice.

Health-related conditions are more detailed. In their first year, children have to undergo bi-monthly medical check-ups. Between their first and fifth birthday, compulsory check-ups are bi-yearly. In addition, in case of pregnancy, recipient mothers are required to undergo a minimum of five medical checks at a public health centre. Furthermore, recipient mothers are invited to attend yearly briefings on family planning together with their male partners.

The discussion of the conditionalities of the BDH shows that the measure of chronological age works as a key technique in the architecture of the scheme. Chronological age demarcates the conditionalities and thereby defines the priorities in young lives. In the early years, these revolve around health-related requirements, which are subsequently replaced by educational requirements. Thus, age-based conditionalities can be said to restructure the condition of childhood in an 'age-normative' fashion (Huijsmans et al. 2014). Based on the measure of chronological age, childhood is conditioned in relation to particular activities and spaces, whereas alternative activities such as children's work are pathologised. As explained above, the reconfiguration of childhood needs to be understood in relation to how the human capital theory underpinning the BDH is mapped onto the life course. BDH is tailored to ensure and protect the human capital formation in children, with the results of these efforts to be yielded when recipient children have achieved the status of productive workers.

This productivist logic and future-oriented approach affect poor people's ideas about social mobility. Parents explained that 'if they [their children] want to succeed in life, they have to study harder than we did'. These shifting ideas on achieving desired futures can be seen as reflecting the government's discourse of *'Ecuador ya cambió'* (Ecuador has changed). This slogan articulates a break with the past. Discursively, development is being disassociated from charity, and the idea is upheld that in the 'new Ecuador', social mobility is achieved through merit and hard work. It suggests that in the past the poor were held back by a lack of knowledge. CCTs fit this discursive scheme by equipping the poor with productive skills and the opportunity to change their lives; in other words, to become autonomous individuals. Social assistance targeting the young is hemmed in ideas of productive transformation, materialised in later stages of their lives—as workers.

In people's popular understanding, this 'new Ecuador' appears mapped onto generations. Some of the girls responded for example: 'Of course mom does not use the BDH money in anything else but our education, she is just a farmer'. Parents also articulated a generational shift. For example, a recipient mother articulated that 'if they [children] study hard, they will succeed in life'. At the institutional level, the discourse of merit and deservedness took shape in the creation in 2011 of an Ecuadorian Meritocracy Institute within the Ministry of Labour, placing emphasis on academic skills as verifiable indicators of effort. BDH recipients were also exposed to this logic through the setting up of a scholarship system based on children's academic performance measured through standardised tests.

Children identified to different degrees with the idea of meritocracy underpinning the construction of the 'new Ecuador'. The variation in responses between boys and girls suggests that gendered norms and opportunity structures work to reinforce the masculine notion of young men as change agents whilst leaving girls uncertain about the effect of human capital investments on their assumed future lives as productive adults.

Boys were generally positive that their futures would be different from their parents' lives because they were getting education and would obtain a degree. Most boys thought that schooling would change them; it would change their conditions and their prospects in life. Boys were looking forward to obtaining a good job, and once that was realised, they would not need any state support. Girls, in general, were more reluctant to embrace the promise of a 'new Ecuador' or even engage in a discussion about it. One of them reacted with discomfort when asked about the future and walked away without answering our question. Diana (eight years old) was also reluctant to respond and disassociated herself by taking out her notebook and starting to do her homework. Diana's mother, then, responded to the question about her future and bluntly stated that: 'when she has grown up, she would stop receiving help and that would be wrong! She would need that money'. Another girl, Martha (ten years old), reacted more mildly and said: 'it is OK if she [her mother] does not receive transfers anymore ... I would not need that money; we would be on our own'. The oldest girl in the group (aged ten) responded in an outspoken fashion to the observation that once children age out of the BDH, their mothers would stop receiving financial support: 'they cannot do that, she needs the money! ... she will be old and will not be able to work and support herself'. These responses from girls contrast starkly with the confidence articulated by the majority of the boys. Indeed, a nine-year-old boy stated firmly: 'when I grow up, my mom would not need it [BDH], because I would be working and taking care of her'.

Co-responsibilities: Reshaping Relations

With that money, the government is supporting us ... the [BDH] money is for us, so that we can go to school ... we should not work, even if we want to help mom, we have to study. (María, 12-year-old girl)

> My mom has to distribute the money among all of us. She has to help us so we can study. She has to buy food and other things for us. (Diana, eight-year-old girl)

Social assistance is an exchange: the conditionalities of the BDH are formally described as *corresponsabilidades* (co-responsibilities in English). Children have to attend school, report illness to their parents, and remain out of the labour force. Mothers are positioned as guardians, ensuring the fulfilment of these requirements, and the Ecuadorian state figures as the overall benefactor. The quotes above illustrate that children are quite aware of the various relations laid out by the BDH and their position within it.

BDH, Poor Children, and the State

The quote from María above articulates a relation of co-responsibility between the children of the poor and the state. This relationship runs as follows: the state is responsible for providing financial support and the recipient responsible for making the 'right' choices in order to lift oneself out of poverty, and the nation to a higher level of socio-economic development. However, the BDH has also transformed the relation of poor children with the state in other ways. Most importantly, the conditionality of the BDH has transformed how poor households experience the state. Recipient households have seen a more intimate presence of the state. Social workers representing the state have become regular visitors and data collection by state officers on poor households has expanded for purposes of monitoring and evaluation. It can thus be said that poor households, and their children, have become more visible to the state, yet the reverse also holds: the state has become more visible to children. Some children would even associate the BDH directly with the president as the key symbol of the state, arguing that the BDH was evidence that he 'cared about the poor'.

BDH and Poverty as a Status

Children had no doubt that the BDH was only extended to the poor, unlike other regional experiences with CCTs, like *Juntos* (Peru), where children remained unaware of the actual purpose of the programme (Streuli 2012). Kevin, a seven-year-old boy, stated for example that: 'My mom receives that money because we are poor. It is very helpful. With that money we can go to school and remain there.' Children also understood that the money came from the government as a relief for the poor, despite its earlier administration by the church.

Amongst each other, most children were aware of who was a BDH recipient and who was not. When asked whether they knew others who received the cash transfer, a common response was: 'yes, there are other poor kids … we all need it'. In general, children were appreciative of the programme, and whilst the BDH is associated with the status of poverty, this did not seem to translate in stigma amongst children:

> my friends [who are not part of the programme] know the BDH pro-gramme is good for us. Other kids are happy with it, because they can buy more things in the family. There are also some disabled children who get money, for medicine and stuff. And it is a good thing that the government helps them too. (nine-year-old boy)

Indeed, since the research was conducted in a relatively deprived *barrio*, the children interviewed appeared more concerned with those whom they knew were poor but not covered by the programme than with the associated connotations of poverty. When children referred to friends who appeared equally poor but were not a BDH recipient household, they would exclaim: 'they need it too!'

BDH and the Rearticulation of Relations Within the Household

'I just administer the money; my son is the recipient'. (mother in her early 30s)

Children are rarely the direct recipients of cash transfers (Barrientos and DeJong 2006). This is part of the making of modern childhood, in which children are placed outside economic relations. Decisions on expenditures are taken by their parents. It is argued that women are better (or rather more altruistic) administrators. Quantitative studies provide evidence that transfers targeted at women are more likely to improve living standards of their children than those targeted at men (Haddad et al. 1997). Some argue cash transfers directed at women have an equalising effect on bargaining power within the household, also benefiting girls (de Carvalho Filho 2012).

The notion of 'co-responsibilities' divides responsibilities between children and mothers in which mothers are the recipients and responsible for managing the cash transfer, whilst it is children who through their activities fulfil the obligations of the BDH. However, as the quote above suggests the fact that mothers living in poverty receive cash only because they have children below a certain age affects generational relations between mothers and children. Children are aware that it is because of them that their mothers receive additional income: 'if my mom were to have had no children, she would be working. She would not need the *bono*' (Cynthia, eight-year-old girl). The BDH, thus, appears to subtly affect children's bargaining position within the patriarchal family.

The co-responsibilities of CCT programmes also place extra demands on recipient mothers. Women are already in charge of most tasks and duties related to social reproduction and are now also made responsible for the facilitating work needed so that their children meet the imposed conditions, for example, by taking the children to medical check-ups. Indeed, when looking for recipient mothers, I could always find them queuing for an appointment at the public health centres. At these centres, appointments can only be made during working hours, preferably in the mornings when specialist doctors visit the centres. Although many poor mothers are not performing paid work, for those who hold a job, these visits cause an absence from work.

When asking mothers why they came to the health centre instead of going to work, this response by a mother in her late 20s is typical: *'You know, children cannot wait.'* Scholars like Montaño (2013) thus wonder about the gendered dynamics of cash transfers: '*Programas de mujeres, pero … para mujeres?*' (Women's programmes, but … for women?). Montaño points at the gendered contradictions characterising many a CCT scheme. Cash transfer programmes not only assume that mothers are solely responsible for the tasks of social reproduction, and naturally place their children's needs above their own aspirations, but also assume that women have ample time to facilitate meeting the imposed conditions. Yet, the ultimate contradiction is that meeting the obligations of the cash transfer comes at a considerable time cost to women, whilst the amount of the transfer does not allow poor women to stay out of the labour market.

Upsetting the Scheme: Teenage Motherhood

Understanding how relations of age work in the constitution of childhood is perhaps best observed in the grey area between childhood and adulthood. It is here that the arbitrariness and the inherent limitations of the unidirectional measure of chronological age to define life phases are most clearly observed as is the friction between normative constitutions and lived experiences.

The documentation about the DHB does not state a minimum age of motherhood. However, I observed that there was reluctance to include mothers who were themselves not yet 18 years of age as recipients. Social workers explained to fear a perverse effect if they were to include teenage mothers: 'we cannot encourage teen pregnancy, only adult mothers receive the transfer' (Fieldwork 2015).

Eventually, I asked about an age limit for mothers' admissibility on social media. In the official response I received through the Twitter account of the Ministry of Social and Economic Inclusion (*Inclusión Social*, May 2015), it was confirmed that mothers have to be minimally 18 years of age. In the BDH, admissible motherhood is constructed not only on the basis of chronological age, but for long also around marital status. For single mothers to be admissible, they had to provide a proof of their situation: a notarised document indicating their spouse had deserted them.

The rigid age-based and marital definition of admissible motherhood fits poorly with the demographic landscape of Ecuador. According to the most recent census data (2010), out of the total population of 14.5 million, 7.3 million are women. About half of these women are mothers (3.6 million): 71 per cent have a partner, whilst 29 per cent are single mothers. Nearly half (44 per cent) of the mothers had their first child in their youth, between 15 and 19 years. Moreover, in the last decade, teenage birth rates have increased from 91 to 111 per 1000 females—the global average stands at 49.

The case of Alicia illuminates things further. Alicia was 19 years old when we first met at the health centre in 2014. She explained that she had her first baby when she was 16; her mother was then just above 60 years old and was a BDH recipient because she also had underage dependent children. Alicia, however, had not been registered although her socio-economic condition would render her admissible. In fact, her friends suggested her to enrol. But she decided not to:

> I am a single mother, like many others are. But I feel ashamed of my condition. I do not want to queue and beg for the *Bono*. I want to work, I have two hands and I will work for my children.

Her mom was proud of her daughter's decision not to enrol in the BDH. In her eyes, Alicia was assuming the 'consequences of her wrong doing'.

Alicia has two children from two different fathers. The father of her youngest child—a two-month-old baby—was the closest to become a husband and continued to provide for her and her children even though he had left her and returned to his parents. 'At least he sends some money for diapers and food, and his parents do so too.' The father of her first child is married and has ignored his legal obligations towards his child. Alicia had nothing good to say about him. It was her mother and younger sister who had pulled her through by looking after her children to allow Alicia to take up a job as a cleaner. 'Where would I be without them?' she asked rhetorically.

Alicia's experience was challenging for herself and her children and also taxing for her mother. Teenage motherhood is a tough job at any income level, but especially so in conditions of poverty. Reports show that teenage motherhood is associated with poverty and low education attainment (Salinas Mulder et al. 2014). To make matters worse, perceptions about teen mothers are very negative in Ecuador, despite a 'modern' approach embedded in politics and formally declared in the 2008 Constitution. Conservative norms are entrenched in society which puts a strong stigma on teenage motherhood. The judgement gets worse if teenage mothers are also BDH recipients. These contextual factors underpin Alicia's refusal to apply for BDH support even when she reached the age of 18 and thus had become formally admissible.

By disqualifying teenage mothers, BDH severely delimits its own potential in breaking the intergenerational reproduction of poverty. In Ecuador, one in five girls between 15 and 19 years is a mother, and most of them are in the lowest income strata (INEC 2015, author's own calculations). As such, the BDH programme is leaving behind one of the neediest segments of the target population. For these young mothers, sharing in the BDH support, which is received by their ageing mothers, as Alicia also does, is the closest they get to receiving state support whilst keeping social stigma to a minimum. In addition, teenage mothers typically start working, leaving their children at home with the grandmothers. The widespread phenomenon of teenage motherhood is, thus, largely invisible to a programme that is meant to support the needy. In addition, being excluded from direct financial support forces young mothers into the labour market, leading them to live motherhood in the margins of their lives (see also Huijsmans 2013).

Age-normativity, thus, shapes the BDH scheme not only in relation to childhood, but also in relation to motherhood. Following Neugarten et al., BDH lays out clear 'expectations regarding age-appropriate behaviour' (1965: 711) stemming from a pervasive system of rules governing the timing of major life events and constraining social interaction. Whereas in the case of children, age-normativity has arguably contributed positively to the lives of children by ensuring school participation and regular health checks, the record looks much less convincing in relation to teenage mothers.

As the responses of the social workers indicate, extending the BDH to include teenage mothers is feared to produce a perverse incentive. This wrongly assumes that becoming a teenage mother is a tactical choice, for example, profiting from the state. Further, since the scheme requires mothers to register and report newborn children, given the social stigma on teenage motherhood, it is unlikely that mothers of minor age would apply even if the age barrier was removed. We can, thus, assume that many young mothers fail to register. They are unable or unwilling to submit the paperwork and therefore remain invisible to the state. Their invisibility, in this sense, can also be seen as a form of resistance, stemming from an intentional silence.

CONCLUSION

In this chapter, I initiated a discussion on some of the many complex relations between age, gender, state, and society restructured through new forms of welfare provisioning, namely by CCTs. The literature on CCTs is dominated by impact evaluations. This includes the effects of CCTs on children's school attendance, performance, and their involvement in child labour. Yet, this concern with children and children's activities is limited to children's assumed future role of productive adults and leaves unaddressed how CCTs reconfigure childhood in a deeply age-normative fashion and how it affects children's relational position in society.

In unravelling the generational architecture of the CCTs, this chapter has traced its theoretical foundation to human capital theory. The mapping of human capital theory onto the life course, linked to a life course approach to the economics of returns to investment, renders the young body a site of investment and the adult body a site of production. The deployment of chronological age as a key technique in the architecture of CCTs weds these age-normative ideas in an inflexible manner to generational categories such childhood and motherhood.

The contradictions and problems of the generational design of CCTs become acutely visible by focusing on teenage mothers. Since the condition of teenage motherhood upsets the normative constitution of the right timing of life events, these young mothers are not admissible to a scheme that is meant to relieve the neediest in society.

In addition, the languages of 'co-responsibilities', I have argued, provides a window into the various webs of relations in which CCTs cast their recipients. This includes relations between receiving and non-receiving children, mother–child relations, and children's relations with the state.

The Ecuadorian CCT discussed in this chapter must also be seen in relation to a discursive reconstruction of Ecuadorian society captured by the government slogan *Ecuador ya cambió* (Ecuador has changed). In this discourse, the young generation is constructed as the first to benefit from a new social contract in which the state is meant to provide all citizens with the minimum conditions in terms of health and education, which citizens are then expected to capitalise on in terms of engaging in productive employment. The interviews illustrated that such a discourse is engaged with very differently by boys and girls. Boys were quick to embrace it as it speaks to masculine notions of men as breadwinners and change agents. Girls, on the other hand, responded with silence and hesitation—indicating doubt whether their increased educational attainment would in fact suffice to lift themselves out of poverty. Batteries of monitoring and evaluation research will, in due course, no doubt show whether these girls' doubts were justified. However, this chapter has made a plea to move beyond such adult-centric and productivist evaluation research and unravel how CCTs reshape childhood and the relational experience of being a child in children's current condition of young people.

Notes

1. It is worth noting the influence of Miguel Kast, who was trained in Chicago and back in Chile produced a national poverty map. This map became a key foundation for geographically targeted poverty interventions implemented thereafter (Lavinas 2014).
2. The Chilean state-planning agency dealing with poverty alleviation.

References

Barrientos, A., & DeJong, J. (2006). Reducing child poverty with cash transfers: A sure thing? *Development Policy Review, 24*(5), 537–552.

Barrientos, A., & Hulme, D. (2009). Social protection for the poor and poorest in developing countries: Reflections on a quiet revolution. *Oxford Development Studies, 37*(4), 439–456. doi:10.1080/13600810903305257.

Barrientos, A., & Villa, J. M. (2014). Economic and political inclusion of human development conditional transfer programmes in Latin America? BWPI working paper no. 200. Manchester: Brooks World Poverty Institute, The University of Manchester.

Cecchini, S., & Madariaga, A. (2011). *Programas de transferencias condicionadas: Balance de la experiencia reciente en américa latina y el Caribe.* Santiago: Naciones Unidas, comision Económica para América Latina y el Caribe, CEPAL Retrieved from WorldCat.

de Carvalho Filho, I. E. (2012). Household income as a determinant of child labor and school enrollment in Brazil: Evidence from a social security reform. *Economic Development and Cultural Change, 60*(2), 399–435.

de Haan, A. (2014). The rise of social protection in development: Progress, pitfalls and politics. *European Journal of Development Research, 26,* 311–321. doi:10.1057/ejdr.2014.

De La O, A. L. (2012). Do conditional cash transfers affect electoral behavior? Evidence from a randomized experiment in Mexico. *American Journal of Political Science, 57*(1), 1–14. doi:10.1111/j.1540-5907.2012.00617.x.

Ferguson, J. (2015). *Give a man a fish: Reflections on the new politics of distribution.* Durham: Duke University Press.

Fiszbein, A., Schady, N. R., & Ferreira, F. H. (2009). *Conditional cash transfers: Reducing present and future poverty.* Washington, DC: World Bank Publications.

Galasso, E. (2006). With their effort and one opportunity. *Alleviating extreme poverty in Chile.* Washington, DC: World Bank.

Gonzalez-Rozada, M., & Llerena-Pinto, F. (2011). The effects of a conditional transfer program on the labor market: The Human Development Bonus in Ecuador. Presented at the 6th Iza/World Bank Conference on Employment and Development, 30 May 2011, Mexico City, Mexico.

Haddad, L., Hoddinott, J., & Alderman, H. (1997). *Intrahousehold resource allocation in developing countries: Models, methods, and policy.* Baltimore/London: Johns Hopkins University Press.

Hanlon, J., Barrientos, A., & Hulme, D. (2010). *Just give money to the poor: The development revolution from the Global South.* Sterling: Kumarian Press.

Heckman, J. J. (2000). Policies to foster human capital. *Research in Economics, 54*(1), 3–56. doi:10.1006/reec.1999.0225.

Huijsmans, R. (2013). Doing gendered age: Older mothers and migrant daughters negotiating care work in rural Lao PDR and Thailand. *Third World Quarterly, 34*(10), 1896–1910.

Huijsmans, R., George, S., Gigengack, R., & Evers, S. J. T. M. (2014). Theorising age and generation in development: A relational approach. *European Journal of Development Research, 26*(2), 163–174. doi:10.1057/ejdr.2013.65.

INEC. (2015). INEC (Instituto Nacional De Estadística Y Censos) (2015). Living Standards Survey Data (Digital Repository). Retrieved from http://www. ecuadorencifras.gob.ec/documentos/web-inec/ECV/ECV_2015/

Jauhola, M. (2011). 'The girl child of today is the woman of tomorrow': Fantasizing the adolescent girl as the future hope in post-tsunami reconstruction efforts in Aceh, Indonesia. *Rhizomes 22.* Accessible here: http://www.rhizomes.net/issue22/jauhola/

Kabeer, N. (1998). Education is my daughter's future. *Index on Censorship, 27*(3), 154–160.

Kingman Garcés, E. (2002, October). El imaginario de la pobreza y las políticas de ajuste en Ecuador. *PROPOSICIONES.*

Krishnan, A., Amarchand, R., Byass, P., Pandav, C., & Ng, N. (2014). "No one says 'no' to money" – A mixed methods approach for evaluating conditional cash transfer schemes to improve girl children's status in Haryana, India. *International Journal for Equity in Health, 13,* 11. doi:10.1186/1475-9276-13-11.

Lavinas. (2014). 21st century welfare. *New Left Review, 84*(Nov Dec 2013), 5–40.

Laz, C. (1998). Act your age. *Sociological Forum, 13*(1), 85–113.

Molyneux, M. (2006). Mothers at the service of the new poverty agenda: Progresa/oportunidades, Mexico's conditional transfer programme. *Social Policy and Administration, 40*(4), 425–449. doi:10.1111/j.1467-9515.2006.00497.x.

Montaño, S. (2013). *Los bonos en la mira: Aporte y carga para las mujeres.* Chile: Naciones Unidas. Informe Anual 2012.

National Statistics Bureau, N. S. B. (2015). [Data base] Retrieved from www.inec.gob.ec

Paxson, C., & Schady, N. (2007). Cognitive development among young children in Ecuador: The roles of wealth, health, and parenting. *Journal of Human Resources, XLII*(1), 49–. doi:10.3368/jhr.XLII.1.49.

Ponce, J., & Bedi, A. S. (2010). The impact of a cash transfer program on cognitive achievement: The Bono de Desarrollo Humano of Ecuador. *Economics of Education Review, 29*(1), 116–125. doi:10.1016/j.econedurev.2009.07.005.

Ponce, J., Molyneux, M., Thompson, M., & Enríquez, F. (2013). *Hacia una reforma del Bono de Desarrollo Humano: Algunas reflexiones.* Quito: Abya-Ayala y CARE Ecuador.

Rosero, J. (2012). *On the effectiveness of child care centers in promoting child development in Ecuador: Jose Rosero* (Vol. TI 2012-075/3.). Amsterdam [etc.]: Tinbergen Institute.

Saad Filho, A. (2015). Social policy for mature neoliberalism: The Bolsa Família programme in Brazil. *Development and Change, 46*(6), 1227–1252.

Salinas Mulder, S., Castro Mantilla, D., & Fernandez Ovando, C. (2014). *Vivencia y relatos sobre el embarazo en adolescentes (Una aproximación a los factores culturales, sociales y emocionales a partir de un estudio en seis países de la región).* Panamá: UNICEF Regional Office for Latin America and the Caribbean.

Schady, N., & Araujo, M. C. (2008). Cash transfers, conditions, and school enrollment in Ecuador. *Economía, 8*(2), 43–70. doi:10.1353/eco.0.0004.

Sinha, N., & Yoong, J. (2009). Long-term financial incentives and investment in daughters: Evidence from conditional cash transfers in North India. Policy research working papers. Washington: World Bank.

Standing, G. (2011). Behavioural conditionality: Why the nudges must be stopped – An opinion piece. *Journal of Poverty and Social Justice, 19*(1), 27–38.

Streuli, N. (2012). Child protection: A role for conditional cash transfer programmes? *Development in Practice, 22*(4), 588–599.

Sugiyama, N. B. (2011). The diffusion of conditional cash transfer programs in the Americas. *Global Social Policy, 11*(2–3), 250–278. doi:10.1177/1468018111421295.

Tabor, S. R. (2002). Assisting the poor with cash: Design and implementation of social transfer programs. Wold Bank Social Protection Discussion Paper Series 223.

Uprichard, E. (2008). Children as 'being and becomings': Children, childhood and temporality. *Children & Society, 22*(4), 303–313. doi:10.1111/j.1099-0860.2007.00110.x.

Young, M. E. (Ed.) (2007). *Child development from measurement to action: A priority for growth and equity.* Washinghton, DC: The International Bank for Reconstruction and Development/The World Bank.

Younger, S. D. (1999). The relative progressivity of social services in Ecuador. *Public Finance Review, 27*(3), 310–352. doi:10.1177/109114219902700304.

Zucco, G. (2011). *Conditional cash transfers and voting behaviour: Redistribution and clientelism in developing democracies.* Accessible here: https://www.princeton.edu/csdp/events/Zucco0021011/Zucco021011.pdf

Growing Up Unwanted: Girls' Experiences of Gender Discrimination and Violence in Tamil Nadu, India

Sharada Srinivasan

INTRODUCTION

Statistical data can provide a good impression of the extent of gender discrimination in various contexts. Yet, such numbers give little insight into girls' lived experiences of growing up under such conditions. This chapter is based on research conducted in Madurai district, located in the South Indian state of Tamil Nadu, which was long associated with the practice of female infanticide and daughter aversion. This chapter asks how girls become aware of, experience and negotiate unwantedness and the associated contexts and structures that (re)produce daughter aversion. More particularly, it analyses how the experience of unwantedness shifts during the course of their childhoods. Analytically, this requires unravelling the interplay between gender and generational dynamics that produce particular age-related forms of gender-based violence.

Rooted in a child-centred perspective, the chapter explores girls' epistemologies, privileging girls' experiences, knowledge, needs and concerns,

S. Srinivasan (✉)
Department of Sociology and Anthropology, University of Guelph,
602, Mackinnon Building, 50 Stone Road East, N1G 2W1 Guelph, ON, Canada

© The Author(s) 2016
R. Huijsmans (ed.), *Generationing Development*,
DOI 10.1057/978-1-137-55623-3_12

267

and draws attention to girls as social actors. By employing intersectionality and attending to the political economy in which daughter aversion and elimination occur, it demonstrates that girlhoods are socially constituted and vary significantly as girls grow up into young adult women. I unravel these dynamics by locating girls' lives within and as affected by various structures, processes and relationships, most notably the intersection of their age-based position with patriarchy, caste and class.

The following section outlines the context of the study and data collection. The third section examines how girls become aware of unwantedness, while the fourth section focuses on their experiences. The fifth section discusses how girls deal with unwantedness. The final section offers some concluding remarks.

Context and Data Collection

According to the Census 2011, the child (0–6) sex ratio in India has declined from 927 girls per 1000 boys in 2001 to 914 in 2011. Much of this deficit is due to daughter elimination in the form of sex-selective abortion, female infanticide and neglect, which in turn is triggered by son preference and daughter aversion for economic and cultural reasons. The non-negotiability of a timely marriage for daughters, the indispensability of dowry and the burden of preserving a girl's chastity top the list of reasons underpinning daughter aversion and elimination. Even when 'unwanted' girls survive, many experience neglect with regard to vital investments reflected in high female infant and child mortality rates (Bardhan 1974; Agnihotri 2001). Adding generational hierarchies to gender hierarchies (Croll 2007, p. 1291) illuminates the gendered nature of child-rearing and processes of growing up. For example, in societies with strong son preference, boys are often seen as objects of affection, as crucial resources for the perpetuation and strengthening of kinship ties, and for old age security, whereas girls may be seen as a drain on natal family resources as they leave the family upon marriage.

Resistance to daughter elimination is idiosyncratic at the local level. This may not be sufficient to challenge the hegemonic norm of daughter aversion. The challenge for interventions is to mobilize disparate acts of resistance to produce a culture of daughter preference. Although current interventions have led to a considerable decline in the practice of female infanticide in the study area, Srinivasan and Bedi (2011) caution that they are unlikely to have succeeded in altering underlying structural factors that lead to son preference and daughter aversion, as none of the interventions is geared towards addressing these.

The study on which this chapter is based was conducted in Usilampatti block in Madurai district in the South Indian state of Tamil Nadu, which reported the first instance of female infanticide in the state around the mid-1980s (Soundarapandian 1985; Jeeva et al. 1998). Compared to all India figures, the child sex ratio for Madurai was 939 girls per 1000 boys in 2011, an increase from 926 in 2001. According to the Census 2011, the district has a female literacy rate of 76.7 per cent, whereas male literacy rate is 86.6 per cent. The study is exploratory in nature and is based on three short rounds of field research in 2006, 2010 and 2012, following the life trajectories of ten girls. Access to the girls was facilitated by an NGO that works on children's issues, yet the research was conducted independently from the NGO. Preliminary discussions were undertaken with about 40 girls in five villages followed by an in-depth research with ten girls who were enthusiastic about being part of the study since our first meeting. Although these ten girls had attended a training programme conducted by the NGO in 2005, this research is not about the programme as such.[1] Familiarity with Tamil and the cultural context, and prior field experience in Tamil Nadu, were important in facilitating fieldwork.

A variety of research methods was used. Suggestions about activities that they particularly enjoyed were solicited from the girls and agreed upon at the start of the research. During the first fieldwork period (2006), I interviewed individually all ten girls, who were then 11–13 years old studying in Classes 6 and 7, and conducted focus group discussions on key issues related to their life worlds such as relationships, aspirations, likes and dislikes with regard to family, friends, school and community. Six girls wrote short autobiographical notes. The girls also prepared and presented a play, and there was plenty of dance, songs and storytelling as part of the research process as an attempt to deal in a child-friendly manner with the delicate issue of experiencing unwantedness. Data collection also included discussions with mothers, teachers and NGO staff. Short revisits were undertaken in 2010 when all girls had attained puberty, and again in 2012 when most girls were legally turning into adults by reaching the age of 18. The village and NGO are not named and the names of respondents have been changed in the chapter.

Given the sensitive nature of the issue under investigation, only girls who had participated in workshops conducted by the NGO were included in the research.[2] The issues discussed in the research were thus not new to them. Two NGO staff accompanied the researcher during the study. The girls and their parent(s) were advised to contact the NGO if they had any concern with regard to the research. At the beginning and at every interaction, girls and their parents were informed that the research was about understanding their views on female infanticide, experiences of growing up in a context where daughters were relatively less valued.

The study village consists of about 2000 households belonging to over ten different castes with *Kallars* as the numerically dominant caste. Whereas a small minority owns most land in this agrarian village, the majority are agricultural wage labourers. Six of the girls studied belong to poor landless *Kallar* families. The remaining four are from poor landless Scheduled Caste (SC) families. SC families are by far the most oppressed, socially and economically. All parents are barely literate and wage labour is their main source of income. All girls have at least one brother; four of them also have sisters.

Knowing Unwantedness

When talking about the issue of daughter elimination, the children referred mainly to 'female infanticide' using the Tamil phrase *penn sisu kolai* (literally: 'female infant killing'). All children I interacted with in the study area—girl or boy—knew about female infanticide, its causes and method of execution. This can to a large extent be attributed to first-hand knowledge because female infanticide occurs post-birth, in the privacy of homes and is therefore less secretive than medically facilitated sex selection (see Srinivasan 2012: 8, 157). As illustrated below, the interpretations of such observations were also reinforced by the NGO activities.

Until the late 1990s, female infanticide was the more widely prevalent form of daughter elimination. In the late 1990s and 2000s, medically facilitated sex-selective abortion was widespread. At present, Census data, NGOs, and local people report that daughter elimination whether in the form of female infanticide or sex-selective abortion has declined considerably. Some of the adolescent girls and boys showed awareness of this shift and knew, for example, the stage in pregnancy when the sex of the foetus was revealed.

To the question, 'When did you become aware of female infanticide (*penn sisu kolai*)?', girls in the study responded by saying, 'from the NGO', 'last year' or 'in the training programme'. The question was then posed in the following manner: 'In your region people kill girls who are not wanted, when did you get to know of this?' The response to this was, 'a few years back', 'when I was in Class 5' or 'last year'. Devi, one of the girls studied, noted that when she was in Class 5 (aged ten), she heard of a female baby's death. Some of the girls had overheard adult conversations on female infanticide; a few of them had heard about the practice from their mothers, neighbours or from their friends. In addition, a few girls mentioned the NGO training programme in the autobiographical notes.

> Devi: People kept saying that the baby had died due to snake-bite, a lizard-bite. Then I heard that the baby died due to drowning, that she fell down. But after the training I know that this is not an accident.

Infant death, and in the study context female infanticide, is often rationalized euphemistically as a natural outcome or event by its practitioners to enable them to deal with the emotional and moral ramifications of the act (see also Schepher-Hughes 1992).

For Devi, Lalita and Jyothi, the awareness of the practice comes from personal experience, as they knew of attempts made to eliminate them at birth.

Devi: I heard from my neighbours, may be when I was in Class 5 (10 years old) that my mother had tried to eliminate me. When I asked my mother about this, she said, 'I was under pressure to get rid of you. Relatives who visited us during your birth advised your father not to have a second daughter. Everybody was asking us to get rid of you. So I tried but in the end we did not'.

Jyothi: I was in Class 3 or 4 (8 or 9 years old). I overheard my mother say to other women that she and her mother wanted to kill me when I was born. It was her elder sister (my aunt) who intervened. My aunt, who did not have a child, said, 'Why do you want to get rid of the child? If you cannot bring her up, I will take her'.

Lalita: I cannot remember when I heard or got to know that my mother had tried to kill me. I heard about it from my mother and her elder sister. My mother would have poisoned me but my *peri-amma* (aunt, mother's elder sister) saved me. During a conversation my aunt said to me, 'Your mother has killed two girls'.

Asha, Lalita and Jyothi reported the elimination of their sisters. In Asha's case, it is public knowledge that her mother killed her older sister and gave away her twin sister. Lalita, who escaped elimination at birth, reported that her mother had got rid of her two younger sisters. When she asked her mother for the reason, she was told, 'We have already done a lot [of dowry] for your sister, we have to do a lot for you. We should have got rid of you too when you were born'. In addition, she insisted that she had witnessed a female baby being buried near her grandfather's house: 'Honestly, I saw it with my own eyes'. Rani wrote that the saddest moment in her life was when her younger sister died soon after birth. In Jyothi's case, two female babies were eliminated after her eldest sister, Sumathi (alive), and she herself had been rescued.[3]

EXPERIENCING DISCRIMINATION

In the context of the study, gender discrimination is relational, based on and reproducing the different values parents attribute to sons vis-à-vis daughters, and the different ways girls and boys (as well as men and women) are positioned in a range of intersecting social relations. Following Bourdieu (1977), social actors (here girls) do not passively mimic the world around them; they interpret, adapt, imitate and resist structures through the process of 'cultural reproduction'. In this study, I present a generational analysis of the cultural reproduction of gender-based violence through a focus on children as they 'negotiate, share, and create culture with adults and each other' (Corsaro 2005: 18). This co-constructive role of children in 'interpretive reproduction' serves to highlight that 'children are not simply internalizing society and culture, but are actively *contributing to cultural production and change*', yet their participation in society is '*constrained by the existing social structure and by societal reproduction*' (Corsaro 2005: 19, italics as in original).

Situating Girlhoods

Friends, play, attending family and village festivals and watching television featured as the girls' favourite activities. Friends were usually from the same class and of the same sex, cherished for laughter, play and support. As most parents are illiterate, friends also help each other with schoolwork. When asked about her friends, Lalita said, 'They are friends for life. It means that we will sacrifice for each other'. The school routine includes 30-minute playtime every day. But girls who had attained puberty did not usually play. Instead, they spent time chatting among friends, and sometimes playing games that did not entail running. Rajeswari and Sumathi were in the same class as the other girls in the study, but they stopped playing with them as soon as they 'came of age'. The group felt that they should continue to play, but the two said that they would be admonished by their parents and other elders in the village if they did so as the social norm for girls who have attained puberty requires them to behave in a 'proper womanly manner'.[4]

Discussions on what the girls disliked about family, friends, school and community (village) turned the spotlight on violence. All girls were unanimous in noting that they did not like their parents' fighting, especially when fathers hit their mothers. When some of them tried to intervene, they also got beaten. A fight with a friend or use of foul language to scold a friend was disliked too, as well as being scolded or beaten at school or at home. Girls were also vocal about violence in public spaces and harassment by boys. This restricted their mobility, denied them safety and a place to play. Both these problems highlight a male domination of public places, making it unfit for women and girls. The girls refer to the village as *yamakundam*, which in Hindu mythology refers to the abode of *yama*, the god of death. Drinking and alcohol-induced violence are reported to occur frequently in public. To avoid physical violence, most people, particularly children and women, do not venture out after sunset.

Being teased by boys (known as 'eve teasing' in India) who are of the same age or are older is reported to be a persistent problem (Derne 1999; Abraham 2001; Rossi 2013). Although school is co-educational, boys and girls sit separately and interactions between them are generally not encouraged. Girls have to confront groups of boys on their way to and from school or village shops and when visiting friends. As one of them said, 'They seem to be everywhere, all the time'. Girls talk back, ignore comments and run away, and have even complained to some boys' parents, but the problem persists. Excerpts from an animated discussion among the girls illustrate much of the above:

Village X is *yamakundam* (Rani, followed by a chorus)

Lalita:	I like the festivals …. I like the temples … I like it when there is calm without conflict, election propaganda ….
Selvi:	Men drink …. If they drink, they should stay in their homes …. Instead they are out in the open ….
Rani:	They [men who are drunk] fight …. The other day they took the empty bottles from the shop and were throwing them at each other …. One of the bottles hit this girl ….

274   S. SRINIVASAN

Jyothi: They are loud, behave badly ....
Usha: They use filthy language and abusive terms.
Asha: Five murders have taken place recently in our village. Did
               you hear about them?
Lalita: Some people from the church talked to us .... People fought
               with them accusing them of spoiling us.
Devi: Another problem we face is being teased by boys.
Sumathi: The guys block our way ....
In chorus: When we pass by them, they say 'Talk to *mama*[5] .... Take a
               look at your *mama* .... Why are you ignoring your *mama*'?
Rani: Sometimes we run away ....
Jyothi: This girl [referring to Devi] talks back and also uses foul
               language ....
Lalita: It is actually very difficult to study in such a place ....
Jyothi: We cannot even walk in peace in nice clothes, putting flow-
               ers on our hair ....
In chorus: They tease us ... 'Come, let's get married .... Are you going
               to get married'?

Exposure to violence is widespread and occurs in different spaces in the
girls' life worlds. The discussions further showed that girls have not only
heard and witnessed violence; often, it is directed at them. Many of the
different forms of violence result from the intersection of gender, caste
and material conditions, and are a major source of unfreedom for girls.
As Derne (1999) notes, such sexual violence is a key source of women's
subordination.

In preparation for the 'good wife' role, all girls were expected to perform daily chores. Fetching water, cleaning the house and utensils and
sometimes cooking are among girls' tasks. Rani cooked every evening after
school as her parents got back late from work. Although the girls seemed
inclined to do chores at home, they wanted to be able to decide when and
what to do, a freedom they felt mothers denied them. Mothers frequently
scolded and shouted at them if they did not work. As one mother said, 'if
you don't shout, they will not work. Only if you scold will they work prop-
erly'. Girls, however, did not like being scolded or beaten. They wanted
their mothers to be patient and talk to them nicely.

Girls reported differential treatment vis-à-vis their brothers, mainly in
food allocation and domestic chores. Boys were generally encouraged to
eat better, and were given better-quality food and food of their choice,
whereas girls had to make do with what was available. Girls performed a

wide range of domestic chores, and in their view, boys are not expected to do much. This view is supported by macro-level data for different parts of India (e.g., Kambhampati and Rajan 2008).

Rani: Boys come back from school, throw their bags down and loaf around. We are expected to carry out chores. If we don't do it, our mothers scold. If you ask why they don't ask our brothers to help out, they scold us even more.

Jyothi: My mother scolds me when I disobey her, don't do the things she asks me to do. I sometimes ignore her and she continues scolding. I am the one who goes to the shop because my brother is a *chella* (favourite) child and my sister has attained puberty. Sometimes I talk back or run away, then, she [my mother] will do the work, but not my brother. She says, 'He is a small child. He is a boy, why should he work?'

Selvi: Once when I came back from school, my younger brother told me that mother had given him something special to eat. When I asked her for my share, she said, 'Why should I give it to you? Are you going to feed me, take care of me in my old age?'

Lalita: My mother says, 'Don't eat like a pig'. My younger brother is always encouraged to eat. She gives milk to my cousin brother. I ask her and she declines. If my father is around, he makes sure I get a share. I fight with her, ask her why she is nice to my younger brother, she says, 'He is a boy, he is a *chella* child. Let him eat'.

Most girls enjoyed going to school and were keen to study 'at least up to Class 12'. Five of them aspired to be teachers, one wanted to be a nurse, another, a doctor and yet another wanted to become a great person. Two of them said they would study up to Class 8 and then engage in wage work. Usha who topped her class said she wanted to be a teacher ever since she became aware of this world:

When the teacher for Class 5 does not come, I teach them. The kids there call me teacher *akka* [elder sister]. It feels very nice.

Violence (or its absence) also featured in the girls' assessment of their teachers. Unpopular teachers were those who got angry, shouted at them and who resorted to beating. Lalita, for instance, said 'I like teacher Vidya because she appreciates my hand writing and is encouraging'. For Devi,

'Just by seeing teacher Vidya you know she is nice. Teacher Anita gets very angry, scolds and shouts a lot and sometimes also hits. Teacher Vidya also scolds but she is a good person'. Asha said, 'If I did a sum wrong, I should not be shouted at. I should be asked to do it again'.

The average level of schooling for girls and boys is low, with most of them studying only up to Class 8 (when they are 12–13 years old), the highest offered by the village middle school. At a global level, improving the education levels of girls is a gender and development strategy to delay their marriage (Plan International 2013). Teachers, as 'agents of development' (Morarji, this volume), reportedly encourage girls to study at least up to Class 12 and go on to train to become a teacher or a nurse or something, instead of getting married with just a few years of schooling. At the same time, they do not intervene if one of their girl students stops attending school as this is not required by the education department. Moreover, teachers who do intervene might face social sanctions from the community. In addition, there were also teachers who felt that girls do not aspire to study a lot or to get a good job.

Childhood studies show that children from an early age are embedded within the gender relations shaping society (Dube 1988, 2001; Hirschfield 2002; Rogers 2003; Corsaro 2005). The girls' responses so far confirm that in a context of extreme gender discrimination, children are acutely aware of the differential treatment meted out to them (see also Papanek 1990; Dube 2001). In addition, the data also show that they question the moral rightness of such different entitlements for girls and boys, even though they may later go on to accept and even reproduce what parents and other adults have done to them—a point I will return to below.

'Becoming a Woman'

Before concluding the discussion on girls' experiences of unwantedness, a brief discussion of the girls' anxiety about puberty is warranted. In 2006, when all the girls except two were on the verge of puberty, none of the girls in the group felt that she was currently happy. Devi articulated that this had to do with worries about 'becoming a *periyamanushi* (woman)'. The following responses reveal the centrality of puberty in the girls' lives and their unhappiness about the status they would shortly acquire.

Devi: I was most happy when I was 3 ½ years old and up to when I was
         7 years old …. Nobody questioned anything I did. [I had a] lot of

> freedom. Now they say I am a big girl. I should stay in the house. This is even before [attaining] puberty .... These days, people are telling me all the time that I am a big girl, I should dress properly .... They talk about my marriage .... It makes me cry.

Asha: My happiest moments were when I was small, I played a lot. Now I have to work. I like my school a lot. When school ends or during holidays I don't like it ... I wonder why the school has to close.

Asked if she had worries, Asha appeared most anxious about losing freedom with the onset of puberty: 'I don't like being restricted when I attain puberty'.

The centrality of puberty in a girl's life finds resonance in the girls' conceptualization of a child. A child, male or female, is described as a person below ten years of age, as the period below this is 'a time of innocence', 'a time of carefree running around' and 'of play'. The formal Tamil equivalent of a child is the gender-neutral term *kuzhandai*. However, in everyday situations, this term is usually limited to refer to infants and babies, and by parents to refer to their own children. The more common referential terms used for children in middle childhood are gendered (*paiyan/pasanga* for boys, and *ponnu/pillai* for girls). In the study context, the attainment of puberty marks the end of childhood in terms of 'social age' (Clark-Kazak 2009), even though according to chronological age, these adolescent girls are still considered children.

Attaining puberty has severe consequences for girls, as an unmarried girl is likened to 'an inferno in the stomach' in the local milieu.[6] 'Control of sexuality is at the core of both patriarchal and caste relations' (Abraham 2001: 135), which often takes the form of early marriage for girls (at around puberty) in spite of the illegality of child marriage (The Prohibition of Child Marriage Act, 2006). Whereas a few girls from well-off *Kallar* families go to university and are employed, for the vast majority of girls, marriage takes precedence over education or a career. Despite these norms, Asha, Jyothi, Lalita and Devi wanted to study and aspired to marry only when they had reached the age of 21. Asha said:

> I will marry my mother's elder brother's son, he is 19 years old, has been to college, and is now a tailor. I will marry when I am 21 years old .... If they ask for marriage immediately after I reach puberty, I will tell them that I want to study .... If my mother refuses, then I have to marry, I cannot protest or fight.

Asha and Jyothi were aware that their plans could fail. In fact, Asha knew that her older sister had to discontinue her schooling following puberty. She was married off soon after and at 15 had her first daughter. Jyothi is to be married to her father's sister's son. She hopes to marry after she has become 'a great person'. She lapsed into silence when asked, 'What would you do if your aunt asks for marriage soon after puberty?' Asha's mother who overheard the question said, 'Then she has to stick her neck out. There is no way out'. Lalita and Devi asserted that marriage would not interrupt their studies.

> Lalita: I do not want to marry till I finish my studies, make good progress and become a teacher. I will not marry till I can stand on my own feet …. My sister used to study well but my parents ignored it and married her off early. My parents regret it now. They will not let the same thing happen to me. My father and *mama* (maternal uncle) are very encouraging.

Devi's observation poignantly sums up the situation for girls.

> Girls of my age face some problems – early marriage, child birth related maternal mortality …. Many girls are married when they are in Class 8. Just the thought of attaining puberty and marriage affect their studies, they do not do well.

DEALING WITH UNWANTEDNESS

Within the possibilities afforded by their contexts, girls find ways to deal with the discrimination and devaluation they experience in the family. This is akin to 'bargaining with patriarchy' (Kandiyoti 1988) where girls rely on a discriminatory patriarchal set up to save them and to get by. The acute sense among girls that they could have been eliminated is apparent even among those who have not experienced it directly. All girls felt female infanticide was wrong; Rani and Devi felt sorry for the female babies that were eliminated. Three girls wrote in their autobiographical notes that they would never eliminate their daughters or granddaughters. One such example is the following:

> Usha: After ten years I will be working as a teacher …. I would be married with two children. I will get them married at the age of 21 and will chose a good boy for them. I will advise them not to kill the girl children and if they did not want one, I will bring her up.

Some of them expressed fear, thinking about the possibility that they could have met with a similar fate. This was evident in discussions with Lalita, who, as noted earlier, could have been eliminated but for her aunt's intervention. As she talked, her eyes filled with tears:

> They should have killed me as soon as I was born.
> [SS: Why do you say so?]
> Living in this village, *oor* is hell. There is too much violence here. When I think of it, it makes me very worried, very nervous.

Devi said that elimination would have been 'better' than the constant worries and difficulties she now confronts routinely.

> It would have been better to have died. [I have] too much of worries. Everybody keeps scolding me. My elder sister scolds me. She says 'Everything is spoilt because of you. They should have killed you'. My neighbours say things to my face. When I did not perform household chores, the old woman in my neighbour's house said, 'Look at you! If they had got rid of you when you were born this would not happen. If I had a daughter like you, I should have poisoned her'.
> My mother scolds me all the time. She always finds fault with me and not with my elder sister. The other day we sat down to eat, she said, 'Why are you sitting there like a corpse? Go bring some water'. When I ask her why she does not ask my sister to work, her response is, 'She is the eldest; you have to do the work'. She does not need a reason to scold me.

In a separate discussion, Devi's mother who is in her 50s talked about the anxiety of bringing up two daughters.

> My first daughter was born after several years of my marriage. Through all that time my husband resisted pressure from his family to remarry to have a child. And then I had another daughter, Devi. Coming under intense pressure I tried to eliminate her. Her father intervened. He said, 'We will bring them up somehow'. Come what may, we want to make them study. The older daughter is studying in Class 10 in Usilampatti. Devi studies well .... My brothers' families[7] don't treat us well. They are extremely well-off. We are poor. They don't talk to my daughters properly. It hurts .... We have to help the girls ashore. We are old, if something happens to us, what will happen to these girls? It makes me worry a lot. If it were a boy, you could send him anywhere to make snacks and sell them. We cannot do that with

our daughters. Girls have to be well-protected till we can marry them off. Thinking of this all the time, I lose sleep.

When asked if she thought Asha was affected by the knowledge about the fate of her sisters, Asha's mother said, 'She (Asha) keeps asking me why I gave her twin sister away'. Lalita also confirms that such knowledge continues affecting children as they grow up.

> Lalita: When you think that parents who give birth to you want to kill you, it feels bad.

The knowledge that mothers tried to eliminate them is probably one of the reasons that girls evaluate their mothers harshly. The view that mothers are more demanding of them (vis-à-vis their brothers) also creates the impression that mothers do not love or want them. Generally, the girls perceived fathers as being more affectionate. This is reflective not only of the hegemonic nature of patriarchy, but also of the disproportionate gender division of responsibility (including blame if girls behave inappropriately) that mothers bear for disciplining their children, particularly girls, and that most fathers are not around the house for much of the time. In addition, elimination surfaces frequently when mothers scold the girls. When Jyothi's mother scolds her for not doing household chores and reminds her that she was spared at birth, Jyothi retorted:

> You keep saying we should have killed you when you were born, so why didn't you? You should have killed me.

Lalita on the other hand threatened her mother.

> My mother says, 'I should have poisoned you'. I tell her, 'You should be killed. I will tell my father, he will take care of you'.

By imagining a future that is different for their daughters, by turning a mother's threat against her, or by ending a play by condemning extravaganza and dowry and exhorting simple living, or as the discussion below shows by choosing factory work over marriage, girls show that they do not simply reproduce structures of gender-based violence. Instead, from their position of relative subordination, they seek change through subtle and direct approaches to bargaining with patriarchy.

MARRIAGE OR WHAT ELSE?

Given the girls' preoccupation with puberty, a field visit was undertaken in 2010 when they were around 15–16 years. None of the girls was yet married, but only two girls—Asha and Rani—were still living in the village and were studying in Classes 10 and 11, respectively, in the school in Usilampatti town, which is about five kilometres away, requiring the girls to commute by bus. These girls were the first among poor *Kallar* families sent out of the village to study. Of the eight girls who were out of the village, two girls—Vani and Usha—were studying. Two—Devi and Selvi—had migrated with their families and had to discontinue their studies after Classes 8 and 9, respectively, to earn a living. The other four worked in various spinning mills in Coimbatore district under what is popularly known as the *sumangali thittam* (scheme). The word *sumangali* is used to refer to a woman's (happily) married status and brokers present the scheme to girls' parents as a way for a poor family to save up money for a daughter's marriage.

Briefly, the *sumangali* scheme is a recruitment strategy used by the mills in and around Coimbatore and Tiruppur. It exploits traditional gender stereotypes and the material realities to draw young unmarried girls into contractual work soon after the attainment of puberty for a period of three years. On the other hand, by allowing girls to earn for their own marriage the scheme arguably also contributes to weakening the image of the daughter as an economic burden and offers girls a small window of freedom to see the world beyond their village and to meet other people (mainly girls). Once a girl turns 18, she becomes ineligible to work under the scheme (Solidaridad 2012). Girls are required to stay in the hostels provided usually within the factory premises for the three-year period. They work for a minimum of eight hours a day or night for a wage of about Rs.500 per week (approximately USD 9 in June 2012) and when the factory receives more orders they are expected to work additional long hours for which they are paid separately. A fixed amount is deducted from their wages for boarding and lodging expenses. In addition, at the end of three years a girl receives a lump sum of about Rs. 25,000–50,000 (USD 448–896 in June 2012).

The disciplinary regime of the factory responds to the anxiety of parents of young unmarried girls: girls are not allowed to leave the factory premises unescorted and are not allowed to talk to or meet any one other than the authorized person (often the girl's father). For instance, when I asked some mothers if I could talk to their daughters on the phone, I was told that my calls would not be allowed. Although no accurate estimate is available, newspaper and anecdotal reports on various forms of exploitation, including sexual violation and poor living conditions, abound; some have called for abolition of the scheme on the grounds of slavery and/or human rights violation (see, for instance, IBN Live 2012).

The possibility of earning a lump sum, however meagre, at the time of a girl's marriage along with the factory's assurance about her safety allows parents to let their unmarried daughters leave home to live and work in faraway factories. The scheme provides many girls from poor families an escape out of early marriage or related domestic pressures and a small window of freedom to see the outside world and to meet other people (mainly girls).

Queried about the welfare of their daughters, some mothers felt that their daughter was better off in the factory than being in the village—she ate well, was healthy (I was shown pictures as evidence), happy and spared the day-to-day domestic worries. Two mothers explained that their daughters *chose* to go away for factory work over marriage as marriageable kin came asking for them once they had attained puberty. The explanation to the prospective groom's family that the girls would work for a while to earn for their marriage appeared to have been acceptable to all parties concerned. Sumathi's mother further explained, 'if Sumathi had stayed at home, these relatives would have come every day asking for our daughter in marriage. Tired of their nagging, we would have also got her married'.

The mothers acknowledged the exploitative nature of the scheme, but argued that this was not true of the companies that they had sent their daughters to. In some instances, factory work even enabled young women to continue their studies. Lalita was said to be working in a factory that allowed her to attend computer classes. In 2010, Usha who had scored 85 per cent in her Class 10 final exams had to discontinue her studies as her father met with an accident and she had to support her mother in earning an income. A year later, she was sent away to a factory where her father said she was allowed to study and sit for Class 12 exams in the summer of 2012.

Selvi's parents were away most of the time, leaving Selvi and her younger brother in the care of their close relative and neighbour. Upon finishing Class 8 in the village school, Selvi joined Asha and Rani to attend the school in Usilampatti town. After a year, just as she started Class 10, one of her female cousins was said to have eloped and got married. Fearing a similar fate for their daughter, Selvi's parents took her and her brother with them to the place where they worked as migrant labourers where she had to work with them for a living.

Although these girls had managed to stay unmarried, for most, pursuing their aspiration to study remained a distant possibility. The intersection of gender, caste and class hierarchies implies that the most realistic alternative to early marriage for many of the girls from poor families is early entry into full-time wage labour. This is facilitated by a highly localized response of capital to the potential of labour exploitation produced by the particular interplay between gender and age when young girls, especially from poor families, have attained puberty.

Turning 18

In 2012, another field visit was undertaken to see how the girls transitioned into legal adulthood. Two girls had managed to complete schooling (Class 12). Whereas Usha continued working at the mill with the possibility of studying further depending on her employer's benevolence, Rani was married a month after her exams and lives with her husband in North India. Not much is known about Selvi and Devi who had migrated with their families. Lalita, having studied up to Class 10, continues to work in the mill as a regular employee after her *sumangali* contract expired.

Of the remaining five, Rajeswari who studied up to Class 8 and is now 18 years came back from the mill after the three-year period. She has been at home since then because of an illness that required surgery. She said she had no plan of going back to the mill and marriage was not likely any time soon. Sumathi was sent off to work in a mill after she finished Class 8, where she worked for four years.[8] She was married to a distant relative when she was 17 years and a year later gave birth to a daughter. When asked how she felt about her newborn daughter, Sumathi indicated that while okay, she would have actually preferred a son. This brings the spotlight back to the unwantedness of daughters. Sumathi's response is reflective of the dramatic transformation that girls undergo with puberty and early marriage. From a very young age, girls become aware of the discriminatory standards that they are subject to, which provide men with freedom, mobility and other privileges while subjugating girls and women at every life stage whether in natal or marital households. The onset of puberty hastens this process through norms and practices aimed to regulate and protect their sexuality (chastity). These not only take away the freedom and mobility that girls enjoyed, but also awaken them to the indispensability of marriage, and that sons are an important resource through which women acquire and consolidate status (see Kandiyoti 1988). Many young women also come to accept that they are vulnerable and in need of male protection, and that far from the futures they imagined just a few years ago, their lives may not be different from that of their mothers or other women in their cultural milieu (see Abraham 2001). Subsequently, this leads many women to decide against daughters: 'We (women) kill her because we do not want her to suffer like we do' (Srinivasan 2012: 189).

Sumathi's sister, Jyothi, who studied up to Class 8 and had finished her three-year *sumangali* contract with a mill, is continuing to work in the same mill for a monthly wage.

SS:	What about Jyothi's marriage?
Sumathi:	There is a *mapillai* (groom). He is related to us, *attai's* (father's sister's) son.
Father:	We are waiting for her to work … to buy jewellery.
SS:	But she will marry a relative.
Sumathi's husband:	So what if he is a relative? Nobody will marry these days without *seeru* (dowry).
Sumathi:	We need to give five *pavun* (One *pavun* = 8 grams of gold).

Vani studied till class 10 and was married when she was 17 years. Asha, whose sister in 2010 explained that she regretted that she could not complete her studies and felt that the family would make sure that Asha studied well, was pulled out of school after Class 11, with one more year of schooling left, to be married to a distant relative. During the field visit wedding preparations were underway. When asked why she could not have waited for a year to get married, both Asha and her sister said that it was her mother who insisted on the marriage and did not listen to anyone. Asha said that she would go back to school after marriage and go on to train to be a teacher.[9] Parents of young girls come under pressure to get their daughters married if they suspect that the girl is seeing someone or if the groom's family is impatient about marriage. In the former, the family honour is said to be at stake, whereas in the latter, the fear is that the groom might look for another bride, which means that the girl's family, especially if they are poor, will have to search for another suitable groom and pay a much higher dowry.

CONCLUSION

At present, approaches to understanding and tackling daughter elimination are adult-centred, focused on adult married women. Toren (1999: 13) has commented on the epistemological dilemma of accessing childhood experiences and children's perceptions from the generational position of adulthood. For this reason, I have treated the girls studied as 'citizens rather than just women-to-be' (Caron 2011: 72), put their voices centre stage in the analysis presented, and complemented these, where relevant, with adults' perspectives.

Conceptually, this chapter has brought into dialogue the idea of 'interpretive reproduction' (Corsaro 2005) coming from the childhood studies literature with that of 'bargaining with patriarchy' (Kandiyoti 1988) from feminist approaches to development. Drawing on Corsaro (2005: 18), the chapter has taken a sociological approach to socialization, treating it 'not only [as] a matter of adaptation and internalization but also [as] a process of appropriation, reinvention, and reproduction'. The lens of interpretive reproduction, thus, warns against a mechanistic reading of the working of unequal relations of power by highlighting the agentic role of young women in the reproduction of daughter aversion. I have demonstrated this by showing how girls from a young age become aware of, reflect on and try to negotiate the differential treatment meted out to them.

Drawing on their differential experiences of gender discrimination, unwantedness and gendered violence, I have shown that cultural reproduction of daughter aversion manifests differently, in the different stages of young women's lives and that children play an active role in these dynamics. This is most visibly observed in the context of the household. Conceptually, this underscores the importance of adding a gender dimension to the interpretation of generation in terms of kinship descent, and taking note of a life phase understanding of generation (see Huijsmans, this volume).

Girls like adult women (e.g., their mothers) acknowledge that female infanticide and daughter elimination should not be practised as well as the factors that cause the practice. But as they negotiate their socio-economic circumstances and cultural norms while progressing through their childhood, at least some of the girls studied seem to have been sucked into the very structural constraints that make women's lives burdensome and daughters unwanted.

The chapter further makes a case for employing the conceptual scheme of 'bargaining with patriarchy' (Kandiyoti 1988) to research with children and youth and extending its analytics with a focus on the role of age and generational relations. Bargaining with patriarchy helps bringing in the structural dimension that is more difficult to capture at the micro-scale at which Corsaro's 'interpretive reproduction' is mostly employed. The *sumangali* scheme is here the case in point. It shows how capitalist dynamics interact with the particular intersection of generational and gender relations that leave adolescent girls with a tough choice between the exploitative relations of capitalism or those of patriarchy.

NOTES

1. The NGO began working in Usilampatti in the late 1980s to prevent female infanticide by setting up women's self-help groups, rescuing female infants under the cradle baby scheme and girl child sponsorship (for more on the work or this NGO, see Srinivasan 2012). The NGO also conducted an adolescent group training programme since 1996, and by June 2006, over 2000 adolescent girls had attended them. The two-day training programme consisted of six modules on health and hygiene, nutrition, women's rights, career guidance, government schemes and maternal and child health. As of 2006, the NGO also started offering workshops for adolescent boys. At present, such workshops are not conducted for boys or for girls.
2. The NGO ran these workshops to train girls to become aware of such practices and to prevent them. The girls who survived female infanticide attempts and went through the workshop were involved in the NGO's awareness raising activities addressing the value of daughters and to prevent daughter elimination.
3. Methodologically, it is near impossible to arrive at a precise assessment of female infanticide and guesstimates are often based on anecdotal evidence, timing and nature of death and birth order of the dead infant. Typically, the first daughter is welcome and never at risk; the risk of elimination increases with the number and birth order of daughters.
4. Notions of the good woman and regulating female chastity as ways to preserve family honour are recurring themes in gender subordination in India. See, for instance, Abraham (2001), Chakraborty (2009) and Lamb (2000).

5. A Tamil woman refers to her husband, as well as other marriageable kin such as maternal uncle or his son, as *mama.*

6. See Abraham (2001), Chakraborty (2009) and Lamb (2000) for a discussion in other parts of India.

7. In Tamil kinship, the mother's brother, *mama,* has a celebrated social and emotional status. He is obliged to protect his sister and her family, especially her daughters. He (and his sons) has the first right to marry his sister's daughter or to decide about his niece's marriage. In recent years, the material and emotional support that a woman and her children can expect from her brother is weakening.

8. The fourth year was on a monthly wage basis.

9. During the third round of fieldwork, a school in district Madurai refused to allow two girls, who were married after Class 10, to join Class 11. This generated considerable debate on the issue of early marriage and child rights, especially the right to education (Imranullah 2012a, 2012b; Kumar 2012; Sinha 2012).

References

Abraham, L. (2001). Redrawing the Lakshman Rekha: Gender differences and cultural constructions in youth sexuality in urban India, South Asia. *Journal of South Asian Studies, 24*(s1), 133–156.

Agnihotri, B. S. (2001). Declining infant and child mortality in India: How do girl children fare? *Economic and Political Weekly, 36*(3), 228–233.

Bardhan, P. (1974). On life and death questions. *Economic and Political Weekly, 9*(32, 33–34), 1293–1304.

Bourdieu, P. (1977). *Outline of a theory of practice.* Cambridge/Oxford: Polity Press.

Caron, C. (2011). Getting girls and teens into the vocabularies of citizenship. *Girlhood Studies, 4*(2), 70–91.

Chakraborty, K. (2009). 'The good Muslim girl': Conducting qualitative participatory research to understand the lives of young Muslim women in the bustees of Kolkata. *Children's Geographies, 7*(4), 421–434.

Clark-Kazak, C. (2009). Towards a working definition and application of social age in international development studies. *Journal of Development Studies, 45*(8), 1307–1324.

Corsaro, A. W. (2005). *The sociology of childhood* (2nd ed.). Thousand Oaks/London/New Delhi: Pine Forge Press.

Croll, E. (2007). From the girl child to girls' rights. *Third World Quarterly, 27*(7), 1285–1297.

Derne, S. (1999). Making sex violent: Love as force in recent Hindi films. *Violence against Women, 5*(5), 548–575.

Dube, L. (1988). On the construction of gender: Hindu girls in patrilineal India. *Economic and Political Weekly, 23*(18), WS11–WS19.

Dube, L. (2001). *Anthropological explorations in gender: Intersecting fields.* New Delhi: Sage Publications.

Hirschfield, L. A. (2002). Why don't anthropologists like children? *American Anthropologist, 104*(2), 611–627.

IBN Live. (2012, April 12). NHRC notice on sumangali scheme. http://ibnlive. in.com/news/nhrc-notice-on-sumangali-scheme/246504-60-118.html. Accessed 15 July 2012.

Imranullah, M. S. (2012a, June 23). Government school slams its doors on married girls. *The Hindu.* http://www.thehindu.com/news/national/tamil-nadu/government-school-slams-its-doors-on-married-girls/article3559934.ece?ref=relatedNews. Accessed 23 June 2012.

Imranullah, M. S. (2012b, July 7). School agrees to admit two married girls. *The Hindu.* http://www.thehindu.com/news/national/tamil-nadu/school-agrees-to-admit-two-married-girls/article3610708.ece?ref=relatedNews. Accessed 7 July 2012.

Jeeva, M., Gandhimathi, & Phavalam (1998). Female infanticide-philosophy, perspective and concern of SIRD. *Search Bulletin, 13*(3), 9–17.

Kambhampati, U. S., & Rajan, R. (2008). The 'nowhere' children: Patriarchy and the role of girls in India's rural economy. *Journal of Development Studies, 44*(9), 1309–1341.

Kandiyoti, D. (1988). Bargaining with patriarchy. *Gender and Society, 2*(3), 274–290.

Kumar, K. (2012, 30 June). A messy corner of India's modernity. *The Hindu.* http://www.thehindu.com/opinion/lead/a-messy-corner-of-indias-modernity/article3585664.ece?ref=relatedNews. Accessed 30 June 2012.

Lamb, S. (2000). *White saris and sweet mangoes: Ageing, gender and the body in North India.* Berkeley: University of California Press.

Papanek, H. (1990). To each less than she needs, from each more than she can do: Allocations, entitlements and value. In I. Tinker (Ed.), *Persistent inequalities: Women and world development* (pp. 162–181). New York/Oxford: Oxford University Press.

Plan International. (2013). *A girl's right to say no to marriage: Working to end child marriage and keep girls in school.* London: Plan International.

Rogers, W. S. (2003). Gendered childhoods. In M. Woodhead & H. Montgomery (Eds.), *Understanding childhood: An interdisciplinary approach* (pp. 179–220). Milton Keynes/Chichester: The Open University Press/Wiley.

Rossi, V. (2013, January 15). Shrouded in patriarchy. *The Hindu.* http://www.thehindu.com/news/cities/Delhi/shrouded-in-patriarchy/article4307378.ece?homepage=true#.UPVhhsF5pAY.gmail. Accessed 15 Jan 2013.

Schepher-Hughes, N. (1992). *Death without weeping: The violence of everyday life in Brazil.* Berkeley: University of California Press.

Sinha, S. (2012, July 6). Teachers should be democratising schools. *The Hindu.* http://www.thehindu.com/opinion/op-ed/teachers-should-be-democratising-schools/article3606726.ece?ref=relatedNews. Accessed 6 July 2012.

Solidaridad. (2012). Understanding the characteristics of the Sumangali scheme in Tamil Nadu textile & Garment Industry and Supply Chain Linkages. Prepared by Solidaridad-South & South East Asia, May 2012.

Soundarapandian, A. (1985, December 4). Varadatchanaikkup payandu pen kuzhandaigalai kolgirargal. *Junior Vikatan (in Tamil).*

Srinivasan, S. (2012). *Daughter deficit: Sex selection in Tamil Nadu.* New Delhi: Women Unlimited.

Srinivasan, S., & Bedi, A. S. (2011). Ensuring daughter survival in Tamil Nadu, India. *Oxford Development Studies, 39*(3), 253–283.

Toren, C. (1999). *Mind, materiality and history: Explorations in Fijian ethnography.* London/New York: Routledge.

CHAPTER 13

Youth, Farming, and Precarity in Rural Burundi

Lidewyde H. Berckmoes and Ben White

Youth, Agriculture, and Precarity[1]

Policy framing and responses to the 'problem' of young people and agriculture in Africa, Sumberg and co-authors argue, are hampered by the lack of 'theoretically and historically informed, conceptually sound and context sensitive' research (Sumberg et al. 2012: 1). Understanding the dynamics and problems of rural 'youth transitions'—a key descriptive notion in policy discourse on youth—requires us to position young people within larger social, economic, and political structures. This relational dimension has been relatively neglected in the social studies of childhood and youth.

The concepts of social reproduction and of generation help to locate young people within larger structures. Social reproduction—'the material

---

This chapter is based largely on an article under the same title that appeared in the *European Journal of Development Research* (2014) Vol. 26(2): 190–203.

L.H. Berckmoes (✉)
NSCR (Netherlands Institute for the Study of Crime and Law Enforcement),
De Boelelaan 1077a, Amsterdam 1008 BH, The Netherlands

B. White
International Institute of Social Studies of Erasmus University Rotterdam,
Kortenaerkade 12, 2518 AX The Hague, Netherlands

R. Huijsmans (ed.), *Generationing Development*,
DOI 10.1057/978-1-137-55623-3_13

and discursive practices which enable the reproduction of a social formation (including the relations between social groups) and its members over time' (Wells 2009: 78)—helps us understand how agrarian societies reproduce themselves on a day-to-day and generational basis, and the continuities and discontinuities in these processes. Generation refers to 'the social (or macro-) structure that is seen to distinguish and separate children [and youth] from other social groups, and to constitute them as a social category' (Alanen 2001: 13). Generation is important in at least two of its many senses (see also Hart, this volume, and Woodman and Wyn 2015). The first involves generation as identity, in the Mannheimian idea of a group that defines itself in terms of common experience (Mannheim 1952). The second is generation as relationship, thus conceptualising young people as participants in, as well as outcomes of social relations between themselves and adults (Alanen 2001). In our view, this should be a core dimension—alongside gender, class, and (where relevant) ethnic relations—in the analysis of agrarian structures and their changes over time. The generational dimension thus needs to be included in standard agrarian political economy questions regarding resource control, division of labour, relations of surplus transfer, and agrarian differentiation (see also Mills, this volume).

Youth unemployment rates in most countries are double the adult rates, and many more are underemployed. Small-scale agriculture is the developing world's single biggest employer, but dominant narratives see agriculture in its present state as so unattractive to youth that they are turning away from agricultural or rural futures (Sumberg et al. 2012; White 2015). Young rural Ethiopians, for example, consider farming as 'a last resort, and for many not an option at all' (Tadele and Gella 2012: 33), and there is a rich emerging literature on young rural–urban migrants, hanging on in cities to avoid returning to their villages, where they will be expected to help with farm work and experience subordination to the older generation (e.g. in Africa, Soares 2010; Mains 2007, 2011). These youth may take on various kinds of casual, short-term jobs, but report themselves as 'unemployed' because they are 'waiting', while looking for what they consider appropriate jobs. This is close to what Standing, following in the tradition of European anti-global and anarchist movements, has called the 'precariat':

> A class in the making, approaching a consciousness of common vulnerability [...]
>
> The precariat consists of those who feel their lives and identities are made up of disjointed bits, in which they cannot construct a desirable narrative or

build a career [...] the precariat cannot draw on a social memory, a feeling of belonging to a community of pride, status, ethics and solidarity. Everything is fleeting. (Standing 2011a; see also Standing 2011b)

Among the many reasons behind young people's apparent turn away from agriculture, we need to take account of the problems that rural youth often have, even if they want to become farmers, in getting access to land while still young (see also Mills, this volume, for the Canadian context, Yagura 2015 for the rural Cambodian context, and FAO et al. 2014, for a global perspective). Reviewing changes in intra-family land relations in sub-Saharan Africa, Julian Quan notes:

> limitations in young people's access to land, land concentration, and land sales and allocations outside the kin group by older generations can become highly problematic where alternative livelihoods are not available, and can trigger wide social conflicts. (Quan 2007: 57)

Georges Kouamé and Kojo Amanor provide examples of such generational conflicts in Côte d'Ivoire (Kouamé 2010) and Ghana (Amanor 1999). The war in Sierra Leone, similarly, has been characterised as a 'crisis of youth' who were frustrated with existing patrimonial forms of resource redistribution (Richards 1996; Peters and Richards 1998; Peters 2011). Important strategies in negotiating youth transitions into social adulthood include education and mobility, which now extends to all social classes and (in most countries) both genders. Youth migrations are not always permanent; we need to explore further the phenomenon of cyclical, part-lifetime migration which may or may not end up with a return to rural communities, and to farming (see, for instance, Temudo and Abrantes 2015, for an example from Guinnea-Bissau).

This chapter explores young men's and women's perceptions of and responses to difficulties in livelihoods building and generational transitions in the aftermath of war in eastern Burundi, a country that has received relatively little scholarly attention. We take as a starting point the need to deconstruct the common assumptions about young people's supposed unwillingness to farm. We describe their 'strategies' of education, marriage, and migration and show how these involve young men and women differently and expose them to new difficulties, while promising little in terms of solutions to the structural problems they face. We argue that a generational approach helps to expose these structural problems of reproduction in rural communities, which often remain neglected in suggestions for improving youth rural livelihoods (see FAO et al. 2014).

The study is based on the first author's field research in a rural area near the Tanzanian border in Burundi, during three research trips between March 2010 and April 2011. The fieldwork was conducted within a larger PhD research project on Burundian (urban) youth (Berckmoes 2014). It took place in collaboration with a non-governmental organisation (NGO) interested in developing a project in rural youth livelihoods building and transitions to independent householding. In-depth interviews and group discussions were conducted with community leaders[2] and experienced NGO facilitators, and with young men and women. A questionnaire survey was carried out by six facilitators with 161 young men and women, in almost equal numbers.[3] Participants were selected on the basis of age (14–25, loosely building on age-based definitions common in development programming), gender (women represented 44 per cent), occupation (76 per cent out-of-school and 24 per cent school-going youth), and location. The average age of youth participants was 19 (20 for men and 19 for women); 35 per cent were 'married', counting both legal marriages ($N = 21$) and non-legal cohabitation ($N = 31$).

The research locations in the provinces Ruyigi and Cankuzo were characterised by subsistence agriculture, large numbers of refugees returning from prolonged periods of exile in Tanzania,[4] and deep levels of poverty. The survey was conducted in three *collines* (administrative units comparable to a village), one of which was formerly inhabited by Tutsi refugees from Rwanda who fled to Burundi in the 1960s and returned after the genocide and subsequent victory of the Rwandan Patriotic Front in 1994. The land left vacant attracted landless families from different regions in Burundi and newly repatriated refugees from the camps in Tanzania.

RURAL LIVELIHOODS IN BURUNDI

At the time of the study, 90 per cent of Burundi's population lived in rural areas, and 95 per cent of the rural employed population worked in agriculture (Ministère de l'intérieur 2010). The total population was estimated at more than 10 million. With an area of 27,830 sq km, Burundi had the third highest population density among African countries (https://www.cia.gov/library/publications/the-world-factbook/geos/by.html, accessed 7 May 2013). High birth rates and substantial flows of repatriating refugees contributed to the pressure on land, and references to the 'population explosion' (Jooma 2005), 'land bomb' (or, *bombe foncière*, ICG 2003) and 'demographic time bomb' (HealthNet TPO IMF 2014; Clark 2013) were common in discussions about Burundi's future. Almost 70 per cent of the rural population lived below the poverty line (IMF 2010).

The youth generation, who grew up during the decade-long civil war (1993–2005), have experienced a 'false start': besides general economic disruption, the war also affected young people's possibilities to obtain education, to save for independent householding, and to invest in land productivity. Also, young unmarried men and women were in a disadvantaged position in terms of access to land due to discriminatory and conflicting aspects of the legal framework. Traditionally, land belonged to family lineages. Married men had the responsibility to ensure access to land for men and women who were not (yet) married. The ideal still was that married sons were to be allocated part of the family's land by their fathers: in most interpretations of customary law, women were unable to inherit or own land, and daughters were expected to live with their husband on the plot he was to inherit. Young men and women were in a vulnerable situation when land disputes arose, for instance, when they were unmarried, when the head of household did not divide land equally between his sons, or when women got divorced. Land regulations introduced during and after the colonial period designated only heads of household as owners of land. The plurality of the legal framework also provoked competing understandings of the rights and duties of the different parties involved. A large number of land conflicts between family members were regularly settled through violence rather than in the courts (Kohlhagen 2012).

In the capital city Bujumbura, the high rate of youth unemployment was one of the main concerns expressed in population consultations.[5] Interviews in Bujumbura suggested that rural youth migrated to urban areas because of the association with modernity and easy access to money. Urban areas were unable to cope with the influx; official urban unemployment rates were high, and especially high for urban youths (Ministère de l'intérieur 2010; CENAP 2010).

Dominant discourses commonly associate Burundi's chronic insecurity and political violence with youth unemployment and restricted livelihoods prospects. This link has been observed elsewhere (cf. Peters and Richards 1998; Utas 2005), but the negative potential of 'idle' youths may be exaggerated in Burundi. The representation of youths as disruptive, violent, and, especially if poor and uneducated, easy to manipulate by the political top has roots in long-term state–society configurations and the involvement of youth militias in violence in the previous decades, and remains salient (Berckmoes 2015).[6] Over the last year, violence perpetrated by, among others, the youth wing of the ruling party underlines how youth embody a generational category easy to mobilise and make conscious of their marginalised conditions; a potential 'precariat'.

Young People and Farming

Young people's apparent turn away from small-scale farming cannot be taken at face value, at least not in Cankuzo and Ruyigi, where farming is still the primary occupation of most young men and women: 'Generally speaking, we make a living with our hoe' (young man, March 2010). Seventy-two per cent of the survey respondents called themselves 'farmers' (*umurimyi*), besides 24 per cent who were still attending school and a very few who reported other occupations. While calling yourself 'farmer' does not always indicate serious or exclusive involvement in farming, 77 per cent of the young men and 85 per cent of the young women reported earning income by selling part of their harvests, and 57 per cent of young men and 39 per cent of young women said that one of their principal sources of cash was working as day labourers on other people's farms. In group interviews, most out-of-school youths envisioned 'farming' as their future way of life, and one of the few realistic options for livelihoods building. Ideas about social reproduction reinforced their attachment to farming: 'Because it is the profession of our forefathers. We grew up seeing our grandparents farm and breed cattle. It is not us now who will just leave this profession like that' (young man, March 2010).

At the same time, young people expressed discontent with current farming conditions. First, because of low crop yields, they often had to work as hired farm labourers, which they would prefer to avoid; it implied that their own or family's plot was not adequately put to use, and indeed their absence, in turn, affected the next season's harvest on the family farm. Second, working as labourers involved them in dependent and hierarchical relationships:

> Because of the bad harvests, we young boys can go work for others. This means that we lose. As we are obliged to work for others, we cannot cultivate our own land (...) We give our strength to someone else (...) When you are used to taking care of yourself, it is not good to go and ask others. (Young man, March 2010)

Independence and self-sufficiency were highly valued in Burundi, and ideas of transition from youth to adulthood, especially for young men, were in large part about achieving these ideals. Formerly, being able to cultivate all you need on your own land was one of the ways in which these ideals were expressed, whereas having to rely on neighbours for necessary food items was seen as humiliating (elderly man, Bujumbura, April 2010).

A second source of discontent was the gap between the norm and the prospects of inheriting land for independent householding. Most young men and women lived with their parents or other caretakers (95 per cent of unmarried youth and 14 per cent of those married and co-habitating). Generally, the plots were owned by their caretaker, although some owned their own plot (21 young men and 24 young women whose husbands owned their own plots). Some lived on land rented from a local land-owner, resident in the city, or a neighbour with a relatively large holding (6 per cent): 'Here a lot of people rent land (…) Here, there are elders [original inhabitants] with large landholdings who rent out [land]' (young man, March 2010). Customarily, parents gave part of their land in use to their children, so they could provide for themselves or prepare for independent householding, which young men would inherit upon marriage or the death of their father. Because these days plots were generally small or because the land was rented, this prospect had become rather unrealistic. As one young man explained: 'we have only a small plot of land on which the house is built, and you, as a boy, you will let your mother stay there and you go find your own land' (March 2012). There was a significant gender difference in expectations regarding land inheritance. 40 per cent of the young men, but only 17 per cent of the young women indicated a firm expectation of inheriting land from their family, while 29 per cent (roughly equal percentages of men and women) expressed the hope of 'maybe' inheriting land, and 32 per cent of young men and 54 per cent of the young women believed they could not count on inheriting land.

Third, all young people were acutely aware of the overall problem of land pressure, declining soil fertility, and other farming-related difficulties: 'As we are all farmers, we face the same problems: limited availability of land, climate change, bad harvests, crop disease' (young man, March 2010). They took worst-case scenarios into account, as shown in a group discussion with youth from previously landless families that had settled in the area:

Lidewyde: Most of you said you were not originally from this commune. Do you plan to stay here in your adult life?

Young man: It is possible, but there is a shortage of land, like before [when our parents decided to move here in search for land]. If there is a place where there is enough land, we go there to look for land for our children. (March 2010)

Non-farm Activities

The response of most youths to problems of access to land and agriculture was not to turn their backs on farming. They sought non-farm income-generating activities, not to replace but to complement and enable farming:

> We wish [a future as farmers], but if we would have other activities to help, that would be better because farming only is not enough. (Young man, March 2010)
>
> Yes, the soil is no longer fertile and there are climatic changes. Therefore we are looking for a profession to combine with farming. (Young woman, March 2010)
>
> Farming only allows one to eat (...) If I have another skill I can move forward, I can develop myself, but with farming only you don't develop. (Young man, March 2010)

Some saw non-agricultural activities as means to buy land while it was still locally available:

> For the boys that will soon become adults, it is possible that you are with seven boys in one family. They will all have to share the same small plot of land. So if you are a boy without a profession you cannot find money to buy land, which is a problem. (Young man, March 2010)
>
> If there was an organization to help us learn a vocation, we could work and have money to buy land before the others do so and there is no more land. (Young man, March 2010)

Professional skills training was seen by both young, out-of-school men and women as a means to achieve income diversification and improve livelihoods prospects: 'We, who have not studied, we are in need of professional skills training schools to be able to survive' (comment noted on questionnaire form, from young man, June 2010).[7]

Just over a quarter of the respondents indicated having some earnings from non-agricultural activities. The most frequent activities reported were petty trade, hairdressing (both young men and women) and brewing or selling alcohol (mostly young women). Yet the numbers of youths engaged in these activities were lower than the numbers reporting non-agricultural skills. When asked about the discrepancies, they reported problems like the lack of starting capital—'I learned a profession [carpentry], but because I have no capital I farm' (young man, March 2010)—as well as problems with the associations they were (supposed to be) working in, most of which were initiated and supported by NGOs.

> There are even a lot [of people who know carpentry] that do nothing. But there is a plan to put us together in an association. We registered, but until today we are waiting. (Young man, March 2010)

Other reported problems within professional associations were geographical distance, lack of guidance in making and implementing business plans, and disputes between members, especially when the groups were made up of youths only:

> Without adults to give advice on how to do things, it is difficult. You quarrel because you are the same age and are without someone who can give advice (…) Adults are like a pillar that hold the house, without them young people will not be together without quarrelling. (Young man, March 2010)

The findings suggest that the young people strongly thought of themselves as embedded within larger social (generational) structures. And, youth saw professional skills training as a way to be better prepared for the hardships of the future, but their pleas for and positive expectations of skills training co-existed with an awareness of its limitations and a view of training as only one step in a highly fragile trajectory away from precarity (see also Utas 2005).

In brief, young Burundian men and women experienced their livelihoods and preparations for independent householding as 'lacking'. They were aware of the unsustainability of current practices of land inheritance and farming, and their concerns about not being able to develop themselves or fulfil their reproductive aspirations oriented them to other livelihood possibilities; but mostly in terms of 'first steps' and with the idea that these 'steps' at some point may lead to possibilities of farming under better conditions. As is noted in relation to rural transformation elsewhere (Bryceson 2002), the young people were oriented towards income diversification but showed ongoing commitment to farming as their (family's) way of life (compare to Rigg 2006: 181).

FORMAL EDUCATION AS PROMISE OF ESCAPE FROM PRECARITY

> If you haven't studied, it is possible that you will always be in the process of 'searching for life' (trying to establish a livelihood). You can be a trader, for instance, and then you may or may not find life – because you may work without making a profit, or you may be robbed. Therefore, you can never say that you 'have your life'. Because at any moment you can fall back to misery. (Young man, March 2010)

In Burundi, the distinction between out-of-school and school-going youth, and the hierarchical relation between them, is pervasive and largely taken for granted. Among the survey respondents, 78 per cent (strongly) agreed that 'students look down on peers who are not educated or have a low level of education' and in group discussions out-of-school youth felt upset about the low regard students appeared to have for farming: 'They [youth in schools] think it is shameful (…) When [a student] passes you… you see, when you go to the farm you do not wear clean clothes. He can pass you and you are dirty with mud, sweat. (…) It is hurtful' (young man, March 2010).

Historically, education in Burundi was for the privileged few and aimed at producing a class of civil servants. After the civil war in 2005, the number of young people enrolled in primary and secondary school significantly increased. This was a result partly of the changes in the selection process, which had barred many (Hutu) youth from (especially post-primary) education[8]; partly of the abolition of fees for primary school and partly of the construction of more local schools, which made it possible for rural youth to continue post-primary education in nearby community colleges rather than in distant boarding schools.

The legacy of education as preparation for civil service, nonetheless, meant that many rural Burundians still imagined (secondary) school to be a sure step to working for the government or other salaried employment. This promise was strongly reflected in the livelihoods aspirations of school-going youth, portrayed in the group discussion excerpts below:

> You will have a diploma and you work and they pay you with money…
> When you finish your studies you become financially independent. You are no longer in need of aid…
> [Without education] you can only enter into a local association, but you cannot have a position with responsibility in those associations.

> I would like to add that if you finish your studies you can find work
> in project businesses that implement big projects like the construction of
> schools and hospitals and you can have them constructed in the area you
> live. (Young men and women, March 2010)

Despite these hopes, education no longer automatically led to salaried employment opportunities. Employment statistics indicated higher unemployment rates among the relatively more educated and in urban areas (Ministère de l'Intérieur 2010). Of course, average education levels were higher in the cities, but a large number of the unemployed urban, educated youth originated in rural areas and came to or remained in the cities in search of employment. They seemed hesitant to return to the countryside, except for an occasional visit to their family:

> I live with my big sister [in Bujumbura] (…) But sometimes I go upcountry
> and pass maybe two months there. My brothers and sisters [who are also in
> Bujumbura] say 'no, really, come back, maybe there will be a job offer and
> you will not know of it'. (Young woman, Bujumbura, June 2010)[9]

Thus, while education may take youth out of the rural margins, it may be only to displace them to the urban margins.

Sending children to school came with substantial costs to their families, both monetary and through the loss of labour. For youth, this underscored that education is a 'privilege', incurring obligations to family and society: 'you can help others, especially those that helped you. You can help their children' (young woman, March 2010). It also rendered school enrolment vulnerable to domestic crises; 12 out of 161 survey respondents reported that they had dropped out of school because of the loss of a parent, another 23 because of poverty in the household. Since education was valued primarily as a requirement for salaried employment, rather than for the knowledge that young people could obtain—'I studied until the sixth grade but six classes are of no use' (young man, March 2010)—the viability of the prospect of a diploma was taken into account in helping or allowing children to go to school. The perception of education as means to an end put particular groups of young people at risk of not starting school (girls in particular) or not finishing (girls, the poor, and those who have difficulty passing tests and have to resit classes):

> What prevents children from going to school is that they are with many
> [children] at home and the parents are poor. They do not have the means

to send all children to school. So the boy may think that 'as my parents are poor and do not have the means to send me to school, I will look for work to finance my own studies', and he loses much time doing that. (Young man, March 2010)

Parents can say that if you study as an adult it is of no use, people that study will do so at a young age (…) they say that to learn how to read and write is of no use (…) They say that at your age you have no chance of even becoming a *chef de colline*. (Young man, out-of-school, March 2010)

When your classmates continue to pass to the next class and you have to redo the year, your parents oblige you to stop and you feel discouraged because they will ask you all the time to drop out (…) because they cannot pay for someone who does not advance. (Young woman, student, March 2010)

In general, rural families were more committed to educating boys than girls.

[Some people] say that school is not for girls. (Young man, March 2010)

[Girls do not go to school] because sometimes girls, when they reach like the 8th year, they get pregnant. The parents think schooling is time lost because instead of coming home with a diploma, the girls come home with children. (Young woman, out-of-school, March 2010)

There are a lot of girls that want to go to school, and their parents refuse it because they have a lot of children and they cannot pay for all of them and the girls have to help them on the land to be able to feed the children. (Young woman, out-of-school, March 2010)

Moreover, on marriage, the girl's family would receive dowry and the girl would then reside with her husband's family; this effectively favours investment in the career prospects of sons.

An additional challenge that female school-going youth emphasised was their dependence on boyfriends and male relatives for items like lamp oil for evening study and cosmetics:

For the girls also, because of poverty, there are times that you go home in the evening and there is no oil for the lamp, and if you have a boyfriend you ask him money to obtain [oil], and he can take advantage of that. (Young woman, March 2010)

Young men expressed related concerns about access to money and goods, and through it, also to girlfriends, whom they were expected to help.

The concerns of young men and women about dependence and dating speak to the fact that both livelihoods perspectives and marriage are important for transition to respectable adult life. School-going youth were deeply concerned about their marriage possibilities after education; for girls, secondary school enrolment prolonged the age of marriage, and the status attached to their education could be threatening to potential husbands:

> If you marry a girl who has studied while you have not studied, she does not respect you, she will call you her wife while you are her husband. (Young man, out-of-school, March 2010)
>
> [What distracts us from our school life is that] you can say that when you finish studies without having a boyfriend or girlfriend you will not find a partner etcetera. [to the group:] Is that not also what distracts us? Who can tell me [if it is true] that if you finish your studies without a boyfriend or girlfriend you will no longer find a partner? (Young woman, student, March 2010)

Conversations with community leaders, parents, and NGO community facilitators highlighted adult concerns about two strategies adopted by young people to deal with their precarious livelihoods and aspirations for independent householding: firstly, unauthorised unions referred to as 'illegal marriages', primarily considered as a strategy of, and a problem for, young woman; and secondly, cross-border migration, deemed important primarily for young men.[10]

DIALECTICS OF MARRIAGE AND PRECARITY

In Burundi, 'illegal marriage' refers to cohabitation of a young woman with a man without fulfilling the traditional ceremonial and legal obligations, which include family consent, payment of dowry, wedding ceremonies, and legal registration of the marriage. These unauthorised unions were in the first place a consequence of poverty and lack of resources for the marriage ceremonies and the dowry. While the amount required depended on the position and characteristics of the families involved and groom and bride-to-be, there were some minimal standards which poor families often found difficult to meet: '[The dowry constitutes of] a cow, and you will find that at your place they have not even a chicken' (young man, March 2010). These unauthorised unions had become quite common; less than half of the 'married' youth respondents were legally married.

Irrespective of its frequency, this form of marriage was publicly denounced. It was also generally believed to leave women and their children in a (legally) vulnerable position. For instance, if the husband dies, wants to take a second wife, or wants a divorce, the woman and children would have no (legal) say and could lose their rights to land and goods. In addition, women who faced domestic violence (a widespread problem in Burundi, Boddaert 2012) had few options for escape; separation had far-reaching consequences for the couple and the young woman's family:

> Normally when a girl accepts that [illegal marriage], it is the start of her problems because when the husband leaves her and she has to return to her parents with a child and without being legally married, the child will not receive any part of the land. This is a problem. The girl will become a menace to her brothers [from whom she will then have to ask a piece of land]. (Young woman, March 2010)

While unauthorised unions put young women and children in a vulnerable position, they were also a response to the precarious circumstances of their parental households. Young people argued time and again that girls felt compelled to get married because of the dire situation at home, sometimes at a very young age. They hoped to find better living conditions with a husband, even if only slightly better:

> Do you know why she accepts? She accepts because then she only has to share the food with her husband, the two of them. It is easier to find food for two [than for a whole family]. (Young man, March 2010)
>
> A girl will marry premature when she is not well treated at home... there are even those I saw who got married at the age of fourteen. (Young woman, March 2010)

This view was corroborated in the survey. Fifty-nine per cent (54 young men and 41 young women) agreed with the statement that many young women like to marry at a young age because they want to escape difficulties in their families; only 29 per cent (young men and women in roughly equal percentages) disagreed.

Another reason suggested in both group discussions and survey responses was that young women worried about being able to find a husband. The majority of the respondents agreed with the statement that 'many girls worry that they won't be able to find a husband', with a somewhat higher level of agreement among young men (85 per cent vs. 65

per cent). Some suggested that these worries were related to the relative surplus of women in the community—allegedly a consequence of the civil war and of migration.

In contrast to the early marriage of girls, the survey respondents confirmed that many young men married late because of lack of resources (91 per cent of young men and women agreed with this statement, in roughly equal percentages). In the group discussions, when asked about the preferred age for marriage, most replied that this is 20 for men and between 18 and 20 for women. The importance of marriage, for both genders, was unquestionable; a necessity for reaching respectable adulthood and ensuring their family's social reproduction:

> When you reach adulthood you want to enlarge your family, because [of] our parents [and] so that our children will also have children when we are dead, [to] ensure continuity. (Young man, March 2010)

While parents generally opposed to illegal marriages, they rarely had power to intervene. First, the cohabitation often took place without advance notice: 'The boy tells the girl to come and when she goes to the market she goes home to the boy, they don't even tell the parents' (young man, March 2010). Second, since the responsibility for costs of the marriage was with the parents, they were hardly in a position to judge their children: 'You do it like that but it is the only way you can. It is them [parents] who have to give the dowry and they do not have it, they tell you to manage for yourself like the others' (young man, March 2010). The traditional expectation of intergenerational ties, through shared responsibilities and parental support, were therewith strongly undermined.

In sum, while marriage for young women could sometimes be an 'escape strategy' from their precarious parental household situation, even if only temporarily, for young men it generally constituted a difficult to reach goal. Young men therefore sought 'escape' or 'first steps' towards improved livelihoods and adult transition often through (temporary) cross-border migration.

Migration as a Last (Temporary) Resort

Forty-two per cent of the survey respondents (61 young men and only six young women) had been to Tanzania to earn income at least once, and more than half of these stated that they had 'often' or 'very often' earned income in Tanzania. Migration to Tanzania was not limited to older segments of youths. Seven young men of 15 years indicated that they 'sometimes' or 'often' had been to Tanzania. In group discussions, common explanations young men gave for going to Tanzania included the following:

> When you are poor, you tell yourself that you can go over there to give your strength in exchange for money, and with the money you look for something to sell here to develop yourself. (Young man, March 2010)
>
> Those who like to go to Tanzania are usually the youth that are preparing for marriage. (Young man, March 2010)
>
> We buy clothes and the rest [of the money] we give to our family. (Young man, March 2010)[11]

The journey to Tanzania could be both dangerous and tiring. One young man indicated that he travelled for three days, on foot and by bicycle. Young people sometimes went on their own, especially when they have been in Tanzania before, as refugees or on previous labour visits. In Cankuzo, youth indicated that Burundians and Tanzanians regularly visit each other's markets. Elsewhere, they usually migrated with the help of a Tanzanian 'broker' who negotiated between employer and employee: 'There are many from there coming here to propose that you go with them. You give them money and they take you' (young man, March 2010).

Because of the costs involved, most young migrants went without papers. Once in Tanzania—without documents—they risked jail, menace by the local population, having their earnings taken by the police or soldiers patrolling the border area, or even getting killed: 'they burn them' (young man, March 2010). The only 'safety measures' youth deemed available were knowledge of Swahili language (spoken in Tanzania), of Tanzanian customs, and of the dangers one might be exposed to, because mental preparation could help one handling the hardships.

Because of the dangers, parents and community leaders expressed great worries about this phenomenon of temporary cross-border labour migration. Yet some parents felt unable to intervene because they had no alternatives, and because 'finding one's own way' was seen as part of growing up, especially for young men. At the same time, some youths migrated without informing their parents, as they knew their parents would oppose.

Both the hardship of the journey and the dangers in Tanzania were seen as making it difficult for girls to participate in temporary labour migration.

Very few female survey respondents indicated an expectation of going abroad (1 'strongly', 4 'maybe'). Group discussions however showed that some young women did go to Tanzania for work. Most of them, allegedly, ended up marrying and staying there: 'Often when the girls go to Tanzania they get married (…) because they [Tanzanians] are rich' (young woman, March 2010). Young women returning to their home communities could expect more stigma than young men: 'boys abandon [school] to go to Tanzania for small jobs but a girl cannot do that kind of job, it is shameful; because parents will not believe that is the reason you left home, they will think that you prostituted yourself' (young woman, March 2010). Cross-border visits by the NGO showed that quite a number of young women ended up in prison, as it was illegal for them to get married to a Tanzanian—another dimension of the precarity of marriage for women.[12] Fifty-three per cent of young men and women (in almost equal numbers) indicated they did not want to count on going abroad for their future livelihoods. Going to Tanzania was for many a last, imagined as temporary, resort:

Lidewyde:	[Given all those difficulties], why do you still go there?
Young man 1:	Because we have no alternatives (*pas autre chose à faire*). When we are in shape we take the risk of getting killed, because we are poor.
Young man 2:	But if you do get the money to eat, if you have a vocation that you do over there, then there is no better life than that, but if you do not have any skill, then you are obliged to go still.
Interpreter (woman):	Even if you are not going to bring anything home?
Young man 2:	Yes, we keep our hopes up. (Group discussion, Cankuzo, March 2010)

Young People, Generations, and Farming in Burundi

Combining ideas from agrarian studies and youth studies, we showed in this chapter that a generational approach helps to expose structural problems of reproduction in rural communities. As we have seen, young Burundians' orientations to their responsibilities for social reproduction—within the household, for themselves and, some day, for their own children—coincided with extremely limited possibilities for improvement. Structural problems such as land scarcity, climate change, population pressure, and a rural economy that offered limited opportunities for non-agricultural income generation stood in the way of successful youth 'transitions' and impeded clear scenarios for ways out.

Young people adopted strategies not necessarily as direct solutions to their predicaments but rather as small steps towards the opening up of future possibilities; fleeting responses. Formal education was seen as potentially offering opportunities, but only after obtaining the secondary school diploma; for young women, marriage could offer more space to explore livelihood building activities; and migration to Tanzania was a temporary solution mainly for young men to raise income to prepare for marriage, to save start-up capital, or to buy land and take up farming so as to 'find a life'. In contrast to dominant narratives about rural youth in Africa, rural (out-of-school) young people's apparent turn away from agriculture was not due to an aversion to farming. They aspired a farming future, at some time and under better conditions.

In reality, the advantages of their strategies were extremely limited: many educated youth faced unemployment in cities; income-generating opportunities for young women after marriage remained inadequate because of restricted access to markets and, sometimes, cultural norms that hampered freedom of movement (see also, FAO et al. 2014); and young men going to Tanzania faced risks of violence, and few were able to save money for more than a piece of clothing or food for the family. In addition, despite the clear indications that the young people thought of themselves as embedded within larger social (generational) structures, the lack of adult support and guidance showed that the youth generation felt increasingly disconnected from their parental generation. In Burundi, this parting should not be seen as a form of rebelling against gerontocratic power and social structures that limited access to resources, as we saw perhaps in several West African contexts (e.g. Vigh 2006; Quan 2007; Kouamé 2010; Amanor 1999; Richards 1996; Peters 2011; Temudo and Abrantes 2015). Rather, there was a sense of abandonment.

The rural Burundian youths knew their strategies were fleeting and recognised that their lives were made up of disjointed bits: 'you can never say that you "have your life"'. Despite their melioristic spirit of 'keeping up hope', as one young man put it—echoing the idea that 'improvement is at least possible' (James in Whyte 1997)—they seemed entrapped in a cycle that reproduced precarity.

NOTES

1. Parts of this section are drawn from White (2012).
2. Interviews with community leaders were conducted in Kirundi, with the help of Burundian interpreters (a woman and a man).
3. The analysis presented in this paper is based primarily on oral testimonies, gathered via different methods.
4. The majority of survey respondents had fled their homes during the war: 44 per cent had spent time in Tanzanian refugee camps; 17.5 per cent had fled but remained within Burundi; only 30 per cent had stayed in their home area.
5. As part of the decentralisation plans, each *commune* in Bujumbura (administrative unit in the capital, 13 in total) conducted population consultations in order to develop a 'Plan Communal de Développement Communautaire'. The reports (most from 2010) indicated great concern with youth unemployment.
6. Burundi has a turbulent history with (postcolonial) outbursts of violence in 1965, 1969, 1972, 1988, and 1991, and the civil war from 1993 to 2005. Since the elections of 2010, political tensions have been steadily increasing. This has led to a severe political crisis in April 2015 which is ongoing. At least 400 people have been killed and more than 240,000 people fled the country (UN estimates, January 2016).
7. The emphasis on training and education may in part have been a result of the research being carried out in collaboration with an NGO. Nonetheless, various other studies on young people in Burundi have also noticed a remarkably high interest in education (Uvin 2009; Sommers and Uvin 2011).
8. Discriminatory governance practices in the past—including genocidal violence—privileged youth from particular regions (South) and ethnic backgrounds (Ganwa and Tutsi) in access to education (Ndikumana 1998). In 2005, when the former Hutu rebel group CNDD-FDD was voted into power, they announced that primary education was henceforth 'free' for all, and selection criteria for post-primary education no longer included background characteristics.
9. Compare with Sommers' observation (2012) that in Rwanda rural youth get 'stuck' in the city because they fear to return home a failure.

10. A third mentioned 'strategy' concerned political participation, at the time in light of the elections scheduled between May and September 2010. However, most youth in these rural outskirts appeared not to be actively engaged in politics. One young man even lamented that youth in marginalised rural communities were 'neglected' in mobilisation campaigns by political leaders from the urban centres. It should be noted that political participation, given its association with wartime mobilisation and violence, was a sensitive topic and may therefore have been under-reported by the youths.
11. Compare, for children and youth's decision-making on migration in West Africa, with Hashim and Thorsen 2011.
12. Conversations and e-mail exchanges with NGO representative and Programme Coordinator, 2012.

REFERENCES

Alanen, L. (2001). Explorations in generational analysis. In L. Alanen & B. Mayall (Eds.), *Conceptualizing child-adult relations* (pp. 11–22). London: Routledge.

Amanor, K. J. (1999). *Global restructuring and land rights in Ghana: Forest food chains, timber and rural livelihoods*. Research report no. 108. Uppsala: Nordiska Afrikainstitutet.

Amnesty International. (2016, January 21). *Burundi: Joint statement on the UN Security Council's visit to Burundi*. N°: AFR 16/3259/2016.

Berckmoes, L. H. (2014). *Elusive tactics: Urban youth navigating the aftermath of war in Burundi*. Unpublished Ph.D. dissertation. Amsterdam: VU University.

Berckmoes, L. H. (2015). Youth, politics and violence in Burundi : Gullible followers or tactics actors? In *L'Afrique des Grands Lacs : Annuaire 2014–2015* (pp. 21–38). Antwerp: University of Antwerp Press.

Boddaert, M. (2012). *Sensibilité au genre des processus de Vérité, Justice, Réparation et Non-Répétition au Burundi*. Rapport de Recherche 'Perspectives Series'. Impunity Watch.

Bryceson, D. F. (2002). The scramble in Africa: Reorienting rural livelihoods. *World Development, 30*(5), 725–739.

CENAP (2010, August). *Défis d'accès au marché du travail: Quelles alternatives pour les jeunes burundais?* Bujumbura: Centre d'Alerte et de Prévention des Conflits.

Clark, H. (2013). Conflict and development. *New Zealand International Review, 38*(6), 2–7.

FAO, IFAD, & CTA. (2014). Youth and agriculture: Key challenges and concrete solutions. Rome, Wageningen, Food and Agricultural Organization of the

United Nations (FAO), International Fund for Agricultural Development (IFAD), Technical Centre for Agricultural and Rural Cooperation (CTA).

International Monetary Fund. (2010). *Burundi: Poverty reduction strategy paper – Second implementation report.* Washington, DC: IMF Country Report No. 10/312.

International Crisis Group. (2003, October 7). *Réfugiés et déplacés au Burundi: désamorcer la bombe foncière.* ICG Rapport Afrique N°70. Nairobi/Brussels: ICG.

Hashim, I., & Thorsen, D. (2011). *Child migration in Africa.* Uppsala/London/ New York: The Nordic Africa Institute & Zed Books.

Healthnet TPO. (2014). Dismantling the demographic timebomb of Burundi. Newsletter June. Accessed 5 Oct 2016, from http://www.healthnettpo.org/ en/1502/dismantling-the-demographic-time-bomb-of-burundi.html

Kohlhagen, D. (2012). *Rapports fonciers et violence au Burundi: Une mise en per-spective socio-historique.* Paper presented at the annual meeting for African stud-ies, 29 November–1 December, Philadelphia.

Kouamé, G. (2010). Intra-family and socio-political dimensions of land markets and land conflicts: The case of the Abure, Côte d'Ivoire. *Africa: The Journal of the International African Institute, 80*(1), 126–146.

Mains, D. (2007). Neoliberal times: Progress, boredom, and shame among young men in urban Ethiopia. *American Ethnologist, 34*(4), 659–673.

Mains, D. (2011). *Hope is cut: Youth, unemployment and the future in urban Ethiopia.* Philadelphia: Temple University Press.

Mannheim, K. (1952). The problem of generations. In P. Kecskemeti (Ed.), *Karl Mannheim: Essays on the sociology of knowledge* (pp. 276–322). London: Routledge.

Ministère de l'intérieur. (2010, September). *Recensement Général de la population et de l'habitat du Burundi de 2008: Analyse des résultats* (rapport provisoire). Bujumbura: Bureau central du recensement.

Ndikumana, L. (1998). Institutional failure and ethnic conflicts in Burundi. *African Studies Review, 41*(1), 29–47.

Peters, K. (2011). *War and the crisis of youth in Sierra Leone.* Cambridge, MA: University Press.

Peters, K., & Richards, R. (1998). "Why we fight": Voices of youth combatants in Sierra Leone. *Africa, 68*(2), 183–210.

Quan, J. (2007). Changes in intra-family land relations. In L. Cotula (Ed.), *Changes in "customary" land tenure systems in Africa* (pp. 51–63). London: IIED.

Richards, P. (1996). *Fighting for the rainforest: War, youth and resources in Sierra Leone.* Oxford: James Currey.

Rigg, J. (2006). Land, farming, livelihoods, and poverty: Rethinking the links in the rural south. *World Development, 34*(1), 180–202.

Soares, B. (2010). "Rasta" sufis and Muslim youth culture in Mali. In A. Bayat & L. Herrera (Eds.), *Being young and Muslim: New cultural politics in the global south and north* (pp. 241–257). Oxford: Oxford University Press.

Sommers, M. (2012). *Stuck: Rwandan youth and the struggle for adulthood.* Athens/Georgia: The University of Georgia Press.

Sommers, M., & P. Uvin. (2011). *Youth in Rwanda and Burundi: Contrasting visions.* Special report #293. Washington, DC: United States Institute of Peace.

Standing, G. (2011a, June 1). Who will be a voice for the emerging precariat? *The Guardian.*

Standing, G. (2011b). *The precariat: The new dangerous class.* London: Bloomsbury Academic.

Sumberg, J., Anyidoho, N. A., Leavy, J., te Lintelo, D., & Wellard, K. (2012). Introduction: The young people and farming "problem" in Africa. *IDS Bulletin, 43*(6), 1–8.

Tadele, G., & Gella, A. A. (2012). A last resort and often not an option at all: Farming and young people in Ethiopia. *IDS Bulletin, 46*(6), 33–43.

Temudo, M., & Abrantes, M. (2015). The pen and the plough: Balanta young men in Guinea-Bissau. *Development and Change, 46*(3), 464–485.

Utas, M. (2005). Building a future? The reintegration and re-marginalisation of youth in Liberia. In P. Richards (Ed.), *No peace, no war: An anthropology of contemporary armed conflict* (pp. 137–154). Oxford/Ohio: James Curry/Ohio University Press.

Uvin, P. (2009). *Life after violence: A people's story of Burundi.* London/New York: Zed Books.

Vigh, H. (2006). *Navigating terrains of war: Youth and soldiering in Guinea-Bissau.* Oxford: Berghahn Books.

Wells, K. (2009). *Childhood in a global perspective.* Cambridge: Polity Press.

White, B. (2012). Agriculture and the generation problem: Youth, employment and the future of farming. *IDS Bulletin, 43*(6), 9–19.

White, B. (2015). Generational dynamics in agriculture: Reflections on rural youth and farming futures. *Cahiers Agricultures, 24*(6), 330–334.

Whyte, S. R. (1997). *Questioning misfortune: The pragmatics of uncertainty in eastern Uganda.* Cambridge: Cambridge University Press.

Woodman, D., & Wyn, J. (2015). Class, gender and generation matter: Using the concept of social generation to study inequality and social change. *Journal of Youth Studies, 18*(10), 1402–1410.

Yagura, K. (2015). Intergenerational land transfer in rural Cambodia since the late 1980s: Special attention to the effect of labor migration. *Southeast Asian Studies, 4*(1), 3–42.

Commentary

CHAPTER 14

Age and Generation in the Service of Development?

Nicola Ansell

The chapters of this book have focused to varying degrees on the ways in which age categories and generational relations are socially produced and on how they work in the governance of societies. Mayall (2002: 27) has used the term 'generationing' to refer to a 'relational process whereby people come to be known as children, and whereby children and childhood acquire certain characteristics'. It is very easy to extend this focus on children to encompass other age categories—as Clark-Kazak (this volume) points out, youth, adulthood and old age are all produced relationally. Importantly, social relations are always power relations, and generationing serves as an exercise of power. It operates in all societies, albeit through different modalities, to achieve social control. This power is not only discursive but also material, shaping people's economic contributions and access to resources. Determining who is a child, what their role is in society and how relationships between generations should be enacted is a crucial part of the way in which social order operates and has significant consequences for people's lives. It shapes people's identities (intersecting with other relationalities including gender and class), is lived by individuals and groups and has material effects. Inevitably, generationing is contested; the outcomes of contestation often lead to change—in some cases, arguably, to development.

N. Ansell (✉)
Brunel University London, Kingston Lane, UB8 3PH Uxbridge, Middlesex, UK

© The Author(s) 2016
R. Huijsmans (ed.), *Generationing Development,*
DOI 10.1057/978-1-137-55623-3_14

Age and generation are deployed by diverse actors for their own ends—by the state, market and civil society as well as within families and communities. Moreover, international agencies and other development actors are increasingly engaged in remaking age and generation across the world. Processes of generationing are important in relation to international development because they help constitute the context in which development policies and interventions operate, as well as serving as techniques or mechanisms through which development is enacted. As such, they shape the ways in which development is experienced, in particular by children and youth, not necessarily, as this volume has demonstrated, in positive ways. Yet hitherto they remain little reflected upon.

This chapter brings together some of the findings reported in the previous chapters to highlight how both age and generation are produced and deployed in the exercise of power in societies. It also examines how age and generation are deployed, purposively or unconsciously, in development policies and interventions, the ways in which these clash with already existing normative constructions and the outcomes for individuals and societies.

THE RELATIONALITIES AND TEMPORALITIES OF DEVELOPMENT

There is growing recognition among academics that development is a relational process. Even the Sustainable Development Goals focus on inequality—a relational measure—and not only poverty. A relational analysis recognises that policies and interventions impact not simply upon atomised individuals but upon the hierarchical relationships of, for instance, gender and class that underlie conditions of poverty (Mosse 2010). In some cases, class relations are reinforced through development policies, which can entrench rather than ameliorate poverty. The major contribution of this volume is to recognise that generational relations may operate in a similar way: affected by policies and interventions, and in turn shaping their effects.

Generational relations are in some respects distinct from other social relations because they embody a temporal dimension. Both development and age/generation are fundamentally temporal and the nexus of these temporalities is significant. Development concerns a process of moving from one situation to another over time—a notion of progress, albeit often contested. Modernisation theory in the 1950s and 1960s seized on the idea that development occurred in a series of predictable, ordered stages. While this idea, most prominently advanced by Rostow (1960), has been critiqued, the imagery remains latent in much development thinking. In recent years, however, the temporalities of development have not been conceptually explored or critiqued in the way that its social relationalities have.

Equally, research focused on social relations has given relatively little attention to human temporality. People are always positioned in a life course; they mature and grow old within and alongside the historical progression of development. As a number of scholars have pointed out (see Cole and Durham 2008; Burman 2008), there are parallels between the 'stage thinking' that characterises development and the approach of developmental psychology towards children. Piaget (1972) and others have argued that children are programmed to progress through a series of developmental stages, with roughly similar timings, but always in the same order. Such ideas lend themselves to categorising the life course—and people—into age groups. The chapters in this volume adopt a more nuanced understanding of human temporalities, recognising that people are positioned relationally—generationally—within their own life courses, but they are also positioned, socially, in relation to other people and their life courses. Age functions to position them, as do generational relationships, between kin or simply between people of different (or similar) ages.

In the sections below, I take relations of age and generation in turn and explore how they are produced, the roles they play in the governance of societies (from within and as imposed from without) and how they are shaped by and shape development.

AGE

Everywhere, the young are expected to behave differently from the old and to have different roles and responsibilities in society. All societies place people into age categories as a means of indicating to them and to others what their roles are (Montgomery 2008). These categories of course intersect with others—gender, class, ethnicity among others. They may be fine-grained categories or broader. They are also always somewhat contested (see Durham 2004), in part because they are also based on different ways of conceptualising age. Age may broadly be categorised on the basis of chronological, embodied or social conceptualisations. While chronological (number of years since birth) and embodied (the body's changing features) age might appear to be founded on objective measures, the behaviours and roles associated with them are certainly socially constructed.

The Production and Power Effects of Age

It is very clear that in any society, the allocation of individuals to age categories, and the ascription of roles and behaviours to these categories, operate as means of achieving social control. In most societies, children are expected—or required—to attend school, whether because they are deemed to be 'children' or 'young' or because they fall into a chronologically defined age group. This requirement positions them in particular ways and enables control to be exercised over them by parents and by teachers. It also defines their function in society, as future economic actors and as human capital meriting investment (see Palacio, this volume). Thus it is in part through age categorisation that social reproduction is achieved and the discursive and material relations of society continue.

The specific ages at which children are expected to attend school (and indeed whether or not school going is strictly associated with particular ages) differ between societies, as do the specific behaviours associated with school-going children. Equally, there are normative expectations as to the roles of persons deemed adult or middle-aged or elderly that differ between societies. However, age does not operate simply as a category to which roles and behaviours adhere. Values attach to age categories and to the relations between them. Horton's chapter in this volume clearly elaborates how the age-based hierarchical structuring of aspects of Vietnamese schooling (relations between teachers and students, older and younger pupils) translates into a pervasive age-based exercise of power. This ultimately legitimates a culture of bullying. Older children exercise agency by bullying those who are younger, larger children bully smaller and stronger bully weaker. Social age is thus intertwined with both chronological and corporeal markers.

In other contexts, the way bodies are experienced and perceived as aged—the corporeal aspects—sit less comfortably with chronological measures. Sometimes it is youthfulness that is most highly valued, though that value does not always adhere to—or benefit—the youthful individual. Focusing on sex work, Coumans (this volume) explains how youthful bodies are deemed attractive and thus valued commercially. The commercial value of youth certainly extends into other domains: there has been a noticeable increase in marketing towards ever younger consumers in Western society in recent decades (Calvert 2008; Deutsch and Theodorou 2010 Coumans). Utrata (2011) highlights how young Russian single mothers' access to marriage and labour markets privileges them in relationships with their own mothers. However, Coumans' chapter indicates that the attraction of youth is not universal—or at least not uniform. Clients differ in their preference for youthful sex workers depending on their own gender and sexual orientation as well as personal preference.

The social age of youth is mobilised in many different contexts and can allow young people to exercise more influence, although it can also prove a basis for their exploitation. Young sex workers are often highly valued by pimps, a situation that may afford them more influence or may make them more vulnerable. Young people also have advantages in other spheres of work. Belay (this volume), for instance, recounts how certain jobs—selling lottery tickets and cleaning shoes—are constructed as suitable for children (or more specifically for boys) but not for adults in Ethiopian society. Boys undertaking such work are able, as a consequence, to make a meaningful contribution to their households and may be taken more seriously, although they remain confined to childhood tasks.

Even more strikingly, Sayibu (this volume) illustrates why, in northern Ghana, children are required as guides for blind beggars. The characteristics associated with children in Ghanaian society attract sympathy. Moreover, the performance of the beggar and their assistant must give the impression that the blind adult has no other kin who could provide care. The presence of an older child or an able-bodied adult would undermine any notion that the beggar was 'deserving'. Blind adults therefore need regularly to change their companions, recruiting new and often unrelated children, creating a market for 'fictive kin'. Ghana's child fosterage tradition makes recruitment of such children possible.

Youthfulness, then, can make young people valuable. There are (socially constructed) advantages to being young. These advantages shape children's role in society and affect power relations, although they need not always work in children's favour. While the children in Belay's research reported positive advantages to their work, those in Savibu's study did not enjoy their roles as companions to beggars. It is important also not to forget that youthfulness can inhibit. In agriculture, as Mills (this volume) points out, young people tend to lack the assets needed to invest. Agriculture has become increasingly capital intensive, which makes it difficult to gain entry when young. In Western society, and increasingly elsewhere in the world, agriculture is becoming the preserve of older people. Mills found, nonetheless, that young farmers in Canada mobilised around their youthful identity in order to seek influence and opportunities.

In all of these examples, it is clear that age and what it means are constituted through market relations (and people's roles as workers and consumers) as well as through government regulation and institutions such as schools. How one is classified in relation to age—and in relation to other age groups—affects the power one may exercise in society, but there is a complex relationship between age and advantage.

Age and Development

While age has always been a significant structuring category in society, in recent decades its role has expanded. Chronological age, in particular, has gained ground as a basis for organising societies. The preoccupation with chronological age has spread globally, in large part through international conventions (such as the UN Convention on the Rights of the Child [CRC]) and through the institutions, policies and practices of international development.

In particular, the age of 18 is becoming progressively more entrenched as a globally recognised boundary between childhood and adulthood. Those below 18 are deemed to possess certain characteristics. Boyden and Ennew (1997) have explained how these characteristics (such as innocence, weakness and passivity) have become incorporated into a 'global model of childhood' which has exported from the West worldwide through the activities of development organisations. Children are seen as possessing certain rights on account of being children—but unlike the rights afforded to adults, these rights are more protective than liberatory and often impose duties upon children (they are expected to attend school) or deny them rights that are available to adults (such as opportunities to earn money through work). The International Labour Organization (ILO) definition of child labour, for instance, offers a detailed prescription as to what constitutes child labour at various chronological ages, but the data it publishes group together large numbers of 17-year-olds within this definition (Bourdillon et al. 2009). Likewise, those who marry below the age of 18 are increasingly classified as 'child brides'.

In some respects, this focus on chronological age has rendered age itself a more important consideration for development. Children and youth are recognised as important categories with their own (albeit largely socially constructed) needs and capacities. Age-based standardisation offers young people enhanced visibility and access to services (Hart, this volume). The use of categories based on chronological age is bureaucratically simple. It makes age legible (Coumans, this volume).

In many cases, however, development policies represent a form of what Huijsmans (introduction to this volume) refers to as age normativity—the global imposition of Western middle-class norms based on chronological age. Often such norms conflict with prevalent age-related norms in non-Western societies. Belay's Ethiopian research for instance draws attention to the clash between recent laws in Ethiopia on child labour (informed by ILO mandates and the CRC) and the everyday lives of street children. While Ethiopian society views some sorts of work as appropriate for children (and inappropriate for adults), the law now takes a blanket view that children should not engage in any form of (market-focused) work. As others have argued in relation to child labour (Bourdillon et al. 2009, 2010), chronological age is a blunt tool for preventing the abuse of the young (or, indeed, the elderly). Laws inspired by international discourse tend to ignore the contexts that propel children into work, and may thereby actually harm children's interests (Haider 2008; Maconachie and Hilson 2016; Okyere 2013). In South Africa, for instance, child labour legislation since 1994 has deepened chronic hunger and child poverty on farms where children previously worked seasonally or part-time (Levine 2011). Moreover, it is becoming very difficult for any organisation to support working children—even those aged 16 or 17 (Bourdillon 2006).

It is not only chronological concepts of age that are deployed to govern young people, and societies, globally. As Coumans points out in her chapter, evidence from neuroscience is called upon in support of regulation based on chronological age (in this case, raising the age at which young people are permitted to engage in prostitution to 21). Neuroscience is similarly called upon to support investment in the 'first 1000 days' (World Bank 2006), a new age category constructed as particularly sensitive in children's development. Clark-Kazak (this volume) points out that the new Sustainable Development Goals (unlike the CRC) are founded in social age insofar as they do not directly reference chronological ages when referring to labels such as 'child' or 'adult'. Nonetheless, they apply clear normative expectations to the age-based categories that they refer to.

Ultimately, through international institutions and development organisations, age is increasingly taking on a governmental function in society. Governments are persuaded to enact legislation that determines what rights one is entitled to or denied based upon chronological age. The Right to Education Project, United Nations Educational, Scientific and Cultural

Organization and Swedish International Development Cooperation Agency published a report (Melchiorre 2004) charting minimum ages for work, marriage and criminal responsibility in 187 countries in an effort to advocate for consistency and (implicitly) higher age limits. Numerous countries have done just this, with India, for instance, introducing a new marriage law in 2015.[1] More broadly, dominant norms are changing worldwide as to what is appropriate for different age groups, and people increasingly police their own behaviour as a consequence, employing their own ideas of age-appropriate behaviours. Age is deployed not only to govern young people on the basis of their age but also to govern what societies are allowed to do with young people, and the function young people play. Societies are expected to invest in future human capital; to grow a differentiated consumer market; and age thereby serves a neo-liberal agenda.

Generation

Generation is a more explicitly relational concept than age: a generation can only exist in relation to other generations. But generation is also about more than simply age. As Huijsmans outlines in the introduction, generation is conceptualised in diverse ways, which can broadly be categorised as cohort (in the Mannheimian sense of a generation of people that share similar attributes and values on account of growing up together, and recognising themselves as distinct from previous generations), life phase (similar to age, but explicitly a person's position within their own life course) and kinship (one's position in relation to one's parents or children, which remains a constant relationship, even as all parties grow older).

The Production and Power Effects of Generation

Generations—however conceptualised—are mutually constituted (Alanen 2009). A cohort comes to see itself as a generation by drawing contrasts with other generations. In this Mannheimian sense, a generation is an identity (Berckmoes and White, this volume), but it is also a position in a power hierarchy in which young people often struggle to exercise greater power. While young people mould identities as generations (that they carry with them in some form through life), adults recognise that generations can take on an identity and challenge conventional attitudes and practices. They therefore seek to shape new generations to mould them to resemble the older generation or what the old want. This might be done through, for instance, the formation of youth leagues, intended to instil the attributes that adults deem desirable, or more mundanely by disapproving of youth subcultural phenomena such as the language they use on social media platforms or the music they listen to.

Generational relations are not simply discursive power struggles though. Generation is also fundamentally concerned with resources and the ways these are distributed. There are established practices through which material goods and forms of knowledge are transferred between generations. In general, resources are transferred from those who are best capable of working and generating income to those who are younger or older and therefore dependent. Transfers from parents to children are reciprocated as the children reach adulthood, and as their parents reach old age. Such institutionalised practices that happen both within households, and increasingly at a societal level, are conceptualised as 'intergenerational contracts' (McGregor et al. 2000). As Huijsmans (this volume) points out, intergenerational contracts are never fixed.

The form taken by intergenerational transfers varies and is strongly shaped by the economic context. In southern Africa, for instance, over many decades, young men had access to relatively well-paid work (as miners in South Africa). This led to the institution of very high bridewealth payments that were transferred by the young men to their wives' parents upon marriage (Murray 1980). Despite young men's access to income, the power of the elderly in rural society persisted sufficiently to enforce significant wealth transfers, in part through control over the sexuality of young women.

Such material relations between generations involve generation in all its conceptualisations. They involve transfers directly between generations of kin; they affect a cohort and position them in a particular way; and they reflect an individual's position in their own lifespan. Berckmoes and White (this volume), for instance, chart how in rural Burundi, today's youth fail to inherit land for independent householding at an age that is normatively expected: the pressure on land is high and it is not relinquished by the older generation. Collectively, the youth resent their situation and resist current patrimonial structures of resource distribution, leading to what is described as a 'crisis of youth'. This contestation over existing relations of generation has the potential to instigate change (Berckmoes and White).

In the rather different context of Nova Scotia, Canada, rural societies are equally gerontocratic (Mills, this volume). Farmers—and rural society generally—are significantly older than urban populations. The urban–rural age structure intersects with generational relations in ways that complicate intergenerational transfers of farming knowledge (Mills).

Generational relations determine obligations between people. To understand when and why children work or attend school, it is necessary to understand their generational roles as dependents or providers within intergenerational contracts. In some contexts, it is necessary for children to perform the provider role at a young age, particularly where numbers of children are very large relative to numbers of adults (Bourdillon 2006). Moreover, sometimes intergenerational dependencies are reversed while children are still very young. As outlined above, Sayibu (this volume) explains how blind beggars depend upon children as their companions.

Generational relations, then, are closely tied to the economic contexts in which they exist. Berckmoes and White (this volume) argue that they should be included in political economic analyses of the control of resources, divisions of labour and relations of surplus transfer. They play a fundamental role in enabling societies to exist in different contexts—in processes of social reproduction. Moreover, struggles to achieve social reproduction in changing contexts require a reworking of generational relations (Berckmoes and White, this volume).

Reworking of intergenerational relations occurs not only at the instigation of young people themselves. Economic and political processes, as well as social processes, intervene. Capital often takes advantage of and reshapes changing generational relations. Srinivasan (this volume) describes the *sumangali* scheme that was introduced in Tamil Nadu, India. This scheme, whereby factories employ girls for a period of three years and dismiss them at the age of 18 with a lump sum payment, relies on and exploits existing institutionalised intergenerational relations. Girls are able to save a lump sum to cover the cost of their own dowry, alleviating their parents of this expense. While on the one hand helping the practice of dowry to persist in a context where it creates social stress, the *sumangali* scheme benefits girls in some ways. It reduces pressure on them from within their families, gives them some freedom for a brief period in their lives, and may weaken the image of daughters as an economic burden on their households and thus prejudice—or 'aversion'—against daughters.

It is not only capital but also the state that manipulates generational relations in its own interests. As indicated above, Horton's chapter (this volume) argues that the Vietnamese state has co-opted generational groupings and institutionalised these as structural aspects of its education system in ways that ultimately sanction the bullying of younger by older students.

Generation and Development

If capital and the state capitalise on and intervene in generational relations, it is unsurprising that development policy and practice—whether driven by the state, international institutions or non-governmental organisations —will do likewise. Since the early years of development practice, there has been an assumption that modernisation will be achieved as new generations—new cohorts of youth—reach adulthood (see, for instance, Blake 1965). Each new generation is expected to have different attitudes from previous generations, and these attitudes are understood to be malleable while the cohort is young. Hence compulsory education in particular is expected to facilitate the transformation of society.

Such generational shifts in attitude inevitably cause friction. Morarji (this volume) examines the framing of educated youth in rural North India as a generational problem. Young people are depicted as failing to contribute to their households and lacking a sense of responsibility. Morarji suggests that this is attributable to the conflicting models of personhood that dominate education (which embraces ideals of liberal individualism) and rural communities (where intergenerational reciprocity is the normative expectation).

Development policies today focus on not only shifting values generationally but also transforming human capital. The early stages of the life course are understood as points for investment in human capital to generate a more productive future adult workforce. Palacio (this volume) explains how conditional cash transfers (CCTs), a rapidly expanding form of development intervention across Latin America, Asia and Africa, are used to promote human capital accumulation. These schemes provide cash income to poor parents on condition that they send their children to school and (in some cases) ensure they receive health interventions such as immunisation and regular health checks. Such practices constitute children's bodies as sites of investment and (by implication) adult bodies as sites of production (Palacio).

CCTs, as rewards for behaviour change, seek to reshape the associations between age and behaviours or roles. They arguably impose Western norms of childhood, dominated by concerns with schooling and healthcare. Enforcement of what Huijsmans (this volume) refers to as normative childhood is achieved through an increasingly intimate presence of the state in young people's lives; through visits by social workers representing the state (Palacio). They constitute both childhood and motherhood in particular ways; children are made aware of their role and significance in both their families and wider society. They are both obliged to fulfil expectations (attending school, for instance) and understand the dependence of their families upon their existence and their behaviours. Yet children are not direct recipients of CCTs. In keeping with Western childhood discourses, they are placed outside economic relations, a situation highlighted by the fact that in Ecuador, although very many young women give birth as teenagers, they cannot receive a CCT for their child (and thus are not counted as mothers within the scheme) until the age of 18 (Palacio).

Beyond specific programmes and policies such as CCTs, Clark-Kazak (this volume) demonstrates that specific constructions of children, youth and generational relationships can be identified in the Sustainable Development Goals. Her content analysis reveals that the international institutions that drew up the goals continue to make particular assumptions about those belonging to familiar age categories. Infants are referred to in relation to health, children in relation to education and young people in relation to training and work. These texts will influence policy interventions over the coming 15 years, and doubtless reinforce expectations as to the roles, behaviours and responsibilities of different age groups. It is noteworthy that there is an explicit exclusion of reference to children in relation to work or to vocational training and that whereas girls and women are often coupled together in the goals, only women are mentioned in relation to decision-making. Perhaps more significantly, the goals refer to age categories but give remarkably little attention to intergenerational or familial relations and do not acknowledge the power relations through which age and generation operate.

Conclusion

The chapters of this volume fall into three sections. The first four chapters explore ways of theorising age and generation in young people's lives. They elaborate a number of different ways of conceptualising both age and generation. All of these conceptualisations reveal that age and generation are both fundamentally relational. Neither has a meaning outside society or without reference to a range of ages or other generations.

Both age and generation exercise discursive power. The allocation of individuals to age categories defined to have particular characteristics, or their generational positioning relative to others, shapes how they are viewed and how they view themselves. In this respect, generationing is fundamental to identity. However, age and generation are also key elements in the constitution of political economic structures. They underlie societal rules and practices concerning who contributes what and how resources are shared out and transferred. They are essential to social reproduction: '[t]he interdependent reproduction both of the social relations within which, and the material and discursive means through which, social life is premised, sustained and transformed over time' (Lee 2000).

Social reproduction concerns both continuity and change. It is fundamentally temporal, as is development, concerned with the mechanisms through which societies are transformed. Relations of age and generation constitute part of such mechanisms. They change over time, partly in response to the actions of institutions including the state and the market. And in turn, change in relations of age and generation bring wider changes to the structure of societies and economies, on a global scale as well as locally.

The second section of the book explores everyday relationalities in the lives of young people that are produced through structures of age and generation. The chapters outline contexts in which the impacts of age and generation on young people's lived experiences, and on how young people see themselves in society, are very clear. As highlighted above, social relations are always power relations, both discursive and material. Examining young people's everyday lives through a relational lens presents opportunities for interrogating how young people are located within webs of power. Significant challenges arise when conceptualising the connections between power and agency, as these chapters make clear. Children and youth often play valuable—arguably pivotal—roles in society on account of their age and the generational relations in which they are embedded. They can perform functions in society that others cannot (working as shoeshiners, accompanying beggars); by virtue of existing (and attending school), they may provide households with access to income and societies with human capital for the future. Berman (2016) argues that being able to undertake activities that are unavailable to adults represents a form of agency associated with (young) age. Schildkrout (2002/1978) illustrates some such roles performed by young children in northern Nigeria. However, while young people may be able to do certain things and occupy powerful positions within the generational structures that hold societies together, these positions do not necessarily confer on them the capacity to make decisions or pursue individual goals. They do not correspond to liberal conceptualisations of individual agency. Indeed, where relations of age and generation allocate significant social or economic roles to groups or individuals (as, for instance, companions to beggars or future human capital), this may represent exploitation rather than empowerment.

The last section of the book examines the negotiation of development. Age and gender shape not just the everyday lives of young people but also societies more broadly. Political economy—and its social reproduction—operates in significant part through the structuring of society by age and gender, and reworking of age and gender relations generates change. This volume contributes in important ways to understanding how the operation of markets and states, and of development agencies and institutions, intervenes in remoulding relations of age and gender. Very often, it seems, development actors are unreflexive about the impacts their interventions might have. Instruments such as the Sustainable Development Goals replicate widespread assumptions about age categories and remain inattentive to generational relations. Through such inattentiveness, and a growing preoccupation with (mainly chronological) age categorisation, 'normative age' is promulgated worldwide. However inadvertent, this is liable to contribute to the reconstruction of age and gender in ways that serve the interests of neo-liberalism. The construction of childhood and youth with particular characteristics (as consumers, as future human capital) plays a role in the construction of society. As Coumans (this volume) remarks, the use of chronological age to determine access to sex work implies that for those who have attained adulthood, it is a rational choice. This obscures the social conditions that propel some young women into it. Whether the restructuring of age and generation brought about by development and its consequences for societies is intentional, or whether it is due to inattentiveness to the relationality of social and economic processes, there is a clear need for these aspects of social change, their relationship to development and to young people's lives to receive greater attention from researchers.

NOTE

1. It is noteworthy that Bolivia has caused controversy by contravening the trend and lowering the minimum age at which children may legally work.

REFERENCES

Alanen, L. (2009). Generational order. In J. Qvortrup, W. Corsaro, & M.-E. Honig (Eds.), *The Palgrave handbook of childhood studies* (pp. 159–174). Basingstoke: Palgrave Macmillan.

Berman, E. (2016). Aged culture. ACYRG blog. http://acyig.americananthro. org/2016/02/08/aged-culture/. Accessed 3 Dec 2016.

Blake, J. (1965). Demographic science and the redirection of population policy. *Journal of Chronic Diseases, 18*(11), 1181–1200.

Bourdillon, M. (2006). Children and work: A review of current literature and debates. *Development and Change, 37*(6), 1201–1226.

Bourdillon, M. F. C., White, B., & Myers, W. E. (2009). Re-assessing minimum age standards for children's work. *International Journal of Sociology and Social Policy, 29*(3/4), 106–117.

Bourdillon, M., Levison, D., Myers, W., & White, B. (2010). *The rights and wrongs of children's work*. New Brunswick/London: Rutgers University Press.

Boyden, J., & Ennew, J. (1997). *Children in focus: A manual for participatory research with children*. Stockholm: Radda Barnen.

Burman, E. (2008). *Developments: Child, image, nation*. Abingdon: Routledge.

Calvert, S. L. (2008). Children as consumers: Advertising and marketing. *The Future of Children, 18*(1), 205–234.

Cole, J., & Durham, D. (2008). Globalization and the temporality of children and youth. In J. Cole & D. Durham (Eds.), *Figuring the future: Globalization and the temporalities of children and youth* (pp. 3–23). Santa Fe: School for Advanced Research Press.

Deutsch, N. L., & Theodorou, E. (2010). Aspiring, consuming, becoming: Youth identity in a culture of consumption. *Youth & Society, 42*(2), 229–254.

Durham, D. (2004). Disappearing youth: Youth as a social shifter in Botswana. *American Ethnologist, 31*(4), 589–605.

Haider, M. (2008). Recognising complexity, embracing diversity: Working children in Bangladesh. *South Asia Research, 28*(1), 49–72.

Lee, R. (2000). Social reproduction. In R. J. Johnston, D. Gregory, G. Pratt & M. Watts (Eds.), *Dictionary of human geography*. Oxford: Blackwell.

Levine, S. (2011). The race of nimble fingers: Changing patterns of children's work in post-apartheid South Africa. *Childhood, 18*(2), 261–273.

Maconachie, R., & Hilson, G. (2016). Rethinking the child labor 'problem' in rural Sub-Saharan Africa: The case of Sierra Leone's half shovels. *World Development, 78*, 136–147.

Mayall, B. (2002). *Towards a sociology for childhood: Thinking from children's lives*. Maidenhead: Open University Press.

McGregor, J. A., Copestake, J. G., & Wood, G. D. (2000). The inter-generational bargain: An introduction. *Journal of International Development, 12*, 447–451.

Melchiorre, A. (2004). At what age?…are school-children employed, married and taken to court? Right to Education Project. Accessed from: http://www.right-to-education.org/resource/what-age-%E2%80%A6are-school-children-employed-married-and-taken-court-2nd-edition

Montgomery, H. (2008). *An introduction to childhood: Anthropological perspectives on children's lives*. Chichester: Wiley-Blackwell.

Mosse, D. (2010). A relational approach to durable poverty, inequality and power. *Journal of Development Studies, 46*(7), 1156–1178.

Murray, C. (1980). Migrant labour and changing family structure in the rural periphery of southern Africa. *Journal of Southern African Studies, 35*(2), 99–121.

Okyere, S. (2013). Are working children's rights and child labour abolition complementary or opposing realms? *International Social Work, 56*(1), 80–91.

Piaget, J. (1972). *The principles of genetic epistemology.* London: Routledge and Kegan Paul.

Rostow, W. W. (1960). *The stages of economic growth: a non-communist manifesto.* London: Cambridge University Press.

Schildkrout, E. (2002/1978). Age and gender in hausa society: Socioeconomic roles of children in urban Kano. *Childhood, 9*(3), 344–368.

Utrata, J. (2011). Youth privilege: Doing age and gender in Russia's single-mother families. *Gender & Society, 25*(5), 616–641.

World Bank. (2006). World development report 2007. Development and the next generation. Washington: The International Bank for Reconstruction and Development/The World Bank.

Index

© The Author(s) 2016

R. Huijsmans (ed.), *Generationing Development*,

DOI 10.1057/978-1-137-55623-3

GPSR Compliance
The European Union's (EU) General Product Safety Regulation (GPSR) is a set
of rules that requires consumer products to be safe and our obligations to
ensure this.

If you have any concerns about our products, you can contact us on

ProductSafety@springernature.com

In case Publisher is established outside the EU, the EU authorized
representative is:

Springer Nature Customer Service Center GmbH
Europaplatz 3
69115 Heidelberg, Germany